FAITH IN THE PUBLIC SQUARE

Faith in the Public Square

Rowan Williams

BLOOMSBURY

LONDON · OXFORD · NEW YORK · NEW DELHI · SYDNEY

Bloomsbury Continuum
An imprint of Bloomsbury Publishing Plc

50 Bedford Square
London
WC1B 3DP
UK

1385 Broadway
New York
NY 10018
USA

www.bloomsbury.com

First published 2012
Paperback edition 2015

British Library Cataloguing-in-Publication Data
A catalogue record for this book is available from the British Library.

Library of Congress Cataloguing-in-Publication data has been applied for.

ISBN: HB: 978-1408-18758-6
PB: 978-1472-92399-8
ePDF: 978-1408-18760-9
ePub: 978-1408-18759-3

2 4 6 8 10 9 7 5 3 1

Typeset by Fakenham Prepress Solutions, Fakenham, Norfolk NR21 8NN

Printed and bound in Great Britain by CPI Group (UK) Ltd, Croydon CR0 4YY

Contents

Introduction

Every archbishop, whether he likes it or not, faces the expectation that he will be some kind of commentator on the public issues of the day. He is, of course, doomed to fail in the eyes of most people. If he restricts himself to reflections heavily based on the Bible or tradition, what he says will be greeted as platitudinous or irrelevant. If he ventures into more obviously secular territory, he will be told that he has no particular expertise in sociology or economics or international affairs that would justify giving him a hearing. Reference to popular culture prompts disapproving noises about 'dumbing down'; anything that looks like close academic analysis is of course incomprehensible and self-indulgent elitism. A focus on what many think are the traditional moral concerns of the Church (mostly to do with sexual ethics and family issues, though increasingly including 'end-of-life' questions) reinforces the myth that Christians are interested in only the narrowest range of moral matters; an interest in other ethical questions invites the reproach that he is unwilling to affirm the obvious and sacrosanct principles of revealed faith and failing to Give a Lead.

Well, archbishops grow resilient, and sometimes even rebellious, in the face of all this. If it is true that religious commitment in general, and Christian faith in particular, are not a matter of vague philosophy but of unremitting challenge to what we think we know about human beings and their destiny, there is no reprieve from the task of working out how doctrine impacts on public life – even if this entails the risk of venturing opinions in areas where expert observers vocally and very technically disagree with each other (such risk is not, after all, a wholly unknown phenomenon in the world of journalism). If it is true that the world depends entirely on the free gift of God, and that the direct act and presence of God has uniquely appeared in history in the shape of a human life two millennia ago, this has implications for how we think about that world and about human life. The risk of blundering into unforeseen complexities can't be avoided; and the best thing to hope for is that at least some of the inevitable mistakes may be interesting enough (or simply big enough) for someone else to work out better responses. The chapters printed here are the result of taking that sort of risk; and they are vulnerable to all the criticisms that I have already sketched. They are offered not as a compendium of political theology, but as a series of worked examples of trying to find the connecting points between various public questions and the fundamental beliefs about creation and salvation from which (I hope) Christians begin in thinking about anything at all.

That being said, in reading them over, I have found a number of unifying threads running through them, which may be the elements of something more like a broader theory about faith and the social order. We have been hearing quite a lot about the dangers of 'aggressive secularism', and the strident anti-Christian rhetoric of some well-known intellectuals is still a prominent feature of our society. But part of what I am trying to argue in several of these chapters is that our problem is *not* simply loud voices attacking faith (and certainly not 'persecution' as some of the more highly-coloured apologetic claims). It is a set of confusions often shared between religious groups and their enemies. For example: it is often assumed that we all know what 'secularism' or 'secularization' means. But there is clearly more than one idea and process involved. Some very articulate debate goes on as to whether we are a 'secularised' society in the way the term was used forty-odd years ago. If the only question is one of public respect for, and more or less active support of, traditional religious practices, it is obviously true that we have, in the UK as in most of Western Europe, moved further down the road already opening up in the 1960s, further away from the observance of public religious orthodoxies. But if the question is about the persistence of popular beliefs and habits, about assumptions concerning non-material powers and presences, we are a long way from being as 'disenchanted' as some would like to think. Public ritual persists, reinventing itself energetically (the flowers at the site of a road accident). Call it what you like, but 'secular' does not quite capture where we are.

And then, 'secularism' as a term is pretty slippery. I've suggested in various places that we need a distinction between 'procedural' and 'programmatic' secularism. Procedural secularism is the secularity proclaimed as a virtue by, for example, the government of India: a public policy which declines to give advantage or preference to any one religious body over others. It is the principle according to which the state as such defines its role as one of overseeing a variety of communities of religious conviction and, where necessary, assisting them to keep the peace together, without requiring any specific public confessional allegiance from its servants or guaranteeing any single community a legally favoured position against others. Programmatic secularism is something more like what is often seen (not always accurately) as the French paradigm, in which any and every public manifestation of any particular religious allegiance is to be ironed out so that everyone may share a clear public loyalty to the state unclouded by private convictions, and any signs of such private convictions are rigorously banned from public space.

The former kind of secularism or secularity poses no real problems to Christians; on the contrary, it is quite arguable that the phenomenon of the Christian Church itself is responsible for the distinction between communities that think of themselves as existing by licence of a sacred power, on the one hand, and *political* communities on the other. Early Christianity demystified the authority of the Empire and thus introduced a hugely complicating factor into European political life – the idea of two distinct kinds of corporate loyalty, one of which may turn out to be more fundamental than the other.

Programmatic secularism, on the other hand, *is* a problem. It defines an exclusive public orthodoxy of a new kind, and works on the assumption that only one sort of loyalty is really possible. Loyalty to your faith will be a matter of private preference, perhaps even very powerful private emotion, but cannot stand alongside loyalty to the state, to the supposedly neutral public order of rational persons. And there are two major issues here. One is that this reduces what will be for a lot of people their most intimate and decisive moral inspirations to the level of private choices, lifestyle choices as you might say; and this 'thins out' the fabric of public debate and of moral passion. The other is that without respect for the possibility of *criticizing* the state on the grounds of a truth that does not change at elections, without the possibility of arguing with some things the state thinks are reasonable or self-evident, the chances of radical social change are threatened. This may not feel like a huge issue in liberal democracies, but the history of the last century should remind us that, in times of political crisis and corruption, we need to know what resources there are to resist what a government decides is 'rational'.

Now, all this has implications both for how the state deals with the question of religious liberty, and also for the basic model of the state itself that we work with. A state that is consistently working with diverse religious groups to make the best use of their resources for the common good and to minimize conflict is a state that sees its remit in relatively modest terms; to use a phrase that will recur in these pages, it thinks of itself as a 'community of communities' rather than a monopolistic sovereign power. This might well suggest to the Christian observer that a pluralist pattern of social life, with a lot of decentralized and co-operative activity, is something inherently more in tune with the reality of the Church's life than a heavily top-down model. And despite the Church's long love affair with absolutism, in Europe and elsewhere, the fact is that some of the most influential Christian political theologians have advanced ideas that come close to this more pluralist ideal – notably Augustine and Aquinas. Furthermore, this is not a vision that is the sole property of left or right in the contemporary context – which is a good sign, if the Church is to continue to be what Karl Barth called an 'unreliable ally' for any and every political system.

Large ethical questions emerge from this, as to how we guarantee the kind of public civility and respect that would express this kind of pluralist conviction and allow diversity to flourish – but without creating ghettoes. Some of these essays touch on these matters as they arise in connection with laws about blasphemy and the various meanings of 'multiculturalism'. If there is to be honest interaction between communities in a complex society, we should not take the pluralist ideal to require a complete absence of challenge between communities, or even challenge from the state in some areas. Pluralism is more than nervous or evasive good manners. *Argument* is essential to a functioning democratic state, and religion should be involved in this, not constantly demanding the right not to be offended. But this equally needs a strong common culture of ordinary courtesy and respect, *and* a sharp awareness of how criticism of certain religious beliefs or practices may come across as simply an expression of the prejudices of the powerful: words and images that seem harmless (however disagreeable) to an established community may feel much more sinister to a minority. It also needs a strong *theological* grounding: religions believe that they exist because of something other than human power and initiative; and this *ought* to mean that they are less anxious about their survival or success, less prone to turn to violence or coercion to secure their position. We all know that this is not how it looks a lot of the time. But the sense of religious dependence on something quite other than coercive power is, in fact, a theme in all the major faiths, and needs to be spelled out again and again, especially given the way in which religions repeatedly face (and give way to) temptations to collude with violence and imperial ambitions.

The sense that human beings are limited and dependent is not, for religious believers, something humiliating or disempowering; it is simply an acknowledgement of the way things are which, like any apprehension of the truth, is liberating because it delivers us from aspiring to mythic goals of absolute human control over human destiny. This bears very obviously on our environmental challenges. A good many advocates and activists in this area have urged people of faith to articulate more clearly the religious imperatives around responsibility for the environment; and whatever the precise scientific predictions around climate change, there should be no debate as to the rightness of a sober and realistic scaling down of our consumption and pollution. As I have argued here, in the wake of many theologians, the persistent recognition in Christian thought of a 'sacramental' quality in the material world, as taken up by Christ and used ritually by his Church, brings some crystal-clear imperatives in this field. It is fatuous to accuse the Church of slavishly following current fashion in this area; a good many theologians and Christian intellectuals (several Eastern Orthodox thinkers, T. S. Eliot and C. S. Lewis nearer home) were making these points long before it became fashionable to talk about ecology. But it is the same concern that ought to inform our response to economic crisis, where it is, once again, a mythology of control and guaranteed security, combined with the fantasy that unlimited material growth is possible, that has poisoned social and political life across a growing number of countries. No theologian has an automatic skill in economics; but there is an ethical perspective here, plainly rooted in theology, that obliges us to question the nostrums of recent decades, and above all persistently to ask the awkward question of what we want growth *for*, what model of well-being we actually assume in our economics. Without an answer to that, we enter just the 'virtual reality' atmosphere that has created (and maintained) financial disaster in the last few years. And this should also give us a clear orientation in thinking through what we mean by 'development' in countries with dysfunctional or immature economies.

This is an attempt to sketch how some of the diverse themes touched on in this book are connected. But these arguments are framed by the two chapters that open and close the collection; and I want to end with a word about these, since they express what I believe to be the most fundamental points of all. First: if there is one thing that is the opposite of one kind of programmatic secularism, the kind that looks for final and decisive accounts of what things are good for in terms of profit and functionality, it is an attitude to the world that acknowledges that there is more to anything and anyone I encounter than I can manage or understand. What I see is already 'seen' by, already in relation to, some reality immeasurably different from the self I know myself to be or even the sum total of selves like me. To grasp this is to see something of what the word 'sacred' might mean. And second: grasping this fully has the effect of what Wittgenstein called having a concept 'forced on you'. To arrive at a belief in God is seldom if ever the end-point of a single thread of argument. It is infinitely more likely to be the outcome of whatever prompts you to let go of the fictions of control, the notion that you 'own' your body, your world, your future or whatever. Such a letting-go opens up the possibility of taking responsibility for meaningful action, action that announces the presence of the fundamental *giving* on which the world rests and entails also taking responsibility for the other, for the suffering, for those experiencing meaninglessness. This can only (if at all) be set out adequately in narratives of the lives that display what it involves; so my final word in this book is about a particular life which by its nature challenges any reductive picture of what human identity amounts to. There is much in this collection that may appear abstract. But the entire argument would be empty if we could not finally tell stories like that of Etty Hillesum: if there are persons who make that kind of room for the meanings of God in their lives, in conditions as extreme as those under which she lived and died, what kind of society and what kind of public discourse will leave us room at least to sense something of why she stands (and kneels) where she does? A society in which the Christian imagination had atrophied to vanishing point would not give us that kind of room. We had better be clear about the scale of the loss and the evasion that would involve; clear too about the scale of the promise opened up by a story and a practice like this.

All of the chapters in this book were originally delivered as lectures. I have not tried to smooth out all trace of the spoken word, but I have attempted to remove references that are too topical or local for a general reader.

Many people have contributed directly and indirectly to these pieces. Madeleine Bunting, Partha Dasgupta, Conor Gearty, John Milbank, Oliver O'Donovan, Bhikhu Parekh, Raymond Plant, Saskia Sassen, Richard Sennett and Andrew Shanks will all have reason to recognize ideas shared or stirred by them over the years; and as always the late Gillian Rose remains a magisterial influence.

Among my past and present colleagues at Lambeth Palace, Kay Brock, Rachel Carnegie, Helen Dawes, Marie Papworth, Richard Chapman, Jeremy Harris, Toby Howarth, Jonathan Jennings, Christopher Jones, Tim Livesey, David Marshall and Guy Wilkinson were tirelessly helpful in commenting on material and suggesting improvements; and Jonathan Goodall has worked particularly hard in pulling this collection together and tidying up its format, and I am enormously indebted to him for this as for much else. My warmest thanks also go to Robin Baird-Smith of Bloomsbury/Continuum for his steady enthusiasm and encouragement.

Rowan Williams
June 2012

PART ONE

Secularism and its Discontents

Has secularism failed?

There are two ways of asking the question about the 'failure' of secularism. You may want to lament a failure to win the human imagination: secularism has been a massive social and ideological project, which now appears in retreat before resurgent religious bigotry. We may not live in a theocratic state, but the global political agenda is being set by the concerns of religious communities, mostly Jewish, Muslim and Hindu. Secularism has not managed to confine these untamed passions in a private space. And it becomes all the more important to resist attempts in our own setting to reintroduce religious discourse to the public sphere. There is a clear connection – if this is your starting point – between 11 September and the controversies around 'faith schools': secularism must not be allowed to fail in this area if we are not to descend into the worst kind of social feuding, justified by the most (rationally) unanswerable grounds imaginable.

But there is another kind of concern, not by any means articulated only by people who have a vested interest in religious institutions, a concern that surfaces every time we (articulate contemporary North Atlantic citizens) witness what we regard as a disproportionate act of barbarity. It may be an especially repellent murder (of a child by a child, or a child by a parent), a narrative of genocide or an outbreak of manic terrorist violence. Have we, we ask, an adequate vocabulary for speaking of *evil*? Does modernity allow for evil or only for a thinly conceived good and bad or, worse still, progressive and reactionary, useful and redundant? If that's the case, secularism, as the necessary companion of modernity, leaves us linguistically bereaved; we are vulnerable because we have no way of making sense of the most deeply threatening elements in our environment. 'Evil' becomes a trivially emotive way of referring to what we hate or fear or just disapprove of (in the style beloved of American presidents), rather than a reminder of – well, a reminder of what, exactly? Perhaps of the fact that there are aspects of human behaviour which we only make sense of when we say we can't make sense; or of an awareness that the roots of motivation aren't exhausted by the sum total of what we can I call reasons.

Both sorts of question, as I've hinted, have come into focus in recent months. While it is lazy chatter to say that 'everything changed' on 11 September 2001 (meaning that quite a lot changed for that small portion of the human race not exposed to daily and intolerable violence), the events of that day concentrated a whole range of bewilderment about faith, morality and tragedy. It is, I think, just possible to connect the two questions in a way that might illuminate these bewilderments; but it will need some stepping back from a good many clichés about sacred and secular, and perhaps some hesitation in moving too rapidly to articulating our worries about theocracy. We need to look harder at the language of the 'secular', relating it to some of our fundamental concerns about both ethics and the arts. As a very brief and superficial summary of where this examination might lead, it's enough for now to say that it's precisely the sense of an imaginative bereavement expressed in the second question that helps us to see why the 'procedural' secularism of Western modernity has difficulty in establishing itself as definitive. But more of this later.

Defining secularism isn't easy (as the foregoing will already have suggested). A secularist set of protocols for public life would rest upon the assumption that our attitudes to one another in the public realm have to be determined by factors that do not include any reference to agencies or presences beyond the tangible. Thus, ideally, attitudes in such a context are a matter of what can be negotiated and successfully sustained between visible agents and groups of agents. Some of these groups will have commitments that can't be ruled 'admissible' in public discourse; if these commitments are to play any role, they must be translated into language accessible to those who don't share them. In its purest form, this would have two quite serious consequences. First, it suggests that the most substantive motivation of at least a lot of agents and groups will be ruled out of public discourse; it will have to dress in borrowed clothes. Second, it implies that the definitive 'currency' of the public realm is to do with calculation about functions: I or we begin with aims that we are out to realize; the other participants in the social or public process are understood in terms of how they further or obstruct those aims. As this becomes clearer, negotiation advances. The social equilibrium is a state in which all significant participants are adequately satisfied that others are serving or at least not obstructing their goals. Successful social performance is measured by this criterion.

I'm suggesting that secularism in its neat distillation is inseparable from *functionalism*; and if so it will generate a social practice that is dominated by instrumental or managerial considerations, since the perspectives that would allow you to evaluate outcomes in other terms are all confined to the private and particular sphere. In practice, of course, neat secularism is not to be found: evaluative discourse leaks out into the public sphere, sometimes in the moralizing rhetoric of political leaders, sometimes in the improvised rituals (of celebration or mourning or solidarity) that sporadically take over some part of the public territory and establish a certain claim to be common speech. But to understand this more fully, we need to follow through the implication of treating secular modernity and functionalism as belonging together; which is that one of secularism's opposites is the resolve to regard the environment, human and non-human, as more than instrumental. And this is where I'd want to step back and reflect for a moment on what this means specifically in the life of the imagination, and how it works in the foundation of a general ethic.

Two pertinent quotations. First T. S. Eliot, in *Burnt Norton*:

... the unseen eyebeam crossed, for the roses
Had the look of flowers that are looked at.

And R. S. Thomas' poem (from a 1972 collection), 'Via Negativa':

... We look at people
And places as though he had looked
At them too; but miss the reflection.

I want to suggest that the imaginative awareness evoked here is what secularism undermines; that the non-secular is, foundationally, a willingness to see things or other persons as the objects of another sensibility than my own, perhaps also another sensibility than *our* own, whoever 'we' are, even if the 'we' is humanity itself. The point is that what I am aware of, I am aware of as in significant dimensions not defined by my awareness. The point may be reinforced in a particularly acute way if I also include my own subjectivity as one of those objects of awareness that elude my possession. Imaginative construction, verbal or visual, works to make present an aesthetic object that allows itself to be contemplated from a perspective or perspectives other than those of the artist's own subjectivity. Art makes possible a variety of seeings or readings; it presents something that invites a *time* of reception or perception, with the consciousness that there is always another possible seeing/reading. Imaginative construction begins in the sensing of the world in this way, a field of possible readings, therefore never reducible to an instrumental account – related to one agenda, one process of negotiation at one time. Instead, there is an indefinite time opened up for reception and interpretation: the object is located outside the closures of specific conflicts and settlements of interest.

The non-secular character of art, in this context, is its affirmation of inaccessible perspectives. It would not be too glib to say that this somehow constituted art as a religious enterprise; I have a strong recollection of an exchange with a British novelist some years ago, who, despite the fact that she wrote on matters to do with religious history, firmly declined to be labelled as 'religious' in her perspective; but, pressed on this, said that she believed she knew what 'blasphemy' was, and defined it in terms of an instrumentalist attitude to the physical and personal world. Perhaps we could propose that art is what resists blasphemy, defines blasphemy by refusing it. But in relation to the large social and political issues we began with, the point is that art is not in the business of negotiating interests and so cannot assume, with 'procedural' secularism, that what is definitive is what a subject brings into the marketplace of competing interest. It is why art is politically unstable and unhelpful (or, of course, depending on your starting-point, essential).

This is also why the contribution of imaginative construction always brings with it a sense of the tragic – an appropriate element to note in any offering in honour of Raymond Williams. Whether Williams really managed to reconcile a tragic vision with the Marxist hope for social self-redemption is a moot point; Walter Stein, in a fine essay on 'Humanism and Tragic Redemption'[1] has some sharp, if sympathetic, questions on this. 'One of the achievements of Williams' work', says Stein, 'is to bring this dilemma, inherent in any messianic secularism, to a sort of phenomenological test – beyond verbal logicalities: the evidences of the tragic imagination'.[2] The hope for a fullness of revolutionary justice within history, however remotely 'within', assumes a possible world beyond tragedy, a future in which redemption has so relocated the history of suffering, guilt and loss that there is a morally definitive story to be told. Stein wants to know if this is meant to be more than a metaphorically intense prescription for revolutionary action, and whether it implies that history exhausts tragedy. If it does, there will be in principle a historical setting in which every loss can be at some level retrospectively justified. Stein thinks that Williams is actually undecided between something very like this and a more nuanced account which would effectively treat the tragic as unavoidable, and the redemptive possibility as a kind of regulative idea. But the way in which Stein sets up this discussion illustrates very clearly the basic argument I have been sketching so far. Is there an historical, intra-worldly perspective that exhausts what can be said about our transactions and perceptions and self-perceptions? Is there a 'seeing' of the world from some vantage point within it that leaves no room for any seeing from elsewhere? If so, on the basis of the discussion so far, that would be a condition without the possibility of art, an ultimate secularity of the imagination.

And if this is correct, secularism fails by bidding for an ultimately exclusive, even anti-humanist closure; it looks to a situation in which we are not able to see the world and each other as always and already 'seen', in the sense that we acknowledge our particular perspective to be shadowed by others that are inaccessible to us. This is a failure because it finally suggests that there is nothing beyond the processes of successful negotiation – or, in plainer terms, no substantive truth but a series of contests about sustainable control and the balances of power. Fundamental criticism – political, moral, credal – is thus rendered impossible. Those religious writers (John Milbank in particular) who have recently pressed the thesis that there is an innate 'violence' in secularism (a striking reversal of the received wisdom of modernity, for which religion is the inherently violent presence in culture) mean not that secularism is an aggressive ideology inviting conflict – it's meant to be precisely not that – but that, in having no criteria other than functional ones, it takes for granted contests of power as the basic form of social relation. And because history obstinately refuses to end and art continues to flourish, secularism in the sense I have been outlining does indeed seem a doomed enterprise, bound to fail in what I have called its 'pure' form.

However, while we might be relatively confident of the moral and imaginative failure in general terms of a programmatic secularity, putting the question about secularism in this way also invites us to think about the varieties of secularist success. The dominance in our culture of managerial standards is too obvious to need much comment; it has changed the face of education at every level, and is the key to understanding why politics has become a mode of marketing. But there is a further and disturbing dimension to this which needs mentioning, and that is the effective secularization of a great deal of *religious* discourse. Secularism as I have been defining it – a functional, instrumentalist perspective, suspicious and uncomfortable about inaccessible dimensions – is the hidden mainspring of certain kinds of modern religiousness. When religious commitment is seen first as the acceptance of propositions which determine acceptable behaviour – the kind of religiousness we tend now to call fundamentalist – something has happened to religious identity. It has ceased to give priority to the sense that God's seeing of the world and the self is very strictly incommensurable with any specific human perspective, and is in danger of evacuating religious language of the pressure to take time to learn its meaning. Wittgenstein's remark that religious language could only be learned in the context of certain kinds of protracted experience, particularly suffering, is a very un-secular insight, since it assumes that to be able to make certain religious affirmations is bound up with how we construct a narrative of difficult or unmanageable times in our lives. There can be no decisive pre-empting of religious meanings by requiring instant assent to descriptions of reality offered by straightforward revelation. All the major historic faiths, even Islam, which is closest to the propositional model at first sight, assume in their classical forms an interaction between forms of self-imaging and self-interpreting, through prayer and action, and the formal language of belief; that language works not simply to describe an external reality, but to modify over time the way self and world are *sensed*. To say that fundamentalism represents a secularizing moment is to recognize that there has been a dissociation here between language and time, so that the primary task (function) of religious utterance is to describe authoritatively and to resolve problems. It is not easy to restore to this kind of religious ethos the awareness of subject and object alike 'being seen' which I have suggested as basic to the non-secular vision.

However, the wheel comes full circle. Secularism fails to sustain the imaginative life and so can be said to fail: its failure may (does) produce a fascination with the 'spiritual'. But its very pervasiveness in the first place means that this spiritual dimension is likely to be conceived in consumerist terms – either in the individualized functionalism of much New Age spirituality or in the corporate problem-solving strategies of neo-conservative religion. Secularism and fundamentalism feed off each other; in reflecting on the first form of the question in my title, the implicit lament for the apparent weakness of the 'modern' project, it wouldn't do us any harm to note that the restriction of religion to the private sphere doesn't necessarily guarantee a moderate and compliant religiosity. The very insistence of the prevailing cultural instrumentalism is just as likely, or more likely, to reinforce elements in religious language and practice that are themselves impatient with inaccessibility, time and growth. A private inflexible faith confronts the managerial public sphere in a mixture of mutual incomprehension and mutual reflection.

This means of course that a religiousness that challenges the dominant instrumentalism will need to be better aware of how pervasive the dominant categories are, and alert to all those aspects of cultural life that implicitly or explicitly resist those categories. Hence my interest here in defending the idea that art is necessarily un-secular. But it is not quite enough to assimilate aesthetic and religious discourses. The roses have the look of flowers that are looked at, and that gives us some sense of the interiority of artistic perception. But how are they looked at exactly? As soon as one can say that they are looked at consistently or patiently, we are on the road to saying, with a consciousness of metaphorical riskiness, that they are looked at *lovingly*. In his remarkable book, *A Common Humanity*, Raimond Gaita observes that such anthropomorphism is nearer the heart of moral vision than principles about recognizing others as rational creatures. Vital morality, he suggests, has more to do with seeing the other as a special sort of object for a subjectivity not your own than with acknowledging another subject: 'Often, we learn that something is precious only when we see it in the light of someone's love',[3] and 'One of the quickest ways to make prisoners morally invisible to their guards is to deny them visits from their loved ones, thereby, ensuring that the guards never see them through the eyes of those who love them'.[4] The un-secular is not only awareness of other possible viewpoints', but of other possible moral relations, not circumscribed by what I as an individual find possible now. Do the roses look as if they were flowers that were loved? And what, specifically, does that mean?

There is a quite complex process going on in such a recognition. I recognize that what's before me, whether rose or person, can be seen from other perspectives than mine. I acknowledge the interiority and inaccessibility that this entails, and the necessary relation of time and understanding in such a light. What would a maximally comprehensive seeing/reading of the person or object be? One that had unrestricted time to look. But unrestricted time to look presupposes a constancy or commitment to looking, thus a self-investment, even self-dispossession, in respect of what is seen or read. If we put the taking of time at the centre of truthful understanding, a certain convergence of understanding and love begins to appear. My own willingness to stay in engagement with what I see is a mark of commitment and so of a certain kind of self-renunciation (I give up the freedom to walk away in search of something more obviously useful to my determinate plans). To entertain the possibility of other perspectives is to grant that more time than mine can be spent on this exercise; my seeing of someone or something as already and otherwise seen is shadowed, so to speak, by the possibility of an always more sustained and self-invested seeing – a greater love. The aesthetic sense of inaccessibility is on the edge of a particular kind of moral evaluation, seeing in the light of someone's (actual or possible) love; it is not the same thing, but it would be hard to make full sense of the one without the other. And the moral in turn borders on the religious, in the sense that the religious believer is committed to affirming the moralist's possible love as actual. There is a perspective that we can only speak of as representing unrestricted time, total self-investment: for the Buddhist, say, that is the perspective of the objectless compassion of enlightenment; for the Christian (or Jew or Muslim) it is the perspective of an active creator – a 'perspective' which can only with some metaphorical license be called that, as it cannot simply be rendered as one viewpoint among others. It is not an historical perspective, though it may have a kind of historical presence as celebrated and anticipated; and it is thus not ever something that offers simple historical closure or exhaustion. It is what offers space for art, including tragedy.

One of the reasons for the incapacity of secularist modernity to ground or welcome imagination in the way I have been conceiving it is also of course the fact that religious discourse is *itself* morally unstable in just this area. The appeal to the unrestricted time and total self-investment of a divine knowing and loving can forget the caveats about how this is not the same as a perspective in the world. It can claim the possibility of historical closure and exhaustion. From early on in Christian history, there has been an urge to declare history over. The seeing and knowing of the world by God can be rendered as a maximal accumulating of information; and so, when the existence of God is challenged or made remote in Enlightenment thinking, largely because it was seen as endorsing oppressive forms of social and intellectual control, there is a temptation to translate the same sort of mythology into worldly terms. There may be no divine perspective, but there can be an aspiration towards an earthly 'panopticon', to pick up Foucault's argument, a human 'view from nowhere' that can claim finality. And here lies the rationale of that comprehensive instrumentalizing of social relation with which we began; this is the essence of public (shared) language, the field within which other discourses must justify themselves. In other words, forgetful religion is itself one of the roots of secularity – just as secularity re-imports itself into religion in the form of fundamentalism. The last thing we should want to argue here is the moral innocence of traditional religion as a whole.

What I think emerges gradually from these considerations is a sense of twofold risk. Secularism fails, and fails dangerously, to allow room for the inaccessible in what we perceive; it can become the vehicle for the most monumentally uncritical political practices in human history, to the degree that it reduces questions of justification to instrumental ones. 'Making the trains run on time: whether they are going to Eden or Auschwitz, and whether this is desirable or undesirable, just depends upon your point of view'.[5] Or, of course nearer home and with a recent governmental consultation paper in mind, developing a vigorous and competitive defence industry in the United Kingdom. But secularism exists because of the ease with which religious discourses have slipped into an assimilation between faith or knowledge directed *towards* God and the knowledge exercised *by* God – and so have become agencies of control and of violence. If we thought that the opposite of secularism was theocracy, we would actually be admitting the victory of secularism in the political sphere; the exhaustion of reading would have been accepted as axiomatic, simply relocated to religious territory once more.

Equally though, as this already indicates, 'victorious' secularism ends up colluding with violent religiosity. If the conflict between secularism and religion is about social power, about secularism's right to legislate religious language and practice out of the public domain, it invites a counter-claim from that secularized religiousness I have tried to outline which seeks to replace secularist certainties with religiously controlled ones. This is probably most evident if we look at the agonized contortions of so many liberals on the subject of Islam; unable quite to grasp why Muslims are not content to be told that their faith is a legitimate private opinion, they fail to *argue* the question of the limits of private and public and the nature of moral motivation in the 'managed' society. Islam is thus defined by liberal rhetoric into a version of individualized Christianity, a set of personal options for leisure time. To be thus defined, in stark tension with the grammar of the faith itself, naturally prompts a political resistance. Neither globally nor nationally have we yet fully understood these issues; some current discussion of 'faith schools' suggests a radical tone-deafness about all this, assuming that partnership between public institutions and religious communities is simply a subsiding of bigotry.

Understand the risks, however, and you're some way forward. Religious language in all the historic traditions has built into it certain critical impulses, certain procedural challenges to the finality of its own formulations. This arises not from a 'liberal' sense that we can't really be sure and we'd better be politely vague, but from convictions about the strangeness of the divine and the dangers of claiming divine perspectives. Orthodoxy goes in tandem with the injunction to the dispossession of all self-centred perspectives, and the language of theology and worship is supposed to enact that dispossession. How does secularism 'dispossess' itself? That is far too large a question to resolve here; but it may be that the recognition of what I have called the 'procedural' aspect of secular language is a beginning. Secularism, in other words, as a characteristic of the public domain, means that there is no legal privilege for any specific religious position; but not that such positions are regarded as simply private convictions. There may be various ways of securing the participation of religious communities in public business – education is only one such. And this entails not a bare endorsement of doctrine on the part of the secular administration, but a willingness to promote argument about the foundations and legitimacy of various public policies in terms broader than those of instrumental reason. Coleridge, writing in the 1830s about the character of a national religious establishment (*On the Constitution of Church and State*), conceived the task of such an establishment as being that of a perpetual friendly opposition, 'the compensating counterforce to the inherent and inevitable evils and defects of the STATE, *as* a State, and without reference to its better or worse construction as a particular state, the Christian Church collects in itself as in a focus, to radiate them back in a higher quality: or to change the metaphor, it completes and strengthens the edifice of the state without interference or commixture, in the mere act of laying and securing its own foundations'.[6] The invitation to religious institutions to take such a share in the public conversation is precisely an invitation to debate about foundations – a debate never to be historically resolved, but equally not to be relegated to privacy.

For that to be a viable and fruitful model, there must be questions asked about how we separate public and private, personal and corporate; questions about how the dominance of a rights culture, however necessary in some respects, intensifies the weaknesses of secularism unless complemented by the cultural and intellectual nurture of imagination, the grasp of the other's perception and perceivedness; questions about what current obsessions with measurable objectives may conceal. But there must also be questions within religious discourse about what most deeply colludes with instrumentalism in its own speech and practice. It is at least worth asking why the most bitterly contested issues within some traditional religions at the moment, certainly in the Christian churches, are not doctrinal in the strict sense but matters on the dangerous frontiers of sexuality and power. I suspect that this is an area where secularism has indeed succeeded rather strikingly in its conscription of religious understanding.

That is not to argue for a distancing from religious tradition and institution in the name of a looser, more entrepreneurial postmodern religious sensibility. Such an argument is made, with great energy and subtlety, by Richard Roberts in a new collection on *Religion, Theology and the Human Sciences*;[7] but I have argued elsewhere that this leaves us with insufficient resources for challenging the consumerist assumption that haunts the world of new spiritualities. These hesitations are echoed in another recent book, Andrew Shanks *What is Truth?*, 'poetic truth ... requires the continued existence of coherent religious communities, in order, as far as possible, to preserve a stockpile of potentially resonant religious vocabulary for its use – a vocabulary still steeped in prayer, which thereby retains something of the accumulated power this sort of truth demands, for its raw material'.[8] Shanks diagnoses with extraordinary perception the risks of religion's failure to be 'religious' enough, religion's poetic inadequacy (its secularism, in the terms of this lecture), but is fully alert to the seductions of various substitutes for traditional religion, as in the post-metaphysical schemes of Heidegger and Nietzsche. Most importantly of all, he identifies the essence of integral religious and artistic vision with what he calls a 'pathos of shakenness', a full exposure to the disruption which truth brings to power. The traditional religious institution and the vocabularies of doctrine may be frightened with much moral ambiguity, but they remain carriers of those practices of facing and absorbing disruption without panic that allow imagination to be nourished.

In short, then, the relation between secularism and the various languages of disruption, inaccessibility, de-centring, or however we put it, will remain radically and necessarily unsettled. Procedural secularism protests at a violence of the imagination which seeks to control all meanings in virtue of its comprehensiveness and intensity; but it must itself be challenged ceaselessly by the bids of the imagination to resource and renew motivation within our common life. To turn to Raimond Gaita again,[9] the aspiration to universal description must be challenged by the localisms of 'natural language' – which, for this purpose, includes the poetic and the religious.

Two concluding reflections. The success of secularism is not only a problem for modern religion; it is manifestly an issue for the arts. David Kennedy, in a scathing essay on 'How British Poetry joined the Culture Club',[10] sets out three lists of assumptions about poetry as reflected in reviews, publishers' blurbs and so on; they represent three stages in the advance of this sort of 'secularism' over recent decades. The first works on the pre-supposition that poetry is meant to be difficult, that – in Brodsky's words – it is 'the only insurance against the vulgarity of the human heart', that it is a deeply un-secular area of language in which 'the moral, the technical, the musical, the erotic, the sexual and the philosophical may all interfuse'.[11] The second illustrates received wisdom about current British poetry – that it is more 'democratic' than formerly, more accessible and relevant, an organic part of a wider cultural industry: The third catalogues what the 'industry' itself now seems to think about art in general – truth may be replaced by 'sincerity or, at least, authenticity', variety and plurality are inherently virtuous, the boundaries between art and entertainment are quite properly unclear and 'The identification of a definite audience dictates the suppression of difficulty and difference'.[12] Enough said, perhaps. If we want to understand secularism, here are some very good working definitions, and I suspect we may learn more from them than from arguments about the statistical levels of belief in religious propositions or self-identification with religious institutions.

And then, invoking again the shade of the writer in whose honour these thoughts are gathered: Raymond Williams belonged in an intellectual world struggling to preserve a commitment to socialism as one of the professed enemies of secularism (as I have characterized it). *Modern Tragedy* and *The Long Revolution* are, as we've already noted, in part essays towards an un-secular socialism; they may be only intermittently successful as such, but they testify to what it is in the socialist tradition that remains passionately discontented with managerial resolutions to social loss or disorder. Answering the question in my title, in both the forms or registers identified, may require us to pay some attention to what has happened to the un-secular socialist voice in recent years. Has secularism failed? The combination of robust poetics, a self-scrutinizing theology and a politics resolved against one-dimensionality suggests at least some ways of answering without resort to Enlightenment placebos or restorationist religiosity. There is still some insurance against the heart's vulgarity.

Secularism, faith and freedom

Most people who would call themselves secularists would probably defend their position with reference to certain ideals of freedom and equality in society. They are opposing, they say, any kind of theocracy, any privilege given to an authority that is not accountable to ordinary processes of reasoning and evidence. A secular society is one in which it is possible to have fair and open argument about how common life should be run because everyone argues on the same basis; the ideal of secularity means that there is such a thing as 'public reason'. Argument that arises from specific commitments of a religious or ideological nature has to be ruled out of court. If arguments of that kind are admitted, there is a threat to freedom because assertions are being made which are supposed to be beyond challenge and critique. Behind all this lies the strong Enlightenment conviction that authority that depends on revelation must always be contested and denied any leverage in the public sphere.

It is a powerful set of presuppositions, whose effects may be read in the work of politicians, columnists and public intellectuals across Europe and North America. It is often allied with some version of the distinction proposed by Isaiah Berlin between 'negative' and 'positive' liberty – negative liberty being what you have in a society where government allows a maximal level of individual choice and does not seek to prescribe moral priorities, and positive liberty being the situation arising in a society where government sees itself as having a mission to promote one or another ideal of emancipation – as having a specific agenda. The true liberal, as opposed to the 'romantic', must be committed to negative liberty. The pursuit of positive liberty leads to ideological tyranny, to the closing-down of argument and the ironing-out of plurality.

This is a distinction that has entrenched itself pretty firmly in some kinds of political discourse, and the suspicion of positive – 'romantic' – liberty is a good deal stronger than when Berlin delivered his celebrated lecture on the subject in 1958. It fits well with the assumption that a 'secular' perspective is the default position for a liberal and intelligent society. The sort of liberal analysis I have been sketching insists that government has no alternative but to take people's accounts of what they want at face value and work to enable them to be realized without interference, simply guaranteeing that individuals and groups do not harm each other in the process. As Michael Ignatieff writes in his biography of Isaiah Berlin, 'a liberal does not believe in a hierarchy of inner selves (higher, lower, true, false) or believe that there can ever be a political solution to the experience of inner human division.'[1] In a climate where the 'end of history' is proclaimed with the same enthusiasm with which the 'end of ideology' was once greeted, there is bound to be a certain wariness about the suggestion that basic critical questions still need to be asked concerning human capacity or destiny as such, or that there is some serious difference between what people claim to want and what is in their true interest.

I shall be arguing that 'secular' freedom is not enough; that this account of the liberal society dangerously simplifies the notion of freedom and ends up diminishing our understanding of the human person. The tempting idea that there is always an adequate definition of what everyone will recognize as public and reasonable argument needs to be looked at hard – not in order to re-establish the dominance of some unchallengeable ruling discourse, religious or ideological, but to focus the question of how a society deals with the actual variety and potential collision of understandings of what is properly human. A debate about, for example, the status of the embryo in relation to genetic research, or the legalization of assisted dying, or the legal support given to marriage will inevitably bring into play arguments that are not restricted to pragmatic assessments of individual or group benefit. While there can be no assumption that a government will or should assume that such arguments must be followed, there must equally be no assumption that these arguments may not be heard and weighed, that an issue has to be decided solely on arguments that can be owned by no particular group.

This suggests that political freedom is more complex than the licence to pursue a set of individual or group projects with minimal interference. It also needs to be the freedom to ask some fundamental questions about the climate and direction of a society as shown in its policy decisions, to raise in the public sphere concerns about those issues that are irreducibly to do with collabo- ration, the goods that are necessarily common. For example, what makes a good educational system for a nation is not a matter best left to any person's or group's private agenda. Likewise, our environmental crisis is perhaps the most dramatic instance of a challenge we cannot manage on the basis of individualism or even with the exiting mechanisms of merely national policy-making. The state cannot just produce answers to such questions on the grounds of defending Berlin's 'negative liberty'. Nor can this answer the question of how the personal liberties of those who cannot exercise what we should normally think of as reasoned consumer choice of the sort we take for granted – the unborn, the disabled, prisoners – can be securely grounded in a philosophy oriented towards negative liberty. A debate that addressed all these concerns at the needed depth would have to draw in larger considerations. A political freedom that was extended to non-choosers or non-consumers, and that included the freedom to push foundational questions about our relation to the rising generation or to the material environment, could not, I believe, be adequately rooted in a view that defined the legitimacy of a state primarily in terms of its ability to defend maximal individual choice.

There is of course, *pace* Michael Ignatieff, a genuine question about how what people say they want, or who people say they are, is manipulated and largely determined by different kinds of economic and political power. With all the necessary cautions one would want to enter against espousing a simplistic view of political emancipation – Berlin clearly has in mind the crassness of Marxist-Leninism as practised in the old Soviet Union – there are surely issues around the questioning and criticism of certain modes of social and economic control without which 'liberal' society becomes as static and corrupt as old-style state socialism. Political freedom must involve the possibility of questioning the way things are administered – not simply in the name of self-interest (as if the sole ground for a legitimate government were its ability to meet consumer wants), but in the name of some broader vision of what political humanity looks like, a vision of optimal exchange and mutual calling to account and challenging between persons, through which each one developed more fully their ability to act meaningfully or constructively. This is a good deal more than the liberty to pursue a private agenda, limited only by the rather vague prohibition on harm to others (always difficult to pin down). And, to take another theme that some have argued to be basic for the understanding of liberalism, it is more than the liberty of a detached individual to 'redescribe' the world in art, imagination and philosophy. Liberty is more than consumer choice; and it is also more than irony. The British Marxist philosopher, Roy Bhaskar, in a detailed critique of the liberal constructivism of Richard Rorty, notes that once we have identified the sources of injustice, cruelty or social stagnation, once we have formulated a language in which to think about them, we are bound to be involved, like it or not, in an incipient process of public change – 'action rationally directed to transforming, dissolving or disconnecting the structures and relations which explain the experience of injustice'.[2] Shifts in language and explanation that arise in the wake of critical understanding are bound to make different kinds of action, and therefore different kinds of decision, possible. Not to act in the public sphere in consequence of such new possibilities is to make an active choice for stagnation. If ironic redescription is no more than words, it is not really ironic at all; it remains dependent on the systems and power-relations it claims to challenge.

But, of course, to speak of a 'vision' of proper exchange and mutuality is to raise the question that obviously worried Berlin. How do we avoid a prescriptive approach, an imposition of one version of what human integrity or flourishing means? This anxiety is one of the driving forces of what I shall call 'programmatic secularism'. This assumes – to pick up again the points made briefly at the beginning of this chapter – that any religious or ideological system demanding a hearing in the public sphere is aiming to seize control of the political realm and to override and nullify opposing convictions. It finds specific views of the human good outside a minimal account of material security and relative social stability unsettling, and concludes that they need to be relegated to the purely private sphere. It assumes that the public expression of specific conviction is automatically offensive to people of other (or no) conviction. Thus public support or subsidy directed towards any particular group is a collusion with elements that subvert the harmony of society overall.

These are the anxieties that have been very vocally shared in the UK over recent weeks and months, and they will be familiar from elsewhere in Europe. At a time of widespread concern about social disruption and worse, it is perhaps inevitable that there should be some anxiety about visible signs of difference. Yet the implication of this secularist rhetoric is complex and deeply problematic. By defining ideological and religious difference as if they were simply issues about individual preference, almost of private 'style', this discourse effectively denies the seriousness of difference itself. Every specific conviction, it seems, must be considered as if it were individually chosen for reasons that are bound to be out of the reach of any sort of public argument. This account suggests that public reasoning is purely instrumental; it is what goes on in the public sphere simply to test more and less administratively successful methods of continuing the provision of undisturbed public order. In other words, there is nothing fundamental to argue about in public. The problem is not only – as Pope Benedict has suggested – that we have lost confidence in reason and its universality; it is also that reason's territory has shrunk. Because there is no tribunal to adjudicate arguments between basic commitments about God, humanity and the universe, it is assumed that there is therefore no exchange possible between them, no work of understanding and discernment, no mapping of where common commitments start and stop. On this account, there is public reason and there is private prejudice – and thus no way of negotiating or reasonably exploring real difference.

If programmatic secularism leads us to this point, it threatens to end up in political bankruptcy. This is why I want to press the distinction between 'programmatic secularism' and what some have called 'procedural secularism'. It is the distinction between the empty public square of a merely instrumental liberalism, which allows maximal private licence, and a crowded and argumentative public square which acknowledges the authority of a legal mediator or broker whose job it is to balance and manage real difference. The empty public square of programmatic secularism implies in effect that the almost value-free atmosphere of public neutrality and the public invisibility of specific commitments is enough to provide sustainable moral energy for a properly self-critical society. But it is not at all self-evident that people can so readily detach their perspectives and policies in social or political discussion from fundamental convictions that are not allowed to be mentioned or manifested in public.

The alternative is a situation in which, for example, religious convictions are granted a public hearing in debate; not necessarily one in which they are privileged or regarded as beyond criticism, but one in which they are attended to as representing the considered moral foundation of the choices and priorities of citizens. This is potentially a noisier and untidier situation than one where everyone agrees what will and will not 'count' as an intervention in public debate; but at least it does not seek to conceal or deny difference. And what makes this more than a free-for-all where the loudest voice wins the right to impose its views is the shared recognition of law, that system of determining the limits of any individual's or group's freedom which represents the agreement in principle of all groups in a society to renounce violent struggle or assertion because of a basic trust that all voices are being heard in the process of 'brokering' harmony.

The degree to which law will reflect specific views and convictions grounded in religious or ideological belief will vary from one society to another, depending on all sorts of factors – most crucially on whether a group is thought to have persuaded a credible proportion of the population at large that such and such a policy is just or desirable. This needs saying so as to avoid any assumption that there are positions that are automatically incapable of being enshrined in law. Thus it is possible in principle to win public arguments about the need to restrict the availability of abortion; and it is possible in principle to win arguments about legalizing euthanasia. The fact that the former may reflect the wishes of religious groups and the latter offend and contradict them is a matter of contingency. It is precisely because such decisions always remain open to argument that they can be lived with; in a society where there were rigidly fixed standards of what could rationally or properly be legislated, there would be the danger of such legal decisions becoming effectively irreformable. It would be harder to reopen questions on the basis of shifting moral perceptions. This is indeed a somewhat high-risk position – but if the alternative is a view that absolutizes one and only one sort of public rationality, the risks are higher.

So it is possible to imagine a 'procedurally' secular society and legal system which is always open to being persuaded by confessional or ideological argument on particular issues, but is not committed to privileging permanently any one confessional group. The recent UK debate about legalizing assisted dying brought into focus many of these matters in a quite sharp way. Considerations based on religious conviction were certainly in evidence in the debate; but what determined the outcome was neither a purely instrumental and 'secular' set of considerations, nor the unequivocal victory of religious conviction, but the convergence of diverse concerns, both pragmatic and principled. It is an interesting model of how, in a working liberal democracy of a 'procedurally' secular kind, there can be interaction and public engagement between varieties of both religious and non-religious argument.

Essentially what I am suggesting is that this alone guarantees the kind of political freedom I am concerned to define and to secure. But what I further want to establish is that – paradoxical as it may seem – such secularism is in fact the outgrowth of a specific religious position. The Christian Church began as a reconstructed version of the notion of God's people – a community called by God to make God known to the world in and through the forms of law-governed common life – the 'law' being, in the Christian case, the model of action and suffering revealed in Jesus Christ. It claimed to make real a pattern of common life lived in the fullest possible accord with the nature and will of God – a life in which each member's flourishing depended closely and strictly on the flourishing of every other, and in which every specific gift or advantage had to be understood as a gift offered to the common life. This is how the imagery of the Body of Christ works in St Paul's letters. There is no Christian identity in the New Testament that is not grounded in this pattern; this is what the believer is initiated into by baptism. And this is a common life that exists quite independently of any conventional political security. Because it depends on the call and empowering of Christ's Spirit, it cannot be destroyed by change in external circumstances, by the political arrangements prevailing in this or that particular society. So Christian identity is irreducibly political in the sense that it defines a *politeia*, a kind of citizenship (*Philippians* 3.20); yet its existence and integrity are not bound to a successful realization of this citizenship within history. There does not have to be a final and sacred political order created in order for the integrity of the Church to survive.

This is the fundamental theme of Augustine's City of God and of much of the mediaeval tradition; its roots are in the complex convergence of Jesus' preaching of a 'Kingdom' to which only trust in his message gives access and membership, and Paul's understanding of the reconstituting of the community of Jesus in and by the cross and resurrection and the foundational gift of the Spirit of Jesus. It was the belief that led the first Christians to deny the authority of the Roman Empire to command their religious allegiance. In response to challenge and persecution, they sought to clarify the strictly limited loyalty that they believed they owed to government. The tension this created arose through the natural assumption that the rival citizenship defined by the Church was simply in competition with the citizenship that Roman law defined. What was virtually impossible for the Imperial administration to comprehend was the idea that there were graded levels of loyalty: that the level of acceptance of legitimate authority which made you pay taxes or drive your chariot on the right side of the road was something different from the loyalty that dictated your most fundamental moral options on the basis of convictions about the relationships between the world and humans – in particular to their creator. For practical purposes, most of the time, ordinary legality would be uncontroversial; the disturbing thing was that Christians believed that there were circumstances in which loyalty to God trumped the demands of the *civitas*. The state's power was not the ultimate and sacred sanction.

What complicated this understanding to some extent in the Middle Ages was the steady growth of practices that made the Church's administration look more and more like a rival kind of state, a system not only safeguarding loyalties beyond those owed to a legitimate government, but apparently erecting a straightforwardly parallel scheme of social relations. The radical turn of the Lutheran and the English Reformations towards an often uncritical religious sanctioning of state power as exercised by 'godly princes' was in part a reaction against this – bringing its own equally problematic legacy. In all of this theological and political history, however, the most significant point was always the recognition that what the state could properly demand of the citizen was limited by relationships and obligations beyond the state's reach; even in the period when Anglicans were most absolute for the rights of the monarch, there was a clear recognition (expressed notably even by Archbishop Laud preaching to the Court of Charles I) that this could not mean that the state was preserved from falling into error or tyranny, or that the state had an unqualified right over consciences. When the state was in error or malfunction, there remained 'passive obedience': that is, non-violent non-compliance, accepting the legal consequences.

One of the clearest and most interesting statements of the nature of these limitations to the state's legitimate demands comes from an unexpected quarter, in the era of the French Revolution and in the wake of the Enlightenment. In 1793, Carl Theodor von Dalberg, Coadjutor Bishop of Mainz and soon to become Archbishop-Elector of that see, published a treatise *On the True Limits of the State's Action in Relation to its Members*. The state exists because of the need of citizens to labour together for their common welfare, and there is therefore no necessary conflict between individual and state. But since the religious commitments of humankind demonstrate that humanity is not characterized simply by 'interest' (that is, by seeking maximal security and prosperity), the state cannot act so as to undermine or deny those aspects of human action and collaboration which express identities and solidarities wider than those of the mutually beneficial arrangements of any specific state. To quote from Nicholas Boyle's lucid summary in his biography of Dalberg's friend Goethe, the limitations of the state 'lie, not in the duty to respect some supposed non-political aspect of the lives of its citizens, but in duties owed to those who are not its members at all: the state may not command or permit to its citizens any action contrary to their obligations as citizens of the world – there are, that is, rights which all enjoy in virtue of their humanity, and it is a distinguishing feature of Christian states, Dalberg believes, to have recognized such rights. Similarly the state may not command or permit any pointless tormenting or wasteful destruction of the non-human creation, animal, vegetable or mineral.'[3]

This is a remarkable perspective whose contemporary pertinence will not need spelling out. As Boyle stresses, it is important that Dalberg is not claiming that there is a non-political sphere of human life that has to be left alone by the state – a tolerated 'Indian reservation' of private conviction. He is arguing for the interpenetration of two sorts of political action, we might say – on the one hand the routine business of a law-governed society, on the other the relations and obligations that exists in virtue of something other than pragmatic or self-interested human decisions, the solidarities that do not depend on human organization. For Dalberg, these are essentially the solidarities of shared relationship to a creator. The state cannot administer what these demand in a simple way – it has a limited and more modest purpose; but neither can it ignore them. We are, in fact, here given a sketch of what I attempted earlier to suggest in terms of the presence of certain sorts of argument and negotiation in the public sphere of a state's legal process, as groups of strong conviction attempt to persuade the state that such and such a proposition would or would not infringe those larger solidarities. Current debates about euthanasia, ecology or the freedoms of religious minorities all in different ways carry elements of this kind of questioning.

Dalberg's great-nephew was none other than Lord Acton – though whether the great historian ever made direct use of his kinsman's work I do not know. Quite early in his political and intellectual career, Acton (writing in 1862 to Richard Simpson) asserted that 'liberty has grown out of the distinction (separation is a bad word) of Church and State'.[4] The mode of expression in this letter might lead us to suppose that he is thinking simply of a liberty of conscience that is basically non-political; but in fact, as his mature writing makes clear, this would be to misread him. He is not advocating a situation where the state conceded certain private rights, but a state that recognizes that it is not in fact the grantor of such rights in the first place; a state that recognizes that it has come into being to serve the diverse human groupings that now constitute it, that it derives its legitimacy from their co-operation and consent as embodied in constitutional form. As such, the state cannot claim to be the source of legitimate behaviour or legitimate modes of association: it has the right from time to time to judge how far particular behaviours and associations adversely affect the coexistence of the communities in its jurisdiction, but not to prescribe in advance that behaviour unlicensed by the state should be publicly invisible or illegitimate. And because the state is always a coalition of groups agreed on a legal structure, it is risky to identify nations and states, let alone races and states. Acton was a good deal ahead of his time in refusing to take nationalism for granted as a natural companion to liberalism.[5] His defence of federalism as a political principle merits some re-examination at a time when what once seemed the inflexible modern notions of national sovereignty are being tested severely by the globalization of markets and cultures; but that is perhaps another story.

What emerges from this reading of the Christian contribution to the history of political thought, a reading shaped by both Roman Catholic and Anglican thinkers (Acton's disciple John Neville Figgis being prominent among the latter; we shall be returning to his ideas frequently in later chapters), is that there is serious case for saying that some aspects of liberal politics would be unthinkable without Christian theology, and that these are the aspects that offer the clearest foundation for a full defence of active political liberty. Faith is the root of freedom and programmatic secularism cannot deliver anything comparable. The Christian presence in the Roman Empire declared that there were solidarities independent of the Empire and therefore capable of surviving political change. Augustine's version of this opened the door to a further refinement, implying that the survival of these 'solidarities' could be a contribution to the reconstruction of political order on the far side of any particular disaster or collapse. And lest that should appear an academic point, it is worth observing that the role of the Church in post-conflict societies in Africa today, dealing with education, the protection of women and children and the maintenance of some forms of trustworthy associational life, illustrates with dramatic and poignant clarity exactly what this means. A 'liberal' politics that depended on the maintenance of one unchallengeable form of administration at all costs, as if no credible political life could survive its disappearance, would risk succumbing to illiberal methods to secure its survival. Whenever we hear – as we sometimes do – of the need to limit some historic legal freedom for the sake of countering general threats to our liberty, from crime or terror, we should recognize the reality of the moral dilemmas here; but also be alert to what happens to our concepts of liberty in this process.

The salient point is that a supposedly liberal society which assumes absolutely that it has (as I put it earlier) the resources for producing and sustaining moral motivation independently of the actual moral or spiritual commitments of its citizens, is in danger of behaving and speaking as if the only kind of human solidarity that really matters is that of the state. Programmatic secularism, as a shorthand for the denial of the public legitimacy of religious commitment as a partner in political conversation, will always carry the seeds, not of totalitarianism in the obvious sense, but of that 'totalizing' spirit which stifles critique by silencing the other. Charles Taylor, writing about de Tocqueville, summa-rizes Tocqueville's concern about a secularized democratic will degenerating 'into a kind of mild despotism (*despotisme doux*) in which citizens fall prey to a tutelary power that dwarfs them; and this is both cause and effect of a turn away from the public to the private which, although tempting, represents a diminution of their human stature'.[6]

Procedural secularism is the acceptance by state authority of something prior to it and irreducibly other to it; it remains secular, because as soon as it system-atically privileged one group it would ally its legitimacy with the sacred and so destroy its otherness; but it can move into and out of alliance with the perspec-tives of faith, depending on the varying and unpredictable outcomes of honest social argument, and can collaborate without anxiety with communities of faith in the provision, for example, of education or social regeneration. Further, the critical presence of communities of religious commitment means that it is always possible to challenge accounts of political reasoning that take no account of solidarities beyond those of the state. Dalberg's awareness of citizenship in a transnational community, and membership within an interdependent created order, offer vivid illustrations of the moral perspectives that state loyalties alone will not secure. And, to move into a slightly different idiom, this poses the very significant question of how 'civil society' is to be understood; the idea that this might have a properly international dimension is, in fact, more and more compelling in our own day.

There is, of course, one set of issues on the border of what we have so far been discussing which demands to be addressed more directly. At the moment, advocates of programmatic secularism are troubled, if not panicked, by the increasing visibility of Islam in historically Christian and/or liberal societies. But even procedural secularists are often disturbed. Islam, so the argument runs, knows nothing of the 'secularizing' element in the history of Christian theology; its political theory asserts the primacy of the *umma*, the transnational community of believers, over every possible political arrangement; but, where Christianity has on the whole settled for ironic distance and the distinction of levels of corporate loyalty, Islam has been understood to assume that it is indeed possible to realize the full political embodiment of revealed law. In other words, it does compete for the same space as the state.

In fact, the distinction in modern democracies between the way Muslims belong and the way others belong is by no means as stark as some ideologues might expect. Some Muslim scholars resident in the West, writers like Maleiha

Malik or Tariq Ramadan, have discussed ways in which Muslim citizens can engage in good conscience with non-Muslim government and law. Some have observed that Islam recognizes law that is compatible with Muslim principles as ipso facto Islamic law so that the Muslim can acknowledge, enjoy and defend full citizenship in a non-Muslim society. Furthermore, there is already in Islam a tradition of plurality in the interpretation of Islamic law, which should make us cautious about assuming that there is one and only one kind of jurisprudence represented by the word *sharia*. And there are also in Islamic history abundant examples of conflict between rulers and religious scholars, government and *ulema*, to the degree that some have spoken of a limited analogy with the Christian tension between Church and state. These are complex historical issues, but there is enough to suggest that we need a nuanced approach to the supposedly monolithic character of Muslim political thought.

That being said, there is one area of abiding difficulty. The Muslim may with a good conscience enjoy citizenship in a non-Muslim society; what exactly does citizenship mean for a non-Muslim in a Muslim society? It is important not just to cast this question as one of simple 'reciprocity', as if both parties shared exactly the same presuppositions and all that was in question was whether these principles were being fairly applied. But to what extent does the Muslim state, acknowledging in more or less explicit ways the sovereignty of Islamic law, employ a notion of citizenship that also allows for legitimate loyalties outside the community of Muslim believers? Historically, there have been impressive examples of something very like this recognition; but there have also been historic examples of severe civic burdens imposed on non-Muslims. Most disturbingly, there is the tension between the great Quranic insistence that 'there is no compulsion in religion' and the penalties associated with conversion and the pressures around mixed marriages in the practice of many Muslim states.

So one of the questions which Christians will want to pursue in their continuing dialogue with Islam is whether the idea of a 'secular' level of citizenship – with all that this implies about liberties of conscience – is indeed compatible with a basically Islamic commitment in the shape of society at large; whether the Muslim state will distinguish between what is religiously forbidden and what is legally punishable as a violation of the state's order – so that adultery or apostasy, to take the obvious examples, do not have to be regarded as statutory crimes (let alone capital ones). Muslim jurists in several Muslim societies are raising these questions already, with much sophistication and sensitivity, and the dialogue between our communities needs to attend carefully to this debate.

I have devoted some attention to this difficult question partly because of its unquestioned pertinence in many parts of the world, partly because of the somewhat inadequate way in which we sometimes discuss it. Reciprocity is a perfectly sensible notion from our standpoint; but we also need to understand why for some Muslims there seems to be no automatic symmetry between Christian and Muslim tolerance. Unless we are able to argue in ways that engage with the distinctive features of Islamic polity and politics, we are not going to connect or to make any difference. We cannot collude with an interpretation of Islamic political identity whose effects for Christians have sometimes been lethally oppressive; neither can we simply expect that an argument assuming Christian and liberal principles will convince. There is ample work to do in this area.

In conclusion, I want to return to the main lines I have been sketching here, and to make one or two final observations on the sort of 'enlightenment' accounts of freedom, faith and the secular with which I began. The case I have argued (by no means a wholly original one) is that a certain kind of 'secularism' has direct Christian and theological roots. By this I do not mean that curious infatuation with the idea of a world devoid of the sacred which preoccupied some theologians of the 1960s, but something almost opposite to this – a culture in which presence and solidarities exist which exceed and escape the conventional boundaries of 'public life', but which thus imbue that public life with depth and moral gravity that cannot be generated simply by the negotiation of practical goods and balanced self-interests. To put it more dramatically, I am arguing that the sphere of public and political negotiation flourishes only in the context of larger commitments and visions, and that if this is forgotten or repressed by a supposedly neutral ideology of the public sphere, immense damage is done to the moral energy of a liberal society. For that ideal of liberal society, if it is to be any more than a charter for the carefully brokered competition of individuals, requires not a narrowing but a broadening of the moral sources from which the motivation for social action and political self-determination can be drawn.

But there is an underlying question prompted by the remark of Ignatieff on 'inner selves', which I quoted earlier. The liberal, Ignatieff claims, is not concerned with 'hierarchies' of true or false selves. But the danger here is surely that of creating a political discourse in which any notion of a self-aware and self-critical person disappears. There is indeed, deplorably, a kind of appeal to 'liberal' ideals which effectively reduces the human self to an economic unit, a solitary accumulator of rights, comforts and securities. But it is an odd sort of liberalism that so dismisses the significance of a freedom learned by social processes of formation and exercised consciously and intelligently for goals that are not exclusively self-interested.

If the three terms of my title do indeed belong together; if a proper secularism requires faith; if it is to guarantee freedom, this is because a civilized politics must be a politics attuned to the real capacities and dignities of the person – not the individual consumer, but the self learning over time to exercise liberty in the framework of intelligible communication and the self-scrutiny that grows from this. Such a concept of the person is, I would maintain, unavoidably religious in character; it assumes that we 'answer' not only to circumstance, instinct or even to each other, but also to a Creator who addresses us and engages us before ever we embark on social negotiation. That, after all, is why we regard the child – or the mentally challenged adult or the dying man or woman who has passed beyond ordinary human communication – as a person, whose dignities and liberties are inalienable. The struggle for a right balance of secular process and public religious debate is part of a wider struggle for a concept of the personal that is appropriately robust and able to withstand the pressures of a function-alist and reductionist climate. This is a larger matter than we can explore here; but without this dimension, the liberal ideal becomes deeply anti-humanist. And, like it or not, we need a theology to arrest this degeneration.

Convictions, loyalties and the secular state

Ana Pauker was a minister in the infamous Stalinist administration that ruled Romania in the early 1950s; she was noted for her unswerving devotion to the orthodoxies of Moscow. A favourite anecdote of the day described how she was seen in the streets of Bucharest on a warm spring day under a large umbrella: why? 'Because', she said, 'it's raining in Moscow.'

Conviction is not always the purely mental business we sometimes assume it to be. Ana Pauker not only had ideas about where the truth lay; she acted as if she were somewhere else, somewhere where this truth was clearer and more tangible. And states have always been suspicious of those sorts of conviction which appear to demand this kind of belonging elsewhere, this additional loyalty. Christians in the eastern Roman Empire of the early fourth century were executed because they were assumed to be agents of the Christian kingdom of Armenia; not much later, they were executed in Persia as suspected agents of the now Christian Roman Empire. Pope Pius V's decree of excommunication against Elizabeth I condemned hundreds of Roman Catholics in the century that followed to persecution and death as agents of a foreign power. Communists in the West, from the 1920s to the 1950s, were widely assumed to have deeper loyalties to the Soviet Union than to their own land. Muslims today in the West and Christians in Iraq are victims of the assumption that they are footsoldiers in the new global conflict between the just society and its enemies.

One of the interesting features of modernity is a suspicion that is related to this, but significantly different. What I've so far been talking about is a situation in which one 'sacred' order, a nation or an empire with a clear sense of its legitimacy and its right to demand loyalty, detects in some of its citizens a loyalty to some rival order that also claims to be legitimate or in some sense sacred. But increasingly what we see, in the actual policies of some states and in the rhetoric of the political classes in other states, is a presumption that the rational secular state is menaced by the public or communal expression of religious loyalty.

It is not a matter of one sacred order (empire, nation state or religio-political unit) facing a rival, but of a sense that the public space of society is necessarily secular: that is, necessarily a place in which no local or sectional symbolic activity is permissible. Conviction is free – that is a foundational principle of modern liberal society; but visible and corporate loyalty to the marks of such conviction is to be strongly discouraged. It puts in question the neutrality of the public space, and can be read as a sort of aggression against other convictions or against the programmatic absence of convictions that the state assumes for public purposes. For statutory authority to collude with, let alone actively support, these loyalties fatally compromises the very basis of legitimate liberal society.

It is the argument of the French government, and of those who, for example, resist the spread of religiously based schools in our own country. It is not trivial or frivolous, but it is important to try and understand what it takes for granted before we accept it as axiomatic. And what it assumes is in fact an aspect of modern Christian rhetoric which has come to speak of religious conviction as essentially a matter of individual option – a rather shop-worn version of the Reformation concern with justification by faith and the Reformation critique of unaccountable Church authority. The modern state presents itself as a guarantor of public order and peace as against religious communities that demand allegiance and come to blows over the terms of that allegiance. In the textbook version of modernity, the Wars of Religion in the early modern age produce a kind of disgust with the claims of public faith, religious commitment that is active in the arena of public life. And those aspects of the Reformation which stress interior devotion and are cautious about the Church as a visible political entity are drawn in to reinforce the argument for a non-confessional state, in which private conviction is free, but public loyalty is exclusively claimed by the state itself. In various ways and in varying degrees, the Christian confessions of the modern Western world accepted this programme over the succeeding centuries.

But the story is not after all so simple. As the American theologian William Cavanaugh has persuasively argued, it would be much more accurate to say that the Wars of Religion arose from the use of religious controversy by political agents to justify military adventures aimed at national consolidation or expansion, which in turn consolidated the new centralized sovereign authorities within nation states. 'Liberal theorists', he writes, 'would have us believe that the state stepped in like a scolding schoolteacher on the playground of doctrinal dispute to put fanatical religionists in their proper place'.[1] But in fact, the development of the belief that the state enjoyed a monopoly of legitimate coercion meant that defining the exclusive boundaries of sovereign territory was far more important than before: the state needs to know whom it can confidently command, whose allegiance it can safely enforce, whom it can mobilize in its defence. Thus the modern state is not in origin a pacific force; it is a system committed to violence as 'the primary mechanism for achieving social integration in a society with no shared ends'.[2]

Shared ends cannot be taken for granted; so particular kinds of social integration are problematic. The state takes each citizen as an agent in need of integration with others, and proposes a concordat to secure agreed boundaries between the interests of these agents. Thus the modern state assumes a direct relation with its citizens, not mediated through other communities – a relation whose contractual quality is already in evidence early on, though it becomes far more evident in the market societies of late modernity. And part of this relation is the state's assurance of individual rights, claims that can be enforced in its courts; among these is the right to freedom of conscience as regards personal belief. However, modern states have not been eager to recognize any priority for personal conviction when this may affect the performance of public duties – as is clear from the varying attitudes to conscientious objection in wartime. While there is usually recognition of a belief system that declares all war illicit, it is far harder to make any case for the person who regards this or that particular war as illicit on grounds of religious belief. Such an attitude suggests that the person's religious commitment involves both an additional level of social belonging, a membership in some other nexus of relations than that of the state, and a formation in critical questioning of the state's decisions, a reluctance to take for granted the legitimacy of these decisions without some further scrutiny.

This whole cluster of issues has become more immediate and practical with the current complexities over the modern state's relation to Muslim identity. Liberal commentators properly concerned to combat anti-Muslim prejudice (Nick Cohen, for example, in an article in the *New Statesman*, 1 October 2004) persist in assuming that Islam is a set of convictions in the mode of much modern Christianity. To suggest that the Muslim owes an overriding loyalty to the international Muslim community, the *umma*, is worrying; it is a factor in Muslim identity (say the liberal commentators) that intensifies suspicion towards the Muslim community in a quite unnecessary way. What is desirable is thus for Muslims to make clear that they have a straightforward primary

modern political loyalty to the nation state, unaffected by the private convictions that individual Muslim believers happen to hold in common.

This means accepting, among other things, the view that the rights conferred
by the modern state are essentially rights accorded to individuals in respect
of their private consciences. And here is where one of the major conflicts in
modern legal thinking comes into focus. The liberal state has repeatedly had to
make accommodation with minority communities, not simply with individuals
– ethnic minorities whose identities have been damaged by state centralism,
religious groups, even those making a specific choice of lifestyle (the fiercely
controverted politics of gender and sexual orientation is commonly cast in
terms drawn from the struggles of ethnic and religious minorities). The liberal
state has made numerous concessions to a multicultural model which is in fact
at odds with classical liberal thinking. And the British state is unusually and
interestingly hybrid in this respect, combining vestiges of a confessional polity
(the establishment of the Church of England) with a generally liberal political
culture and an increasing pragmatic acceptance of multiculturalism.

Maleiha Malik, a professional jurist of Muslim allegiance, has recently
written at length on this conflict, arguing that, since we cannot just go back
to conservative nationalism, and since the interests of minority groups are not
adequately safeguarded by classical liberal principles of individual entitlement
and non-discrimination, we need a more sophisticated model of the relation
between the state and its minorities, which in turn requires some rethinking
of the original picture of the state contracting with a mass of atomised
individuals. Her conclusion is that the state cannot avoid legislation about the
rights of communities; but that there then needs to be a pathway for minority
communities to find new ways of identifying with public processes and social
institutions, so that (instead of making the main form of protection against
discrimination the guarantees provided by the courts, and so consuming
immense energy in litigation) specific groups may play a positive role in
framing policy before legislation is finalized. And this needs more developed
representative institutions of consultation. The issue of 'rights' for a minority
religious community thus comes to be allied with a wider set of questions
about local democracy and the weaknesses of an 'elective dictatorship' model of
parliamentary rule.[3]

What this implies is in fact a subtle reframing of the issue of loyalty. Loyalty
to a sovereign authority is replaced by or recast as identification with a public
process or set of public processes; the simple question about loyalty, 'Are you

with us or against us?' becomes a question about adequate and confident partic-ipation in a law-governed social complex. We are taken beyond a polarized picture of exclusive loyalty to the state menaced by mysterious fifth column-ish affiliations elsewhere. Loyalty to the *umma* is not necessarily in competition with dependable citizenship in the state if the state's practices of consultation and acknowledgement of communal identities remove the threat of a total and terminal privatizing of religious conviction – the individual believer facing the state which tolerates his or her belief system but cannot deal with them as they concretely are, embedded in the specific relationships that in fact constitute the believing identity itself.

In the same book as Maleiha Malik's essay, there is also a piece by Tim Winter, one of the foremost expositors of Islamic thought in the UK, on 'Muslim Loyalty and Belonging', in which he argues that the danger faced by Muslim communities from within is a primarily negative model of Islamic identity, a model lacking 'cultural embeddedness'. Alienated equally from familial tradition (usually regarded as hopelessly compromised), from a living tradition of reflective exegesis and from the environment fostered by global capitalism, the Muslim radical recognizes the essence of Muslim faith and law only in what totally negates all these; and this, says Winter, is 'a religion of the gaps, a kind of void ... a list of denials, of wrenchings from disturbing memories'.[4] But the implication of this is that a secular state that fails to address Malik's agenda about participation for minority communities is one of the factors that intensifies pressures towards such a negative definition of religious loyalty; more seriously, it may intensify the sense that there is indeed a compe-tition between two comparable loyalties.

Now there are certainly features in classical Islamic political thought that lend themselves to the notion that the 'House of Islam' is always and neces-sarily a clearly defined positive political unit; but there is also a long tradition of reflection on what it is to be a minority in a non-Islamic setting. Part of the problem in all this is precisely the modern assumption that political belonging itself is always unitary and clearly defined. The Islamic model is perhaps best thought about not as creating a parallel state, but as positing a loyalty to divine law, variously incarnated in different concrete political units, but always having a claim even when imperfectly realized.[5] Such a loyalty is indeed about the possi-bility of critical participation in the institutions of a secular state; but it requires the state to think clearly about what it understands by religious belonging and not to reduce it to the level of a private voluntary association of the like-minded.

This particular discussion ought to sharpen the agenda of Christian theologians, and to send them back to some foundational texts. Early Christianity, as we have seen, is a communal phenomenon proclaiming an allegiance that is deeply threatening to the unitary and sacred identity of the ancient city and the ancient empire. I have argued elsewhere that what we find in some of the records of the martyrs is in fact a surprisingly novel account of political loyalty: the accused refuse to treat the emperor as divine, but they accept the duty of paying taxes and praying for the public good. Thus they see themselves as participating in a public process, not as rebels against existing order; but they will not regard their loyalty to the state as a matter of exclusive and absolute obligation, religious obligation. They are, it seems, trying to clarify the sense in which political loyalty and religious loyalty are not in direct competition – though they may be in conflict if the former makes claims appropriate only to the latter. Similar points are made in the famous second century Letter to Diognetus, in which we find a clear affirmation of the Church as a distinctive community with different moral horizons, but also a denial that this means a visible separation from public life. The lapidary statement in the Epistle to the Philippians that the *politeia* of Christians is in heaven (*Philippians* 3.20) is evidently taken to imply both that Christian belief is a form of participatory citizenship and that this exists in parallel, and sometimes in tension, with the forms of citizenship that exist in any given social order.

It is a less clear-cut picture than we find in classical Islam – or perhaps we should say, a more sceptical one, in which hopes for the realization of an actual state embodying the law of God are far more muted. But we should not therefore conclude that the difference between the two traditions of faith is between a public and a private or a corporate and a personal ideal. The modern Christian tendency has indeed been to stress, as Reinhold Niebuhr so eloquently did, the way in which faith can purify motivation and reinforce the standards of moral commitment that prevail in a liberal society; but an increasing number of Christian moralists have observed that this leaves no role for the Church as a body with its own integrity and peculiarity, as a community whose end is to form human lives according to some model (and by some power) other than that of the individual agent of the liberal ideal. Stanley Hauerwas has recently characterized Niebuhr's view as effectively 'a complex humanism disguised in the language of the Christian faith';[6] the liberal Christian approach assumes that the business of Christian commitment is not to produce lives that participate in the holiness of Christ so much as lives that can be lived with a fairly easy conscience within the arrangements of the modern state, motivated by a rather unspecific inspiration.

This takes us back to the sort of case made by Cavanaugh in the work referred to earlier. He identifies with some sharpness the way in which the modern state generates what he calls a 'state-society complex', defining what is culturally acceptable or dominant. 'What is permissible as public discourse increasingly obeys the logic of accumulation; state-funded school lunch programmes are defended in terms of increasing students' performance and thus enhancing the country's position in the global economy vis-à-vis the Japanese'.[7] This cultural hegemony is deeply hostile to the practice of communities that do not begin from the same standards of instrumental rationality; it insists upon the naturalness and indisputability of this sort of rationality, and increasingly affects the concrete practice and the rhetoric of religious communities themselves. Cavanaugh, like Hauerwas, denies that the 'public space' of contemporary culture is in any meaningful sense neutral or free, and insists that the Christian community must be distinguished by the telling and enacting of a story that is different from that propagated by the modern state. This, of course, involves exposing the fact that the modern state does in fact tell a story: that is, that it is not the embodiment of a timeless rationality. In the face of the narrative of modernity, the Church declares that its account of human nature, calling and possibility is constituted by a set of highly specific events, figured forth in sacramental action. And the community that gathers around these actions is one in which human beings are deliberately shaped in the likeness of one particular form of life, the form that is defined in the story, the identity, of Jesus Christ.

Thus Cavanaugh goes on to say that the activity of the Church in the public sphere should not, and indeed cannot, be confined to 'lobbying'. Helpful as this is in some circumstances, the main task is to create 'spaces' for an alternative story – to challenge the self-evidence of the narrative of secular modernity. This is in no way a bid for religious takeover or confessional monopoly, but it does make a claim for the visibility of Christian community – and other religious communities. It assumes that the state does not have the right to demand a sort of secrecy on the part of religious groups, a contract by which no sign of particular religious loyalty is admitted in the public space. But it means that the religious community needs to be clear about its primary responsibility as a place where people are formed in moral vision by shared practice; and such practice, says Cavanaugh, is both the ritual practice by which the basic story

is learned and repeated and stories of alternative human behaviour shaped
by this. Christian involvement in the public sphere is a visible celebration of
the sacramental reality by which believers live, and the devising and implementing of usually small-scale projects suggesting possibilities for human
beings different from those assumed by contractual and acquisitive stories.
Cavanaugh's book ends with a moving narrative bringing these two elements
together: following the murder in 1977 of a Salvadorean priest who had resisted
government injustice, Archbishop Oscar Romero had decided that the requiem
for this priest should be the only mass celebrated in the diocese on the Sunday
following, so as to 'collapse the spatial barriers separating the rich and the
poor'.[8] The reader will recall Romero's own death not long afterwards, in the
context of another eucharistic celebration: drawing rich and poor together in
this way is also to draw near to real danger in some political contexts.

This is a dramatic example – too dramatic almost to be helpful. Drama is
always attractive for a variety of questionable reasons, and it is important to
remember the caveat long ago entered about a particular kind of socially-
conscious British theology or spirituality – that it borrows the language and
imagery of more tragic and serious situations to glamorize its well-meaning
reformism. Yet we need some stories of alternative possibility, even in the less
apocalyptic atmosphere of modern Britain: perhaps the church-based mass
campaigns around international debt and, currently, trade justice provide
something of this, especially since they have not been by any means confined
to 'lobbying', but have been regularly linked with concrete policies and actions
by local churches (commitment to the use of Fair Trade goods, for example).
When all the cautions have been entered, the point still stands: the Church as
a political agent has to be a community capable of telling its own story and
its own stories, visible as a social body and thus making claims upon human
loyalty. While not a simple rival to the secular state, it will inevitably raise
questions about how the secular state thinks of loyalty and indeed of social
unity or cohesion. To this degree, it is not in a different case from the Muslim
umma.

But the overall picture begins now to look very complicated. The defender of
public secularity might well say, 'This is precisely what we need to worry about:
social cohesion is threatened by highly visible religious groups. This is not an
issue about some sort of sinister totalitarian uniformity, only of the conditions
for public stability, dependable order.' The concern is a serious one. The apologist
for a robust account of religious visibility in the public sphere has to do some

work to clarify the role of the state in such an argument, and the character of the stability or 'social integration' that might be hoped for. It will not do, surely, to rest content with a sort of Hobbesean situation in which strong, community-based ethical frames of reference simply fight it out between themselves.

In what remains of this lecture, I want to try and suggest some ways of responding to this concern. The first thing to say is that no one begins with a clean slate in this context: we are not seeking to develop a polity out of nothing. The modern state has developed for reasons that represent irreversible trends in social history, trends to do with vastly expanded population levels, the universal administration of welfare and the exigencies of defence. As has been argued at length in some recent writing, the shift from 'nation state' to 'market state' represents an intensifying of the contractual element in modern polity, to the degree that national government is both pressed to increase its responsiveness to consumer demand and eager to devolve some of its duties to private contractors. Its actual sovereignty is also deeply compromised by global economic forces. Yet it remains, even in 'market' form, a system for guaranteeing at least two things: a structure that determines the economic standing of every person within defined geographical boundaries and thus provides a clearing-house of comprehensive information (and often, in consequence, a comprehensive welfare scheme); and a monopoly of legitimate force, as expressed in a legal system and a defence budget. In a world in which populations are mobile as never before, and in which there is therefore bound to be wider ethnic and religious diversity in any area than hitherto, there is no possibility of dismantling either of these. Government needs to know whom to tax, and in some circumstances whom to conscript, and who has a claim to be defended. The apparatus of the modern state is essential for a law-governed society in which diverse communities exist side by side.

The modern state thus realizes, however unsatisfactorily, one central element in any corporate religious vision: it militates against simply forgetting any person, treating individuals as dispensable. Since every religious system considers that the existence of each person is non-contingent, an expression of positive divine will, this has to be a basic religious concern. In this respect, modern polity and the religious communities we are familiar with stand together against, for example, ancient slave societies. And, as hinted earlier, this allows us to see political loyalty as bound up with the claims of law rather than mere geography or ethnic history (the emotional loyalty felt towards place and history is another matter, of course, and not our primary focus here): the state apparatus is a means to secure certain rights and liberties, which, whatever exactly we might want to say about them, at least represent a statutory seriousness about each human subject as citizen.

The state thus implicitly proposes a kind of minimum level for political virtue – the keeping of the law as a form of acknowledging the basic claim of other agents to the same stability or security as you desire for yourself. It is not quite the same as the all-important liberal principle of toleration; more a bare recognition of mutual limits between agents and of a certain conceptual space occupied by other agents in respect of an order not determined by either you or them in isolation. Our problems arise when this bottom line of political virtue is fleshed out by some more definite philosophy – often derived from specifically non-religious axioms (Cavanaugh's 'state-society complex'). And the religious apologist ought to be able to say something like this. 'I accept the universality of the rule of law in this specific contingent setting, and the monopoly of force, internal and external, which it entails. I do so because of the irreducible commitment of my faith to the non-contingent quality of each agent. But this is still mostly a procedural or formal acceptance. As a religious believer, I have some matters of content to propose here as representing what my tradition sees as appropriate virtues, or even as making for holiness. And my task becomes one of negotiating how much of that content a diverse population can own for itself.'

Thus, the state will formally be bound to provide for the nurture and formation of children. The religious person will want to argue for this to take the particular form, say, of state support for monogamous marriage. For the believer, this is something enjoined by basic beliefs – that human fidelity is an imaging of divine covenant with the community, for example. But the public argument has to be that this might be a desirable framework for maximal stability for the growing child; and there would need to be statistical work to support this as a negotiating position. Likewise, the state provides protection against homicide. The religious person sees this as grounded in the divine relation to each person, from conception to death, a relation that sets up certain indestructible inter-human relations also; and is therefore extremely suspicious of the limitations on protection involved in the legalization of abortion or euthanasia. But the public argument will be about whether these limitations involve so deep a contradiction that the actual principle is undermined.

The point is that the religious 'negotiator' in such cases (which are, as you will recognize, far from academic at the moment) accepts that much of the argument will be pragmatic – but acts and argues from a position that is not pragmatic, and that is formed by specific narratives and practices. S/he does not seek the right to impose those narratives, but, by engaging in public dispute on these matters, denies that there is a simple and neutral resolution. Even as arguments of contingent evidence are deployed, the believer's own position is not finally dependent on them, and the motivation for pursuing a critical debate arises from loyalties that are bound up with narratives of God's commitment to the believing community. It is thus equipped to survive particular defeats within the system; it insists that majority votes do not specify what is true, even if they determine what is, descriptively, at any moment lawful. And this is a significant critical element in any society, which, if it is not to be at the mercy of pure legal positivism, needs some vantage point from which it is possible to discuss moral questions in terms that go beyond the constraints of a majority vote alone.

This is to fill out somewhat an argument sketched by Raymond Plant. Specific communities of religious commitment can go a fair way to accepting the common rule of law as enshrining something central for them; but they will inevitably be seeking to 'thicken the texture' of law in the continuing process of public argument over political and social virtue. A society that is rich in settings for such public argument is one in which the participation of diverse religious groups will not threaten the basic acceptance of law, but will seek to persuade a hybrid public of the possibilities of putting fuller content into its common life – at least to accept or endorse policies that keep open such possibilities, even for those who do not share the beliefs and practices that ground them. We return to Maleiha Malik's case for a constant strengthening in a mature modern democracy of the openings for substantive debate, involving communities of commitment – not only individual bearers of legal rights. 'Institutional identification is more likely where substantive issues concerning the common good are discussed.'[9]

A final word: I do not intend to comment in detail on the various proposals about legislation against 'religious hatred' discussed in recent years; but I note that their critics are mostly secular liberals and conservative Christians. Secular liberals fear the restriction of critique and challenge, including satire; conservative Christians fear the restriction of seeking conversion or open debate with members of other faiths. And while I am not wholly sure of the rightness of the legislative proposals in question, all I have said in this lecture is meant to question the presuppositions of such critics. The secular liberal may need convincing that a stronger, more publicly recognized community will be less rather than more likely to fear public discussion, even satire. The conservative Christian may need convincing that the law is capable of recognizing specific and active difference and disagreement without assuming that it will always issue in violent or prejudicial action. But this will not happen for either of these unless there is a general climate that understands the public character of religious loyalty, even in the secular state – and that is prepared to work with the visibility of such commitment without panic. The signs in our own political milieu are not wholly discouraging by any means, but we need more thought about the basis of co-operation, if 'faith communities' are to be more than a pool of cheap labour for projects of social integration. But ultimately we do not have to be bound by the mythology of purely private conviction and public neutrality; and, if my general argument is right, the future of religious communities in modern society should show us some ways forward that do not deliver us either into theocracy or an entirely naked public space.

Law, power and peace

The Iraq War was fought for the sake of freedom and democracy, so we are insistently told. And just as insistently, the news from Iraq tells us that, whatever else may have resulted from that ill-fated enterprise, the present situation is not exactly 'freedom and democracy' in the sense that the war's apologists probably had in mind. 'Democracy' is a word that we take to mean a certain sort of political accountability: government is made to answer to the will of the people, regularly and routinely, so that particular interest groups cannot cling unchallenged to power. But the tormenting problems over the shaping of an Iraqi constitution have brought to light very clearly some of the central tensions in understanding democracy. What if the popular will is overwhelmingly in favour of a form of government that does not correspond to our ordinary liberal assumptions? And what is to be done to secure the rights and liberties of minorities in a context of significant religious or ethnic diversity, where a majority vote may be the accurate representation not of arguments won, but of a demographic advantage?

Most of us in the West would probably want to argue that democracy needs to be more than the guarantee that majorities have their way. This means that we have to introduce into our discussion the idea of 'lawful' democracy, democratic institutions that earn credibility not just by corresponding to 'popular will' but by placing themselves under law. But how we understand lawful democracy requires some reflection: if we are to avoid the self-defeating definition that law is what a majority says it is, we must clarify what it means. And in what follows, I want to connect this question with a set of issues much illuminated by David Nicholls' work and the tradition it represents, issues around the concepts of sovereignty and the state. This tradition has rather a lot to say to a range of current questions; and following this through will, I suggest, help us clarify at least some of the ways in which our present political conundrums need to be better anchored in a history of practice and theology that is normally ignored these days.

David Nicholls wrote, eloquently and pungently, on 'pluralist' theories of the state, following through and elaborating the insights of J. N. Figgis and Harold Laski in particular among twentieth-century theorists. Roughly speaking, this defines a state as a particular cluster of smaller political communities negotiating with each other under the umbrella of a system of arbitration recognized by all. These smaller communities may be of very diverse kinds – trade unions, ethnic and cultural groups, co-operative societies, professional guilds (universities, the BMA, the Bar Association) and, of course, churches and faith groups; what they have in common is that they are what we might call 'first-level' associations, groups of agents dealing with the questions of self-regulation and self-defence that arise routinely in work and life together. They represent relatively unstructured forms of belonging, some of them chosen, some of them not. What is significant for the wider political scene is that they assume they have a right to exist and to take corporate action to keep their common life going in a reasonably orderly way.

But no one of them occupies the whole political and social territory; belonging to the Methodist Church and the BMA doesn't exhaust who you are in your daily business and interaction. So there has to be something that deals with your life when you are not acting specifically as a Methodist, something that clarifies what is everyone's business in the public sphere. And there may have to be 'brokerage' between different communities where diverse sorts of belonging provoke conflict. There have to be taxes, speed limits, a monopoly of legitimate force or restraint. The law of the state is what provides the stable climate for all first-level communities to flourish and the means for settling, and enforcing, 'boundary disputes' between them. The law does not attempt total regulation of how these communities govern themselves (though it may, as with British charity law, require certain standards of accountable practice); Nicholls quotes from William James,[1] who insists as a metaphysical principle that 'there is always some self-governing aspect remaining, which cannot be reduced to unity', and notes that Figgis and others use philosophers such as James to provide a base, or at least an analogy, of some sort for political pluralism. What the law of the state does is to create the conditions, within a complex social environment, that allow each group to pursue what it sees as good. And if any group's notion of what is good veers towards anything that undermines the good of other groups, the law's task is restraint and control of any such tendency, as well as the defence of the whole network against destabilizing from outside. If pluralism is understood in this way, then, as Nicholls points out, it is a great mistake to think of Hegel as some kind of an apologist for monolithic centralism. English Idealists who were influenced by Hegel were glad to point out Hegel's critique of the French political system because of its lack of intermediate civil society associations.[2]

The pluralist tradition contrasts this vision of diffused governance and interdependence with a rival idea of state and law, in which what comes first, conceptually speaking, is a single sovereign power, beyond challenge, something that is not only a final court of appeal but in some sense a source of legitimacy for other groups. Here the law of the state is a universal and impersonal tribunal, before which every individual stands on a perfectly equal, neutral footing. If legal citizens decide to associate with each other in some way, they need the licence of the sovereign authority; unauthorised associations are by definition problematic, and the state has the right to suppress them. In the public sphere, all citizens are just that – individuals who have certain civic rights and duties. Nothing else should impinge, visibly or conceptually, on this public space.

Figgis, like his German inspiration Gierke, tended to identify this latter model with 'Roman' law and the former with the laws of the Germanic peoples. This is not a very easily defensible historical model; but it reminds us that Roman law was indeed intensely centralized, and that it was systematically suspicious of private societies – which is why the early Christians suffered. As an empire, the Roman state granted equality of status to people of all nationalities, and imposed upon all nationalities an absolutely uniform culture, reinforced by a formidably organized army drawn from all regions. The collapse of the empire left a dangerous void; into that gap stepped, simultaneously, the new Germanic kingdoms and the early mediaeval Church. The latter became the inheritor of the basic principles of Roman law, with a centralized system of courts and a universal sovereign authority, the Pope. But as this system lost much of its effectiveness and credibility in the later Middle Ages, it came to be replaced, not by some version of the looser systems of the old kingdoms, but by a new phenomenon, the nation state under its all-powerful prince. The sixteenth-century monarch (Henry VIII, Philip II or whoever) was the single source of all legality and jurisdiction within the 'empire' of his or her territory (Henry VIII's legislation explicitly declared that 'this realm of England is an empire' – a single sovereign jurisdiction). And that territory was increasingly likely to see itself as a community with a single history and destiny, a nation whose members were united in a sort of racial distinctiveness. It is worth noting that the first openly racialist laws were passed in Spain in the sixteenth century.

Now the detail of this is, again, vulnerable in a good many places; it is a broad sweep of argument, against which several points can rightly be made, about the other elements in the medieval papacy's practice, about the survival in Renaissance states of older feudal patterns and so on. But in outline it remains a powerful analysis, and is not unrelated to the very detailed and nuanced historical picture lately painted by Philip Bobbitt of the progression from princely state to nation state, and thence ultimately to the modern 'market state'. There is, though, one more point to note, one that is more likely to slip the attention of a contemporary commentator. Figgis and Nicholls both give it suitable priority. I mentioned that the idea of the Roman state was intrinsically hostile to the presence of the Christian Church as an unlicensed association. The effect of this was to set a question mark against the sacredness, the ultimate claim, of the Roman state; its lawfulness could not be seen as absolute and universal. The state has a proper power (early Christians are careful to say that they are quite content to pay taxes), but it is not a holy power. It can be challenged, and its finality can be contested. It has become secular, as we say. And across the centuries the effect, most noticeably in Western Christianity, was to build in to a lot of Christian thinking a certain scepticism about political power in itself. The state administration might be good or bad, but it was not the dispenser of heavenly law.

This was frequently taken to mean that the Church could claim to offer what the state couldn't, a focal, omnicompetent authority; but there are some signs in the Middle Ages and after of a theological awareness that the whole idea of sacralized central authority, a single source of law, might be questionable, in the visible Church as much as in the state. At the Reformation, what happened all too often was that the all-powerful Pope was simply replaced by national sovereigns, and later by nationalism, the idea that this mysterious entity, 'the nation', was a God-given, unquestionable unit whose freedom to do what it collectively wanted had to be secured at all costs. Nineteenth-century romanticism (and racism) did a great deal to make this seem self-evident; twentieth-century history ought to make us wonder. We are now, in fact, in quite a good position, historically and culturally, to revisit the original theological impulses of the secular state, and to understand more clearly the relation between belief in a divinely revealed order of community and the actual business of any state in the world as it is. And we have perhaps learned the dangers of imagining that the divinely revealed order can simply be made the material of legislative dominance in a complex society, of diverse convictions and practices. We are more likely to grasp the irreducibility of negotiation, tension and diversity, with communities of religious conviction playing their part in the middle of it all.

Out of this a number of points emerge with some clear contemporary relevance. One of them I have already tried to outline at some length elsewhere, and I shall touch on it here only briefly. If the pluralist account is to be preferred, it is a mistake to suppose that a healthy or just society can be sustained where there is a systematic attempt to restrict religious belonging or identity to the private sphere. The faith community, like other self-regulating communities, has to be seen as a partner in the negotiations of public life; otherwise, the most important motivations for moral action in the public sphere will be obliged to conceal themselves. And religious identity, pursued and cultivated behind locked doors, can be distorted by its lack of access to the air and the criticism of public debate.

But there is another implication that needs a little longer to tease out. In the pluralist thesis, state government makes provision for what is agreed to be everyone's business. There are areas of our social life where you can't begin to make a sensible case for different communities legislating their own preferences. In some degree, you could say that the state here protects the very conditions for there being any coherent action by anyone at all for the sake of a social good. If there are no taxes, speed limits or entitlements to medical care, there is no dependable social environment. No group will be able fully to achieve the goals that their particular association has in view because of the absence of certain general social conditions of stability. When the diverse first-level communities of the pluralist theory accept the arbitration of the state, they do so because they recognize the need for someone to address the necessary agenda which no one of them can manage – and indeed which no one of them has any obvious right to manage. The 'lawful' state is not one in which sovereign authority delegates downwards, but one in which the component overlapping but distinct 'first-level' communities and associations that make up the state are assured that their interests are both recognized and effectively brokered, so that none of these communities is threatened in its pursuit of social good by others.

Now, when we turn to the vexed questions around international law, we often come up against the idea that international law represents some deeply dangerous infraction of the sovereignty of the actual national jurisdictions that govern us in our daily lives. But there is an obvious analogy between what the pluralist says about the state and what needs to be said (with some urgency these days) about international law. Just as the particular state has the task of addressing issues that no one community can tackle, so in the global context there are issues beyond the resource, the competence or the legitimate interest of any specific state. The most blindingly obvious at the moment is the ecological crisis, the complex of challenges around degradation of the environment, access to water, global warming and so on. It would be absurd to think that these matters could be dealt with effectively by any one jurisdiction; but if they are to be dealt with at all, then there must be some transnational authority capable of implementing 'pollution taxes', controls on deforestation or overfishing and a range of similar measures. This is the most extreme case of a power that secures what I have just called 'the very conditions for there being any coherent action by anyone at all for the sake of a social good'. Enough and more than enough has been written in recent years about the middle and long term effects on health and social stability of a process of environmental abuse developing at the present rate. The catastrophe of Hurricane Katrina made these concerns very immediate in the US in the middle of the first decade of the twenty-first century, and reminded us of the social crises that come in the wake of environmental disaster.

But there are other issues of this kind. The Geneva Convention acknowledges that the ethics of international conflict cannot be regulated simply by individual nations; there has to be a compact that has some binding force – even if, in this case, it is not clear how much more than moral force is involved. The International Criminal Court is at best patchily effective, but it has at least kept on the table the notion that there is such a thing as a criminal way to conduct conflicts and that this can be adjudicated. Recently, the ICC has begun to take some steps towards identifying forms of the arms trade as criminal complicity in unacceptable forms of conflict. There is an issue over the sale of small arms that relates directly to the use of child soldiers in certain regions, and this has rightly been seen as a prime example of such complicity. The UN has encouraged regional agreements on this, and has lent its weight to proposals for new conventions that allow higher levels of tracking and monitoring of small arms. It may well be too little and too late, but once again the issue is at last within the horizon of public discussion.

These examples are meant to show that we are increasingly aware of living in a world where the independence of nation states is severely limited – by economic globalization, by the uncontrollable spread of pollutants, by the regional effects of local conflicts. And as we become aware of this, we realize that a tight definition of national sovereignty simply does not fit this kind of world. We can hang on to a conception of national interest and hope for the best; or we can grasp the various nettles involved in ideas of transnational jurisdiction – precisely on the analogy of the pluralist thesis about national government itself. We need a clear vision not only of the lawful state, but of the lawful international system. There are things that are appropriately dealt with at different levels, and it is essential to recognize what no single nation or national jurisdiction can manage. There are issues that have to do with the security of any imaginable political and social environment, safeguards without which no individual state can realize its own conception of the good.

It could be said to be a version of the familiar principle of 'subsidiarity' – except that the term, and to some extent the theory, still seems to envisage a sort of delegation downwards of responsibility, as opposed to the referral 'upwards' to transnational level. The way we discuss sovereignty is often in terms of Renaissance debates – the illegitimacy of thinking there is any court of appeal higher than the national jurisdiction. This was, after all, at the heart of Henry VIII's changes to the medieval system. To be sovereign is to be inviolable, beyond challenge. But this works on the assumption that the rival to national sovereignty is supranational sovereignty of the same sort – a single jurisdiction from which authority flows downwards. The princely state and the nation state take their character from their reaction against a version of papal jurisdiction. So now, ideas of 'world government' provoke profound anxiety; and the British nervousness about 'Europe' as some sort of unitary political or economic reality is a local version of this (understandable) fear of local decision-making being trumped by a higher court.

But if we have clarified our understanding of what sovereignty means within the state, it should be easier to talk about international law without these myths. The sovereign power is the power that is lawfully equipped to arbitrate among actual first-level communities on matters that affect the viability of any and all of them to exist securely and usefully. Comparably, an international juris-diction is the power lawfully equipped to secure co-existence among nations in those matters outside any particular state's responsibilities or capacities. And this is perfectly compatible with the recognition that there are areas in which those responsibilities and capacities are and should be clearly in unchallenged operation. Where transnational jurisdictions are rightly suspect is when they assume rights to some degree of 'micromanagement', cultural or economic; Europe has not always had a good record in this respect, but the European Union in its original vision seems to assume at least some of the pluralist's principles.

To go back to our starting point: if democracy in any one state is not merely a recipe for majoritarian dictatorship, if the sovereign power is more than just the will of a majority, it should be possible to think of the international scene in a similar way. The unchallenged dominance of one national interest will always need restraining. Equally, international institutions damage their legitimacy if they become a context where majorities can enforce their group interests on particular states. If there is to be international intervention, it presumably has to be in a situation where a specific state has become manifestly dysfunctional, terminally incapable of securing the lives and welfare of its citizens, to the degree that their corporate interest, their common good as a state, has no organs for its expression. It is, in fact, not an easy discernment; though Rwanda in the 1990s remains one of the obvious test cases (and one where international institutions did not by any standard cover themselves with glory). There remain questions about whether it is ever proper for a state to intervene in another on behalf of an international moral consensus, or to salvage any remains of civil order in a situation of chaos (Tanzania's intervention in Amin's Uganda is a case in point). It is not a matter that invites a brief answer; I shall say only that such action needs, at the very least, a high level of explicit international assent, even if not a fully formal level, if it is not to be seen as self-serving and so to undermine its own purposes.

Let me return for a moment to the theological thesis outlined earlier. If one of the effects of Christian theology and practice is the emergence of the 'secular' state, the state that has no absolutely given claim on ultimate loyalties yet can rightly claim to be 'lawful' to the extent that it faithfully enables the negotiation of diverse communities in a peaceful context, it is important to exercise the same kind of theological reserve about international order. It is a secular matter, a matter of the network of political virtues like prudence and justice that enables the recognition and arbitration of conflict and the securing of an environment that is for everyone's good. There is a proper 'justice' in the attempt to guarantee that all specific states have access to environmental goods and protection against unrestrained trade in weaponry. There is a proper 'prudence' in seeking enforceable controls upon environmentally dangerous practice, and limits to acceptable methods of coercion within states and in conflict between states (so that torture, genocide and germ warfare are outlawed). But this is good and defensible not because there is a sacrosanct universal power imposing political morality; it is good because it is good for every participant in the negotiations of the international political world. When a transnational jurisdiction steps beyond the limits of what can be shown to be good for any state, and seeks to prescribe what is good for this or that particular state, it is right to raise questions. This is, as I have said, not an easy distinction to apply; but it is important to have the distinction to hand.

A pluralist model of political life can thus, I believe, make sense of international law without binding us to the undoubtedly risky idea of some kind of universal sovereign state. The Christian denial of sacred 'givenness' to any political order should make us as wary of any such universal sovereignty as of any sacred claims for this or that national polity. There is, ultimately, only one sovereignty which is theologically grounded, and that is Christ's. To quote Oliver O'Donovan's sharp formulation, 'the only sense of political authority acknowledged within Christendom was the law of the ascended Christ, and ... all political authority was the authority of that law'.[3] And the legacy of 'Christendom' to modernity was the notion that particular administrations are open to challenge because they are there to implement a law they have not made and do not control.[4] The law of the state or of the international system exists to serve the variety of specific goods that are being pursued and often argued about in actual complex societies. When it appears to serve the interest of any of those specific groups in an exclusive way or, in the international context, the interests of one nation or federation of nations, it betrays its purpose and risks reducing the idea of law to the safeguarding of power, that ancient distortion defined by Plato.

The pluralist vision has been questioned by some because it leaves the state as such without a goal, a specific good. Matthew Grimley in his excellent recent monograph on *Citizenship, Community and the Church of England*,[5] observes how the pluralism of Figgis, for example, came to look far less attractive in the course and in the wake of the First World War because the crisis seemed to demand a more robust affirmation of the goods upheld and pursued by all British citizens. The nineteenth-century confidence, rooted in the tradition of Hooker and Coleridge and refined by English Idealists like T. H. Green, that the state had the right to require and pursue its own moral goals, that it was itself a moral community, received a considerable shot in the arm between 1914 and 1918, and, as Grimley shows, it survived the 1930s with great resilience – only to collapse surprisingly quickly after 1945.

But this is only part of the picture. It is true that the pluralist model assumes that the state is in no sense an interested party, and so that it cannot in any simple sense have goals of its own, goals that are potentially in competition with those of its constituent communities. However, the very idea of the coexistence of moral communities in a complex state could be seen as itself a convergent morality of sorts, and one with a theological underpinning. It is good for first-level communities to see their account of the social good set in the context of other such accounts, good for it to have to argue its case, expose itself to the exchanges of the public forum. It is good that the peace of a society or of an international system should be more than the juxtaposition of wary and rather distant units, generally sealed off from each other, occasionally petitioning the state's tribunal for its rights. It is good because it represents the best security we have against uncriticized, sacralized power in the political realm. In the actual historical world of existing societies, the good is something that gets argued about. Certainly, societies regularly become impatient with argument and hungry for an account of the social good that is final and obvious – theocracy in past ages, ideological systems of left or right in the twentieth century, programmatic secularism in our own day. But this is to seek an escape from history; as we have seen, the fundamental vision of Christian theology both claims that the future has arrived in the assembly of believers around Word and Sacrament, and warns against supposing that this future can be rendered now as a public system, a regime, within the political world. When this happens, the Kingdom of God becomes a contender alongside others for the control of debated territory; it becomes less than itself.

This is a little different from the simple commendation of pluralism on the basis of a multiculturalist philosophy. That can in practice mean not much more than what I called the juxtaposition of mutually non-communicating groups. More can be said. If the state does indeed have a kind of moral interest, as I have been suggesting, it is twofold – an interest in securing the liberty of groups to pursue their own social goods, and an interest in building in to its own processes a set of cautions and defences against absolutism. But, to use the phrase yet again, in a complex society, groups may need each other's co-operation to pursue their own social goods. And one of the things that the state can do is to facilitate such co-operation through its own sponsorship and partnership. A proper development forum in a city or region is one of the ways in which people build up an environment within which it is easier for all to pursue their goals, which is why it needs the co-presence of representative community bodies, commercial concerns, interest groups and faith groups. Education is an obvious context in which the state has a moral interest of the kind I have outlined in nourishing co-operation. To pick up a currently controversial issue, the state's assistance to 'faith schools' is not the subsidizing of exclusivism but the bringing of communities out of isolation to engage with the process of maintaining what they and other communities together need, and to argue and negotiate. The state is thus more than a tribunal; it exercises its lawful character by promoting and resourcing collaboration.

And so, to return to our earlier analogy, international systems of various sorts can properly address those conditions that affect all states; they can seek for covenants of restraint over arms sales and pollutant emissions, even unregulated capital flow. The concept of a form of taxation recognizing the transnational costs of some practices (the 'Tobin tax', the Contraction and Convergence proposals on pollution) is one that reappears more and more frequently in current discussion; and it is important to give a rationale for this independent of any fantasies of universal sovereign jurisdiction, a world super-state. What I have been suggesting is that the pluralist critique of certain ideas of national sovereignty offers a way forward in helping us see lawful authority as, at every level, what secures the bare conditions of any social good.

So if we go back to where we began, to the complications of how we understand the word 'democracy', we have perhaps a fuller sense of what is fundamental. Representative institutions and elective practices are no more than a means of majoritarian dictatorship without a robust account of what lawfulness means in society. Unrestricted liberty for any individual or group is unfeasible in any stable setting; but law is the bid to identify what everyone can recognize as guaranteeing stability and an equitable distribution of the freedoms of groups to pursue their goals. And this has a great deal to do with the way in which a state authority establishes dependable public institutions and infrastructures and guarantees due public process to deal with criminal offences. This helps, incidentally, to explain why military intervention to promote 'democracy' is so seldom anything other than hugely counterproductive: large-scale degra-dation of an infrastructure, almost inevitable in prolonged warfare, especially involving modern techniques of aerial attack, is itself an immediate obstacle to creating a trustworthy and thus lawful system of administration. As we have seen in Iraq in recent months, the setting-up of representative institutions alone fails to solve anything so long as there is no confidence that a system exists to secure the social environment and to act as a disinterested broker between communities. Despite careful and costly negotiations about the representation of diverse religious groupings within the Iraqi constitution in the wake of the military action against Saddam Hussein, a proper recognition of one aspect of the pluralist concern, even this will not automatically outweigh the sense of a lack of public dependability, visibly embodied in failures in security, medical care, education, water supplies and so forth. Occupying troops are placed in an impossible and highly vulnerable position, expected to maintain an order that really needs so much more development of a firm infrastructure in the whole of the society. The struggles of Iraq in the post-invasion years should serve to make us more attentive, please God, to the gap between slogans about democratization and the hard work needed to secure a reliable material environment for civil society to mature, and thus for a fully lawful state apparatus to be shaped.

To try and sum up. Lawful democracy is a situation in which the ordinary associations of human life, largely self-regulating, sometimes voluntary (credit unions, the Bar), sometimes not (ethnic groups, say, or the 'community' of those who suffer disablement of some kind), sometimes hybrid (religious groups), are held together in negotiation and limited but significant interaction through an administrative system that can plausibly claim to be defending the conditions needed for any one of these groups to do what it seeks to do. This system does not legislate provisions that directly attack the beliefs and goals of its constituent communities, except insofar as there may be any such beliefs or goals that threaten the existence of other groups. It is also careful in its legislation to conserve certain basic principles of human dignity: it safeguards life and it prohibits the deliberate degradation of, or of causing of pain to, any person in the name of the state (hence the now practically universal prohibition of torture in legal systems – despite the countless outrages in practice). In all these ways, the lawful state embodies the possibility of its being held to account; it denies its own invulnerability from criticism. Its sovereignty is not a claim to be the source of law, but the agreed monopoly of legal force and a recognition of where the ultimate court of appeal is to be located for virtually all practical and routine purposes. This does not and cannot preclude consideration of how the state's own conditions for effective existence are taken care of by instruments that deal with those matters, like the conduct of conflict and the defence of the environment, that are indisputably beyond any local jurisdiction. And the pluralist account of sovereignty and law within the state allow us to think this through without invoking the hugely risky resort of a proactive transnational sovereign power.

But the finally significant point remains the theological ground of all this. Despite its regular collapse back into theocratic dreams, the Christian tradition rests upon a strong conviction that no political order other than the Body of

Christ can claim the authority of God; and the Body of Christ is not a political order on the same level as others, competing for control, but a community that signifies, that points to a possible healed human world. Thus its effect on the political communities of its environment is bound to be, sooner or later, sceptical and demystifying. In spite of the massive counter-movements of the twentieth century, Communism and the Third Reich, the drift of modern society seems inexorably away from any commitment to the state as morally purposive reality. In this context, we have a choice. We can look to what I have called 'programmatic' secularism as a solution: public life as a sphere of rational negotiation according to universal enlightened principles, with a strong commitment to equality before an impartial tribunal as the essence of citizenship. We can embrace a multiculturalism which seeks to keep the peace between essentially separate social groups or interest groups, with minimal government and much reliance on private initiative. Or we can explore the tradition I have been trying to work with here and ask what an 'interactive' pluralism would look like, that had thought through what was involved in the state's arbitrative and balancing function in a way which allowed active partnership and exchange between communities themselves and between communities and state authority. I have argued that this is a viable moral definition of the lawful state, profoundly linked with the Christian, certainly the Augustinian Christian, sense of the hopes and limits that can be seen in political life. I have also suggested that the pluralist vision will help us tackle the overwhelmingly urgent issues around global justice and prudence which seem so often to be thought about these days with inadequate conceptual tools.

The Church, like all other 'first-level' communities though for dramatically different reasons from other groups, does not exist by licence of the state. And that fact gives both reinforcement and limit to the state – reinforcement to the state as a system of lawful brokerage and stable provision, not threatened by theocratic claims; limit to the state as an atomistic sovereign system answerable to nothing outside itself. The tradition of theological and political thinking to which David Nicholls contributed so fruitfully offers a perspective uniquely equipped in our own chaotic political and international setting to provide a rationale for effective work towards justice and peace.

5

Europe, faith and culture

A lot of what gets said about Europe these days suggests that we are better at saying what it isn't than what it is. We say 'Europe' when we mean 'not Britain' or 'not America', sometimes 'not the Islamic world' or even 'not the developing world'. But we need from time to time to try and rescue a positive definition of some sort; which means a bit of history and a bit of political philosophy, and some of that will be around in this lecture. My main point, though, will be that to understand some of the most basic things for which the word 'Europe' stands when it's used positively, we need some thinking about religion as well — specifically about Christianity. And if the presence of Europe in the world hasn't been and isn't now exclusively a source of good things, it may be, I'll be suggesting, that we find the problems appear in proper perspective only when we've thought harder about these religious issues; and that therefore we may find a way forward from some of our world's most stale and destructive situations only when this work has been done.

Let me start by listing five things that are often associated with Europe when people seek to identify what it has contributed to world history and culture since roughly the early seventeenth century (the significance of this particular time scheme should be clearer as we go on). And I should add before proceeding that I'm treating a great deal of what the US presents as its unique contribution to the world as derivative from certain trends that began in Europe. First, then, is a doctrine about human rights. Gradually, from 1600 onwards, and most rapidly from about 1800 onwards, distinctively European political thinking developed the assumption that human beings were born with entitlements to certain kinds of freedom, more and more envisaged as freedom of access to what would make each human being content with their situation and would permit no potential in human beings to go without being developed. Recognizing a right in this sense is recognizing that people are properly seen as being able to claim the resources they need to make them both happy and in control of their lives. How exactly this has evolved into the contemporary idea of rights as claims that can be enforced in some sort of political tribunal would take a long time to spell out. But the fundamental point is that modern Europe, Europe after the Reformation and the wars of religion, came to take increasingly for granted this model of individuals as endowed with the right to win control of their environment as far as possible.

And this connects with a second feature of 'European-ness': the assumption that freedom understood as the absolute liberty to choose between alternatives is an unqualified good. If the goal is maximal control over the environment, then we need to be sure that everyone has an equal chance of selecting what they want from the possibilities that life in this world offers. To have your choices made for you is degrading and inhuman; the ideal human subject is one who has a clear view of alternative possibilities, a clear understanding of the pathways by which these can be made real and a clearly definable means of access to these pathways. And this of course involves the third European differential: democracy. If no individual or group or class has the right to define what is going to be possible for others, the organization of social life has to be by means of the widest possible consultation about people's preferences, with the option of changing those who administer the law and policy of society when change is desired. Although monarchies of various sorts survived and still survive in Europe, what steadily disappeared was any conviction about a 'right to rule'.

But this creates something of a dilemma. Democracy seeks to consult everyone, but it cannot guarantee the enactment of everyone's wishes and preferences. It is bound to enact the desires of a majority, and this seems to threaten the universal liberty of access and control we have spoken of. What then emerges is a fourth feature of European public culture: the distinction between public and private. This means encouraging people to think in terms of a sort of contract by which the greatest benefit to the greatest number is assured by majority decisions, and individuals accept that their specific choices may rightly be limited when they have possible consequences for others that would limit the liberty of those others. But this is offset by the agreement of public democratic authority to allow an almost unqualified freedom in those areas where there are no obvious public consequences for choices. Modern democracy brings with it a pluralist assumption about personal morality.

All this takes for granted a certain sort of 'story' about human beings and how they behave and are expected to behave; and the last aspect of European distinctiveness I want to mention at this point is the character of modern European art and literary culture. This is something that focuses intensely on the complexities of the individual's awareness and emotion. It appears in musical Romanticism, in a variety of modernist movements in visual art, but above all in European (and American or Australian) drama and fiction. What people look at and think about when they read novels or watch plays and films is the records of specific individuals making their choices, experiencing the effect of their choices, battling often to secure the right to choose and so on.

Basic to all my five proposals for identifying what is different about modern Europe and its post-colonial legacy across the Atlantic and elsewhere is the belief that what is most uniquely human is a capacity for 'self-creation' – for the making of choices that will establish a secure place in the world and shape an identity that is not determined from outside, determined by social power that acknowledges no accountability or by doctrines and models that have no public evidence to support them. If an individual decides to allow their identity to be so determined, that is no doubt their business, but it isn't something that anyone can rightly expect public authorities, governments, to support or enforce. Public life organizes the aspirations of individuals in such a way that they don't interfere with each other too dramatically, and leaves what is supposed to be a reasonable amount of private space in which various individual preferences can be exercised.

It is this sense that the essence of the human task is *defining yourself* that is at the heart of the modern European enterprise; and it is what sets it apart from both traditional societies and modern ideologically defined societies. In traditional societies, a human being would be defined in relation to other human beings and their given roles and tasks, and the whole complex of human relations defined in relation to a 'sacred order', the balance of things as defined by the will of God or the gods or the eternal harmony of all beings, the *Tao* of Chinese philosophy or the *logos* of the ancient Stoics. Within such a framework, there might well be a strong affirmation of the person's freedom to adopt or reject this or that way of living out the given order in which they existed; but there would be no assumption that each person would have to decide who and what they were and work out that decision more or less from scratch. And insofar as the project of 'self-creation' challenges the priority of an eternal creating purpose outside this universe, it looks as though European modernity is basically hostile to any religious sense of the world and of human destiny.

For many in the modern West, that is not of course a problem; it simply reflects the unstoppable advance of the demystifying of the world and the removal of authorities that work without any rational accountability. The obvious direction of human history is towards a world in which there is a level playing field, a universal space into which any individual may move and stake out their territory, while government restrains excessive bids or claims that threaten others within this territory. But this tidy summary conceals two major problems that we cannot indefinitely avoid looking at. The first is simple: the fact that this model remains the preferred world view of a prosperous minority of the human race, and shows little sign of being voluntarily adopted by others. The sociologist Grace Davie has written of the 'European exception' in discussing the patterns of religious commitment and practice in our world. She is of course saying this in the light also of the statistically high level of religious practice in the US; but I'd want to suggest that since religion in the US is characterized by many deeply untraditional features, by a sort of market principle of maximum variety and choice, it is itself as untypical as Europe in the context of what the rest of the human race thinks about religion. If religious commitment is first and foremost an individual's private choice, then, never mind whether the choice is yes or no, the principle is the same.

But the second problem from which we are tempted to turn our eyes away is the internal strain that is manifest in the way in which the 'European' model works at home and, more significantly, abroad. Some recent historians of Christian mission have located the missionary movements within the context of what they call the great European migration – the immense cluster of social and economic processes which, from the late Middle Ages onwards, took Europeans to other parts of the world, most often as conquerors or colonisers. The emergent culture of Europe assumed that it had universal validity; but in practice this also meant that those who knew this culture as insiders, those who 'owned' it for themselves, had the right to decide how it should work, while those outside the European household had to be content with the structures imposed by insiders (occasionally with the promise held out that outsiders might one day become insiders).

The effects were dramatic. The slave trade developed as a major international commercial concern at just the time philosophers were becoming increasingly eloquent about the universal human birthright. Racial superiority was, for the first time in human history, defended on abstract philosophical grounds. The process began by which local economies were inexorably drawn in to the mechanisms of transnational business and the material resources of the globe came to be seen as a virtually limitless warehouse for development. And one of the deepest tensions in the modern mindset emerged as the pressure for national self-determination as an expression of the basic conviction about self-creation rubbed up against the pressures towards unfettered global competition in the market. European universalism ended up producing a world in which immense inequality was created, and in which the degree of that inequality seems to become yearly if not daily more marked. The great European migration (which itself includes the rise of North America as a global power) has irreversibly altered the nature of the human world, bringing, undeniably, new levels of prosperity to some and new levels of political self-determination; but it has a massive shadow. And to understand what is going on here, I want to return to the question of Europe's religious roots to see if we can gain any perspective on the huge moral ambiguity of Europe's cultural exports.

As is widely recognized, the European mindset I have been describing has its beginnings in certain aspects of Christian language and belief – but also in the sheer social fact of how the Christian Church thought of itself in its earliest years. Christianity was always a religion of *conversion*: and that means that it has always proposed to human beings that what has been taken for granted about their identity, their possibilities or their relationships isn't necessarily fixed and final. Conversion is *choosing to be different*; it is a step out of the culture you once belonged in. And the early Christians had to wrestle a good deal with the question of how this could be announced and offered in the highly controlled and religiously policed environment of the Roman Empire without inviting the conclusion that Christians were automatically out to subvert the entire fabric of social morality.

What this involved in practice was, for many of the earliest generations, martyrdom – the ultimate countercultural statement. And what this came to mean was that, for Christians, choosing to be different might not make any instant and visible difference: martyrdom claimed that there was a hidden reality, deeper and more lasting than the culture that currently prevailed. The martyr witnessed to what was and remained true whether or not it could command a majority vote. And the ordinary Christian, living in this rather precarious setting, would have a sort of double vision – the world, the prevailing culture as it actually was, and the Kingdom of God by which the current order of things was judged. The cultural and political climate in which the Christian lived might be the reality for the majority, completely taken for granted, even regarded as sacred – but the Christian would know that it was still under judgement and that what seemed natural and beyond question in this environment was still open to question by the standards of God, the 'hidden God' who was at work in the most conspicuous human failures, in apparent defeat and death, as he had been at work in the death of Jesus.

Now the relevance of this for our main subject is in this aspect of Christian language that involves what I've called double vision. Christianity at first refused to allow believers to take things for granted, and it gave believers the conviction that their own choices could bring them into a different order of things, invisible but ultimately decisive for the whole universe. It encouraged questioning of certain kinds – the questioning of how things were done in the Roman Empire, but also the questioning of oneself: how far did a believer still act as if he or she were simply an inhabitant of the 'given' world of Empire? And even when Christianity became socially and culturally the majority view, the 'normal' position in Europe, the tension did not go away. Church and government still argued about who set the boundaries for public morality; and, very importantly, the monastic movement enshrined a degree of tension at the very heart of the Church's life. 'Conversion' came to be the technical term for opting to become a monk or nun, because such a decision once again affirmed that you didn't have to live in the place where you were born, culturally and spiritually speaking. The Christianized world might go on its way fairly smoothly, but there was always a hidden and more drastic way of being a disciple. Even in a 'baptized' society, there were still questions to be asked.

Gradually in Western Europe during the Middle Ages, thinkers developed the implications of this. St Augustine, at the very end of the era of the old Roman Empire, had starkly denied that any social arrangements, even the most apparently Christian ones, could satisfy the radical desires of the soul for God's love and justice; the Christian was defined as someone always refusing to settle down. And a few centuries later, something not unrelated was being worked out by St Thomas Aquinas in his scepticism about the divine authority of kings. Christianity might have been the system taken absolutely for granted by the society of Western medieval Europe, but it still contained the seeds of deep cultural unease, an *irony* and a scepticism about existing situations and systems in the light of God's action in the cross of Jesus and the revelation of what God's justice really meant. At the time of the Reformation in the sixteenth century, this scepticism exploded as a protest about the institution of the Catholic Church itself.

But it was never a matter of Protestant liberty versus Catholic tradition and stability. Protestants sadly often ended up reinstating an uncritical veneration for the state; Catholics produced, especially in mystical writings, a profound analysis of the anarchic possibilities of the inner life of human beings. But what is hard to deny is the fact that after the Reformation, that unease and unsettlement, that sense of the 'homelessness' of the human self in a world where you couldn't take for granted that society (even Christian society) would tell you who you were and what your task was, became more and more sharply marked. The double vision of the early Church and of St Augustine was increasingly in evidence.

But – and here is the crucial twist in the plot – all this coincided, not entirely surprisingly, with a loss of focus and nerve among many European thinkers where God was concerned. It is one thing to reflect on and nurture a scepticism about the appearances and conventions of society when the other world of God's character and Kingdom is clear and compelling, however mysterious. But what happens when unease and scepticism spills over into this area as well? A double vision in which both aspects are equally questionable leaves the human spirit homeless in a far more radical and threatening sense. To question myself in the light of the mystery of God's justice revealed through the death of Jesus, to decide for self-sacrifice, whether as martyr or as monk, on the basis of the doctrine that self-sacrifice is the hidden law of all things, rooted in the self-forgetfulness of divine love, is a long way from questioning myself simply because *nothing* is secure, anywhere. To find out who I might be or become cannot rest on anything outside; it will require introspection, the exploration of what St Augustine had called the inner 'caverns' of the self.

This can be traced in the increasing anxiety among philosophers about how we can be sure that we know what we think we know; but it can also be traced in the growth of what I identified earlier as one of the distinctive cultural creations of the modern European mind – the novel.

Novels are records of how selves are shaped. The earliest novels, especially in the English-speaking world, were very much focused on how individuals found their way to security – economic security, sexual stability, a sense of confidence in their worth. The nineteenth-century novel pushed the boat out rather further in exploring alienation from the roles prescribed by society and the consequences of nonconformity, and it increasingly offered diagnoses of the ills of society and recipes for its reformation. The twentieth century intensified the ways in which alienation was understood, but also pushed the form of the novel into new territories as the whole idea of a unified self evolving in time was confronted by new varieties of philosophical scepticism, with the 'death' of both author and subject being confidently announced. Yet the novel remains one of the most persistent vehicles in the European and American cultural environment for understanding human decisions and conflicts.

Quite a lot has been said over the years about the origins of the novel in Puritan and Pietist journals, in the habit of self-examination and the laying-out in story form of how God's leading Providence might be traced in a life. But, as I hinted earlier, this is not an exclusively Protestant story: the 'mystical' autobiography (for example, the memoirs of a Teresa of Avila, an Augustine Baker or even the fragmented personal reflections of a Pascal) provides some of the background as well. For an earlier age, introspection, looking at the inner world, meant essentially coming to understand what *kind* of thing a human being was; from the seventeenth century, it meant coming to understand who *this particular subject* might be or become. The philosophical question, 'What can I be sure of?' was complemented by the psychological question, 'Where can I take my stand as a unique agent in the world?' The Puritan writing his or her journal, the mystic writing an account of the discovery of God's overpowering darkness, are both seeking a way of establishing that God is the foundation on which they stand, even when outside events don't instantly enforce this as a natural conclusion. But the novel cannot take for granted that there is a foundation in God; and so it dramatizes the search for other sorts of security – or, later on, shifts the focus from the goal to the search itself. And this shift is of course reflected in other art forms in the European context, in drama and eventually film as well (although it might be more accurate to say that European drama in its supreme phase in the sixteenth and seventeenth centuries had already set some of the agenda for the novel's development).

So one way of understanding the ambiguous impact of Europe on our world is to see the modern European mind as the detached half of a complex reality that Christianity helped to bring to birth. The homeless soul, uprooted from its apparently natural habitat in an inherited culture so as to be replanted in the soil of God's universal community, the homeless soul obliged in an imperfect world to look beyond appearances and to suspect the claims of culture and society to final authority – this soul once cut off from the narrative of God's action in the cross and resurrection will find a home nowhere in earth or heaven. In the Christian context, self-questioning is the discipline of stripping away all external circumstance or internal habit that makes us simply feel good or safe for the sake of discovering a good that cannot be defeated by the world as we experience it or by our own failures. It sets out for the human self a journey that is a sort of reflection of the definitive story of faith: the 'Son's Course', the 'journey of the Son of God into a far country' and his return home (both phrases from great and very different twentieth-century Christian commentators, Gerald Vann OP, and Karl Barth) – this is the story that for Christian believers establishes once and for all the rhythm of the world's life. God 'abandons' the life of an isolated heaven to work out and define what divine life might mean in the conditions of a compromised and tragic world; and this definition leads to the utter failure and darkness of the crucifixion, leaving only the bare fact of indestructible love; and that indestructible reality recreates the whole world in its refusal to be enclosed by death. It is a story that insists that God is not to be found in the world except when human beings are ready to lose all that is less than God so that the indestructible may take root in them. It is a story, therefore, that naturally generates its own culture of restlessness.

But if that restlessness is separated from any sense of the indestructible, then what in a Christian context is the motive power for creative irony, critical freedom and hope becomes a ceaseless, obsessive wondering whether I as an individual have yet understood my nature and my needs and whether I have yet found the resources to satisfy them. Criticism will focus on the dissatisfactions of the individual; rights will be conceived in terms of the expectations of the individual; and, to pick up the controversial but immensely illuminating language of the American political historian and analyst, Philip Bobbitt, we end up with the 'market state' of the late twentieth and early twenty-first century, drawing its legitimacy from its capacity to satisfy the consumer demands of its citizens. In the global context, this brings with it just the tensions that we looked at earlier around the competitive and acquisitive models that have dominated Europe's engagement with the rest of the world.

But the past century, perhaps especially the past 60 years or so, has given an extra focus and an extra sharpness to some of these concerns. The cultural world we have been thinking about, individualist, pluralist, absorbed in the analysis of the self and its multiple possibilities, has been brought up against two powerful alternatives to its certainties. For a great deal of the twentieth century, the West was confronted by a philosophy and a social system claiming scientific foundations, completely irreligious, indeed anti-religious, in its understanding, yet having many of the characteristics of monotheistic faith – Marxism and its outworking in state socialism. As the Cold War era ended, there were those who very publicly assumed that there could be no serious alternative to the North Atlantic world view; but within a very short time indeed, a very different presence was making itself felt in a new way: Islam, the historic sibling and sparring-partner of medieval Europe, long ignored or despised by badly-informed Westerners as culturally and intellectually static, emerged again as a partner in debate – and potentially or actually a partner in conflict.

Both Marxism and Islam are, in their basic conception, morally serious and philosophically sophisticated visions which seem on the face of it to have relatively little place for pluralism or irony on the classical European model; both assume that the presence of a finally satisfactory human order sanctioned by God or by the objective forces of history is at least a possibility within the world we know, and both are critical of the 'interior' focus of Christian language and the pessimism or even passivity which this can, in their eyes, generate. In both cases, the experience of searching dialogue with Christianity makes it quite clear that we are not talking here about worlds that simply can't communicate with each other; but there is no doubt that the divergences are plain and significant. Even when the Marxist or the Muslim shares substantial aspects of the cultural inheritance of the European world, they will write very different kinds of novel or drama.

This is nothing to do with the clichés about clashing civilizations that we regularly hear, nor to say that Islam is always going to be 'other' to Europe: Islam has long been bound up with Europe's internal identity as a matter of simple historical fact, and it stands on a cultural continuum with Christianity, not in some completely different frame. It is simply to underline that there is a genuine distinctiveness about the cultural mindset that most directly inherits the Christian perspective; whether this is good or bad, true or false, we ignore the distinction only at the cost of honest and effective conversation across boundaries. More to our present point, we ignore the *history* of this distinction at the same cost. If we want to know why Europeans and their cultural relatives take it for granted that appearances can be deceptive and that we always need to 'decode' even the most innocent-looking claims, why we take it for granted that even our talk about what is most sacred and serious carries a shadow of incongruity, the answer is in a theology that has encouraged us to think of the world around us as never being a place to settle down for good. In this context, the challenge posed to the classical European legacy by Marxism or by contemporary Islam is important and constructive; a growing number of European thinkers in recent years have acknowledged that the pure pluralism of some sorts of postmodernist theory does not provide a very robust or compelling alternative to the 'monotheistic' certainties of other philosophies, even within the historic territories of Europe itself. If Europe is to go on being culturally alive, it will need to ask if it has understood its own legacy too narrowly and exclusively.

And there, of course, lie some of the great risks of our day. A completely fragmented cultural world, in which we no longer have any certainty about what is and isn't valuable and serious, will not generate cultural depth or excitement. The long-term fruit of a purely postmodern climate is a world of imitation, endless self-reflection which doesn't do much to take forward the creative project. It is tempting to react to this by looking for a style or a set of convictions that will liberate us from the maze of uncertainties and reinstate a clear view of how sacred or unchallengeable authority is present in history. This is very unlikely now to be the old Communist scheme, morally and intellectually discredited as it is. But it can surface in various ways within the West. Apart from those who simply turn to religious systems of unquestionable security, to fundamentalisms of various sorts, the still powerful idea that we have reached or are in sight of reaching an 'end of history' is another form of the same thing – the idea that debates about essential moral, social and spiritual issues is really over and that the global market has won all the arguments by default. Here we see two apparently diverse trends coming together – the radical individualism of our culture and the belief that there can be no rational argument about the sovereignty of the global market: consumerism and a kind of 'soft' totalitarianism go together.

Sixty years ago, in the wake of the Second World War, the Catholic historian and philosopher, Christopher Dawson, wrote, 'A society which has lost its religion becomes sooner or later a society which has lost its culture.'[1] When the processes I have been describing take over, what is lost is ultimately not only the culture of Europe and its cultural family, but also the idea of culture itself. The end of history is a situation in which nothing remains to be discovered about human nature and the possibilities of human relationships and language. Like any other fundamentalism, it assumes that the interesting questions have been answered and what remains is only an assortment of ways for whiling away the time. It is the mirror image of what many have found most disturbing in both the old Marxist world and the rhetoric of so-called 'radical' Islam today. Communism in its heyday resisted anything that looked like innovative or questioning art and restricted the artist to work that would reinforce the social message of the Party. Some of it was highly competent, and some of it managed to be skilfully subversive, but the political framework was designed to freeze out real creativity. And to turn to the other great alternative to the Christianity-haunted West, one of the tragedies of our time is that an Islamic world which has historically produced a vastly sophisticated material and poetic culture is threatened from within by those who acknowledge only the bare word of the sacred text, divorced from learning and interpretation; the paradox about Islamic primitivism is that it seems to arise not from the strength of faith, but from its weakness by dismissing out of hand the capacity of faith to engage transformingly with the social and imaginative world. A confused or weak faith produces a cultural loss of nerve, and that cultural loss of nerve impacts in turn on faith itself, generating the frantic anxiety that clothes itself in violence.

I've suggested elsewhere that for the European tradition of political liberalism to survive – the tradition of civic freedoms to criticize and reshape government, and to allow for genuine public debate about what is good for a society – we need a clearer awareness of the Christian heritage that, silently and in hidden ways, has produced that tradition through its commitments to abiding human dignity and the possibility of justifiable dissent from a ruling philosophy. When we reflect on faith and culture in Europe today and tomorrow, we need to think about a good deal more than just persuading European people back to Christian worship (though that would be a good start ...). There is something to be said about how Europe continues to contribute to the rest of the world a certain kind of moral awareness grounded in the critical spirit of Christianity and its conviction that conversion is possible, and thus that the present organization and appearance of the world isn't everything. But (and this is really the main point of what I have been arguing here) if this spirit is to be critical, a means of proper *judgement*, it can't be endlessly suspicious, it can't settle with the notion that there is nothing to trust anywhere. Christian faith tells us that, because God is to be trusted, we can be very bold indeed about the degree of scepticism we give to what is less than God. In the context of faith, this is the 'unbearable lightness' that is given to us in relation to the systems and expectations of the world around, the irony that is still compatible with love and commitment in God's name.

It is something that may be slightly clarified by setting it alongside what Christians have called 'negative theology' across the centuries. In this theological tradition, thinkers and writers have insisted that no human form of words captures what God is; but this doesn't lead them to conclude that nothing can be said of God. What they affirm is that no form of words, however true as far as it goes, is going to be fully *adequate*; there is always more to say (even in heaven). This is a theology that is hopeful because of the conviction that there is always more, and that this 'more' is always more compelling and wonderful — and so perhaps in the Christian's attitude to culture. We want to say of human achievement and creativity not 'this is false and empty', but 'this is not yet all that could be'. The Christian approaches culture, society, art, politics, not with a negation and a demand for a *rival* culture or society, but with the readiness to question in the name of a something more that God alone opens up and makes possible. And even those who don't quite know what they believe may perhaps understand a habit of questioning that works not to dismantle all certainties and leave us isolated choosing machines in a market-shaped wilderness, but to open further horizons, further depths of understanding of both the comedy and the tragedy of human existence.

At the start of this lecture, I sketched out five features of European cultural distinctiveness, all of them to do with how the modern European soul sees itself as called to 'create itself'; and later on, we looked at the ways in which this could have crippling and ruinous effects on our world. But when we see our souls as called to create because they come from the hand of a creator, as creative in the degree that they are aligned with a mysterious and indestructible loving purpose, we have something of immeasurable value to inform and sustain our culture. And it may be that we shall discover a notion of human rights that is not just about enforcing my own claims, but about the demands of dignity in all persons; a notion of freedom that sees it as freedom for the other, not from them; a vision of democracy that is about the constant search for ways of ensuring that even the most marginal and deprived has a voice; a search for a convergent morality in public life, not a separation between minimal public order and private moral preferences; and a climate of artistic creation that evokes something of the richness of the human subject when it is opened up to the holy. That would be a true culture of life; a worthy goal for this great community, this year and every year.

6

Religion, diversity and tolerance

Recent discussions about the admission of Turkey to the EU have brought into the open all sorts of concerns about the historic Christian identity of Europe; and these in turn have given a little more focus to the wider issue of what exactly Europe thinks itself to be in the current global context. In what follows, I want to suggest a way of understanding Europe's Christian heritage that may open some doors for a common vision. Our international situation is at the moment deeply uncertain and fluid. There is widespread impatience with transnational institutions, from the EU to the UN, yet equally widespread anxiety about the dominance of a single power. We are increasingly aware of the issues that cannot be solved by single sovereign states on their own – ecological crisis, terrorism, migrancy – yet are uncomfortable with any notion of global jurisdictions. We in the Northern/Western sphere are conscious of facing (to put it as neutrally as possible) a highly critical, if internally diverse, global 'opposition' in the shape of the Islamic world, and we do not know how best to respond to its presence outside and inside our own borders. Enlightenment liberalism, the self-evident creed of reasonable people, now appears as simply one cultural and historical phenomenon among others. Its supposed right to set the agenda for the rest of the world is no longer beyond question, however much the American Right or the European Left assume that their positions are the natural default beliefs of intelligent human beings, and that cultural and religious variety are superficial matters of choice or chance.

In short, we need some thought about European distinctiveness and whether it has any specific moral substance. In the absence of any such thinking, we end up in a very typical postmodern trap – argument replaced by parallel assertions; and, as several recent theologians have argued, what is left if we refuse to discuss moral and spiritual foundations is simply violent competition for the power to set agendas, political, economic and cultural, with religious commitment seen as at best a 'lifestyle option' chosen for its ability to enhance individual effectiveness or comfort.

Sociologists writing about religion in Europe [as noted in the last chapter] have taken lately to referring to the 'European exception': everywhere in the world except in Europe, the public visibility of religion has increased and is increasing. The picture, popular a few decades ago, of a universal drift towards secularization (that is, the virtual disappearance of religious belief as a significant factor in either personal commitment or public policy), has had to be modified. This may be deplorable to the self-consciously progressive Western mind; and attempts to reintroduce religious considerations into public debate can prompt savagely hostile comment – as recent British debates about euthanasia have shown. But there is at the very least a problem here that needs analysis. And I want to suggest that the solution of the problem is a rather teasing set of ideas, which may not comfort either the secularist or the believer in religious domination in society.

The solution requires us first to retell the history of Europe. What we mean by 'Europe' culturally speaking tends to be the complex of civilizations and language groups brought into political relationship by two factors – the great Germanic, Turkic and Slavonic migrations that destroyed the Roman Empire, and the emergence of new institutions that sought to salvage the legacy of that empire. Among the latter, the Christian Church is quite simply the most extensive and enduring, whether in the form of the Western Papacy or of the 'Byzantine Commonwealth', the network of cultural and spiritual connections in Eastern Europe linked to the new Roman Empire centred on Constantinople. As some historians have argued, the emergence of Islam in fact produced a third competitor for the imperial Roman legacy; but we shall be returning to that notion later on.

In the West, the new Germanic kingdoms, governed by tribal law and feudal obligation, engaged in a centuries-long conflict with the renewed system of centralized Roman administration whose supreme court of appeal was the Pope. For the Roman-centred Church, the fact of Christian identity was a theoretically universal thing, which made it possible to legislate across cultural, linguistic and economic frontiers, and which generated an international civil service. Throughout the Middle Ages, the two models jostled, bargained, quarrelled and reshaped each other; by the sixteenth century, a new configuration was emerging, as the political world we recognize as 'modern' was born.

Although some scholars in the last century and a half have argued as if the battle had been between a damaging centralism and a healthy local independence, the truth is much more complex. The Roman system worked on the basis that any local jurisdiction was subject to a higher law; the local power of a monarch or an aristocracy could not be the last word, and tribal or familial loyalties should not determine people's possibilities. It was this spirit that, for example, enshrined the principle that consent was necessary for a valid marriage, challenging, if only implicitly, some of the prevailing assumptions about the status of women. It was this spirit that, in the hands of Thomas Aquinas, reserved for citizens the right to criticize, and even in some circumstances to replace, a monarch on the basis of universal law.

At the same time, the problematic result of the system was a legal language that gave no place to concrete local tradition and the networks of semi-formal mutual obligation which actually make up specific societies, and a stress on the absoluteness of the ultimate sovereign court as religiously sanctioned. Centralized religious authority was bound to appear as a sort of 'super-state', a political system which trumped the claims of other political organizations. And this provoked increasing unease as some people in Europe became more aware of certain biblical themes, of the Christian tradition of foreswearing force or compulsion, and the primitive Christian suspicion of worldly authority.

The Reformation produced a new map of the political territory. The evolving nation-states of Europe were eager to appeal to local sentiment in support of new levels of political independence, affirming the right of the state to assert its own jurisdiction as beyond appeal. But in so doing, they not unnaturally produced what might be called a 'papal' model of royal authority, a view of the monarch's status as source of legal validity which reinforced the sense of the 'sovereign' state in an unprecedented way. The new princely regimes (Catholic as much as Protestant) reproduced within their borders the model of a centralized system, treating citizens as abstract possessors of legal claim before the state's tribunal. Both feudal survivals and foreign ecclesiastical jurisdiction came under attack. The Roman Catholic Church emerged as still a resolutely international body as against the new national Churches of the Reformation, but with no very clear account of how it saw the legitimacy of the new states. In due course, the final revolt against traditional forms of authority, feudal or ecclesiastical, led to the Enlightenment model of universal secular legality – the principles of the French Revolution and, in modified form, the Napoleonic Code. Both Catholic universalism and the remnants of 'common-law' custom and mutuality were removed from public life in the name of a universal system of legally conceived equality and freedom, divorced almost entirely from religious sanction.

Now the point of this rather breathless (and by no means uncontroversial) tour of Western European history is to try and identify what the argument is that has made Europe the way it is. The history just summarized tells us that the conflict of the so-called Dark Ages, the encounter between the tribal kingdoms and the Church, the tangled relations of common law, canon law and Romanized civil law guaranteed that political power in Western Europe was always a matter of negotiation and balance. Despite what some historical caricatures have maintained, sovereign state power in Europe was never consistently treated as a sacred thing. It could be challenged by the Church's authority; it could be checked by feudal obligations. And when we speak of the Christian heritage of Europe, what we should have in mind is not just the story of a faith-dominated society, homogeneous and pervasively spiritual, but a history of political argument – with the implication that forms of government are rightly the raw material of contests about legitimacy. Political power is answerable to law and to God, and it is therefore right in some circumstances to challenge it.

This is what I should regard as the central conviction of political liberalism (as distinct from theological or social liberalism) – the idea that political life can and should be a realm of creative engagement. It is not, notice, a principle simply of democratic rights, nor of individual liberties; it affirms rather that loyalty to the state is not the same thing as religious belonging: not that the state has no claims, but that it is a mistake to see those claims as beyond challenge in any imaginable circumstances. And in this sense, to the extent that Europe has pioneered such 'liberalism', Europe is what it is because of its Christian history.

Let me elaborate this a bit further. The Church of Christ begins by defining itself as a community both alongside, and of a different order to, political society. Its membership is not restricted by race, class or speech, and in that way it puts questions against the absoluteness of any local and tribal identity. Yet it does not seek to set up another empire on the same level as the Roman imperium. It has 'citizens', but their citizenship is not something that requires them to set up societies in rivalry to the existing systems. Until the state makes ultimate claims which Christians cannot obey, Christian citizenship is largely invisible; in the Roman Empire, when the Emperor requires worship from citizens, the hidden potential for dissent appears. Martyrdom establishes the distinctiveness of Christian belonging over against all other kinds.

That model of an alternative citizenship is what gradually produced the systems of ecclesiastical law. But when the Western Empire collapsed, it was only the Church that retained any sense at all of a unifying legal frame of reference. It was inevitable that it should emerge as something very like an empire itself. Yet the fact that this represented a compromise with its own most formative traditions led to a steady stream of protest – internal protest like the monastic movements, separatist protests like those of the Waldensians and Wycliffites. 'Secular' power, the authority of local rulers and feudal aristocracies, could be a useful ally against a Church authority that had become too much of a universal state. So the tension continues, not so much between 'Church' and 'state' as between different models of securing the independence of the body of believers, the hidden alternative citizenship created in the fellowship of Jesus Christ. And so long as the Church is faithful to the New Testament's scepticism about any final victory of the Church within history, the very fact of the Church is the ground for scepticism about any regime that pretends to offer ultimate solutions or permanent stability.

In practice, of course, the Church has most often been an enemy to what we should instinctively see as democratizing or liberalizing moves in a nation's history. It seems odd to ascribe to the Church the ultimate ideological responsibility for argument and pluralism in European politics. Yet the Reformation and Enlightenment protests upon which much of 'modernity' in Europe rests did not come from nowhere; they were centrally theological disputes, even when they were resolved in ways inimical to the authority and public influence of faith. If we are unaware today of this background, we shall misunderstand where the liberal tradition comes from; and we shall be more vulnerable than ever to the sort of unhistorical optimism which has characterized far too much of Western involvement in the complexities of non-Western societies.

But this means that Western modernity and liberalism are at risk when they refuse to recognize that they are the way they are because of the presence in their midst of that partner and critic which speaks of 'alternative citizenship' – the Christian community. What I have been arguing is that the distinctively European style of political argument and debate is made possible by the Church's persistent witness to the fact that states do not have ultimate religious claims on their citizens. When the Church is regarded as an enemy to be overcome or a private body that must be resolutely excluded from public debate, liberal modernity turns itself into a fixed and absolute thing, another pseudo-religion, in fact. It is important for the health of the political community that it is able to engage seriously with the tradition in which its own roots lie. To say this is not to demand the impossible, a return to some past age when the institutional Church claimed to dictate public policy. But without a willingness to listen to the questions and challenges of the Church, liberal society is in danger of becoming illiberal. Wholesale secularism as a programmatic policy in the state can turn into another tyranny – a system beyond challenge. The presence of the Church at least goes on obstinately asking the state about its accountability and the justification of its priorities. It will not do to forget that the greatest and most murderous tyrannies of the modern age in Europe have been systematically anti-religious – or rather, as I have already hinted, have become pseudo-religions.

What I am arguing is that the virtues we associate with the European identity, the virtues of political liberalism in the sense I have outlined, will survive best if they are seen as the outgrowth of the historic European tensions about sovereignty, absolutism and the integrity of local communities that were focused sharply by the Christian Church and its theology – a theology that encouraged scepticism about any final political settlement within history. The Christian presence challenges the crude Marxist notion that the end of history has arrived in the shape of the Socialist state; it also challenges any assertion of the end of history in terms of the triumph of market capitalism. The Church's presence and voice in any society, especially in 'liberal' Europe, leaves politics quite rightly under scrutiny and declares its commitment to a history that is still unfolding, still unfinished. The state, whatever its ideology, is never again to be a sacred thing. If I may refer back to an earlier essay on this subject, I would suggest that 'Unless the liberal state is engaged in a continuing dialogue with the religious community, it loses its essential liberalism. It becomes simply dogmatically secular, insisting that religious faith be publicly invisible; or it becomes chaotically pluralist, with no proper account of its legitimacy except a positivist one (the state is the agency that happens to have the monopoly of force)'.[1]

We should note one important implication of the model that has been sketched so far. If the state has no sacred character, it is not the sole source of legitimate common life: intermediate institutions, guilds, unions, churches, ethnic groups, all sorts of civil associations, have a natural liberty to exist and organize themselves, and the state's role is to harmonize and, to some degree, regulate this social variety. I have mentioned already the risks of 'chaotic pluralism'; but pluralism of some sort is implicit in any political philosophy that rejects a sacralized sovereignty. The challenge is for a state apparatus to become a reliable and creative 'broker' of the concerns of the communities that make it up – not simply a dependable tribunal before which rights may be argued, but a legal and (in the broadest sense) moral framework within which communities may interact without the fear that any one may gain an unjust or dispropor-tionate power. This 'interactive pluralism', rooted, as we have seen in earlier chapters, in the liberalism of thinkers like Acton, Maitland and Figgis, would see the healthy state neither as an alliance of suspiciously coexisting groups, nor as a neutral legal unit whose citizens all possessed abstractly equal rights, but as a space in which distinctive styles and convictions could challenge each other and affect each other, but on the basis that they first had the freedom to be themselves.

This is therefore the basis upon which a European political philosophy is able to embrace religious variety and to practice cultural hospitality. Europe, as a cultural reality existing because it has been addressed by the Christian gospel and is historically confronted by the challenge of the Christian Church, is not thereby made into a uniform society, a new Christendom. Quite the contrary; the characteristic European state, in dialogue with the Church, is able to consider its cultural life as always under renegotiation, as its demography changes. At the same time, while it is essentially hospitable to the stranger and the migrant, it has to confront the risk that it may find itself being hospitable to some sort of bid to alter the foundational idea of Europe as a sphere of 'liberal' interaction between communities within the frame of law.

And this, of course, raises the spectre that haunts so much of our discussion, the fear of a militant Islamic ideology that seeks to replace liberalism with a new theocracy. I noted earlier that Islam itself was culturally and historically one of the systems that replaced the Roman Empire, providing, only now on a profound religious base, the same sense of belonging in a single culture of equality and justice. To be a member of the *umma* was to be assured in principle of belonging to a reality for which nationality and class were irrelevant to the theological and legal status proper to a believer. It is true to say that Islam is in its most robust historical form, both 'Church' and 'state'; and thus it is a challenge to any Muslim to make sense of living outside that unitary reality. The uneasy and sceptical relationship between the political community and the community of belief that has characterized the Western Christian world (and often even the Eastern Christian world as well) is, at first sight, largely foreign to Islam.

Yet, in fact, Islam has had a history outside its historic majority cultures. It has had experience of negotiating its way in other settings. Its celebrated principle that there is no compulsion in religion means that it is not absolutely and theologically committed to an imposition of specifically Muslim law even in majority contexts – or so some would argue. The work of Muslim thinker like Tariq Ramadan on the identity of Western Muslims spells out some of the principles by which a Muslim identity outside a Muslim majority state can be understood. On the basis that cultural habits that do not directly conflict with Islamic precept become Islamic in virtue of being practised by Muslims, it is possible for a Muslim to see his or her Western cultural identity as integral to their Muslim identity. There is, says Ramadan[2], no single 'homeland' for Muslims: they can be at home in any geographical and political environment, and they need to avoid 'self-ghettoization', becoming 'spectators in a society where they were once marginalized'.[3] They need to be arguing and negotiating in the public sphere. But the acceptance of such argumentation is undoubtedly a development, as Ramadan agrees – a necessary recognition of distinctions between primary and secondary concerns in social life, a following-through of principles rooted deeply in classical Muslim thinking about ijtihad, the labour of interpretation.[4] In modern conditions, this labour is something needed not simply in the context of jurisprudence within Muslim society, but in relation to an irreversibly plural and complex environment.[5] Ramadan can even say, surprisingly for the Western reader, that the Muslim distinction between religious and social authority, between what is enjoined for the good of the soul and what is ordered for the stability of an external environment, is really much the same as the Christian distinction between Church and state. What is different is that the Islamic world has never gone so far as to sanction the absolute institutional separation that emerged in the Christian world.[6]

I have devoted some time to Ramadan's discussion of Muslim identity in the West, partly for its intrinsic interest and partly to reinforce the main argument of this chapter. 'Europe' has introduced into the cultural map of the world a particular habit of argument, a particular recognition of diversity which carries with it also a certain recognition of the limits of the state's authority. By denying to the state an unquestionable freedom to reshape the conditions of social life, by giving place to arguments that call the state to account in the name of a higher law, this political and philosophical tradition assumes that the political realm will always be one in which mediation and mutual listening will be normal and in which law exists as a means of such mediation. Where the state is not an essentially religious unit, and where the religious community does not seek to become a universal executive, diversity is inevitable. However, this does not imply the necessity of relativism, or of what is sometimes called 'consumer' pluralism (the availability of a plurality of lifestyle choices). If religious communities are acknowledged as participants in public argument, they are bound to some level of creative engagement with each other and with the secular voice of the administration, so as to find a solution that has some claim to be just to a range of communal interests. Ramadan, it seems, agrees that this is precisely the path that must be taken by Islam in the context of modernity. And he pleads for better and more constructive alliances between diverse religious communities on common concerns – not to impose a theocracy by stealth, but to ensure the fullest possible statement of shared moral goals and anxieties in the public debate.

We misunderstand our situation, then, if we imagine that the world's current problem is a neat binary opposition between a totalizing religious culture (Islam) and a single 'enlightened' or 'democratic' world of rational neutrality. The reality is a lot more interesting – and it is interesting precisely because of the theological roots of modernity. A Muslim thinker like Ramadan helps us to see that, while it was Christianity, for a variety of internal reasons, that crystallized in its most extreme form the idea of the state's relativity and secular character, Islam itself acknowledges the same tension between levels of human identity and aspects of human virtue, and implies the same liberty of criticism against specific political systems. But both equally allow that loyalty to these systems is not inconsistent with the loyalty of faith; commitment to the lawfulness of the processes of argument in a society and acceptance of the outcome of ordered negotiation is presupposed by the political ethics of both traditions. Without that, we should simply revert to the ghetto ethics from which Ramadan is seeking to liberate his co-religionists.

So if Europe is historically a Christian-inspired culture of argument and what a theologian would call 'eschatological reserve' about excessive political claims (reservation in the light of the inevitable imperfection of all that is achieved within history), there is nonetheless a European future for Islam within this discourse. The liberal heritage as we have been defining it, the welcoming of creativity and diversity in the political process and the social map, is not a polar opposite to the classical Muslim understanding of social identity. The real opposition is between a classical Muslim and Christian acceptance of interpretation and reflection in charting the believer's duties in the public sphere, and the crude and violent absolutizing of a single narrow cultural expression of faith, devoid of any positive sense of history. The Islamist extremist is not a traditionalist in the proper sense, but someone who has simply fixed on a moment in the living tradition and frozen it.

But we cannot leave the subject without revisiting the dangers of a secularism that is equally forgetful of history. The political style that seeks to keep religious communities in the private sphere, insisting that religion is always and primarily an individual option related only to the supposed well-being of that individual and like-minded private persons, is at risk, as I have said earlier, of becoming itself a pseudo-religion, a system that is beyond challenge. A mature European politics will take another route, seeking for effective partnership with the component communities of the state, including religious bodies. It will try to avoid creating ghettoes. It will value and acknowledge all those sources of healthy corporate identity and political formation (in the widest sense) that are around. The agnostic German philosopher, Jurgen Habermas, said in a discussion with the then Cardinal Ratzinger in January 2004 that the liberal state needed resources with which to confront the depersonalizing effects of globalization, and should 'treat with care all cultural sources on which the normative consciousness and solidarity of citizens draws'.[7]

And perhaps this is the central contribution to be made to a future European identity by the Christian tradition. It challenges the global socio-political juggernaut – consumer pluralism combined with insensitive Western promotion of a rootless individualism, disguised as liberal democracy. It affirms the significance of local and intentional communities, and their role in public life. It is able to welcome the stranger, including the Muslim stranger in its midst, as a partner in the work of proper liberalism, the continuing argument about common good and just governance. When it is allowed its proper visibility, it makes room for other communities and faiths to be visible. By holding the space for public moral argument to be possible and legitimate, it reduces the risk of open social conflict, because it is not content to relegate the moral and the spiritual to a private sphere where they may be distorted into fanaticism and exclusion. For Europe to celebrate its Christian heritage in this sense is precisely for it to affirm a legacy and a possibility of truly constructive pluralism. And for the Church to offer this to Europe (and from Europe to the wider world) is not for it to replace its theology with a vague set of nostrums about democracy and tolerance, but for it to affirm its faithfulness to the tradition of Christian freedom in the face of the world's sovereignties.

The spiritual and the religious: is the territory changing?

1

'I'm not into religion. I am completely anti-religious. Religion is a term for a collection, a denomination. I am interested in personal experience of God'. This remark from no less an authority than Bono of U2[1] elegantly sums up a view that has become increasingly widespread in Britain and in much of contemporary Northern Europe: substantial numbers of people identify themselves in questionnaires and surveys as 'spiritual but not religious'. The spiritual dimension of all sorts of things, from school education to business practice, is recognized more and more seriously. But all this is distinguished sharply from adherence to any specific religious tradition and community. While the spiritual may be a resource for health, even for 'capital' (as in the title of a recent book by Danah Zohar and Ian Marshall, *Spiritual Capital: wealth we can live by*), the 'religious' is seen as ambivalent at best, dangerous at worst.

If we ask why exactly the religious is so unattractive in the eyes of many, including so many iconic and opinion-forming figures, the answers are not too difficult to work out. Bono's remarks provide an obvious starting-point. Religion is a matter of the collective mentality, with all that this implies about having to take responsibility for corporately-held teaching and discipline; so religious allegiance can be seen as making over some aspect of myself to others in ways that may compromise both my liberty and my integrity. It may be seen as committing myself to practices that mean little to me, or subjecting myself to codes of conduct that don't connect at all convincingly with my sense of who I am or what is creative and life-giving for me. It may mean being obliged to profess belief in certain propositions that appear arbitrary and unconnected with the business of human flourishing. The spiritual, in contrast, is what opens up and resources personal integrity at a new depth, developing and not frustrating the sense of personal distinctiveness and allowing ordinary human activities to be understood afresh against a broader background of 'sacred' meaning. Such a vision doesn't commit you to believing six impossible things before breakfast, signing away your liberty or becoming locked into a tribal mentality, hostile to other sorts of meaning and commitment.

If we wanted to identify the two most significant grounds for objection to religion in this connection, they would, I think, be the claim to some kind of exclusive truthfulness (with the implication of the untruthfulness and thus illegitimacy of other convictions), and the demand for an abdication of personal liberty. If we are looking for spiritual resources in our modern environment, they have to be inclusive and generative of liberty. So Danah Zohar can write, in the introduction to the book just referred to:

> My use of the word *spiritual* here and throughout the book has no connection with religion or any other organized belief system. Religious organizations and religiously based cultures have undoubtedly built some genuine spiritual capital. But they have done so within the limitations of belief systems that exclude those who hold other religious beliefs and those who have no religious belief. The broader kind of spiritual capital needed for organizations, communities, and cultures participating in today's pluralist and global society must draw on deeper, non-sectarian meanings, values, purposes, and motivations that might be sacred to any human being.[2]

2

Behind all this lies a broad historical trajectory which has been skilfully mapped by sociologists like David Martin and Grace Davie. Martin has identified it as the process of a 'loosening of monopoly':[3] the historic Churches and the historic nation states alike, and often in collaboration, provided for all citizens a narrative within which they could live and die, a narrative that justified discipline, sacrifice and solidarity. As the economic power of the average individual changes and thus the availability of a wider assortment of chosen identities opens up, 'monopolistic' claims about what constitutes identity lose their social and imaginative plausibility: we are always going to be aware of perfectly credible and attractive alternatives to the demands made by traditional forms of belonging. It is no longer obvious why we should live like *that*. Thus what remains of traditionally shaped identity will slip further and further towards a reservoir of material which people can draw on as they put together an identity they have *chosen*. Socially speaking, this is not just a description of what happens when 'religion' encounters 'modernity', and it has little to do with any supposed erosion of religion's credibility by science.[4] It is part of the general shift in economically developed societies away from the idea of a controlling narrative, a story about shared meanings and goals.

This is one of the most pervasive changes in the shared mindset of the modern West. As Martin, Davie and others have insisted, it is a different thing from secularization. It does not mean that people have stopped asking the questions which were once framed by religious narratives or looking for sources of significance in their lives beyond the realms of measurable worldly success. The difference is, to use a distinction sometimes made in this connection, that we generally prefer these days to be patrons rather than subscribers: we reserve our liberty in regard to our various affiliations rather than committing ourselves to regular and unquestioning support. Parish clergy will probably note with wry familiarity this shift in attitude and how it impacts on regular church attendance; and another of the substantive cultural changes that we have seen in our lifetimes has been the gradual spread of the 'patron' mentality in Catholic as well as Protestant environments. The patron remains in control and his or her relation to the community of affiliation is one in which questions will regularly be asked about how well the patron's needs are being recognized and met. The subscriber characteristically considers himself or herself bound in important respects by the needs of the community or organization. Quite apart from the problems of the Christian Church in contemporary Britain, the almost insoluble challenge for many charities these days, competing as they have to for support, is how to persuade people by what are essentially market methods that they should take up a very non-market-minded position of committed involvement.

So the challenge to those of us who maintain our involvement in traditionally conceived religious communities is not just an assault by principled secularists on all religious belief – though that is hardly insignificant. More immediately in most contexts it is that we can't help being committed, like the charities I mentioned a moment ago, to living with a market mentality. We have to learn how to make ourselves look credible and attractive, marketable. We cannot avoid a deeper examination of what it is that is said to make 'religion' problematic or even threatening. We have to work out how just such an estimate might be, and we have to argue what it is that the search for 'spiritual capital' independently of corporate religious affiliation leaves as unfinished business.

These are complementary challenges, of course. In trying to meet them, I want to be clear that I have no desire to belittle the concern people have for spirituality, or the importance given to discovering a vision that can be held and acted on with personal integrity; nor do I want to suggest any idealizing of uncritical religious allegiance (as we shall see, the word 'religious' has its own shadows and pitfalls for believers). But I do want to confront the idea that the future of human spiritual awareness and maturity can lie only with a post-religious consciousness, with what might be 'sacred to any human being', over and above the affirmations of any specific religious body.

3

Religion as understood by those who find it unacceptable in the way Bono outlines is something seen essentially in terms of an appeal to the will: *decide* to believe these propositions and to obey these commands. Heard in this way, the appeal to religious faith invites the response, 'Why should I?' It seems like a simple bid for power, an appeal to irrational submission. The more religious commitment is seen in this essentially *political* mode (something to do with securing conformity to a system of ideas and government), the less it connects with any aspiration to personal integrity as most people now conceive it. But one of the peculiar curses of modernity has been to create in this particular area of human reflection a series of false polarities. Because pre-modern religion did indeed often represent patterns of authority beyond accountability and challenge, the connection of religious affiliation with an abdication of responsibility was not difficult to make. The result has been the classic Enlightenment stand-off between a faith which refuses criticism and questioning, and therefore refuses real self-knowledge as we understand it, and the realm of critical rationality, in which every assertion is justified by argument and evidence that is in principle accessible to anyone. At its crudest, this can be stated in terms of religion offering poor and unreasonable explanations for phenomena that science can explain reasonably. But even at a more sophisticated level of argument, we still hear the same underlying theme: religion introduces an alien element into reasonable human discourse; it makes life difficult for anything approaching a *universal* language of rights and liberties, law and equity, a language to transcend the various forms of murderous tribalism which afflict our world. Against this background, it is very naturally viewed by many as something which may be tolerated as a purely private matter of conviction, but no more. When we talk about the public sphere (education, business, rights) we may need a spirituality, but it will have to be of the Zohar/Marshall variety, freed from the shadow of 'sectarianism'.

But what if it is wrong to see traditional religious affiliation as a matter of deciding like this, as if we were just talking about 'lifestyle choices'? Traditional styles of religious commitment were nothing much to do with *resolving* to think or do this or that: they were environments in which people were supplied with a set of possible roles within a comprehensive narrative, a set of possible projects shaped by the governing story. The aim of life was to act in a way that lets the story come through, that shows to the world what we believe is most real. Freedom was imagined as *the liberty to embody an objective truth*. Freedom was what happened when we were delivered from a state of illusion and unreality, the unreality of letting our lives be shaped by nothing but instinct or arbitrary choice.

And here is the salient point in response to what can be claimed for post-religious spirituality. The spiritual intelligence outlined by Zohar and Marshall perceives the interconnectedness of things and the consequent imperative of acting responsibly, acknowledging that level of interconnectedness. But it also begins with the assumption that human beings have, so to speak, already decided on the range of activities they will undertake, so that the only question is how to perform them more responsibly. Acquiring spiritual capital, as Zohar and Marshall clearly admit, is an aspect of acquiring sustainable wealth for the greatest possible number; hence the illustrative stories of how spiritually alert people in global organizations[5] can improve the performance of the organization, qualitatively and even quantitatively.

There is a perfectly proper warning here against the easy assumption that some kinds of organization are just too evil to merit the engagement of spiritually serious persons. But at the same time, it is hard not to feel that something has been left out of the picture, some question about the overall worth of what we have already decided to do. What is it that makes, say, a global fast-food enterprise a proper enterprise in shaping a life that expresses a larger, interconnected truth to which we are answerable? How deep is the spiritual question allowed to cut? It is possible to recognize interconnectedness and yet to miss a major moral point. It isn't just a matter of how we do the things we've already decided to do; it's also what sort of things we have already decided to do, and how or whether those things could possibly be signs of the interconnectedness of things, or indeed of that relation to the 'sacred' as something beyond our individual minds and feelings.[6]

There's the problem; if you can recognize patterns of cosmic interconnection and yet not know how to start asking questions about what sort of actions are revealing of the sacred order of things, something is missing, something that has to do with motivation for radical challenge and possible change in what we take for granted. Deciding that you are obliged to be responsible is not something you can instantly derive from belief in an interconnected universe. Responsibility has about it an irreducible element of being called to 'answer' for and to other agents; its roots have a lot to do with the sense of being the recipient of something at the hands of another. Something is bestowed which both enables and requires an answer. Yet to speak like this of 'bestowing' or 'endowing' is to move immediately into a realm in which I confront something like another personal presence. A generalized 'sacred' dimension of reality may be independent of my mind, but doesn't in itself need or suggest this language of 'bestowal'. Talking about God, not just about the sacred, assumes, on the contrary, that there is not only a sacred reality, but an initiating agency that is independent of anything in our world. I am invited to make myself answerable for the good, the human welfare and spiritual health, of the human other, to make myself disposable in some measure for them, in part because of how I have learned to 'read' the world around, reading it as suggesting that an agency independent of any circumstance within the world has 'taken responsibility' for *my* welfare – has not only given life in general, but put at my disposal the life that is its own.

Religious traditions that speak about an active divine presence thus maintain that my responsible action is in some way a reflection or even continuation of the foundational act which initiates everything we perceive. And that act may be discerned vaguely and generally in some aspects of the world; but it is not given precise shape in terms of freedom and initiative without some more specific story that can be told about the free self-communication of the sacred which makes this act visible. Morality becomes not a matter of compliance with arbitrary rules enforced by threat, but the struggle to identify and move with the direction of fundamental creative action as it has shown itself to us. Freedom is indeed the freedom to be in union with this act; anything less is going to be ultimately frustrating and self-destructive. But freedom in this sense, a freedom that allows for radical change, is triggered only by the clear representation or realization of an unconditional divine gift within the world's own story. And this at once involves us in claims about uniquely revelatory or transforming events, in dealing with questions about where we can best stand in order to see, with some measure of authoritative clarity, the direction, the 'flow' of things with which we seek harmony.

Religious identity that works in this way allows for a complex of elements that 'post-religious' spirituality cannot easily deal with or accommodate. There is, most obviously, the whole world of language and feeling that connects with personal relation – supremely with *love*, in the Christian tradition. The process of exploring the 'endowment' offered is more like the discovery of a person than anything else, and the responses we develop are closely analogous to the kinds of self-examination we may undertake in the light of a serious and lasting relation with another human being. Yet when this has been said, what comes most sharply into focus is a vastly intensified sense of what can also appear in human intimacy – the inadequacy of thinking and responding as if the other were simply a version of oneself. And so, while Christian theology in particular gives unique privilege to this language of the personal and of love, it also constantly reminds the believer that the analogy is partial; we do not know what it might mean for an infinite agent utterly outside our frame of interlocking, interdependent reference to be 'personal'. We have no other framework that can carry the truth of what we want to say, but we cannot specify exactly how what we say correlates with how it is with the divine. The confident deployment of the language of love always goes along with the critical awareness that the words take us to the edge of what we normally think of as knowledge, not to a clear position from which we can authoritatively survey the truth.

4

Interpersonal imagery, then, combining with the recurrent and unavoidable recognition of its incompleteness, is regularly part of what the 'religious' as opposed to the 'spiritual' entails – at least in the Abrahamic traditions. The specific reality of the human self is not abolished, but it is dethroned or decentred. To discover who I am I need to discover the relation in which I stand to an active, prior Other, to a transcendent creator: I don't first sort out who I am and then seek for resources to sustain that identity.

What I am trying to convey is what the creative imagination of the 'mystical' writer most fully embodies, an awareness that the policy of living in faith and worship constantly opens upon a landscape still to be explored, resisting mastery and mapping, yet also authoritative in its distance from what the individual or collective human will produces. The traditional religious marks of gratitude and obedience can be translated, in this register of writing, simply as what an enjoyment of the real entails – an 'enjoyment' which is also a comprehensively and painfully self-displacing process, allowing what is there, and prior to us, just to be itself. Anyone who concluded that the risks of exclusivism, 'sectarianism', were too high and that the future had to lie with non-revelatory, non-dogmatic spirituality, would need also to acknowledge that a particular register of speech and understanding would have to disappear – all that evokes this complex blend of joy, yielding, relational intimacy and so on, all that it is tempting to call, in the broadest sense, the 'erotic' in spiritual imagination, which has figured so largely in historic practice. Redefinition in terms of spiritual capital has a price. And part of the price is the loss of the unqualified enjoyment of what is there for what it is ('We give thanks to Thee for Thy great glory'). Whether it is a necessary price to escape from the evils of exclusivism is a matter I shall come back to before finishing.

But all I have said highlights the point briefly touched on above: practitioners of traditional religion are generally, if they think about it, reluctant to reduce what they do to the model of a corporate adherence to a set of doctrines and policies. They sit uncomfortably with the very category of 'religion', largely because it has been so trivialized by this kind of reduction. To turn specifically to Christian identity (though others may want to spell it out in terms of their own narratives or communal practices), the idea of 'the Christian religion' is a late and weak formulation: what first exists is the Assembly, to give the literal meaning of the Greek word for 'Church', as a fresh configuring of the whole of experienced reality – a new set of human relations, a new horizon for what human beings are capable of, a new understanding of the material world and its capacities. The Christian involved in the celebration of the Eucharist is not affirming a set of propositions with the help of an audio-visual programme, but inhabiting, in speech and action, a drama which purports to 're-locate' him or her in the space occupied by Jesus Christ in his eternal relationship with the Father, a relocation which is enabled by his sacrificial death and his rising from the grave and ascension into heaven. 'The Eucharistic sacrifice represents the cost of love's unarmed appeal to the city and of what followed from the rejection of the sign of the peace ... [A]ll the ordinary citizens of the city are able to become a brotherhood by a sharing in the broken body and the shed blood. They are made whole and peaceful again by absorbing and imbibing its brokenness and its violence'. This is part of David Martin's summary of what it is that the 'Assembly' offers the 'city', the society in which it is set: not first a complex of doctrine and regulation, but a ritual of healing through being drawn into a common space, a 'Kingdom', an alternative City.[7] And this ritual of healing claims to be effective because of an actual event or set of events in history, in which the sacred reality from which everything derives freely identified itself with the victims of human violence so as to absorb and swallow up the cycle of violence once and for all. Doctrine is indispensable for the statement of this, and regulation and moral valuation flow inexorably from it; but *first* it is exposure to an action believed to be effective in altering the world we experience, human and non-human.

In other words, the Christian alternative to the post-religious spirituality outlined earlier is not simply 'religion' as some sort of intellectual and moral system but the corporately experienced reality of the Kingdom, the space that has been cleared in human imagination and self-understanding by the revealing events of Jesus' life. Standing in this place, I am made aware of what is fundamental and indestructible about my human identity: that I am the object of divine intention and commitment, a being freely created and never abandoned. Standing in this place, I am also challenged to examine every action or policy in my life in the light of what I am; and I am, through the common life of the 'Assembly', made able to change and to be healed, to feed and be fed in relations with others in the human city. Faced with the claims of non-dogmatic spirituality, the believer should not be insisting anxiously on the need for compliance with a set of definite propositions; he or she should be asking whether what happens when the Assembly meets to adore God and lay itself open to his action looks at all like a new and transforming environment, in which human beings are radically changed.

5

We have noted the large-scale cultural shift which has made post-religious spirituality seem in some ways better adapted to contemporary conditions than classical religious practice; but we should also note some encouraging signs which suggest that the movement is not all one-way. The growing presence in Europe of a substantial and confident form of classical religious practice in the shape of Islam has put the quest for detached non-sectarian spiritual capital in perspective: post-religious spirituality has to compete with an articulate corporate voice which stubbornly resists being made instrumental to the well-being of an unchallenged Western and capitalist modernity. The natural and instinctive reaction of government is to attempt to co-opt the strong motivations of such corporate vision into the project of strengthening social cohesion. Yet, as we noted earlier, it, like much of our current culture, still tends to view religious belonging as simply a form of private lifestyle option, and finds difficulty coping with the fact that there will be areas of stand-off between the practices of the community and the assumptions of the culture at large.

There is a fair amount of confusion in all this, and it will take time to clarify and find our way through. Still, the gradual and cautious welcome given in official vocabulary to what 'faith *communities*', rather than just spiritually sensitive individuals, may contribute to the strengthening of motivation towards mutual support and nurture suggests that the picture has altered a little in recent years. When the great German philosopher Jurgen Habermas acknowledged some years ago in debate with the then Cardinal Ratzinger that traditional religion offered necessary resources to the construction of social reason and just practice, he was paving the way for some such approach on the part of secular government. There is an implicit acknowledgement, it seems, that what religious affiliation of a classical kind offers is not to be reduced just to an enhanced sense of the transcendent or of the interconnection of all things. Mark Thompson of the BBC observed in a lecture in 2008 that there is evidence of 'not just a persistence but a sharp revival of interest in the spiritual potential of traditional religious practice and belief.'

This is not, as I have stressed earlier, a reason for the traditional believer to dismiss the role of the post-religious 'spiritual' sensibility; but it is important to be clear, so far as we can, about where the differences lie and precisely what critical questions might be put to the advocate of the non-sectarian spiritual in terms both of the roots of motivation and of the scope of moral challenge within the framework of global capitalism. And, as again we observed earlier, there is at least a shared concern for more than the enhancement of the individual's self-awareness. In the Zohar/Marshall book (chapter 10), there is even a proposal for a sort of elite network of disciplined strategists, aware of something like a vocation to change the moral complexion and culture of their organizations. The rather unhappy analogy used is of the Order of Knights Templar; but the salient point is the recognition that shared discipline and a sense of calling, of a kind typical of traditional religious practice, are a necessary undergirding for any sustained attempt to question and transform institutions at more than a surface level.

But what, finally, about the issue of the innate exclusivism of revelation-based faith and communities of faith? We have noted that *any* claim about what is good for humanity as such will have about it an element of exclusivity: it is the reverse side of trying to hold to a perspective of universality and equality in the human world. We cannot, however passionately we want to avoid 'sectarianism', settle for a philosophy that believes radically different things are good for different sorts of people, different races, sexes, classes, without entrenching a politics that would be rightly objectionable to most of our contemporaries and which would make nonsense of any discourse of rights. David Martin notes, in his *Does Christianity Cause War?*, that 'universality itself sets up a boundary … the announcement of peace sets off a profound tension',[8] and concludes that such conflict is an inescapable aspect of our human condition. No-one can identify the argument that will establish convincingly for everyone that their variety of universalism is correct (and this holds for post-religious spirituality as much as for anything else). The question is, Martin suggests, less about the universal character of the claim than about how we imagine (that word again) our methods of commending the vision.

The better we understand the distinctiveness of religious claims, the better we understand the centrality within them of non-violence. That is to say, the religious claim, to the extent that it defines itself as radically different from mere local or transitory political strategies, is more or less bound to turn away from the defence or propagation of the claims by routinely violent methods, as if the truth we were talking about depended on the capacity of the speaker to silence all others by force. Granted that this is how classical communal religion has all too regularly behaved; but the point is that it has always contained a self-critique on this point. And that growing self-awareness about religious identity, which has been one paradoxical consequence of the social and intellectual movement away from such an identity, makes it harder and harder to reconcile faith in an invulnerable and abiding truth with violent anxiety as to how it is to be defended.

In short, as religion – corporate, sacramental and ultimately doctrinal religion – settles into this kind of awareness, it becomes one of the most potent allies possible for genuine pluralism: that is, for a social and political culture that is consistently against coercion and institutionalized inequality, and is committed to serious public debate about common good. Spiritual capital alone, in the sense of a heightened acknowledgement especially among politicians, businessmen and administrators of dimensions to human flourishing beyond profit and material security, is helpful but is not well equipped to ask the most basic questions about the legitimacy of various aspects of the prevailing global system. The traditional forms of religious affiliations, in proposing an 'imagined society', realized in some fashion in the practices of faith, are better resourced for such questions. They lose their integrity when they attempt to enforce their answers; and one of the most significant lessons to be learned from the great shift towards post-religious spiritual sensibility is how deeply the coercive and impersonal ethos of a good deal of traditional religion has alienated the culture at large. But, more importantly, if we who adhere to revealed faith don't want to be simply at the mercy of this culture, to be absorbed into its own uncritical stories about the autonomous self and its choices, then we need to examine the degree to which our practice *looks* like a new world. And if this debate drives us Christians back to thinking through more carefully and critically what the great Anglican Benedictine scholar Gregory Dix meant by describing Christians as a new 'species', *homo* eucharisticus, a humanity defined in its Eucharistic practice, it will have served us well. 'The unleavened bread of sincerity and truth' is the gift of the Easter Gospel, we are told in the liturgy; 'Lord, evermore give us this bread' (*John* 6.34).

PART TWO

Living within Limits:
Liberalism, Pluralism and Law

Multiculturalism – friend or foe?

1

We seem to be worried about multiculturalism; but we seem to be equally unclear about what the word means. Not too long ago, it could be used relatively neutrally, as a description of a society in which you could no longer take it for granted that there was a dominant or normative 'culture' (whatever exactly 'culture' itself means) – a society which many recognized as that of Britain in the late twentieth century. The level of variety in dress, cuisine, music, language, in the world of literary and visual images, in the heritage of social custom and sexual convention, within the national social unit had become so high, we were told, that we could no longer think of a canon of information or protocol or literary and historical reference that everyone could reasonably be expected to work with. An acute sensitivity grew up to aspects of our educational system and to the visible icons in our public space that seemed to assume that there was indeed one normative story to be told of our society. At its most crass and shallow, it showed itself, and still does with weary predictability, in attempts to excise culture-specific words like 'Christmas' from the public language of bureaucrats. At its most serious, it has been apparent in efforts to challenge an uncritical celebration of the national heritage without recognizing its moral shadows, and to draw out the diversity of strands that in fact have made up what we think of as a single national cultural history.

But more recently, the word has become for some commentators a way of designating a serious social dysfunction. David Cameron has associated it with the 'Balkanizing' of society – with a set of policies, more or less deliberate, which leave culturally diverse communities cocooned in their own frame of reference, in such a way that they never engage honestly with one another and there is no clear focus for social or national loyalty. Talking about this is frequently, of course, a coded way of talking about one kind of perception of Islamic groups in the UK: this perception is of communities indulged by nervous authorities, increasingly isolated in their educational practice, allowed to flaunt symbols of their faith while others are attacked for doing so, virtually encouraged to live in a 'state within a state' where loyalties are not to the 'host' society (a complex idea, as we shall see), but to a nebulous and alarming international network of believers. Thus multiculturalism understandably comes to be defined, as it is by David Cameron in the speech referred to a moment ago, as one of the 'walls of division' that must be torn down for the sake of a secure and just society.

The response to multiculturalism seen as a problem in this way is often to appeal to some sort of integrationist strategy that would provide a clear benchmark for belonging within our society – whether a reaffirmation of our Christian roots, a citizenship test of some kind, or a return to a style of teaching literature and history that stressed a central, definitive story. This is often the point at which discussion of that elusive thing referred to as 'Britishness' enters the field. A lot of this discussion is muddled and unhelpful; but it does focus on a significant question. Is there an identity beyond that of the immediate ethnic or religious group that provides a straightforward link of common interest and common loyalty with the rest of a society? And can such a link be established without reviving an agenda that would override the reality of ethnic difference and diverse religious conviction, without endorsing a model of society in which the only kind of belonging that could be publicly affirmed and supported was a strictly secular citizenship? The latter is on the whole what France has taken as foundational; but it is not obvious that either in theory or in practice this offers a defensible solution.

In considering the current debate about multiculturalism, then, we need to distinguish a number of different questions. Is there such a thing as national identity? Can and should a state recognize the rights and liberties of interme-diate groups within it, in addition to the rights of individual citizens? Should our educational system be promoting some ideal of integrated national belonging? But if we are to have any intelligent perspectives on these issues, we must go back a bit further, I believe, and ask a few questions about the language we are using.

2

What exactly is culture? A little earlier, I referred to the sorts of thing we probably most readily think of when the word is used – costume, custom and cookery. These days, as I have suggested, the word is also quite often and rather confusingly a roundabout way of referring to religious diversity. Vaguely in the background for some will be the sense of a whole intellectual trend in the twentieth century which has emphasized cultural diversity across both geographical and historical gaps, and has created an awareness of the cultural relativity of much of what any particular group might take for granted; and this spills over into a sense of the difficulty of defining absolute standards or values once you have noticed this relativity. Hence the phenomenon of cultural relativism, often invoked at some point in these discussions.

The trap in this is the assumption that a culture is both fixed and imper-meable. When we encounter a cultural 'other', our first reaction may well be the recognition of sheer difference; and this may lead us to exaggerate the degree to which we think of that other as enclosed in itself. It is the way it is, with no reference to the way things are with me or with us. And whether we are thinking of seventeenth-century travellers trying to make sense of East Asian societies or twentieth-century anthropologists trying to make sense of pre-modern societies, the natural reaction is to see the object as self-contained, on the other side of a barrier.

The same can apply to studying societies in the past: earlier European (and indeed non-European) societies tended to assume that the past was not at all foreign and that the values held and the arguments going on in the present were the same as those in previous centuries. A massive intellectual revolution, from the late seventeenth century onwards, has produced an increasingly 'anthropo-logical' view of history: 'the past is a foreign country.' And if you think about popular current attitudes to the past as illustrated, for example, by historical dramas on television or film, the problem becomes very clear. People in the past are shown either as having more or less contemporary attitudes and habits, thinly veiled in costume, or else as holding completely incomprehensible and irrational beliefs (especially religious ones). It seems there are things from the past which are almost incapable of being presented in popular entertainment; to take just one fairly harmless example, the recent television adaptation of *Mansfield Park*, eminently jolly and enjoyable in itself, revealed painfully just how completely it had been assumed that most of the motivation of the novel's characters would have to be written off for televisual purposes. The past is a foreign country and foreigners, as English people have always suspected, are peculiar. Speak to them slowly and loudly enough and you may be able to get them to understand you (since there is no real chance of your understanding them).

Can you really expect to have a conversation with the other, in their historical or geographical distance, in such a world? Combine this problem with a relativist assumption that no-one is really 'right' in an objective sense, and the result is a slightly uneasy intellectual map on which numerous diverse 'cultural' units coexist; the political task is to guarantee that no one of them suffers because of unfair power exercised by another group and that all are respected or tolerated by a state apparatus which seeks to reduce potential conflicts between them. Each takes its own frame of reference for granted and shies away from real challenge at the level of intellectual exchange; what could this be, after all, in a context where there is no common view of what counts as reasonable? In a modern state, this means a very strict separation between what might be called private plurality and public conformity. Public life will inevitably tend to make diversity publicly invisible or at least simply decorative when it becomes visible (celebrations of ethnic diversity as no more than a manifestation of the level of generous tolerance shown by public administrators).

But because that public-private distinction is unsafe and unstable for quite a lot of cultural communities, and because its effect will frequently be to convey to specific groups that their specificity is precisely what isn't wanted in the public square, this can be alienating. Hence the anxiety about a 'Balkanized' society. And since the tendency in this attitude is towards leaving cultures as they are, you can find a problem arising when public relativism ends up reinforcing the most inflexibly conservative elements in a culture by treating it as fixed. You may even have a vicious circle set up whereby an ethnic or religious group will find it in its interest to maintain the unchanging stereotypes held by outside authorities. If their identity as a tolerated group seems to depend on their being seen in a certain way by a benevolent administration, access to that adminis- tration may depend on continuing to be seen in the same way. This accounts for some of the frustration felt by those who are regularly spoken for in public by 'community leaders' who fit a certain stereotype, but do not represent the diversity or the pressure for change within the actual community.

The point that needs drawing out is that there is something odd about regarding culture as a fixed and given matter. At the most basic level, 'culture' is a word that refers to the particular sort of impact a group of human beings makes on its environment. Its origins lie in the same group of words that includes 'cultivation'; one of the most basic forms of culture is agriculture, since that is near the foundation of the human impact on the environment. And, as Timothy Gorringe traces in his very valuable book, *Furthering Humanity: a theology of culture,*[1] the use of the word predictably diversifies as it is applied to very different ways of affecting the environment, including our imaginative and intellectual work on the environment, creating 'culture' in the modern sense of mental and artistic sophistication. It ceases to be just about negotiating the challenges of a physical environment and becomes something to do with meanings and values, with the patterns of words and pictures through which we make the world around us ours and express our priorities and expectations, identifying what has weight, authority or worth for us and gives shape to our lives.

Words and pictures: as soon as we see culture in these terms, we move away from any assumption that a culture is necessarily static. People use words to reflect on other words, pictures to comment on other pictures. Who you are talking to changes as time passes; cultures meet and trade, literally and metaphorically. The current exhibition of the sacred texts of the Abrahamic faiths at the British Library prompts the question of the common origins of some spectacularly distant 'cultural' phenomena – the so-called carpet pages of decoration in Celtic gospel books and the same sort of pages in manuscripts of the Qur'an. Cultures borrow idioms and conventions equally in methods of producing artefacts and in philosophical speculation. It is a peculiar form of modern snobbery to think that in the pre-modern world people universally lived more enclosed lives.

If culture is a word for making things and making sense of things, it is never something that can be abstracted from history. The changing potential of technologies and the shifts of populations over centuries create new environ-mental possibilities and linguistic opportunities. People learn to make different things and say different things. To freeze the frame at any point is to make nonsense of the process – which is why some ways of talking about national identity or the essence of a local cultural world can't be sustained. The historian Jonathan Clark, writing about the uses and misuses of history in respect of Britain's identity, has this to say: 'Britain was not invented; it developed. It was not devised by a small number of cultural entrepreneurs, acting as advertising executives to package and market a new product; it grew, the often unintended result of actions by men and women in many walks of life and often, too, the result of conflicts and cross-purposes.'[2] Clark notes, very interestingly, how Britain generally avoided being captured by a crude appeal to racial unity, and how the lack of a race myth enabled it to make the most of its historical diversity (he has helpful things to say too about the overwhelmingly modern and even

Enlightenment origins of racial philosophies). The result, he argues, has given Britain a more durable national cohesion than might have been expected, precisely because it has not bound its unity to a tight and inflexible account of race or culture.

In theory, British society ought not to be easily panicked about its identity; it has lived through a history which exemplifies in marked fashion the way in which cultures are shaped by changing populations, languages and technologies. And the salient point for our wider discussion is that there is no useful way of talking about 'Britishness' without telling a specific story – a story which is about how both invasion and foreign adventure created a flexible and hybrid language, how a particular kind of concordat between royal, feudal and ecclesiastical power outlasted a brief experiment with royal absolutism in the early modern period, how the reaction against absolutism moulded a set of legal standards and protocols (habeas corpus, jury trial), how lessons were learned and not learned in the treatment of subject societies through England's relations with its Celtic neighbours ... and so on. It is not a story of unbroken success or virtue: the imperial episode is not very edifying in its origins and much of its working out, and the economic effect of rapid industrialization was wealth for some and a colossal alienation between classes on the other. 'Britishness' still includes a set of tangled class relationships that surprises many other nations. But we can talk about a legal and political 'way of making sense' that remains overall a striking and rather unusual achievement.

The errors that Clark has in his sights are, however, not only racial myths but, importantly, what he calls a 'presentist' mentality which assumes that constructive historical conflict and negotiation are essentially over and that there is now a self-evident state of political rationality prevailing, which lays down clear and universal principles for social stability and equity. Because it obscures the particular story of how current political practices and assumptions came into being, it effectively creates a new dominant and unquestioned culture against which others are to be authoritatively measured; it colludes with the mindset that blithely presumes its own universal mission to civilize with as little self-doubt as High Victorian imperialism. It uses history selectively, with the simple aim of illustrating its own superiority and the inevitability of its triumph. Against this, Clark sets the difficult but genuinely transforming task of engaging with a history in which things might have turned out differently, and in which apparently clear ideological settlements turn out to have manifold and even contradictory roots. As he argues (in chapter 4 of the same book), the automatic modern association of universal suffrage with challenges to landed interest, criticism of the confessional state and support of individual enterprise and a high level of free trade is the product of a long historical story in which theological themes and controversies play a surprisingly large part. In other words, the self-evidence of the modern Western democratic package is put in question by the fact that it represents a gradual and not at all obvious coalescence of various political ideals. It may well be a good and humane outcome, but to understand it, let alone defend it, we need some sense of what made it what it is.

We are beginning to see, I hope, what might be one helpful orienting principle in thinking about multiculturalism. If culture is a mode of making sense of the world, by material and intellectual labour, it is inherently changeable. No such mode is going to be eternal and self-sufficient, and to speak of cultures is not to speak of non-communicating units, whether across time or in space. It is possible to understand each other; it is possible to understand the past. And both understandings are liable to shift and adjust as time goes on and the agenda alters. The changeability of different cultures reinforces the perception of relativity; but paradoxically it works against relativism, because it allows for mutual adjustment in a long process of settling how we corporately frame more adequate and durable strategies for mapping our place in our environment. In short, multiculturalism will indeed be a recipe for Balkanization or ghettoization if it ignores history and denies the possibility of cultures affecting each other, changing themselves and the other and sometimes creating new and hybrid forms.

3

Static pluralism is not a healthy condition for a society; and the well-intentioned eagerness of some in recent decades to compensate for insensitive cultural hegemony by treating all clusters of cultural and religious expression as equally worthy of abstract respect and equally distant from the public square has not delivered quite what was intended. Likewise, a 'clash of civilizations' model assumes a spectacularly non-historical view of how cultures work and is easily conscripted into the service of new imperialisms incapable of questioning their own legitimacy or adequacy.

But how does this impact upon our local and practical challenges – on the vexed question of group rights or on the foundations of an educational curriculum? In a finely nuanced discussion of the state's relations with the minority group, Maleiha Malik, a legal and political scholar of Muslim allegiance, seeks a way between, on the one hand, privileging group minority identity in such a way as to offer no intelligible account of the majority's proper interest or of a wider 'belonging to the polity' of a state overall, and, on the other, leaving intact a secular and neutral public sphere in which no form of belonging other than the abstract legal and civil identity of the citizen is of political significance. It should be possible, she argues, to define a common public culture in which the needs and priorities of minorities are openly discussed and negotiated but with a clear sense that it should be possible for the minority to be able to identify with the institutions of society as a whole. 'For the minority', she writes, 'this means that their private identity cannot automatically be reflected in the public sphere without some limited assimilation to the shared values that are the agreed basis for a common public life. For the majority, this re-negotiation carries with it significant costs. These costs will be an inevitable outcome of attempts to transform the public sphere and institutions: from exclusively reflecting the dominant culture, towards a common culture which also seeks to accommodate some of the most urgent needs of minorities'.[3] What Malik is trying to clarify in this and other seminal papers is the idea that negotiation over the participation of minority groups in representative political processes is not the same as seeking a situation where those processes are mortgaged to the veto of the minority – a situation which human rights legislation can tacitly encourage, she suggests. The problem is that this model, by continuing to treat the minority as a political 'other' in need of protection, gives no path to authentic participation with the possibility of reciprocal influence: that is, of proper political agency.

Thus talk about 'group rights' will not take us beyond the static models we ought to leave behind; but public practice needs conventions for engaging with communities of conviction over its policies, rather than assuming that all choices boil down to individual lifestyle options. And the implications of Malik's discussion for education are interesting. A good education for a shared culture such as she outlines would be one in which students were indeed educated about the history and convictions of the majority. In the case of Britain, that would mean an education that laid out the features I mentioned earlier about the mingled political and religious roots of the British understanding of legality and constitutional balance. It would present the social and political elements of 'Britishness' not as a timeless orthodoxy, but as the outcome of a long process in which many factors are involved other than the narrowly political. It would enable a measure of literacy in respect of the language and imagery of the majority. And it would also set out an understanding of the way in which historical processes shape culture that itself becomes an important element in resourcing dialogue between majority and minority culture. Worrying that it presupposes an unquestioned privilege for the majority culture is missing the point and fighting the wrong battle.

So if there is a 'curriculum' implication here, it is about a sensible historical grounding for everyone in what happens to have brought us here. Nothing is served by the kind of half-hearted half-relativism that is unwilling to foreground this. And a good exposition of these processes will say something about the fluidity of cultural identities over long periods. It becomes an education in resisting static ideas about cultures, while at the same time affirming the need for understanding of the roots of a culture and a national identity.

But looming up behind these issues is the larger one hinted at earlier. The processes by which cultures take shape are many-layered, and the engines of development are varied. Some are contingent and pragmatic – a literally changing physical environment; but some are to do with a changing sense of what needs to be secured in order for human beings to be as human as they can be. Christianity (like Islam and Buddhism, a faith that began as a reforming and innovating movement) introduced into the Mediterranean world a much enlarged sense of what was 'due' to human beings, a set of convictions about freedom and the unique vocation of each person and a set of expectations about mutual responsibility. Understanding cultural history is emphatically to do with understanding how people decide what is due to persons – how they settle on accounts of minimal regard to human dignity or worth. History once again displays, uncomfortably, just how non-self-evident such minimal accounts are and how easily they are overridden (by religious believers as well as others, it must at once be said).

Gorringe, in the book I quoted earlier, argues, following the magisterial work of Bikkhu Parekh on the subject, that intercultural argument about what may or may not be good for human beings is bound to take account of irreversible moments in global history that make the denial of, say, equality between the sexes indefensible, even on the grounds of respecting diversity. Similar points could be made about the rights and dignity of children; no-one ventures to defend child soldiering, child labour or the genital cutting of teenage girls on the grounds of cultural relativity. The argument cannot be settled from a point outside all human cultural specifics; but it is an argument that moves on, nonetheless, and creates areas of consensus that cannot easily be imagined as up for renegotiation. In Gorringe's terms, the 'furthering' of a human agenda shaped by converging and negotiating convictions, offers a moral touchstone for intercultural debate that may not be clearly identifiable in the abstract, but emerge in the historical encounter between cultures as a common ground that allows both agreement and further exploration of disagreement. And he very carefully contends that Parekh's own dismissal of 'moral monism' (the idea that there is one and only one form of human life that is maximally good for humans) still leaves open the possibility of defending the view that there are capacities in all human beings that need development if a properly human life is to be lived and understood[4] – that, in Christian terms, there are some things that are unequivocally good news for any imaginable human being because they allow this sort of development.

On this basis, there have to be questions about any picture of cultural diversity that simply regards it as a pattern of chosen private differences that have no place in the neutral space of modern secular society. The supposedly neutral space of secularism, as I have argued in other places, carries its own legacy and its own assumptions about what is due to human beings. To the extent that it deliberately avoids commitment about what human flourishing looks like and contents itself with managing as fairly as possible the resources of a society, it will risk at least two things. The first is the deficit in motivation that results when there is no accepted, conviction-based and widely approved rationale for taking responsibility for others. The second is the reduction of all major moral questions in society to questions about the management of fixed and finite resources, so that issues around what is needed for morally desirable ends are sidelined. The culture (if one has to use the word in this context) of public neutrality is going to be in some degree parasitic on more three-dimensional cultures if it is not to dissolve into functionalist and bureaucratic tyranny.

The strength of an interactive and historically educated multicultural social life – one in which cultural diversity is worked through in active conversation and co-operation between communities of conviction, against the background of a properly understood political and legal tradition – is that it helps to resource us all in the struggle against a managerial and impersonal politics which very few people actively want. If we can distinguish between a multiculturalism that is simply a minimal public tolerance for eccentric or exotic private diversities and a multiculturalism that brings into public democratic debate the most significant motivating elements in people's convictions about human dignity and destiny, we shall have moved on significantly from some of our current deadlocks.

4

And this brings me to my last consideration. If a culture is a way of making things and making sense, then from one point of view we live in probably the least multicultural human environment there has ever been. The global market has canonized once and for all certain ways of making: industrialization is everywhere, the network of global communication is everywhere, the effects of market forces are felt by everyone on the face of the globe. To quote Nicholas Boyle's words in his magnificent essay on European cultural identity, *Who Are we Now?*, 'no human life can now be led in total isolation from the ever denser global network and no organised human intrusion from outside it is now possible ... Governments, anxious to reduce imports or to meet some other norm set by international competition, make their presence felt by imposing (de-) population programmes or changes in age-old cultivation practices ... The more you have in common the more you have to compete about, and vice versa.'[5]

There is indeed one dominant culture in the world, and that is the exchange system of the market, which transforms every local history. It isn't surprising that the climate this has produced has led some to speak of the end of history – as if, again, we now had a state of affairs that could forget how it came into existence because it is really the obvious position for human beings to be in and needs no argument, no defence, no ancestry. It may be benevolent to some aspects of local cultures; it may learn to speak in local accents for certain purposes, advertising or decoration (Macdonald's offers some ethnic variation in outlets across the globe), but it works in one mode of production, employment and marketing, and assumes that everyone is a potential customer. It is as universal as ever Christianity or Islam aspired to be, but the substance of its universality is a set of human functions (producing, selling, consuming) rather than any sense of innate human capacity, and of the unsettling mysteriousness that goes with that.

The market, as we are repeatedly told, is the major – and inevitable – engine for democratization and economic liberation for the world's societies. Granted, more or less, given rather a lot of qualifications about what is necessary to establish fair trading conditions for the dramatically powerless and marginal economies of the globe. But how do we live with what seems to be universally the result of the dominance of the global market – the erosion of particular identities, local ways of making sense and things which change at a human pace and on a human scale, not as part of a single, increasingly irresistible and rapid process of homogenizing human beings? There are at least two signs of a counter-trend that deserve mention in this connection. The first, a very familiar one, is the steadily diffusing impact of various kinds of environmental consciousness. To take a simple example, the growing concern about 'food miles' in relation to what is available in the local supermarket suggests a developing awareness of what the actual capacity and the actual limits of a local economy are. The concern has led to the revival of farmers' markets in some places and to the recognition that the demand for a universal availability of maximal consumer choice has consequences for producers both near at hand and in the developing world. Combined with the similarly growing pressure about 'fair trade' conditions of production, there is a potential here for keeping a marker firmly in place about diverse economies, diverse rhythms of production, diverse seasonal harvests and so on. Alongside the vaunted 'multicultural' sign of varied ethnic cuisine in the streets of Britain, there is a proper concern about the globalization of food production and distribution which acts as a necessary warning for those who imagine that they can without cost live in a global 'non-locality' where all consumables are equally accessible.

In something like the same way, the growing reach and capacity of microfinance institutions, not only in the poorer parts of the globe, offers an alternative (or at least supplementary) model for economic growth and security. It is worth noting that the most successful of these enterprises, Muhammad Yunus's Grameen Bank, owes something to a Muslim economic tradition, and that some of the major organizers of credit unions in Ireland, Canada and elsewhere have been Catholic clergy and laity. Once again, there is an awareness of the cost of abandoning entirely the various kinds of local loyalty and direct accountability which global economics threatens. Against the monoculturalism of the global market, these affirmations of the local are of real significance.

Others could be cited, but the point is that our discussions of multiculturalism are too often conducted in abstraction from thinking about the economic culture we all inhabit, whether we like it or not. And an appreciation of what is possible to strengthen a sane pluralism and localism in our approaches to local economies and local politics needs to be part of any reflection on what it means to be a multicultural society that goes deeper than slogans. Cosmetic, external variety underpinned by a wholly uncriticized globalism is a very unpromising future. A plurality of cultures that did not involve some real diversity in ways of making, marketing, saving, and organizing the conditions of material life would be superficial; we should all still be locked into a basic sense of sameness.

So my conclusion is that for a sensible discussion of multiculturalism we need to leave behind the assumption that what we are talking about is nothing but a world of unbridled and uncritical cultural diversity which undermines any possible commitment to overall social cohesion in a state. First, we need to be as clear as we can be about what culture is. And as we gain greater clarity about this, we ought to see how it is shaped in history, and how it is therefore a dangerous fiction to stick with an absolute and timeless account of any cultural unit, modern or pre-modern, eastern or western. We need a strong commitment to interaction between diverse cultures, including the possibility of reasoned criticism. We should not see a problem with an educational curriculum that traces the distinctive lines of a society's development in its arts and products, its legal institutions and its religious imagination; to teach these is not to say, 'This is the only acceptable way of being a human person here' – simply, 'This is how these specific human beings in this place understood their humanity; this is the deposit on which people here are drawing, knowingly or not'. And finally, we need to find how such particular traditions of being human help us question the largely unseen forces that flatten the surface of the human world in the name of a universal market that is notably empty of resources for moral motivation, communal loyalty and creativity.

None of this (as we've seen) commits us to relativism, only to a properly mutually engaged discussion in public about what is good for corporate human life. It will have been obvious that I am taking for granted that religious diversity is part of this picture – and that religious communities will play a focal part in resisting the 'flattening' effects of modernity on the human profile. If we are talking about how human beings make sense as well as making things, there is no way in which this dimension can be bypassed. It is true that most of the great faiths set themselves to create a universal 'culture', convinced that they have a truth relevant and transforming for all humans – and that therefore they will experience conflict between themselves. But if that conflict is always approached not with the aim of literally or metaphorically eliminating each other, but with the expectation that the mixture of 'civic' collaboration and intellectual and spiritual exchange in the public sphere will ultimately enrich all participants, we need not fear breakdown. Forget 'multiculturalism' as some sort of prescription; begin from the multicultural fact. We are already neighbours and fellow-citizens; what we need is neither the ghetto nor the reassertion of a fictionally unified past, but ordinary intelligence, sympathy and curiosity in the face of difference – which is the basis of all learning and all growing-up, in individuals or societies.

Faith and Enlightenment

Isaiah Berlin is, for most of us, one of the leading canonical voices of liberal modernity; all the more interesting, then, that some of his best work is about the shadowside of the Enlightenment legacy. In his celebrated essay on 'Two Concepts of Liberty',[1] and in several discussions of 'Counter-Enlightenment' figures like Vico in Italy and Herder in Germany, he sets out with great clarity the quagmire into which the first generations of enlightened thinkers were blithely advancing, unaware of the horrors their ideals were to generate in more recent times. The paradigm of enlightened rationality was inseparable from a set of convictions about universal human values: whether at a distance of space or a distance of time, human beings were fundamentally the same and their needs could be worked out by the application of universal, reasonable principles, accessible to all. Acquaintance with these principles would guarantee the freedom to direct my life in accordance with my true nature and my deepest wants. But what Berlin draws out is the process by which this universalist utopia can become a totalitarian nightmare; because when decision-makers have determined what is rational, they are bound sooner or later to regard opposition as irrational and so without legitimacy. They will embark on a coercive political pedagogy, to make citizens rational and capable of exercising 'positive' liberty, of realizing their 'true' nature; and that entails sanctions against those who refuse to be taught. Not only does this enshrine 'the rule of experts'; it leaves no final possible appeal to any individual right to freedom of conscience, since the irrational conscience has to be educated out of its error. 'I issue my orders and, if you resist, take it upon myself to repress the irrational element in you which opposes reason'.[2]

Thus the conviction that rationality is one and the same in every human situation is politically and ethically perilous. Those who resisted enlightened universalism may have done so with various agendas that are no less perilous, but a mature liberal view has to reckon with their arguments. Thus Berlin identifies in Herder three governing notions clearly 'against the main stream of the thought of his time'[3] – 'populism, expressionism and pluralism'. Populism is a commitment to the positive valuation of local and specific identity, to an historically and linguistically continuous culture. Expressionism (as Berlin grants, a rather unsatisfactory term, given its more technical meaning in the history of art) is the belief that culture is always expressive of systems of communication between persons or agents; that artefacts, patterns of behaviour and custom, artistic idioms and so on cannot ever be abstracted from the networks of meaning they inhabit and from their claim to embody fundamental identities for individuals and groups. Pluralism is the belief that different cultures or societies have not only diverse but incommensurable systems of value, so that there is no way in which we could identify a single universal definition of the good life. As Berlin put it at the end of his 'Two Concepts' essay, 'To assume that all values can be graded on one scale, so that it is a mere matter of inspection to determine the highest, seems to me to falsify our knowledge that men are free agents, to represent moral decision as an operation which a slide-rule could, in principle, perform. To say that in some ultimate, all-reconciling, yet reliable synthesis duty *is* interest, or individual freedom *is* pure democracy or an authoritarian State, is to throw a metaphysical blanket over either self-deceit or deliberate hypocrisy'.[4]

What this perspective reintroduces into political discourse is a sense of the tragic: rational universalism cannot deliver what it promises in terms of a resolution of every conflict that honours every positive moral principle, and so the decisions that are made in the public sphere are always going to involve loss, compromise, some degree of failure in response to rational ethical imperatives. If '[w]hat the entire Enlightenment has in common is denial of the central Christian doctrine of original sin',[5] counter-Enlightenment pluralism brings back a sober recognition if not exactly of original sin, then of 'original finitude', of the limits of human aspiration. The problem is that so many of its advocates do so with the aim of discrediting or paralyzing any idea that planned social change is possible; beginning from a deeply pessimistic assessment of human capacities, counter-Enlightenment theorists will regularly argue for high levels of social control, harsh penal systems and minimal social mobility. Berlin's challenge is to construct a politics that secures not only basic 'decency' (a favourite word), but the greatest possible freedom for debate between advocates of diverse projects and priorities; the society worthy working for is one in which diversity is tolerated – and therefore criticism is always possible.[6] And this aim is not vitiated or undermined by clarity and honesty about the incompatibility of certain goods with each other in any finite political settlement.

This kind of chastened liberal realism is an impressive attempt to hold a very difficult balance. It embraces wholeheartedly Enlightenment scepticism about unquestioned authority and the need for reasoned justification of belief and obedience. It repudiates wholeheartedly Enlightenment optimism about the possibility of a conclusive rational 'roadmap', as we might now say, for social organization. Reason is a powerful tool for critique, and its power in this context habitually leads us to mistake it for an unproblematic guide in constructing social paradigms. Society is organized not by the discovery of some ultimately unifying principle that will guarantee the fulfilment of all rational aspirations, but by an endless series of 'treaties' between aspirations, imagined goods, desirable states of affairs. There is no social settlement without loss; but that does not mean that any and every social settlement is a radical failure or that – to pick up another of Berlin's leading ideas – it is unworthy of rational commitment. Such commitment allows us to recognize that our ideals may not be universally and eternally valid within a clear, comprehensive scale of values ('Principles are not less sacred because their duration cannot be guaranteed'[7]), without making us practically indifferent. We choose our priorities for defensible, discussable reasons, but we know that the discussion goes on and that what we have rationally chosen, defended and worked for may well appear differently in a different moral or intellectual environment.

Implicit in this is a deep scepticism about whether there is anything that could be called a final or optimal social settlement. With the terrible language of 'final solutions' ringing in our ears, we are likely to find this scepticism irresistible; properly so in many ways. Yet it is difficult for someone approaching these matters from a position of religious commitment to be wholly satisfied; and I want to reflect a little on just why this is and whether there is an unbridgeable gulf not only between classical universalist Enlightenment politics and faith, but also between even Berlin's revisionist Enlightenment and the language of traditional religious belief.

One of the paradoxes in this particular bit of intellectual history is that Enlightenment does not give up the register of *eschatology* in its language, the hope of a final resolution to historical conflicts, even when that register is drastically reimagined as the coming reign of universal reason. The French Revolution, of course, deliberately mythologized its own processes, with the enthroning of 'Reason' in Notre Dame and the recalibrating of the calendar.

History was over; the bloody birth pangs of the new order were still going on, but a new age had definitively begun. And a significant part of what Berlin is doing is to wean us away from eschatology of any kind. There is no end of history – whether this delusion is proclaimed by communist or capitalist (and Berlin would have been surprised and, I think, amused to hear the capitalist versions of it that gained currency in the 1990s), it is always mistaken and almost always oppressive in its implications. We have no handle on the future and we have to accept that the 'judgement of history' is entirely inaccessible to us. In the light of this, even our dearest convictions have to be held with some degree of ironic self-consciousness.

But for the Abrahamic religions, eschatology is a major aspect of their frame of reference. Sometimes it has been used in corrupt and corrupting ways – either as an excuse for not addressing injustice now (because it will be sorted out hereafter) or as a way of giving a theological gloss to some sort of religious tyranny claiming to be the ultimate and definitive state of human politics. But at least as often it has been a negative and critical element: every imaginable 'judgement of history' is overridden by something on another plane; no imaginable state of society will deliver what the true apocalypse promises, because no human power can anticipate the judgement of God. There is, you could say, just as much room for irony here as in secular scepticism. But there is also something that is on the far side of irony. There is indeed an optimal or final human condition, a state of affairs in which human agents are related to each other and to their world in the way they were meant to; and that optimal condition depends on the realizing of a relation to the maker of the universe. Because this relation is always in process of formation, vulnerable and fragile, while human life continues, it is never going to be simply and solidly fleshed out in a social settlement within history. It is not even the case that successive settlements can be guaranteed to create a gradually improving approximation to it: our capacity for brutal and radical error grows no less as time goes on. Yet there *is* an imagined state of affairs, one day to be realized but not in any way we can anticipate or control, by which we map and assess our current achievement. And that means that we can't afford an unqualifiedly ironic attitude to our convictions. Or rather – because that phrasing in itself could be misleading – we cannot afford a wholly ironic attitude towards the hope of something like comprehensive healing or homecoming. What our current ideals, convictions and policies have to be tested for is how far they take us towards or away from the reintegrated relations we imagine in the context of restored relation to God; how far they take us 'homewards' or otherwise.

I want to argue that this is a very different way of characterizing the idea of a 'unified' social settlement from the one used by Berlin. Typically, Berlin's case rests on the impossibility of simultaneously realizing *ideals* – optimal freedom, optimal equality and so on. He assumes, absolutely correctly, that we could not ever provide a coherent account of a society in which there existed both unqualified liberty and unqualified equality. And on that basis he concludes that any notion of an optimal social settlement is bound to be incoherent in theory and totalitarian in practice. But what if we come at this from a different angle? What if the unity we are looking for in society is not the realization of an abstract ideal, but a condition in which each person is fully cognisant of what is needed for each specific neighbour's welfare and committed to make it possible? This is not to measure social achievement against correspondence to an ideal embodiment of some supreme good (freedom, equality and so on), but to think critically about it in the light of what the maximal welfare of each citizen, *within* the constraints of shared life, potentially competing needs and finite resource, might entail. It is also to assume a shared willingness to bracket any fantasies of what would maximally fulfil *my* wishes as an individual and to allow these to be overridden by the vision of a possible common good equally owned by myself and my neighbour. And for each social agent, the potential sacrifice this entails is made imaginable and bearable by the confidence that the whole interlocking pattern of social relations will secure attention to my interest in the same terms as I give attention to the neighbour's.

Building on ideas eloquently developed by the Chief Rabbi in numerous books over recent years, I believe that this offers an account of optimal social unity in terms of covenantal mutuality. What I have called the 'revisionist Enlightenment' model of Berlin's liberalism very importantly rules out defining an optimal social state as one in which a rational solution to all problems has been permanently established, so that any opposition can be discounted as irrational or worse. But we are not then restricted in our discussion of social goods, simply to an unending series of short-term compromises. It is possible to think about a convergent condition of society not in terms of something delivered by universal reason, but as a habit of commitment to the good of the other, which creates and sustains mutual trust – not, curiously, a virtue celebrated by the Enlightenment. To be 'covenanted' to each other is to promise that no-one's interest is written out of the social script and – crucially – that a long-term perspective on social needs is being taken for granted (not just an electoral cycle). In practice, this will of course involve what I have called 'treaties', just like Berlin's scheme, carefully crafted compromises in which there is a serious effort to avoid unfair distribution of the cost and enough of what everyone needs and hopes for to make a settlement sustainable. The difference is that, approaching this from a standpoint of faith, the overriding imperative is to scrutinize the way in which any settlement deepens those relations which will do the active sustaining – and, more deeply, how far such relations are likely to shape the habit of attention to the neighbour, the habit of *promised* attention that gives some long-term ground for trust. Or, in other words, the aim is not simply pragmatic avoidance of unmanageable conflict, but the formation of political character; and in the fullest religious context, the formation of political character is an aspect of developing a relationship with God, upon whom ultimately depend those other dimensions of healed or healing relation.

One of the weaker points of Enlightenment politics, classical or revisionist, is the absence of much interest in political virtue, in the question of what kind of human agent is being nourished and encouraged by this or that piece of public policy. Recently there has been a welcome revival of interest in such questions, strongly spurred on by the perception that economic habits in particular had long since ceased to be related to questions about what kind of human being it might be desirable to nourish in society. Berlin's ironic and modest pluralism is extremely suspicious of any political philosophy that promises to deliver a new kind of human being; and that is understandable, given the aspirations of a certain sort of radicalism to reinvent the human. But without some compass here, political decision-making becomes no more than damage limitation. To say that a society can and should allow considerations of what human character is being formed by its public practices as part of its decision making does not mean that societies should adopt an orthodoxy about what is best for all human beings (the corruption of the ideal of 'positive liberty' that Berlin so vigorously resisted in the great essays of his maturity). It is simply to be aware that there are public policies and habits that significantly close down possibilities – sometimes by neglect, sometimes by assuming the most selfish or short-term motivations in citizens. To take some examples that are not just academic in the light of the last decade or so, this 'closing down' of possibilities might be evidenced in policies that restrict access to or support for public educational facilities like libraries and galleries; in employment regimes that reward patterns of work that undermine family life; in the encouragement of unmanageable debt; in the scapegoating, in general social attitudes or in policy, of refugees; or in the pressure for the kind of savings in health care budgets that further centralize and bureaucratize contact with physicians and narrow the pastoral or personal responsibilities of the nursing profession.

These are the sort of issues that are not well dealt with in the framework of a purely liberal political culture; addressing them adequately requires a clear sense both of the nature of a strictly social good (one that can only be achieved by mutual collaboration) and of some picture of human flourishing that is not reducible to a fairly peaceful adjustment of competing individual needs. They require a political perspective in which the quality of relations features; and this is not provided for in any clear way by a discourse in which 'value pluralism' is left as an unquestioned and fundamental feature of social thinking. In line with what social scientists like Michael Sandel have argued very recently, a lively and critical political discourse is more likely to be one that draws in discussion, even argument, about optimal patterns of human habit and character than one in which value is left entirely as a matter of individual conviction. To allow for this is not to succumb to the toxic universalism that ends up excluding or penalizing dissent. It is does not oblige us to believe that we are capable of realizing an optimal moral society according to principles that everyone ought to be able to assent to. It simply invites us to include in political argument considerations about how a particular course of action, individual or public, impacts on the character and habits of social agents and how far it reinforces those habits of mutual attention that provide the only secure ground for trust.

The Enlightenment society, whether in classical or revisionist style, does not pay a great deal of attention to this issue of social trust; after all, rationality is not a matter of trust but of clear demonstrability. Because invitations to trust were in the pre-modern period so closely allied with appeals to irrational and oppressive systems of authority, early modernity turned away from such language. But the result is a twofold problem. On the one hand, truth comes to be seen as something discoverable by essentially impersonal means, by arguments and observations that anyone can utilize. Each individual may calculate their duties and their rights without having to relate in any particular way to anyone else except within a general rubric of tolerance. The notion that there is a kind of epistemological distortion, a skewing of perception, that comes with purely individual accounts of who and what I am and what I want is alien to this way of thinking. And whatever one makes of Hegel as a social philosopher, one of his cardinal insights was that our original pre-reflective, self-determined and self-oriented account of who we are is precisely what has to be dissolved as we learn what it is to *think*, and therefore to act, humanly.

Scepticism about authority, in other words, can lead into a sort of unexamined fundamentalism about individual rights. And the answer is not to turn the clock back to authoritarianism, but to work at social and personal practices of mutual challenge and scrutiny, with the assumption that relations of a certain kind are inseparable from access to certain kinds of truth. On the other hand, impersonal truth implies that particular personal and local perspectives are bound to be at best decorative extras, and at worst distortions. This is partly where the 'end of history' language comes from: to say that you believe something because of what you or your ancestors have learned informally and unsystematically over a long historical period is never good enough as a justification.

From these two elements in the Enlightenment spirit come the opposite menaces of individualism and totalitarianism. Berlin is eloquent as a diagnostician of the second, but less alert to the first, and thus to the risks of a society in which everyone's relations to everyone else are essentially formal, legal or commercial, the relations of self-contained agents negotiating their separate space. Various forms of contract stand in for a background of trust that can be taken for granted; suspicion is endemic; and a crisis in language itself threatens in the longest of perspectives, as people come to assume that every utterance is about a tacit bid for power. And while it is (to repeat the point) impossible just to speak or act as if this substantial cultural change had not occurred or could be quickly reversed, this doesn't mean that we are now in permanent thrall to formal and individualist pictures of our relations. Intentional communities still exist which do assume trust and which do also assume that language can be a vehicle of plain celebration rather than just negotiations of power and advantage. There are practices in society that work in blithe disregard of the dominant paradigm – the learning of crafts, the making of music, even non-professional sport. But it is hard even for the most dedicated secularist to deny that communities of faith are the most durable contexts for relationships and habits that exist at right angles to functional and individualist models of human society.

The Enlightenment turned on religious dogma as the single most offensive example of irrational and tyrannical assertion. The reaction was quite intelligible in many ways. But the effect was to confuse unchallengeable authority with the unavoidably social elements of learning and discovering one's own humanity, and by rejecting the first to obscure the importance of the second. The counter-Enlightenment often tried to salvage the second by reversing the first; and 'revisionist Enlightenment' thinking like that of Isaiah Berlin in his most famous work accepts the counter-Enlightenment critique of rational univer-salism but without identifying whether there are other sorts of universalism possible. My contention so far has been that the relation of religious faith to the post-Enlightenment agenda is a more complex one than has sometimes been acknowledged. It is not a matter of straightforward opposition: faith should in fact be sympathetic to the critique of ungrounded authority; and, as the present Pope is fond of pointing out, the very idea of universal reason has theological roots – though the definition of reason is not quite what a Voltaire might be happy with. The idea that human maturity involves challenges to unchallenged power (as with the stories of Daniel in Hebrew Scripture or the records of the Christian Church in the Roman Empire of the first three Christian centuries) is not at all inimical to faith. That power has to explain itself and justify itself to all through recognizable public arguments is a sound moral and religious principle. But what religious practice claims, and what separates it from some sorts of universalism, is that public argument need not rule out discussion of tradition, of the histories of learning and usage that locate certain ideas in the fabric of corporate life, of the images we inherit and develop of human life well-lived and human relations working creatively. The universal horizon is a vision not of finally agreed rational discourse guaranteeing a right answer to everything and the fulfilment of all reasonable aspirations, but of a corporate work of discernment in which no voice is silenced in advance and in which each participant is able to trust that they are the object of a measure of unselfish attention. The Jewish model of a community of covenant is fundamental for such a vision; and the Christian model of the Church as Christ's Body builds on this and takes the metaphors of organic interdependence to a new level. The universal horizon is one of sustainable mutual generosity – understood, by individuals of faith, as part of the journey from and towards integral relation with the maker of the universe.

But why exactly does it matter to keep some sort of universalism on our intellectual or moral radar? Because once we give any house-room to the idea that certain claims about humanity are open to radical revision, once we leave any negotiating space around commitments to human dignity as a fixed matter, we risk making human dignity a matter of our choice. This is how we elect to see the world, and it is simply a fact about how we see fit to live our lives. But if so, then defending human dignity becomes entangled with defending ourselves, our freedom to choose; it becomes bound up with issues of power and competition once more, insofar as it is a form of self-assertion. Human dignity understood as beyond negotiation is something that demands our loyalty quite independently of our interest or advantage. It allows us to contemplate the idea of human fulfilment, an 'optimal' state for human beings as a vision that could survive any amount of pragmatic defeat and any amount of local and cultural diversity in expression. In religious terms, it appeals not to some static definition of human nature in the abstract, but to the conviction that God values human persons without limit or qualification – that divine wisdom, in the words of *Proverbs* 8, 'rejoices in humankind'.

Charles Taylor, a critical admirer of Isaiah Berlin, in his enormously wide-ranging study, *A Secular Age*, examines what motivation might be discovered for systematic and unrestricted love for humankind. 'How can we become agents on whom misanthropy has no hold, in whom it awakens no connivance?' he asks.[8] Part of his very subtle and engaging answer is that a motivation which stresses the uncaused or gratuitous nature of philanthropy, the nobility of its willingness to do without metaphysical grounding or transcendental reward, actually privileges a certain kind of virtue – an individual heroism that may be admirable but is essentially a solitary achievement. 'The heroism of gratuitous giving has no place for reciprocity', he argues; 'This unilateral heroism is self-enclosed'.[9] Taylor wants us to think about a love for humankind that is thoroughly bound up in a sense of continuing reciprocal work on each other's human flourishing, and so has to be imagined as resting on something more than an individual's noble and disinterested decision. Instead, love of humankind or reverence for human dignity is (you might say) a routine response to what is perceived to be the case: no more *heroic* than any other clear-eyed submission to the facts of the case. But on any other basis, in Taylor's argument and mine, radical and non-negotiable reverence for human dignity becomes vulnerable in all sorts of ways to distortion. And while it is possible simply to assert that such dignity is unarguably present in every human person, the only rationale for this that does not collapse is the belief that this dignity is specified and required by the relation in which every human being stands to its maker – a relation completely unaffected by any particular way in which things turn out in the history of this world. And this is the foundation of trust, both in terms of our cosmic context and in terms of our mutual connectedness: there is something that cannot be denied by anyone we encounter because we are able to *recognize* one another, literally or metaphorically to speak with each other in the confidence that communication is possible, across both temporal and cultural gaps. It is the confidence that enables us to write history (the past may be a foreign country but we can still discern how its language makes sense) and to *argue* across cultures about the requirements of the good.

Religious faith sustains the possibility of talking intelligently about what some have called 'the solidarities we did not choose'. It insists that those solidarities are not transient matters, vulnerable to cultural changes, but equally are not simply biological matters. Czeslaw Milosz, in his essay, 'Speaking of a Mammal'[10] discusses Bertrand Russell's appeal to recognition of our solidarity as 'members of a biological species' as the ground of universal sympathy, and counters Russell's brave if naïve position by insisting on the ineradicable presence of culture and politics in our account of humanity. 'No prisoner in a concentration camp of our era', he says, 'would dream of asking pity for himself in the name of biological kinship with those who condemned him; he knows that he was discarded by them as historically harmful, and it is that harmfulness which defines him in the first place, and not his membership in the tribe of *homo sapiens*'.[11] Something more than biology is required, some imagined community of universal *recognition*; and that is what faith proposes, in various forms, but always steering us towards the realization that we are recognizable to each other because we are first recognized (affirmed, valued, loved) by God.

This is the point at which religious discourse has to be acknowledged as neither pro- nor anti-Enlightenment in the usual sense. It steps around some of the Enlightenment's central tropes as misconceived: if we are faced with a choice between coercive universal rationalism and pre-critical authority, it may well be time to ask if the argument has been properly set out in the first place. And if the only third alternative in view is a pluralism that cannot ultimately give an account of convergent and mutually constructed goods for humankind, an account of character and habit formed by participation in communities of meaning and cultural symbolism, the outlook is not promising. Religious faith – and in a very particular way the 'Abrahamic' faiths – should be capable of absorbing the critique of unchallengeable human authority in the name of the transcendent moral reality that cannot be either fully expressed or overridden and relativized by the pragmatic calls of the moment or the immediate setting in human history. Because the idea of a *calling* is so fundamental to all the Abrahamic languages, there is always a dimension of faith that acknowledges simultaneously an agnosticism about the full and exact scope of what we are summoned to and an austere appeal to obedience and self-forgetfulness. That appeal cannot ever be reduced, though plenty of attempts have been made, to a simple defence of the positive law of the religious institution – partly because eschatology keeps coming back, the conviction that the final resolution of the world's crises is not in human hands.

Which is why, finally, post-Enlightenment religious faith is both a possible and a complex matter. Once the Enlightenment questions have been asked, there is a loss of innocence: even the religious traditionalist is now a traditionalist because he or she has in some measure chosen to be so. The inhabitant of pre-modern tradition simply occupies what is believed to be the natural and obvious space for the human mind; which is why fundamentalism, in any faith, is a quintessentially modern thing, the self-conscious and reactive choice of supposedly traditional positions in a way that tears them from their context and makes them an aggressive assertion over defined alternatives. But fundamentalism is not the only religious response to 'enlightened' modernity. And neither is revisionism, the theological modernism that accepts the judgement of that optimistic rationalism which Berlin invites us to take with a substantial pinch of salt. A post-Enlightenment faith that has integrity and intelligence will need to push back at some of the myths of rational universalism as toughly as Berlin ever did, and it will be no stranger to the tragic dimension which he gently but inexorably brought back into the foreground of political discourse. But it will equally want to challenge too quick an adoption of pluralism, in the name of certain stubborn convictions about both God and God's human creation; it will, as many have argued in recent decades, need to work hard at defining the rationalities and the universalities that are not just stalking horses for incipient totalitarianism. To recover the connection between doctrine, narrative, reason and virtue is not a project to abolish Enlightenment, simply because it assumes some of the Enlightenment's own categories, above all the patient business of requiring any human authority to explain and vindicate itself and of creating the context in which open and respectful argument can take place. But in recognizing that reason and argument are learned and matured in the specifics of cultural conversation – including the conversations of faith – the religious interpreter is still able to return the challenge to the Enlightenment and its heritage and ask if its framing of intelligent human options has not been shadowed by gravely mistaken assumptions.

At the end of his superb essay on Tolstoy, Berlin describes the Russian novelist and the French counter-Enlightenment polemicist Joseph de Maistre as both 'observers utterly incapable of being deceived by the many subtle devices, the unifying systems and faiths and sciences, by which the superficial or the desperate sought to conceal the chaos from themselves and from one another'.[12]

What I have hoped to suggest is that faith, while offering a unifying perspective and a unifying goal for the human community, need not mean adopting a superficial or desperate concealment of the difficulty of hearing one another and working with one another. If – and it is admittedly a large if at times – faith is a unique resource for the nourishment of political as well as private virtue, and if such virtue requires us to make sense of our solidarities and our traditions rather than either discarding them or fighting for them, there is a step that can be taken beyond Isaiah Berlin's scepticism; a way of allowing some critical solidarity, as we might say, between faith and Enlightenment after all.

Pluralism – public and religious

1

The word 'pluralism' has come to mean an uncomfortable variety of things in both the political and the religious sphere. In reference to religion, it is most often used to mean the conviction that no particular religious tradition has the full or final truth: each perceives a valid but incomplete part of it. This sort of pluralist perspective implies that no faith can or should make claims for itself as the only route to perfection or salvation. In the political context, it can refer to at least two positions. The first is an analysis of the state associated with political theorists like Harold Laski and John Neville Figgis in the early twentieth century. According to this approach, we must think of the state not as the all-powerful source of legitimate community life and action, but as the structure needed to organise and mediate within a 'community of communities', a plurality of very diverse groups and associations of civil society, ranging from trade unions and universities to religious bodies. And a second political meaning is the one given currency particularly by Isaiah Berlin in his writings on political liberty.[1] There is a genuine plurality of human goods, and they are not all compatible in any given situation: doing the right thing may involve the sacrifice of one desired good for the sake of another, and we must not deceive ourselves as to the cost, pretending that there is some ideal condition in which all genuine human moral goals are realized harmoniously. If there is such a diversity of human goals, the most realistic political aspiration is for a liberal state that does not seek to advance by legislation a programme for this or that specific vision of human improvement or self-realization.

Diverse as these definitions are, there are clear areas of overlap. If it is true, as some claim, that no religious tradition possesses ultimate truth, no religious tradition can claim the right to be legally enforced. If the state has to broker relations between different communities, it must itself be ideologically neutral.

If a religious body exists within a pluralist state, it must at least recognize that it cannot expect the state to legislate as though its religious and ethical claims were beyond dispute. It has to understand that, while it may still make the same truth claims, they are now open to scrutiny, rebuttal and attack, and cannot be taken for granted. And the interweaving of all these themes is perhaps more evident in India than in many places in our world. For example, India, in declaring itself a secular state at independence, was making a clear option for a certain kind of public and political neutrality, acknowledging that to be a citizen in India could not be something that depended on any particular communal identity, and that the state could not intervene in religious disagreements except insofar as they became socially disruptive. Furthermore, the religious context and history of India are bound to pose questions to any simplistic religious absolutism; and the oldest traditions of India have a good deal to say about the elusiveness of the divine as well as its revelation. Which is why modern India is such a fruitful context in which to examine understandings of pluralism – how they apply in practice and the questions they raise.

2

I say this because it is easy at times to take the language of pluralism in any or all of the above senses as an unexamined aspect of what social modernity means; yet both conceptually and practically, there is unfinished business. I do not expect to finish it in a brief lecture; but it may be useful to notice where the unfinished-ness can seriously mislead, with risky consequences both for faith and for politics.

In what follows, I want to offer some thoughts about how religious pluralism might be understood in a fresh way that will not simply leave us with relativism or indifference. And I shall be trying to connect this with some thoughts about the character of a well-functioning modern democracy that seeks to secure equal liberties for diverse communities. I believe that the history of reflection on these questions in India has considerable relevance for our general thinking about the issues of religion in the modern state.

Part of what was taken for granted in the formation of modern independent India was the conviction that the state had to create a new kind of loyalty – not replacing or destroying the more basic kinds of belonging associated with religious history or ethnicity, but securing for everyone a degree of equal access to social goods: to fairness before the law, the chance of economic liberty and protection from the violence of other groups. A proper political pluralism works with, not against, the grain of local and specific identities, but it still has to assert certain values and standards for all. Whatever may be said of the 'value pluralism' argued by Isaiah Berlin, it cannot mean that the state has no moral commitments. It is at least committed to seeing everyone as deserving of legal protection and capable of sharing in democratic decision-making. But in basing itself on assumptions like these, it also recognizes that the law and the state cannot just treat a population as a collection of individuals; their actual identity is already bound up with values and beliefs. As Sunil Khilnani writes about Nehru, he 'saw cultures as overlapping forms of activity that had commerce with one another, mutually altering and reshaping each other. India was a society neither of liberal individuals nor of exclusive communities or nation-alities, but of interconnected differences.' This last phrase is of great importance, and we shall be coming back to it later in this discussion.

So part of the modern political story in this context, a story played out very clearly in India, is one of making the connection between communal identity, religious or otherwise, and the new, constructed loyalty that is political affiliation as a citizen. Rather than trying to build civic loyalty from nothing, a sympathetic state will build on the experience of co-operation and passionate concern for the common good that is nurtured in particular communities, especially by a religiously formed ethic of self-giving, so that this sense of mutual 'investment and mutually created well-being can carry across into the wider political realm.

In this context, how should we understand and speak about religious pluralism? The pluralist state takes religious belonging seriously and sees itself, as a state, as serving the healthy coexistence and interaction of diverse communities of conviction and loyalty by creating for all of them a 'civic space' where all can find a voice. It is a system of legal universalism and a morally serious and committed project of securing every particular community's liberty to express itself and argue about shared concerns and hopes. This is what is commonly meant by calling states like India 'secular'.

But part of what this also means is that the real differences between communities and their claims are not seen as unhappy survivals of a less enlightened age that really need to be eradicated. A secular democracy can perfectly well benefit from the serious arguments that may be generated between these communities about shared goods and concerns and the moral and religious basis on which goals are pursued in society; the state's job is not to silence all this, but to ensure that there is a space in which the argument can be pursued with civility.

3

Religious pluralism is not, of course, strictly or necessarily 'relativist'. It generally assumes that there is some reliable common ground in claims to knowledge of God or the sacred, even if it is sceptical of more particular doctrinal formulations – the Christian doctrine of the Trinity, for example, or the Muslim commitment to a direct and final divine communication in the Qur'an. But it may still be agreed that the sacred reality surrounding this universe is benign, that human beings have some share in, or natural capacity for knowing, the divine character, that meditative practice in silence and asceticism brings us closer to the divine and that universal compassion and the quest for universal justice is a natural expression and consequence of knowing the divine. All these things may be affirmed as holding true in every human situation. But as to the distinctive assertions of each of the faiths, these (we are told) must be regarded as at best uncertain or perhaps as diverse attempts to express what is in fact the same vision or message. They may be helpful vehicles for local religious expression or devotion, but they cannot be treated as holding true in all situations; properly understood, it is argued, they cannot even be regarded as serious candidates for being believed as universally true.

But whether religious pluralism of this kind is relativist or not, it still carries with it some unresolved problems. The 'universal' truths on which all major religious traditions are alleged to agree are all embedded in, entwined with, the specific convictions of each faith: and so the *reasons* given for affirming the universal truths will vary. It is not as though belief in a benign sacred power is simply innate in everyone and is clothed with different cultural forms from which it can be painlessly separated. Such beliefs are grounded in the narratives of encounter between the divine or the sacred and the human, the narratives which are embodied in scriptures or rituals and commonly spoken of in the language of 'revelation': that is, they are represented as connected with moments in history and language, their credibility and intelligibility is bound up with history and language, and their expression is determined by these stories of encounter and enlightenment. Of course, different traditions approach these matters in diverse ways: there is a sense in which the historical experience of Gautama is indeed identical with the enlightenment attained by the Buddhist practitioner in any and every human setting: that is, it is presented as universally available and, in an important sense, not dependent on any particular supernatural agent who can only be 'contacted' or activated by a person holding correct theoretical or theological beliefs. But this example reinforces the point. The experience may be universal and the enlightened practitioner may be in principle 'equal' to the Buddha; but the character of the experience is once and for all specified by the narrative of how the Middle Way was discovered and realized by Gautama.

The point is that, while it may be possible to distil a fairly general core of common wisdom from the diverse languages of faith throughout the world, each will provide a different rationale for believing – and, even more importantly, a different discipline of life and practice for becoming aligned with it, living it out effectively. This diversity cannot be reduced to what 'suits' regional, cultural or even individual temperaments. It has been noted that what is often left out of accounts of the intellectual problems around certain classical theological formulae in Christianity like the Nicene Creed is a proper account of how the formulation actually took shape, in response to what specific pressures – in other words, how it was *learned*. The issue is the same in this wider context. We cannot avoid asking how a particular system of belief is 'pressured' into existence, how what is claimed as a truth is learned. And, as the observations on Buddhism in the last paragraph imply, the story of how a religious world view emerges into being is closely bound up with how the believer now becomes fully assimilated to that world view, how he or she comes to live it as true or real.

So a religious 'pluralism' that seeks to identify a core of common insights as opposed to a diversity of ways in which these are clothed is in danger of ignoring not only the narratives of origin which all faiths appeal to, but also the narratives of personal development and transformation related by believers. The 'common core' approach cannot become an embodied practice, except in terms of ethical recommendations of a pretty uncontroversial kind; and such recommendations have usually been regarded by religious people as impossible to sustain independently of the practices (and thus the narratives) of particular religious commitments. It is not realistic, either intellectually or practically, to see religious 'pluralism' in its frequently used sense as a straightforward programme that can guarantee peaceful coexistence between faith

communities on the basis that they all come to regard their distinctive narratives as non-essential and culturally-conditioned 'extras' to a basic common
vision.

But this need not mean that we are left either with a world, or a society, of
mutually uncomprehending systems or with a bitter competition for supremacy
between the 'religions'. Apart from the critical fact that the whole idea of
'religions' as parallel systems all seeking to conquer the same territory and
answer the same questions is a hugely unhelpful place to start, we need to
recognize that what confronts us here is a complex map of stories and rituals.
They are shaped and expressed in such a way that they inevitably make implicit
or explicit claims about what is the fullest or most effective way to secure and
understand contact between humanity and the sacred. But they also (and conse-
quently) make some claims about whether and how the sacred order of being
might *act* towards us in making such contact possible and real. In the nature
of the case, there will be no 'neutral' evidence that will settle this question; but
that does not reduce us to hopeless agnosticism. Instead, it prescribes, I would
argue, a careful and attentive interaction between communities of religious
practice, so that we can raise questions like, 'How does this tradition deal with
such and such a particular aspect of human experience?' or 'How does this
practice actually connect with what are claimed to be the fundamentals of the
original narrative?' – and 'Are these two or more traditions addressing similar
or different concerns when they use language and imagery that seems to be
closely similar?'

This is close to what the Jesuit scholar Francis X. Clooney describes as
'comparative theology'. 'In our religiously diverse context,' he writes, 'a vital
theology has to resist too tight a binding by tradition, but also the idea that
religious diversity renders strong claims about truth and value impossible.
Comparative theology is a manner of learning that takes seriously diversity and
tradition, openness and truth, allowing neither to decide the meaning of our
religious situation without recourse to the other'.[2] Clooney defines a method
in theology that does not seek to keep itself at a distance from particular rites,
idioms and narratives, but rather seeks to learn what may serve the goal of
spiritual maturity within the commitments already undertaken and accepted.
Instead of proposing a theology of inclusion on some sort of a priori basis, it
simply performs 'acts of including'[3] by engaging carefully and imaginatively
with other voices and habits. It is a theology that still retains its fundamental
understanding of how its own vision or world view is learned and how that

learning is constantly reproduced in the believer's life, and it does not shrink from making claims for the truth of what is thus learned. But it also opens up new kinds of relations between the believer and the rites and stories of another faith – and with the persons who hold to another faith. Clooney speaks of a 'new community' emerging in this process, even of a degree of 'multiple belonging'.[4] The comparative theologian seeks to enter into the world of the believer in another faith, to experience some of what they experience as a genuine and personal spiritual discipline and means of discovery and growth, and so to understand more fully the relation between basic narratives and daily practice. The simple polarity of insider and outsider is no longer adequate to describe these relationships. Yet to say this is not to abandon the claim that there is still one narrative that offers the comprehensive perspective in which others may most truthfully and rightly be read.

4

At this point, it may perhaps be possible to see how the political and religious aspects of the present discussion begin to converge. I have suggested, in effect, that interreligious conversation needs to beware of two misleading perspectives – on the one hand, the idea that any encounter must always be a contest between two or more self-contained rival systems, offering clear alternative answers to the same set of questions so that only one of them can be regarded as ultimately true; and on the other hand, the belief that all specific narrative and doctrinal schemes are variant expression of the same underlying conviction or convictions. In other words, interreligious conversation and encounter seeks to avoid assumptions both of 'zero-sum' conflict and of the possibility of a final dissolution of real otherness. For this to happen, there has to be a secure space for genuine exchange and exploration: there has to be a 'civil space' for religious communities to meet each other. This is in some ways a distinctively modern challenge. There have been many pre-modern societies in which diverse faith communities live alongside one another in varying degrees of sympathy or harmony; but there was generally a single dominant religious presence, allied with political power. In this perspective, what the neutral or secular modern state makes possible is a deeper and more empathetic encounter between religious discourses and systems. The secular public sphere provides the space for civil argument.

Earlier in this paper, I spoke about the new *loyalties* created by a properly pluralist law-governed democracy. By establishing a situation in which genuine diversity in society can be acknowledged and worked with through a shared loyalty to legal institutions that protect all, a degree of *mutual* loyalty develops, a sense of shared interest and investment in the neighbour's well-being. This is the civic ambition of modernity. But we have noted already that it is a serious and damaging mistake to think that the identity so created is something which replaces other identities: as I said above, no-one is *just* a citizen, and the project of a blanket promotion of secular civic identity at the expense of actual communities of habit and conviction is one of the less liberal aspects of some contemporary liberalism. Part of what consolidates civic loyalty is the confidence that the state and its law recognizes the real plurality of the communities that compose the state, rather than working only with abstract models of legal identity. So the challenge before the healthy pluralist state is to maintain a robust defence of universal civic liberties and universal access to legal process and legal protection, while seeking to work with the grain of existing loyalties and solidarities to secure a better settlement for all, not just for a majority.

This has been precisely India's agenda from Independence onwards. It has consistently tried to define a 'secularism' that is not hostile to multiple religious identities; and it has had to struggle repeatedly with pressures and temptations in the direction of communalism, to avoid the state becoming only a harassed referee between sometimes violently competing identities and claims. In this sense, India's political history is a good deal more central to the understanding of the basic problems of religion and politics in modernity than some have thought; and the success or otherwise of India's capacity to manage 'interconnected differences', in Nehru's pregnant phrase, will have significance well beyond India's borders.

But my point here is that this significance is not only to do with the political management of an unusually complex society. The success of the project is also to do with the viability of the model of interreligious encounter I have been outlining. Where religious identities and political power are intertwined, conversation is always affected and usually distorted by the awareness of these issues of power and advantage; a civic or civil space for encounter and proper mutuality is not created. The secular environment in which religious identities are recognized but not privileged allows for mutual questioning, mutual influence and a degree of change in how each party sees its own identity. The secular assumption in the government of the state is not necessarily hostile to religious faith, but neither does it simply leave every self-specified identity beyond challenge or critique.[5] The very fact of the civil space guarantees that there will be critique; it should also guarantee, by means of the educational and civic policies of the state overall, that such a critique is reasoned and non-violent.

In such a context, it is possible to see how the sort of encounter envisaged by Clooney can flourish through 'acts of including' and mutual discovery which may modify and enlarge the original self-definitions of a religious tradition without evacuating it or threatening to submerge it into generalities. I said earlier that religious identities were shaped by narrative and by ritual and spiritual practice. Granted that there are foundational stories and patterns of practice that are at the heart of a tradition, it is also true that there is a continuing narrative, a developing process of 'receiving' and realizing afresh those founda-tional matters. And if the continuing narrative takes in the practices of civil encounter and reasoned argument, this in itself begins to modify some of what might originally have been seen as essential to an identity. Such a process, of course, happens whenever any religious tradition moves into a new cultural situation and seeks expression in a new language; Christianity, which has never had a single sacred language, has particularly varied experience of this, but there are parallel stories to be told in each of the world's major traditions.

In both the political and the religious context, we can see the importance of creating a set of loyalties that are not exclusively communal and local in order for those communal and local identities to speak to each other and to argue without fear or panic. The civic space is in one sense artificial: but in a complex society it is a necessity not only for order and social collaboration, but also for the intelligent discussion and appropriation of more basic loyalties and affilia-tions. I don't think this necessarily implies that civic identity always 'comes first' or matters more – that a religious believer is simply an Indian who *happens* to be a Jain or a Briton who *happens* to be a Muslim (and here I am less happy with Amartya Sen's analysis[6]). The kinds of belonging involved are sufficiently different for us not to have to see them as competing. To be a Christian, Hindu or a member of any distinct religious body is to inhabit and accept an identity that is believed to be in tune with how the universe most deeply is, or with what God intends and desires. This will therefore mould personal options and practices in a comprehensive way, consciously and unconsciously. To belong in this way is to be a particular kind of human being, with the added hope and trust that *this* mode of human existence will most fully correspond to what reality itself requires of us. The facts and the claims of civic identity and loyalty are not put forward as a way of living in accordance with transcendent truth, but as forms of social life that recognize diversity of conviction and secure protection for the voices of all. These claims and social forms can be accommodated along with, even within, the wider claims for truth, since they allow for belief to be articulated while controlling violent conflict. And, although this would be too large a topic to address here, the forms of civility and exchange can themselves be incorporated into the forms and claims of religious belief as representing a new form of old virtue. It is striking that every major religious tradition now proclaims that it prizes tolerance and peaceful diversity. It was not always so; but the pressure of modernity, in a wholly positive way, has made certain kinds of civic charity native to the religious narrative itself.

'Pluralism' is, as we have seen, a slippery word, but in both the political and the religious context it has a positive sense that needs clarifying and defending. It denotes the refusal on the part of political authority to seek legitimacy by simple appeal to one tradition of faith. It denotes a self-awareness on the part of the state, a recognition that actual civil society is composed of a variety of groups with a variety of convictions and habits, moral and ritual, so that the state's task is to seek the best possible co-existence and interaction between them for the attainment of goods that no one group can secure alone. It denotes a recognition also that religious diversity is neither a problem to be overcome nor a threat to be controlled. Properly understood, I suggest, a political pluralism that is fully conscious of the potential of interactive variety (a refinement of 'interconnected difference') is a fruitful context for an interreligious encounter that does not compromise convictions, but is also ready to envisage growth and change. Both political and religious pluralism acknowledge the reality of *history*: identities, however deep and passionately adhered to, do not make decisions and self-determinations unnecessary. There are dimensions of identity that we create as well as inherit. Amartya Sen speaks of 'the long history and consummate strength of our argumentative tradition':[7] my contention has been that our best political future lies with what I have elsewhere called 'argumentative democracy', and that religious integrity is well served and not undermined by such a vision for our society. India has struggled to put flesh on these abstractions for over half a century, and, if I am right, its continuing struggle with the challenge is a matter of concern and importance for us all, caught as we often are in the contemporary world between renewed bids for theocracy and anxious efforts to secure the complete privatizing of faith.

Religious hatred and religious offence

The question of whether and how a society should defend religious belief against attack, 'defamation' or abuse became more and more current in the first decade of the twenty-first century. The creation of a criminal offence under British law of incitement to religious hatred provoked bitter and sustained controversy; anxiety was expressed on the one hand by committed secularists who feared some kind of limitation on the freedom to criticize or satirize religious belief in general, and on the other by Christians who were apprehensive that the legislation might be used to restrain the preaching of Christianity as unequivocally true and to prohibit any public statement that questioned the validity of other faiths. Both suspected, not without reason, that the main motor of the legislation was a wish to respond to the frequently expressed complaint that existing blasphemy laws in the UK did not adequately protect all non-Christian faiths. And while this is in fact a debateable reading of the blasphemy laws in the light of what the courts have said in the twentieth century, there was undoubtedly a strong perception that Muslims suffered relative disadvantage and an equally strong political resolve to minimize the sense of exclusion felt by many British Muslims in this regard. But this reinforced the anxieties of those who believed that disproportionate attention was being given to a hypersensitive minority: surely, it was argued, those whose beliefs were at odds with those of the majority in a basically liberal society could not claim immunity from public criticism.

The debate revived many of the themes that had been around in 1989 and 1990 in the wake of the tumult over Salman Rushdie's *Satanic Verses* and the *fatwa* of the Ayatollah Khomeini against the author. It was further complicated by the publication in Denmark of cartoons that were widely seen as insulting to Islam and by the very different decisions taken by publishers internationally as to whether they should be reproduced. This fierce conflict renewed the unease (to put it no more strongly) about free expression being 'held hostage' by the sensitivities of a particular group in such a way that the basis of liberal society could be compromised. And the application of blasphemy laws in other contexts did nothing to help. A succession of cases in rural Pakistan involving the use of blasphemy laws to intimidate local Christian communities drew international attention some years ago when local tensions overflowed into rioting and violence against Christian minorities; and towards the end of 2007, the imprisonment of a British woman in Sudan under local blasphemy laws on what was generally recognized as a preposterous charge provided further ammunition to those who were most concerned about the possibilities of abuse and moral/legal blackmail in laws to do with religious sensitivities.

The announcement in January 2008 of a consultation on the abolition of the offence of blasphemy in English law was a predictable step towards what proved to be an eventual rationalizing of the previous legal position; but it opened up a number of questions about the nature and significance of offence to religious belief and the ground for legal restraint – as also the broader and vexing question of what a society might properly expect *morally* speaking of its citizens in regard to religious belief and practice. In what follows, I shall concentrate on this borderland between the legal and the moral, in the hope of clarifying a little the social meanings of anti-religious language or behaviour. This lecture was originally delivered some few days after Holocaust Memorial Day: and it is important to underline that there is a sense in which the foundational form of religious hatred and religious offence in our culture has been and remains anti-Semitism. Its history in Europe shows how the slippage can occur from abusive words and images to assumptions about the dangers posed by a community stigmatized as perpetual outsiders to actions designed to remove them for good. The lethal mixture of a Christian tradition of anti-Jewish polemic and routine humiliation – interspersed with murderous outbreaks of popular violence – and a post-Christian, pseudo-scientific philosophy of race illustrates how religious hatred can be generated by both intra-religious and secular forces; one of the most demanding aspects of trying to make sense of this set of problems around religious offence is the clarifying of where the border lies between criticism and contempt and between contempt and violence. The history of anti-Semitism does not suggest that we shall find a comfortingly clear answer.

But to return to the broader issue: as David Nash has pointed out in a compre-hensive, if rather disjointed, survey, recent discussion has been pulled in sharply contradictory directions.[1] The liberal concern for the rights of minorities has been in tension with the liberal commitment to free speech. Nash quotes David Lawton, who wrote a study of blasphemy in 1993, saying in 2002 that 'laws intended to protect minorities would curtail freedom in the name of multi-culturalism'.[2] And what has been in evidence recently has been a hardening of attitudes on both sides of the debate, with more and more aggressive statements of the overwhelming claims of universal and non-negotiable liberties, and more and more heated and sometimes violent assertions of the right of religious groups not to be publicly insulted or traduced. It is a dramatic instance of the way in which a discourse focused on rights can lead us into unmanageable conflicts if it is isolated from other considerations about the foundations of law; but that is something I shall come back to later. As things stand, the right to religious freedom – that is, to adopt and practice whatever religious system you choose – is axiomatic in all Western conceptions of human rights, and is indeed given a very clearly privileged place in European Human Rights legislation as trumping other considerations in situations of conflicts of right. But the same principle of freedom to believe what you choose dictates the right to hold and express views critical of or hostile to any or every religious system. In legal terms, there is also the tangle of issues around how the law recognizes 'group rights', the claims of a community rather than just an individual to sustain its own convictions and practices – a much-controverted area, as it raises questions about how we assess the compatibility of a community's practices with the rights otherwise recognized in all citizens.

Broadening the view still further, we need also to acknowledge that the last couple of decades have witnessed a sharp rise in awareness of the potential seriousness of 'offence' in general. Legislation against racist language and behaviour became a model for identifying varieties of harassment and discrimi-nation in the workplace and in the public arena of comment and discussion; pressure has increased for what might be called an 'isomorphic' approach in law to any act or form of words that could be interpreted as stigmatizing others or demeaning their human dignity – hence the 'Single Equality' legislation developed and debated under the Labour administration of Tony Blair and his successor. Conservative Christian activists (along with some other religious voices) regularly express their concern about how this could impact on any public statement of traditional Christian sexual morality or any policy designed to guarantee that such morality should be observed in overtly Christian institutions; and while some of this argument is frankly alarmist, there is under-standable concern among those who are responsible for Anglican and Roman Catholic Church schools, for example, about their freedom to require certain standards of candidates for employment. And behind some of the worries over the idea of religious offence lie deeper worries about the 'victim culture' – a sense that we are moving into an atmosphere where every citizen is encouraged to see himself or herself as constantly vulnerable to being undermined by others, where dignity has to be constantly secured by the threat of litigation.

But before exploring this further, we should also note the way in which, in the modern period, legislation about blasphemy or religious offence has been defended from the point of view of public order. This was the position taken by legal authority in declining to prosecute the BBC over the broadcasting of *Jerry Springer: the Opera* under the blasphemy laws; the criterion of risk to public order was defined as the central issue, and it was determined that such a risk was insufficiently high to justify legal action. As many have pointed out, the English law of blasphemy has its origins in an era where the criticism of religion was tantamount to a criticism of legal order itself. Sir Matthew Hale, Lord Chief Justice in the late seventeenth century, famously declared in 1675 that an attack on religion constituted a threat to 'dissolve all those obligations whereby civil societies are preserved'.[3] But even when this strong association between religious belief and the very notion of civil obligation had largely disappeared, there remained a clear sense that attack on religious belief *could* be productive of such a level of public disorder that a prosecution would be justified. Last year's decision of the Administrative Court in *R v the City of Westminster Magistrates' Court* spelled this out carefully, distinguishing between threats to society in general and perceived offence, however serious, to personal beliefs, and concluded, interestingly, that offence was not *as such* an infringement of the right to believe and practice religious faith.

From all this, it emerges fairly clearly that the former blasphemy law, in setting the criterion of threat to public disorder very high, made it impossible to pursue any legal action exclusively on the grounds of perceived offence; and the 2006 legislation which defines the crime of inciting religious hatred attempted to bind offence to criminal intent, the desire to generate active menace towards a group with certain convictions such that their civil liberties might be at risk. In other words, whatever the anxieties of some, religious offence is not being defined simply as anything that a person or group happens to find offensive. The abolition of the common law offence of blasphemy, it seems, does not substantially alter the extent of the protection afforded to religious communities and individuals; nor does the new legislation offer an unlimited charter for the hypersensitive. However, this leaves some serious issues still open. In what way precisely can we fix the point at which offence affects the civil liberties of religious believers? How clearly can we distinguish an intention to refute or belittle religious convictions from an intention to threaten people who hold them? Does the right to free expression of 'offensive' sentiments have the same moral quality as the right to belief itself? Julian Rivers notes in his 2007 guest editorial for *Religion and Human Rights*[4] that the apparently attractive idea of an offence of 'defamation of religion' is less specifically helpful than might at first appear: defamation is indeed the core of what concerns many in regard to discriminatory behaviour, but it proves difficult to see it as in itself a violation of human rights, isolated from practices of discrimination, threat or active hostility. In respect of some of these questions, as far as the law is concerned, we shall have to see how the courts respond; but I shall argue that there are certain considerations, not all that widely discussed, which ought to affect the way the law is seen and, more importantly, ought to pose some questions to too simplistic a liberal approach in this area.

Briefly, my points have to do with two aspects of the question. The first is the way in which discussion of these matters has so often been conducted in complete abstraction from considerations of what is socially desirable or constructive; the second, related to the first in obvious ways, is the isolation of the discussion from the realities of cultural and political power in various contexts in our world.

On the first, Richard Webster, in his immensely intelligent and independent essay on the Rushdie affair, observes that absolute freedom of speech is not in fact either a possible or a desirable state of political affairs. The fact is that 'in the real political world which we all perforce inhabit, words *do* wound, insults *do* hurt, and abuse, especially extreme and obscene abuse, *does* provoke both anger and violence.'[5] An abstract discussion of free speech, in which, to quote Webster again, no distinction is made 'between the freedom to impart information and the freedom to insult,'[6] is in effect a strategy which isolates the would-be 'blasphemer' from the actual historical and interpersonal constraints which secure a reasonable level of civility in human society (after all, we do restrain freedom of speech by laws about libel and slander). The creation of avoidable resentment, never mind avoidable suffering, does not seem like a positive good for any social unit; and the assertion of an unlimited freedom to create such resentment does little to recommend 'liberal' values and tends rather to strengthen the suspicion that they are a poor basis for social morality and cohesion.

That is not a fair conclusion, but it is equally not a surprising one, given the way the argument has gone (and Webster, who is not a religious believer of any kind, offers some extraordinary examples of 'liberal' aggression and ignorant bigotry in his account of the reactions in 1989 and 1990 to the furore over the *fatwa* against Rushdie). What this analysis obliges us to think about is some of the things which much of the classical liberal case for freedom to offend takes uncritically for granted. It assumes, for example, that any pain caused by offensive language or behaviour is so superficial as not to be significant; if you feel hurt, wounded, by abuse, it is a mark of undue or even immature sensitivity ('Grow up!' 'Get used to it'). Furthermore, to pick up a regular defence of the admissibility of anti-religious abuse, it is commonly said that since a religious believer chooses to adopt a certain set of beliefs, he or she is responsible for the consequences, which may, as every believer well knows, include strong disagreement or even repugnance from others. But this assimilation of belief to a plain matter of conscious individual choice does not square with the way in which many believers understand or experience their commitments. For some – and this is especially true for believers from outside the European or North Atlantic setting – religious belief and practice is a marker of shared identity, accepted not as a matter of individual choice, but as a given to which allegiance is due in virtue of the intrinsic claims of the sacred. We may disagree; but I do not think we have the moral right to assume that this perspective can be simply disregarded. Both the dismissal of the possibility of actual mental suffering and the assimilation of belief to a matter of choice reflect a worryingly narrow set of models for the human psyche – or, in plainer English, a lack of imagination.

Webster hints more than once that such a lack of imagination is an ironic backdrop for the arguments of writers or dramatists defending the right to present religious subjects offensively. But more significantly, he notes that if this sort of argument is taken for granted, it points to a coarsening of general sensibility: in the potent image he takes from some remarks by Anthony Lejeune, we are getting into the habit of 'burning your enemy's flag' – belittling symbols which other human beings have loved and even died for.[7] We need to be aware of the implicit cruelty and the dehumanizing potential of such assumptions. It is one thing to deny a sacred point of reference for one's own moral or social policies; it is another to refuse to entertain, or imagine, what it might be like for someone else to experience the world differently. Spectres of colonialism, 'Orientalism', and, once again, anti-Semitism are roused when this insensibility to the otherness of the religious other goes unquestioned. And behind this is the nagging problem of what happens to a culture in which, systematically, nothing is sacred. We may have moved on from the confidence of Chief Justice Hale

in claiming that civil loyalty of any kind had to be built on religious foundations; but the uncomfortable truth is that a de-sacralized world is not, as some
fondly believe, a world without violence, but a world in which there can be
no ultimate agreement about the worth of human or other beings. There may
be a strong, even practically unbreakable, consensus about the wrongness of
torturing prisoners or raping children; but there will be no very clear sense of
what, if anything, beyond the dignity of an individual is being 'violated' in such
cases. This is not to make the facile claim that morality needs religion, only
to note that a morality without the sacred is bound to work differently. And a
post-religious morality that has simply lost any imaginative understanding of
what the sacred once meant is dangerously impoverished. I referred in Chapter
1 to my recollection of correspondence with a British novelist who claimed
that, while she had no belief in God, she needed something like a concept of
blasphemy to express her sense of a violated order when confronted by gross
military extravagance or environmental exploitation.

The liberal apologist might reasonably come back at this point to object that,
while the point may be well taken about coarsened sensibility or even about
the inappropriateness of a simplistic choice model for religious allegiance, the
issue about 'hurt' needs very careful handling. No doubt there were profound
and genuine feelings of hurt among white Americans in the South during the
Civil Rights campaigns of the 1960s: not everyone who accepted the appalling
conventions of the day was personally wicked, deserving, so to speak, to have
their feelings disregarded; yet without the shock of the campaign, with its
cost in terms of personal upset, change would not have occurred. The same
arguments are, painfully close to home, often at work in debates in the Church
about the ministry of women or the acceptance of homosexual people. In
arguments about what is true or what is good, the feelings of the other can't
determine what is said. And if I believe that religion in general or some religion
in particular is actually deplorable or destructive, I must insist upon my liberty
to say so, whether or not it causes pain. It is, ironically, precisely the argument
that many religious people would themselves use in claiming the liberty to state,
for example, that abortion or euthanasia is morally unacceptable, even though
realizing that such a statement would cause real pain to some; it is a liberty not,
for some reason, readily acknowledged by some vocal advocates of other kinds
of free speech.

The appeal to the moral imperatives of truth telling for the sake of justice is a
fair point so far as it goes, but there are still questions being begged; and to see

what those questions are will take us on to the issue of power in this context. The simplest response to the defence in term of the requirements of abstract justice is to recall the difference between critique and abuse: it is one thing to say that someone may be deeply and dangerously wrong, even to say it with anger, and another to say or imply that if someone is wrong it is because they are infantile, wilfully blind or perverse. A polemical strategy that refuses from the start to accept that anyone could have *reasons* for thinking differently is a poor basis for civil disagreement (in both the wider and narrower sense of the adjective); it is a way of denying the other a hearing.

And this at last brings us to how power is at work in all this. The classical free speech arguments were largely formulated against a background of resistance to a dominant culture administered by non-accountable authorities: blasphemy functioned as one form of protest against tyranny, and the hagiography of militant anti-religious prophets presents, fairly enough, a picture of brave individuals or small groups standing up to the consolidated power of one or another kind of religious establishment (Nash's book gives ample illustration of this). The emotional colouring of anti-religious polemic is still rather Voltairean – certainly part of the tribal memory of a courageous and persecuted minority.

And that is why the instinctive reaction of most *bien-pensant* commentators, of the right as much as the left these days, when issues of religious offence are being discussed, is to revert to the tribal memory: religion is a powerful and mostly malign presence, at the very least a presence unwelcome in the public sphere, which needs to be kept in its place so that the hard-won triumphs of Enlightenment are not jeopardized. But what is harder to cope with is a situation in which this kind of folkloric, David-and-Goliath pattern is not really applicable. Yet again, we should remember some of the history of anti-Semitism. Some of the passionate polemic against Jewish people in the New Testament reflects a situation in which Christian groups were still small and vulnerable over against an entrenched religio-political establishment; but the language is repeated and intensified when the Church is no longer a minority and when Jews have become more vulnerable than ever. It is part of the pathology of anti-Semitism (as of other irrational group prejudices) that it needs to work with a myth of an apparent minority that is, in fact, secretly powerful and omnipresent. It is the pattern we see in the workings of the Spanish Inquisition, searching everywhere for Jewish converts who might be backsliding; it is the myth of the Elders of Zion and comparable fantasies of plots for world domination; it is the indiscriminate attribution (not only by certain Muslims) of all the evils of the

Western world to an indeterminate 'Zionism'. A rhetoric shaped by particular circumstances has become so embedded that the actualities of power relations in the real world cannot touch it. There are many instances where the habit of imagining oneself in terms of victimhood has become so entrenched that even one's own power, felt and exercised, does not alter the mythology.

Something of this kind is often going on in discussion about anti-religious polemic in the modern Western world. Many religious believers will respond with wry amusement to the survival of an eighteenth- or nineteenth-century rhetoric about the malign influence of religion in the state; even a state like ours with a religious establishment is not exactly a theocratic prison house, if the trend of recent legislation is any sign. But the issue is rather sharper where the religion in question is not the historic religion of the nation. In recent years, even more than at the time of the Rushdie controversy, many commentators have fallen into the classic 'anti-Semitic' trap: Islam is perceived worldwide as an organized, coherent and omnipresent danger, and Islam as a local reality in the UK is seen exclusively through that prism. If that is the world you inhabit, then something like *The Satanic Verses* or the Danish cartoons becomes a brave assertion of the right to attack the symbols of an oppressive global hegemony.

But the local reality is different. Webster points out how in 1989-90 Muslim groups in the UK took to a relatively militant response to Rushdie as and when it became clear that the literary and political establishment had nothing to say to their sense that their faith had been publicly and damagingly misrepresented and their sensibilities shaken. For groups like those in West Yorkshire who were at the forefront of militant reaction in Britain, the overwhelming feeling that animated their protests was that they, as a disadvantaged minority with the most limited access to any sort of public voice, were being left at the mercy of a powerful elite determined to tell them what their faith really amounted to, and to remind them that they had to get used to being seen, never mind the realities of their social and economic position here, as essentially the representatives of a foreign and threatening power. The same is true of the furore over the Danish cartoons: the Muslim community in Denmark is neither large nor militant, yet the cartoon issue was framed as if these products were a sign of courageous defiance towards a hegemonic power.

Now I recognize the qualifications that have to be entered at once. Some anti-Muslim images or words (foolish or insulting as they may be) may well exhibit courage in a world where terrorist violence reaches across every national boundary and intimidation is more and more common; no-one will forget in a hurry the murder of Theo van Gogh in the Netherlands. Likewise, we can't overlook the ways in which offence can be deliberately exaggerated for the purposes of fomenting greater violence (as was the case with the Danish cartoons, where some extremist groups circulated far more offensive images than those that had actually been published). But what if we exercise a little imagination again? What Webster describes as the insensitivity of an elite means that those who lack access to the subtleties of the English language, to the means of expressing their opinions in a public forum or to any living sense of being participants in their society know only that one of their most overpoweringly significant sources of identity is being held up to public scorn. This feeling may be the result of misunderstanding or misinformation, it may even be in some cases linked to a failure or reluctance to take the opportunities that exist to move into a more visible role in the nation's life, but it is real enough and part of a general conviction of being marginal and silenced. It is not a good situation for a democratic society to be in. The belief becomes entrenched among minorities that the majority in this society have decided to understand you and your faith exclusively in their terms. In the case of the bitter controversy in the Sikh community over the play *Behzti* in 2004, it was clear that many deeply intelligent members of the Sikh community in Britain were torn between the belief that the play would cement in the minds of audiences largely ignorant of the Sikh religion a distorting and negative set of images and the gloomy conviction that violent protest against the play would have exactly the same effect:[8] very much a no-win situation. Once again, there is the disconnection between the firm claim of an artistic establishment that protest against oppressive systems is justifiable, even imperative (and *Behzti* had identified a real and too-often buried concern among Sikh women), and the counterclaim that this kind of representation of a religious culture in front of what was likely to be a fairly religiously illiterate audience would be experienced as a straightforward flexing of the muscles by a hostile, alien and resourceful power. The British Muslim legal theorist, Maleiha Malik, invariably a voice of sanity and perception in these matters, has written of the way in which tendentious or positively misleading presentations of religion affect both 'insiders' and 'outsiders': 'Reflecting back to an individual a distorted or demeaning image of themselves will influence not only the perception of outsiders, it also impacts on the self-understanding of "insiders".'[9]

Abuse as something that can result in internalizing a poor self-perception is a familiar matter, not to be taken lightly. When we read some of the literature

of earlier centuries, we are likely to be taken aback by the casual way in which
the disabled are mocked and belittled; some of Shakespeare's scenes remind
us that a blind or mentally disturbed person could be seen, even by the most
humanly sensitive of all artists, as an occasion for cheap laughs. We have on
the whole come to recognize that insults directed at people with disabilities
are unacceptable, because the people involved are at a disadvantage, may be
liable to internalize what is said, and are likely to lack access to at least some
of the more obvious means of articulating and defending a position that would
be enjoyed by those likely to be making the dismissive or offensive comments.
Similarly, we have left behind the era when it was unproblematic to make fun
of other races or nationalities. Most would now acknowledge that offensive
and belittling ways of talking about individuals, groups or classes of people
presuppose that the object of such talk is *absent*. And if they are absent, they
have no voice. They may in some way or another have a chance to react but
not, within the same conversation, to interact and set out in that context who
they actually are. So that the moral question raised by some kinds of claim to
unbridled free speech is how far it can license the sort of language that assumes
the absence or powerlessness of the other. It is abundantly true, unfortunately,
that Christianity, like some other religious traditions, has itself at times in its
history been scandalously bad about this, and has established models of abusive
and demeaning talk about 'the other' (Jewish, Muslim, heretical, unbelieving)
that are as bad as anything that any contemporary Christian might complain
about in the mouth of a militant atheist. But the moral question remains.

And that is where I want to place the emphasis of this reflection. The grounds
for *legal* restraint in respect of language and behaviour offensive to religious
believers are pretty clear: the intention to limit or damage a believer's freedom to
be visible and audible in the public life of a society is plainly an invasion of what
a liberal society ought to be guaranteeing; and the obvious corollary is that the
creation of an offence of incitement to religious hatred is a way of avoiding the
civil disorder that threatens when a group comes to feel that it has been unjustly
excluded. Since the old offence of blasphemy, as we have seen, no longer works
effectively to do this, there is no real case for its retention. How adequately the
new laws will meet the case remains to be seen; I should only want to suggest that
the relative power and political access of a group or person laying charges under
this legislation might well be a factor in determining what is rightly actionable.

But beyond this is the larger issue of what is actively desirable for a liberal
society. We regularly treat discussion about the law as discussion about what we

can get away with, in all sorts of contexts, as if the law existed to define a 'lowest common' content for social morality. But, as most of us equally recognize in some part of our consciences, what is legally permissible is not necessarily thereby made desirable, acceptable or, simply, good. We may decide, as on the whole we have decided, that religion should not be protected by law over and above the ways we have just been summarizing; but that does not close the moral question of what are the appropriate canons for the public discussion of belief. I have suggested two points to ponder here. The first is to do with the far more general issue of civility in controversy: a coarsening of the style of public debate and a lack of imagination about the experience and self-perception of others, especially those from diverse ethnic and cultural contexts, the arrogant assumption of the absolute 'naturalness' of one's own position – none of this makes for an intelligent public discourse or for anything like actual debate, as opposed to plain assertion. I've sometimes used the term 'argumentative democracy' to capture what a genuinely plural social discourse might be. The law cannot and should not prohibit argument, which involves criticism, and even, as I noted earlier, angry criticism at times; but it can in some settings send a signal about what is generally proper in a viable society by stigmatizing and punishing extreme behaviours that have the effect of silencing argument. Rather than assuming that it is therefore only a few designated kinds of extreme behaviour that are unacceptable and that everything else is fair game, the legal provision should keep before our eyes the general risks of debasing public controversy by thoughtless and (even if unintentionally) cruel styles of speaking and acting.

But the second point is to do with what can sometimes underlie the thoughtlessness or cruelty. The assumption of the naturalness of one's own position is regularly associated with an experience of untroubled or uninterrupted access to the dominant discourse and means of communication in one's society. If I can say what I like, that is because I have the power and status to do so. But that ought to impose the clear duty of considering, when I engage in any kind of debate, the relative position of my opponent or target in terms of their access to this dominant means and style of communication – the duty which the history of anti-Semitism so clearly shows European Christians neglecting over the centuries. I have intimated that I think the law could and should take this into consideration where 'incitement to hatred' is concerned; but it is again primarily a moral question, the requirement in a just society that all should have the same means to speak for themselves. It can reasonably be argued that a powerful or dominant religious body has every chance of putting its own case, and that one might take with a pinch of salt any claim that it was being silenced by public criticism; but the sound of a prosperous and socially secure voice claiming unlimited freedom both to define and to condemn the beliefs of a minority grates on the ear. Context is all.

In this lecture, I have attempted to go a little below the surface in the discussion about what protection religious believers should enjoy from the law of the land, in order to pinpoint some of the related issues around what is actually desirable and morally defensible in a society that is 'procedurally secular' but genuinely open to the audibility of religious voices in public debate. It is clear that the old blasphemy law is unworkable, and that its assumptions are not those of contemporary lawmakers and citizens overall. But as we think about the adequacy of what is coming to replace it, we should not, I believe, miss the opportunity of asking the larger questions about what is just and good for individuals and groups in our society who hold religious beliefs. As a believer, I think, of course, that what is just and good for such persons is also crucial to the justice and goodness, indeed the sustainability, of the whole society, in a very strong sense. But I also think that even the unbeliever or agnostic might reasonably ask how authentic are the claims of our society to proper democratic pluralism if we cannot do justice to this particular kind of variety in our public life and conversation.

Do human rights exist?

Twenty-seven years ago, Alasdair MacIntyre in his seminal work on the foundations of moral discourse, *After Virtue*, declared that human rights did not exist.
'Rights which are alleged to belong to human beings as such and which are
cited as a reason for holding that people ought not to be interfered with in their
pursuit of life, liberty and happiness' are a fiction: 'there are', he says, 'no such
rights, and belief in them is one with belief in witches and in unicorns.'[1] The
language of rights emerges, MacIntyre argues, at a time when people need a fresh
moral compass in the wake of the dissolution of much traditional morality; like
the concept of 'utility', which is another characteristic notion developed in the
modern period as a touchstone for moral decision, the idea of 'rights' is meant to
act as a trump in moral argument. The trouble is, MacIntyre argues, that rights
and utility don't get along very well together in argument: one is essentially about
the claims of the individual, the other about the priorities of administration. The
result is the familiar modern stand-off between the individual and the bureaucratic state. The state is both the guarantor of rights – more clearly than ever with
the emergence of the 'market state' in which the most important reason for recognizing the legitimacy of a state is its ability to maximise your choices, as Philip
Bobbitt has demonstrated – and the authority that claims the right to assess
and on occasion overrule individual liberties. Hence the tension between the
state and civil society which has been so explosive a theme in twentieth-century
politics. The lack of mediating concepts to deal with this tension was identified
by Hannah Arendt, echoed more recently by Gillian Rose, as one of the roots of
totalitarianism. But Rose notes also the same problem identified by MacIntyre,
the way in which the stand-off between rights and utility leaves the path open
to an exclusively *managerial* account of political life, in which 'expertize' about
process is allowed to short-circuit proper discussions of corporate human goals.

MacIntyre's point is not, therefore, to deny the reality of human rights in
the name of some kind of absolutism; quite the contrary. He is anxious that

the language of rights and the language of utility are, as typically used in the modern world, no more than assertion – stop-gap notions to avoid complete relativism in public morality. This is one of the undoubted complexities in contemporary discussion of rights. On the one hand, 'human rights' is habitually used as a discussion-stopper, as the way in which we speak about aspects of social morality that are not up for negotiation or compromise. 'Human rights abuses' are widely seen as the most damaging weaknesses in a state's claim to legitimacy, and in extreme cases may be used as part of an argument for direct intervention by other states. On the other hand, what is often discussed in connection with both the Universal Declaration of Human Rights and the specifics of current human rights legislation is, in fact, a hybrid mass of claims to be decided by the state through its legislative apparatus; it is a quintessentially bureaucratic or managerial business, weighing various supposed entitlements against each other. If we speak without qualification of the right to life, the right to a fair trial, the right to raise a family and the right to a paid holiday under exactly the same rubric, it is very hard to see how this language can plausibly be understood as dealing with moral foundations. Fundamental issues blend with reasonable contractual expectations in a confusing way, and the idea of a list of entitlements dropped, as it were, into the cradle of each individual is deeply vulnerable to the charge of arbitrariness. MacIntyre's scepticism is well placed.

But if we are to salvage something from this, what do we need? Salvaging is important, if only for the reason that, if the language of rights is indeed the only generally intelligible way in modern political ethics of decisively challenging the positive authority of the state to do what it pleases, the only way of expressing how the state is itself under law, then this language needs to be as robust as it can be. In these remarks, I want to propose two ways in which a particular religious tradition may offer resources for grounding the discourse. There is now an abundant literature on religion and human rights, and a certain feeling in some quarters that there is a tension between rights and religious belief. It has been a good deal discussed in the context of Muslim critiques of the Universal Declaration, but Christian theologians have also voiced some unease about a scheme of ideas that places claims ahead of duties or even dignity. But I do not believe that this supposed tension is as serious as it is made out to be – so long, that is, as there is some recognition that rights have to be more than pure assertion or, as some would now have it, necessary fictions to secure a maximal degree of social harmony.

As Roger Ruston has argued in a very important study of the development of rights language,[2] the idea of irreducible or non-negotiable liberties for human beings has a strong theological basis in medieval thought. Paradoxically, it is in part the result of Christianity's confused and uneasy relationship with the institution of slavery. As is often pointed out, slavery as such is not condemned in Scripture, and is taken for granted, with varying degrees of regret, as an unavoidable social institution by most if not all Christian thinkers of the first millennium and a half of Christian history. However, from the first, the Christian community included both slaves and slave-owners; the letter to the *Ephesians* in the New Testament touches briefly on their relationship (6.5–9), as does *1 Peter* (2.13–25). The slave must give service as if freely to the Christian slave-owner, not as a response to compulsion, and being willing to serve the harsh master as willingly as the kind one; and the slave-owner must remember that s/he and the slave are alike bound in 'slavery' to one master. This last point relates to a passing remark made by St Paul in *Romans* 14.4 about refraining from judging another believer: you are not entitled to assess the satisfactoriness of the behaviour of someone else's slave.

The point is that the slave-owner's relationship to the slave is severely complicated by the baptismal relationship. The slave is no longer simply the property of the master or mistress, but 'belongs' to the one divine Master and is ultimately answerable to him, in exactly the same way as is the Christian slave-owner. As the Christian community develops and reflection about these issues continues, some implications are tentatively spelled out. In a world in which the slave-owner had powers of life and death over the slave, the Church determines that it is sinful to kill a slave (though the penitential tariff for this doesn't seem appropriately high to a modern reader). In a context where the slave-owner was assumed to have unlimited sexual access to slaves, sex with a slave is treated on the same basis as any other sexual misdemeanour; and marriage between a slave and a free person is recognized by the Church.

Stoic writers like Seneca had made it a commonplace that the master had no power over the mind of the slave; but no philosopher attempts to limit what ownership of the body might entail. The Christian attempt to think through the implications of slave and slave-owner as equal members of the same community inevitably qualified what could be said about absolute ownership, and offered minimal but real protection to the body of the slave. So it is not surprising that Thomas Aquinas, discussing the limits of obedience to earthly masters or sovereigns,[3] say explicitly that while 'a human being is bound to obey another in matters external to the body, in those things that affect the nature of the body, no one is bound to obey another human being, but to obey God alone – for instance, in matters to do with the body's sustenance or the begetting of children.' A slave cannot be commanded, for example, to starve to death; nor can he or she be prohibited from deciding on marriage or celibacy.

The principle that has been established is that the human body cannot in the Christian scheme of things be regarded as an item of property. It is not just that I have an 'ownership' of my body that is not transferable, though some moralists (including a few recent Christian writers) have tried to argue something like this; it is rather that the whole idea of ownership is inappropriate. I may talk about 'my body' in a phrase that parallels 'my house' or 'my car', but it should be obvious that there is a radical difference. I can't change it for another, I can't acquire more than one of it, I cannot survive the loss of it. The body (and this is where Aquinas and the tradition associated with him significantly refuses to accept a separation of 'soul' and 'body' as entities existing side by side) is the organ of the soul's meaning: it is the medium in which the conscious subject communicates, and there is no communication without it. To protect the body, to love the body, is to seek to sustain the means of communication that secure a place within human discourse. And so a claim to control the body absolutely, to the point where you could be commanded to deny your body what is needed for its life, would be a refusal to allow another to communicate, to make sense of themselves. The ultimate form of slavery would be a situation in which your body was made to carry the meanings or messages of another subject and never permitted to *say* in word or gesture what was distinctive for itself as the embodiment of a sense-making consciousness.

My own relation to my body is not that of an owner to an object; and to recognize another material thing as a human body is to recognize that it is not reducible in this way to an object among others. In that it is a means of communication, it cannot be simply instrumental to another's will or purpose. It is significant that Aquinas uses the examples he does. The nurture of the body is, for humans, more than an instinctive business; it requires thought and a measure of liberty. And the sexual involvement or non-involvement of the body is a primary locus for the making of sense; denial of this liberty is the denial of something absolutely fundamental (which is why sexual abuse is indeed a prime instance of rights being violated, the body becoming an instrument for someone else's 'meanings', a tool for the construction of another person's sense-making). The recognition of a body as a human body is, in this framework, the foundation of recognizing the rights of another; and to recognize a body as a human body is to recognize that it is a vehicle of communication. It is not a recondite point. The state of mind in which someone is unable to grasp that another's body is a site of feeling and so of consciousness and so of communication is routinely regarded as seriously distorted, whether we are talking of the difficulties of the extreme end of the autism spectrum or of the plainly psychotic. Our ordinary human interchange simply and straightforwardly depends upon understanding any apparently human body we encounter as in some sense a potential communicator with me. And when in the past people have sought to justify slavery or other forms of institutionalised dehumanizing, it has been necessary to restrict, often expensively and dramatically, their opportunity to communicate and to belittle their ability to do so. In George Steiner's extraordinary story 'The Portage to San Cristobal of A.H.', in which a group of Jewish agents have been given the task of kidnapping an aged Hitler from his South American hideaway, they are strictly instructed not to allow him to speak to them, because that will force them to see him as a human like themselves.

One advantage of putting the issue in these terms is that it takes us away from the more unhelpful aspects of those rights theories that stress the grounding of rights in human dignity, but then associate human dignity with a particular set of capacities. The danger of these is that, by trying to identify a list of essential capacities, it becomes possible to identify criteria according to which full claims to human rights may be granted or withheld. The right of the imperfectly rational person – whether the child or the person with mental disabilities – may be put in question if we stipulate a capacity for reasoned self-consciousness as a condition for acknowledging rights. And to speak of the right of the body as such casts a different light on the sensitive issue of the right of the unborn; the unanswerable question of when embryonic material becomes a 'person', let alone when it acquires a soul, still assumes a basic dualism about the body and its inhabitant or proprietor – where the way in which we ought to be framing the question is in terms of what counts as bodily continuity and what can be said about the 'communicative' dimension of the organic life of the unborn, how even the foetus requires to be seen and understood as expressing something to us in its character as an individual human organism.

But that is a complex set of arguments, and my aim for now is simply to establish that recognizing the human body as a human body, that is as a system of communication, by no means exclusively rational, let alone verbal, is fundamental for understanding why we should want to speak of rights at all, of equal liberties that are rooted in the liberty to 'make sense', that is to engage in communication. As I have said, it is in one way only to spell out the act of faith we make every time we engage in human communication at all. Yet behind that routine act lies something else, given that many human societies have in practice assumed that some human bodies are not worth communicating with or receiving communication from. Hence the point of excavating the theological insights that have moved us irreversibly in the direction that leads towards universal doctrines of right. Grasping that the body cannot be an item of property is one of the things that is established by the Christian doctrine of communion in, and shared obedience to, Christ. The doctrine affirms that the body of every other individual is related to its maker and saviour before it is related to any human system of power. This in turn implies that there is a level of human identity or selfhood that cannot be taken over by any other person's will – a level of human identity both bodily and subjective or interior. And this belongs with the recognition that the body *speaks*, that it is the way I make myself present to myself and to others. This holds true even for the most inarticulate, or those whose communications are hardest to decode: to put it as vividly as I can, they still have *faces*. Over against those who want to locate human dignity in the distinctive structure of the human self, a position which still skirts the risks of setting *conditions* for dignity, I want to propose that the character of the body as the vehicle of language is what is basic here.

Michael Zuckert, in a careful and interesting essay entitled 'Human Dignity and the Basis of Justice: freedom, rights, and the self'[4] makes a strong case for beginning from the character of the self as a mental structure allowing human beings to understand themselves as agents with an identity that continues through time and a capacity for envisaging future situations as resulting from present decisions. This is surely what is most irreducibly unique about us, and thus what grounds a universal moral code. But I believe he weakens his case by speaking of the self (following Locke) as proprietor of its experiences ('The relation of the rights-bearer to his property is remarkably parallel to his relation to his self'[5]). The embodied self as communicator, I suggest, is more than the self-conscious organizer of experience into patterns of continuity through time, past and future; it can survive the absence of this sort of self-awareness without forfeiting its claim to be treated as possessed of equal liberty in the basic sense defined earlier. Given the much-chronicled history of the abuse, psychological, physical and sexual, of the mentally challenged, of small children or sufferers from dementia, it is crucial to clarify our grounds for regarding them as protected from being made the carriers of the desires and purposes of others; if we begin from the recognition of them as embodied in the same sense that we are, we have such a clear foundation, in a way that I am not sure we can have even on so sophisticated a version of capacity-theory as Zuckert's.

If this is correct, the irreducible core of human rights is the liberty to make sense as a bodily subject; which means that the inviolability of the body itself is where we should start in thinking about rights. 'Man is "created equal"', wrote the poet and artist David Jones in the early 1940s, 'in the sense that all men belong to a form-creating group of creatures – and all men have unalienable rights with respect to that equal birth right';[6] and that form-creating character is anchored most simply and primitively in the character of what we mean by the very notion of a body (as opposed to an object). It is true, of course, that while the sort of Christian thinking represented by Thomas Aquinas laid the founda-tions for this, it still accepted extreme physical punishment, including death, for transgression, and of course did not understand the necessary freedom to determine the pattern of one's sexual life as a charter for everyone to shape their own destinies irrespective of the Church's teaching. The implications of Aquinas's view still allow the state to say that it will limit the bodily freedom of some of its citizens when that freedom threatens the freedom of others – though, centuries on from Aquinas, we have taken on board more fully the need for punishment both to respect the essential physical dignity of the punished, and to be capable of rational communication to the punished. The basic concept of right with which Aquinas works itself puts in question capital punishment or humiliating and damaging physical penalties. It is what grounds the modern refusal of legitimacy to torture, degrading or humiliating punishment or even indefinite detention without charge; significant markers in the age of Guantanamo or Abu Ghraib, and at least a significant part of the argument about the time limits for detention now being discussed in our own legislature. Likewise, this view allows the Church to say that there is a limit on morally acceptable options for sexual life; although we would not now understand this as licensing a restriction by law on the decisions people may make in this area. We are free to make bad or inadequate sense of our bodily lives, and the legal restriction of this, beyond the obvious protections of the vulnerable, would have to be seen as outside the powers of rulers. If the state legislates against sexual violence and abuse, as it must, it is because of the recognition that this is an area in which the liberty to make sense of or with one's own body is most often put at risk by predatory behaviour on the part of others.

So: equal liberty is at root inseparable from the equality of being embodied. Rights belong not to the person who can demonstrate capacity or rationality, but to any organism that can be recognized as a human body, at any stage of its organic development. If the body cannot be property, it will always be carrying meanings or messages that are inalienably its own. And this opens up the second area in which aspects of Christian theology offer a foundation for a discourse of universal rights. Thus far, the emphasis has been upon the view from within, as it were – the body as carrier of the soul's meaning, the body as 'formed', given intelligible shape, by the continuing self called into being by God. But the process by which the body realizes its communicative nature, by which it becomes concretely and actively a locus of meaning, is a process in which the body *receives* and digests communication. The individual communicates meaningfully when s/he is decoding and responding to the meanings that are present to him or her; the full development of the particular body's freedom to communicate is realized in the process of understanding, managing and responding to the communications that are being received.

The human other is thus essential to my own growth as a communicative being, a bearer of meaningful messages that cannot be silenced; my own liberty not to be silenced, not to have my body reduced to someone else's instrument, is nourished by the equal liberty of the other not to be silenced. And, in the framework we have been using, this is identified as the central feature of the community created by the Christian gospel. Slave and owner are not merely bound to a common divine Master, they are bound in a relation of mutuality according to which each becomes the bearer of necessary gifts to the other. The relation of each to the Master is such that each is given some unique contribution to the common life, so that no one member of the community is able fully to realize their calling and their possibilities without every other. Not abusing or killing the slave is, for the slave-owner, the necessary implication of recognizing that the slave is going to be his or her benefactor in ways that may never be visible or obvious, but are nonetheless vital.

The dignity accorded to the human other is not, then, a recognition that they may be better than they seem, but simply a recognition that what they have to say (welcome or unwelcome, intelligible or unintelligible, convergent or divergent) could in certain circumstances be the gift of God. Not every human other is a fellow-member of the Body of Christ in the biblical sense; but the universal command to preach the gospel to all prohibits any conclusion that this or that person is incapable of ever hearing and answering God's invitation, and therefore mandates an attitude of receptivity towards them. Not silencing the other or forcing their communication into your own agenda is part of remaining open to the communication of God – which may come even through the human other who is most repellent or opaque to sympathy. The recognition of a dignity that grounds the right to be heard is the recognition of my own need to receive as fully as I can what is being communicated to me by another being made by God. It compels that stepping back from control or manipulation of the other which we so often seek for our security, so as to hear what we cannot generate for ourselves. And it should be clear, incidentally, that this is an argument that also grounds whatever we might want to say about the 'right' of the non-human world to have an integrity not wholly at the mercy of human planning.

To found human rights on the body's liberty to express its own message, and the need for all embodied human beings to receive each other's meaningful communication in order for them to be who and what they are, removes from the argument those elements of conditionality which can creep in if we speak too glibly about capacities, whether rational or moral. Nicholas Wolterstorff, in the special issue of the *Hedgehog Review* already quoted, notes the way in which some other contributors insist that the discourse of human rights and dignity expresses simply 'an explication of what it is to treat humans as humans'; but he very reasonably goes on to ask why in particular circumstances I should treat *this* human being as a human being, if, for example, I conclude that s/he is a poor or inadequate specimen of humanity. If the appeal to treating humans as humans is not to be purely assertive or tautologous, we need more.[7] Something related to language about the image of God seems called for – but we need also to be aware that this language can't just be 'mentioned' as if it instantly provided a clear rationale for rights as we understand them.[8]

My purpose in these reflections has been to suggest precisely what might be involved in doing more than 'mentioning' the biblical themes. Is this, then, to argue that we simply cannot talk about human rights intelligibly if we do not have a religious or even a Christian foundation for doing so? Given that there is already more than one essay in grounding human rights in traditions other than Christianity (Abdulaziz Sachedina's work is a case in point, as seen in his contribution to the *Hedgehog* symposium quoted), it may be rash to make excessive claims for Christianity here. But the fact is that the question of foundations for the discourse of non-negotiable rights is not one that lends itself to simple resolution in secular terms; so it is not at all odd if diverse ways of framing this question in religious terms flourish so persistently. The uncomfortable truth is that a purely secular account of human rights is always going to be problematic if it attempts to establish the language of rights as a supreme and non-contestable governing concept in ethics. MacIntyre's argument, with which we began, alerts us to the anxiety and the tension that is hidden within the classical Enlightenment discourse of rights, the sense of having to manage the effects of a moral bereavement; and the development of that discourse in the ways we have witnessed in the late twentieth century does little to diminish the anxiety or resolve the tension. The question of whether there is anything at all that is quite strictly non-negotiable about human dignity –whether, for example, we might be permitted to revisit the consensus about torture when faced with the 'captured terrorist and ticking bomb' scenario beloved of some political ethicists – is not academic. Our instinct seems to be that something has to be secured over against the claims of *raison d'etat* in the name of a human 'form of life' beyond choice and convenience.

Sabina Lovibond, in her brilliant essay on *Realism and Imagination in Ethics*, has some pertinent reflections on Wittgenstein's remark that 'justification comes to an end': that is, that there comes a point where we have to stop arguing and accept that we have reached a level that is recognized as basic for any kind of human thinking.[9] 'Justification', producing reasons for doing this rather than that, comes to an end, she argues, 'not because we get bored with it, but because rational discourse unfolds within a setting not chosen by ourselves' – a setting which she, with both Wittgenstein and Hegel, associates with the fact of embodiment. When we grasp that our embodied state is the condition of everything else we might want to say about thinking in general and ethics in particular, we have arrived at the point where it no longer makes sense to ask for 'justification'. To speak of non-negotiable rights is to attempt some explication of this 'not chosen' dimension of our reality. And to be able to assess or even prioritize the wildly varied entitlements that are currently called 'rights' means developing some means of seeing how far, in a specific social context, this or that claimed entitlement reflects what is required for participation in any recognizable thing we could call human culture and discourse; how far it is inseparable from the imperative to allow the body the liberty to say what it means to say. We may, for instance, feel instinctively that the right to a paid vacation belongs to a different order from the right to fair trial; yet in certain economic conditions, guaranteed freedom for leisure is an intelligible aspect of possessing adequate bodily/communicative liberty.

The idea of a pattern of embodied interaction in which every body, literally, is equipped to 'say' what it has it in it to say, in intelligible exchange (which means more than a chorus of individual self-expressions), is, for Lovibond, the heart of an ethic that can seriously claim universality and objectivity, 'realism'. I would only add that, while this is an absolutely accurate account of the formal shape of a universal ethic (and thus one that can do justice to the language of inalienable right) it still leaves some unfinished business. I have interpreted the New Testament texts about slavery so as to suggest that the recognition that it is impossible to own a human body is rooted not only in the recognition of how the body works as a communicative organism, but in the conviction that the bare fact of embodied reality 'encodes' a gift to be offered by each to all, a primitive communication by the creator; the inviolability of the body is ultimately grounded in the prior relation of each embodied subject to God. And, as I have hinted here (and developed further elsewhere, as in the essays in this book on environmental issues), this has some application for the rest of the material order as well.

Political and legal philosophy is unlikely to arrive at complete convergence with theology in any imaginable future; but the way in which a theology may propose a frame for political and legal questions is not the less important for that. The theological perspective as I have tried to outline it here is, at least, a way of insisting that we should not pretend that the discourse of universal ethics and inalienable right has a firmer foundation than it actually has. If the Enlightenment has left us in some measure bereaved, it is important to accept that, and to ask what are the most secure foundations that can still be laid for our universalist aspirations. We should beware of looking for easy refuge in bare assertion or brisk functionalism about rights: but it is also important to grasp that universalism itself is not a simple and self-evident idea and that there are various ways of conceiving it outside the strict Enlightenment framework. Among those ways will be the various religious modes of imagining universal destiny or equal human dignity. These, I suggest, need to be engaged with, rather than dismissed as irrational or regressive. It may be that the most important service that can be offered by religious commitment where human rights are concerned is to prevent any overlooking of the issue of how to establish a 'non-negotiable' foundation for the whole discourse. As in other areas of political or social thinking, theology is one of those elements that continue to pose questions about the legitimacy of what is said and done in society, about the foundations of law itself. The secularist may not have an answer and may not be convinced that the religious believer has an answer that can be generally accepted; but our discussion of social and political ethics will be a great deal poorer if we cannot acknowledge the force of the question.

Reconnecting human rights and religious faith

The Universal Declaration of Human Rights is unquestionably a landmark in the history of moral consciousness, one of the factors that has consistently given hope and purpose to political life throughout the globe since it first saw the light of day in 1948. It has offered a global benchmark for identifying injustices to those who have never been able to make their voices heard. And, for all the challenges (which we shall come back to in a moment), it has been an energizing force in the witness of more than one community of faith in their struggle against arbitrary oppression and for the protection of the vulnerable. Yet the language of human rights has, surprisingly, become more rather than less problematic in recent years. The 'human rights record' of certain states is (very understandably) deployed as a factor in calculating political and economic strategies of engagement; but this has its impact on any idea that the language of human rights is, so to speak, 'power neutral'. For some, it can reinforce the notion that this language is an ideological tool for one culture to use against another. We have heard over a good many years arguments about the 'inappropriateness' of human rights language in a context, say, of mass economic privation, where it is claimed that a focus on individual rights is a luxury, at least during the period when economic injustices are being rectified. Both the old Soviet bloc and a number of regimes in developing nations have at times advanced this defence against accusations of overriding individual rights. But more recently, questions about human rights have begun to give anxiety to some religious communities who feel that alien cultural standards are somehow being imposed – particularly in regard to inherited views of marriage and family. And so we face the worrying prospect of a gap opening up between a discourse of rights increasingly conceived as a universal legal 'code' and the specific moral and religious intuitions of actual diverse communities.

In what follows, I shall be suggesting some ways in which we might reconnect thinking about human rights and religious conviction – more specifically,

Christian convictions about human *dignity* and human *relatedness*, how we belong together. Similar points may of course emerge from other kinds of religious belief. I believe this reconnection can be done by trying to understand rights against a background not of individual claims, but of the question of what is involved in mutual *recognition* between human beings. I believe that rights are a crucial way of working out what it is for people to belong together in a society. The language gets difficult only when it is divorced from that awareness of belonging and reciprocity. This is not just to make the obvious (and slightly tired) point about rights and responsibilities. It is to see the world of 'rights' as anchored in habits of empathy and identification with the other. And I shall also argue that a proper understanding of law may help us here. Law, I believe, is not a comprehensive code that will define and enforce a set of universal claims; it is the way in which we codify what we think, at any given point, mutual recognition requires from us. It will therefore shift its focus from time to time and it cannot avoid choices about priorities. To seek for legal recognition of any particular liberty as a 'human right' is not to try and construct a universal and exhaustive code, but to challenge a society that apparently refuses full civic recognition to some of its members.

The 'universal' aspect of rights, though, is a central element. What makes the gap between religion and the discourse of rights worrying is that the language of the Universal Declaration is unthinkable without the kind of moral universalism that religious ethics safeguards. The presupposition of the Declaration is that there is a level of respect owed to human beings *irrespective of their nationality, status, gender, age or achievement*. They have a status simply as members of the human race; so that this language takes for granted that there are some things that remain true about the nature or character of human beings whatever particular circumstances prevail and whatever any specific political settlement may claim. While this is not, as a matter of fact, a set of convictions held uniquely by religious people, religious people will argue that they alone have a secure 'doctrinal' basis for believing it, because they hold that every human subject is related to God independently of their relation to other subjects or to earthly political and social systems. Human beings are held to be created by God 'in the image and likeness of God', as the Jewish and Christian Scriptures insist; they are seen as having a responsibility to reflect in their lives the love, fidelity and justice of God – hence the Torah, the law in the Hebrew Scriptures and the various concepts of mutual nourishment and support in Christian Scripture, such as the language of membership in a single organism.

From one point of view, therefore, human rights has to do with the individual person, establishing the status of the person as something independent of any society; from another, it is a doctrine deeply opposed to 'individualism', since it locates this status of the person within a scheme that (logically) requires any person to acknowledge the same status in every other person, near or far, like or unlike. Every individual's account of their own needs or desires has to be thought about and negotiated in the context of this mutual recognition, this assumption of a basic empathy between persons living out the same human condition. Take away this moral underpinning, and language about human rights can become either a purely aspirational matter or something that is simply prescribed by authority. If it is the former, it is hard to see why legal systems should be expected to enshrine such recognitions. If it is the latter, its force depends on the will of some actual legal authority to enforce it; the legitimacy of such an authority would have to be established; and there would be no inbuilt guarantee that the *unconditionality* of the rights in question would always be honoured. The risk would be that 'human rights' would be seen as a set of entitlements specified by a particular political authority, and thus vulnerable being redefined according to that authority's convenience and preference and circumstances. It is not an academic point: in the last century, the Church in South Africa or the Democratic Republic of Germany, to take just two examples, was perhaps the most significant context in which universal, non-negotiable human dignity could be affirmed and defended. The struggle against apartheid in South Africa would have been very different without what the Church contributed; and in East Germany, the Church was almost the only place where free discussion was possible and different futures could be imagined, welcoming all who wanted to ask the questions that were prohibited in the public square. For rights language to lose the link with religious language and institutions would be for it to lose something historically crucial.

It is important for the language of rights *not* to lose its anchorage in a universalist religious ethic – and just as important for religious believers not to back away from the territory and treat rights language as an essentially secular matter, potentially at odds with the morality and spirituality of believers. As I have hinted, I think that we may be helped by some serious engagement with the question of the character and foundations of *law*. And, if we begin from there, we may find some directions for thinking about human rights that will help overcome some of the current confusion around this discourse and refresh our commitments. Odd as it may sound, a better account of how human rights relates to our thinking about the function of law could save us from a danger-ously thin version of rights as a primarily legal category, and from some of the confusions that come with that.

Law sets out what is expected of the citizen and what the citizen is entitled to expect. As legal systems develop, they codify in increasing detail these basic expectations, and affirm that such expectations are not simply at the mercy of what happens to suit a ruling authority or elite at any given moment. A law-governed society is one in which anyone belonging to the community has certain guaranteed liberties of access to protection against assault or to redress after injury. An important advance in principle was the abandonment of the idea that someone may be punished by having the protection of the law withdrawn: in early modern practice, outlawry disappears as a sanction, and the offender undergoing punishment retains a claim to some kinds of protection. While law is made and enforced by local juridical authorities, it is always bound up with some sorts of universalist claim. Within one jurisdiction, 'equality before the law' as a principle implies that the law deals with any imaginable subject of the jurisdiction on the basis that they are *recognizable* as belonging to a single community, and that this belonging is unconditional, whatever sanctions may be imposed by the legal system. Thus in modern legal practice, we generally work on the assumption that the wrongdoer's civic identity is to be preserved intact. In other words, the bonds that connect us are not to be broken by any arbitrary exercise of power: law affirms that something is owed to the fellow-citizen whatever may happen to either the society or the individual. But in a similar way, the idea of a 'law of nations' arises from the acknowledgement that different law-governed societies can recognize in each other comparable needs and dignities. The direction of development in all this is clearly towards some kind of universal principle, based on *the mutual recognition of a shared human condition.*

One implication of this is that every member of a society has the liberty to *argue* for proper protection if it seems not to be forthcoming. Law does not offer a comprehensive definition of the answers to such claims, but establishes a process for scrutinizing them and a way of ending debates by way of public decisions announced by recognized authorities. In this sense, law is bound to be 'reactive': what people think about themselves changes, what they think is possible changes, and the law has to assess whether any particular fresh claim that protection is inadequate is a reasonable one. And this is triggered by the kind of public argument that, if we look at recent and not so recent history, leads to major shifts in what we think is necessary to overcome the exclusion of certain people from the society to which they think they belong.

The point can be illustrated in many ways. The advance of legislation around the protection of ethnic minorities, not only from very specific kinds of practical discrimination, but also from demeaning public speech, reflects such a reactive move: 'civic discourse and practice', the developing moral and imaginative awareness of a society, lead us to recognize that certain ways of speaking and behaving habitually restrict the possibilities of certain groups, implicitly as well as explicitly. Where it has been commonplace to use stereotypic words and images of others, we come to see that by using such words and pictures we are in effect treating some person or group as people we need not fully *recognize* as fellow-humans and fellow-citizens, people who do not *belong* in the same way that we do. And once that is acknowledged, the law properly steps in to do what it is there to do to secure recognition. Again, in the last century or so, the principle has been increasingly applied to women as well as ethnic 'others': bit by bit, the law has identified some of the ways in which women receive less than full recognition in society, how employment opportunities are skewed by assumptions about the superiority of men, how the imbalance of power leaves women vulnerable to sexual exploitation or harassment. The law steps in to assert that women have received less than is due to them, and that practices that perpetuate this are now proscribed. Probably more rapidly than anyone expected, the same principles have led, in many parts of the world, to various enactments for the protection of sexual minorities (and it is important to put on record the consistent support of the Anglican Communion, in successive international meetings at the highest level, for such protection from violence and intimidation). At the moment, the vulnerable position of religious minorities is fast becoming a matter of urgency in many contexts. This is particularly acute where there is a vague tradition of tolerance towards a minority that has never *quite* amounted to full civic equality; heightened political tensions mean that this is now an anomaly that has to be sorted out. And in the light of all these issues and more, there is a growing set of questions about the proper protection of migrants, including asylum seekers. It is an area in which regression to attitudes of suspicion and harshness is in evidence in more than one society. It is going to need some stubborn arguments from those who believe that the sense of belonging *within* any one state or society and a sense of belonging *between* diverse human communities have to be kept together. And this is one area where religious traditions of hospitality, based in universal acknowledgements of human dignity, have particular weight.

The unifying conviction in all this is that, once we have acknowledged both that a person or group is properly part of our community and that they are *inadequately* protected, the law has to rectify the situation. The fundamental point is not so much that every person has a specific set of positive claims to be enforced, but that persons and minority groups of persons need to be recognized as belonging to the same moral and civic world as the majority, whatever differences or disagreements there may be. And I want to argue that a proper consideration of human rights has a better chance of sustaining its case if it begins from the recognition of a common dignity or worthiness of respect among members of a community than if it assumes some comprehensive catalogue of claims that might be enforceable. This implies that the language of human rights is an aspect of *culture* – what has been helpfully called 'a culture of dignity': it is the outworking of a steadily intensifying and more inclusive habit of acceptance, a wider and wider acknowledgement of belonging. The Australian ethicist Sarah Bachelard, in a perceptive paper on 'Rights as Industry', published ten years ago in Australia,[1] takes this further and argues that a sustainable and morally 'dense' commitment to human rights must have in its background the possibility of *love* – in the sense of a felt urgency about how human lives 'matter', how they are 'unique and irreplaceable'.[2] If it is seen first and foremost in terms of an agreed set of specific entitlements, there is a real inadequacy in this sense of uniqueness, of lives mattering. Instead of the language serving an awareness of infinite human distinctiveness, it can be boiled down to a strictly calculated set of claims, equally distributed to all.

I referred earlier to the Universal Declaration of Human Rights as a landmark in ethical development that has strengthened the hand of countless protesters against injustice, religious and secular. But it is still possible to misread it as just such a catalogue of entitlements, especially in a cultural setting where individualist assumptions rule. Take, for example, Article 23 of the Declaration, a very significant statement about economic life: 'Everyone has the right to work, to free choice of employment, to just and favourable conditions of work and to protection against unemployment'. Now, if we take this to mean that every individual is literally and legally entitled to a job (in the same sense that he or she is entitled as a citizen to a fair trial, say), there is no possibility of any universal assurance that such a claim could be met. Article 24 speaks of a right to paid holidays: even more of a problem if seen as entitlement. And what imaginable entitlement is there (Article 28) 'to a social and international order in which the rights and freedoms set forth in this Declaration can be fully realized'? We need to translate a bit. A 'culture of dignity' is, for example, one in which a person's freedom to work or access to employment is a significant moral touchstone; or it is one in which the conditions of work are not such as to prohibit leisure and self-care; or one in which the imperative to create a just and sustainable international order is given proper priority. We cannot pretend that gross inequalities in access to employment are really compatible with a proper sense of shared belonging; we cannot argue that a lack of international justice and stability have nothing to do with whether we are living with an adequate degree of respect towards each other. When we are speaking of 'rights' in the context that these Articles of the Declaration have in view, we have I think, to reconfigure the argument in more positive terms – in terms of what sort of considerations would be at work in a society (and a global 'society of societies') that assumed the need for maximal mutual recognition.

All of this implies that the law comes in at the point where there is a particular case in which some person or group is able to argue that they are insufficiently protected relative to others in that society. Thus, in an economically stringent situation, the law cannot create jobs; but it may remove unfair restrictions on who can apply for jobs in particular circumstances. The rest of the work has to be done by the 'culture' overall – the work that will secure educational opportunity and keep up the pressure for economic justice. The law responds to the cultural context when it can be shown that people have unequal expectations of how they will be treated. The claim that is being enforced is not a claim to some specific good (a job, a particular kind of education, a paid holiday), but the claim to be treated on the same basis as other citizens, to be protected against unfairness, because unfairness entails a failure of recognition, a lack of mutual acknowledgement.

All of which should make us cautious, I believe, about legislation that begins from a presumed *specific* right that calls for enforcement. At the moment, there is a good deal of discussion, for example notably in the UK, of whether there is such a thing as a 'right to die' (and thus to request legally recognized assistance in dying) as an aspect of the right to be spared intolerable pain or humiliating disability. But the problem that faces the legislator (and the judge) is this: legal recognition of a liberty to decide the moment of one's death, and to require professional assistance in securing this, shifts what we might call the 'default setting' of a society. It declares that securing this liberty by a change in the law is necessarily more urgent than securing the protection of, for example, elderly, disabled or seriously ill individuals who may be pressured to think themselves dispensable, encouraged to see their conditions as rendering them burdensome or substandard – or of practising physicians who are called on to make what are admitted to be highly complex decisions about the irreversibility of a medical condition or about a patient's state of mind. If we ask what is *protected* by a change in the law, it is not easy to answer. One might say, 'the liberty to choose to avoid suffering that could be terminated'. But if protecting such a liberty entails substantive threat to a significant quantity of other people, and if changing the law has the effect of changing an *assumption* that deliberately inducing premature death is not admissible, it cannot be reasonably argued that the 'right' in question must on any account be honoured.

What we are really talking about is, once again, a set of cultural issues and conundrums, not least about how much as a society we invest in care for those terminally sick or disabled, so that they do *not* experience anything that could be described as cruel or degrading treatment. There are real and tough arguments to be had about how we show adequate respect to a person dying in circumstances of unmanageable pain and loss of dignity; about how we properly value lives lived in circumstances of dramatically restricted comfort and mobility; how we avoid an attitude to medical care that seeks to prolong life at all costs, in a kind of technological triumphalism. There are delicate issues over what the attitude of the law should be in practice to people who resort to unlawful expedients in extreme situations. There is the fundamental question of what it is to die well. To none of these is there an instant and simple answer that would imply a right to 'assisted dying'. Arguments about all these questions are profoundly serious, and not everyone will begin, as most religious believers would, from the assumption that life is not to be surrendered in this way because every imaginable human condition is capable of being lived through in a way that relates it to God. But even without that assumption, the problem remains: faced with the possibility of a change in the law that is designed to protect a supposed liberty at the cost of removing a highly significant protection for the most vulnerable, I do not believe we can claim that this is straightfor-wardly about honouring a universal entitlement.

What this brings into focus is the anxiety that law is being used proactively to change culture – one of the chief anxieties of some religious people faced with developments in the application of rights. But surely it will be said this is exactly what is happening anyway when law establishes protection for previously unprotected or under-protected person or groups? Not exactly: when the law establishes protection or equality of access to public goods for a previously disadvantaged person or group, it declares that an agreed aspiration to a culture of dignity is damaged or frustrated by unequal protection and access. It secures what the very institution of a law-governed society is intended to embody, and it identifies as inconsistent or corrupt the refusal to extend recognition to particular persons or groups. Now laws change as societies become more conscious of what they are and claim to be; as I have said, it may take time for a society to realize that its practice is inconsistent – with respect to women and to ethnic, religious or sexual minorities. Law may indeed turn out to be ahead of majority opinion in recognizing this, but it has a clear argument to advance – that the failure to guarantee protection and access is simply incompatible with the very idea of a lawful society. But this falls short of a legal charter to promote change in institutions, even in language. Law must prohibit publicly abusive and demeaning language, it must secure institutions that do not systematically disadvantage any category of the community. But these tasks remain 'negative' in force. If, for example, a change in the law on assisted suicide is argued for on the grounds that the present situation unfairly stigmatizes those who seek to help a loved relation to die, because it exposes them to the risk of prosecution, it is important to ask whether it is the law's job (once it has secured the basic *safety* of every citizen) to accelerate changes in the social and cultural attitudes in this area that have traditionally supported the existing legislative position. The same question arises in regard to the demand for 'gender-neutral' marriage, if it is pressed on the grounds that the existing legal status of civil partnership implies a more marginal social position than marriage: the question has to be asked whether the law, once it has secured what it is there to secure, should be used to address perceptions of 'cultural' rather than directly legal status. Are these matters that need to be addressed at the level of culture rather than law, the gradual evolving of fresh attitudes in a spirit of what has been called 'strategic patience' by some legal thinkers?

But on such a basis, it ought to be possible to revisit the connection between religious belief and the discourse of human rights with an eye to avoiding the dangerous stand-off that threatens. The existence of laws discriminating against sexual minorities as such can have no justification in societies that are serious about law itself. Such laws reflect a refusal to recognize that minorities *belong*, and they are indeed directly comparable to racial discrimination. Laws that criminalize certain kinds of sexual behaviour need the most careful scrutiny: legislation in this area is very definitely to do with the protection of the vulnerable from those with power to exploit and harm. Sexual violence against women and children of both sexes is a tragic fact, especially in conflict-ridden societies, and the law's protection is urgently necessary. Go beyond this, and the territory is a lot more slippery. Many societies would now recognize that legal interference with some sorts of consensual sexual conduct can be both unworkable and open to appalling abuse (intimidation and blackmail). This concern for protection from violence and intimidation can be held without prejudging any *moral* question; religion and culture have their own arguments on these matters. But a culture that argues about such things is a culture that is able to find a language in common. Criminalize a minority and there is no chance of such a language in common or of any properly civil or civic discussion.

It is just this issue of language in common which belongs in the centre of a discussion of rights. Too often, the presentation of human rights as a set of entitlements to be enforced in law suggests a division between the routine language of an actual society and a universal and abstract account of human identity, as if there is a single universal positive jurisdiction that trumps every particular social and cultural order. The challenge for a mature political philosophy that seeks to avoid this abstract universalism is to hold together the proper universalism that accords everyone dignity and security with the diversity of actual social institutions, including religious institutions, that form our identities. What the law does, I have argued, is to insist that for a society to be worth the name of a *legitimate* society (one that doesn't rest only on the interest and success of the strongest), it must embody mutual recognition, the assumption that the other's experience is comparable to mine to the degree that we can talk about it. Legal equality is the way the space is secured for this kind of civil discourse. Rather than silencing the particularities of diverse communal identities, it allows them to come forward into a safe space both to argue and to collaborate. The shared acknowledgement of 'human rights' is, among other things, a guarantee that there is a shared social agenda to collaborate about – a common practice of scrutinizing what is going on with an eye to who is being left out and how they might be integrated better into the common activity of a community.

As I have argued elsewhere, following the seminal studies of Roger Ruston (principally *Human Rights and the Image of God*),[3] this takes for granted that every human agent is potentially a free contributor to a creative social practice, endowed with the capacity to make a difference to a shared social world. This is about the capacity not to enforce rights, but to be actively involved in *right* itself – in the struggle for justice. And this capacity is the ultimate foundation of 'rights' in the plural: what we recognize in one another is the creative capacity, as material, bodily presences, to make some kind of difference.[4] But, lest that formulation lead us into the error of making rights conditional on some sort of effective performance as a difference-maker (so that the child, born or unborn, the disabled, the aged, the mentally challenged and so on, are ruled out), we have to define the making of a difference in terms that bring in the sort of thing that Sarah Bachelard draws attention to in the paper cited earlier – the 'difference' that is my sense of wonder at the unique otherness of the other. Moral differences are effectively made in our world only when something of that wonder is activated; and the apparently powerless or silent human person (the child, the elderly person, the person with disabilities ...) has a profoundly powerful role in maintaining the moral intensity of more active agents *through whatever relations they make possible by their bare physical existence.* To put it as strongly as possible, it is about how certain persons are receivers as well as givers of *love* and make a difference, as both receivers and givers of love. For the believer, though Sarah Bachelard does not spell this out in these terms, it is rooted in the conviction that they are objects of an unconditional divine love.

And we are now bordering on the issue touched on at the start of these reflec-tions. The language of human rights becomes manifestly confused and artificial when divorced from our thinking about belonging, recognition, dignity and so on. It is vulnerable to being seen as a culture in itself – usually an alien culture, pressing the imperatives of universal equality over all local custom and affinity, all specific ways of making sense of our world. But what is it that grounds the moral vision that belongs with these things – belonging, recognition, dignity? The truth is that mutual recognition is a fragile thing: social exclusion and political oppression begin when the imperative to care only for those who appear instantly and obviously like us takes over; and it recurs constantly in human history. What Freud called 'the narcissism of small differences' translates into political terms when near neighbours sharing territory and often even language are driven towards mutual hostility by wider circumstances – food or water shortages, demographic projections, the suspicion of the other that is intensified at times of general social disintegration. The effects are horribly familiar: at worst, genocide, at the very least, the enshrining of massive discrimination.

To acknowledge the dignity of another person is in effect to admit that there is something about them that is, so to speak, *beyond me*: something to which my individual purposes, preferences, fears or hopes are irrelevant. The other is *involved* with more than me – or indeed, more than people that I think are just like me. Mutual respect in a society, paradoxically, means both the recognition of another as mattering in the same way that I do, sharing the same human condition, *and* the recognition that this entails their not being at my disposal, their independence, their distance from me. And this is where Christian theology comes in. Roger Ruston, in the book mentioned earlier, proposes that speaking about the 'image of God' in human beings puts 'the human person into a set of relationships: first with God, a relationship of filial adoption and answerability; second, with one another, relationships of equality and reciprocity; third, with the non-human creation, which may be understood as a relationship of stewardship and freedom of use.' And, as he goes on to say, these relationships are seen accordingly not as extraneous or accidental, but as constitutive of what human identity truly is.[5] What makes this theological principle so significant for 'human rights' is that this nest of relationships means that we cannot separate any human individual from a 'morally charged' environment, rooted first and foremost in relation with the Creator. Their life, and the lives of groups of such persons are of significance in the eyes of God; what I recognize in recognizing the dignity of the other is that they have a standing before God, which is, of its nature, invulnerable to the success or failure of any other relationship or any situation in the contingent world.

For human rights to be more than an artificially constructed series of conventions, embodied in a set of claims, there has to be some global account of what human dignity means and how it is grounded. It cannot be left dependent on the *decision* of individuals or societies to act in this way: that would turn it into a particular bundle of cultural options among others – inviting the sceptical response that it is just what happens to suit the current global hegemonies. It has to establish itself as a vision that makes sense of the practice of law *within and between societies* – something that provides a general template for looking critically at the claims of any particular society to be equitable and inclusive, not something that just represents the preferences of the powerful. A credible, sustainable doctrine of human rights must therefore be both modest *and* insistently ambitious. It must be modest in seeing itself as the legal mopping-up of issues raised in the context of a broad-based struggle for social equity and consistency – the negative face of what appears positively as the capacity to work for justice in a spirit of mutual reverence; but it must be ambitious in insisting on the dignity of every minority and their consequent claim to protection, to be allowed to make their contribution, to have their voice made audible.

The mistakes sometimes made are to be ambitious in the wrong areas and modest in the wrong areas – to be ambitious for human rights as a universal programme for what might be called affirmative action; to be modest about the uncompromisingly metaphysical or religious foundations that the discourse needs and about the 'humane' education of the emotions that is involved. Sarah Bachelard, mentioned earlier, quotes a poignant passage from Simone Weil in which the great French thinker observes that talking about a violation of 'rights' is 'ludicrously inadequate' to the situation of a victim of sexual abuse: 'That language', says Bachelard, 'gets no grip on the desecration of the fragile and vulnerable heart and body of a young girl through rape, ... the refusal to acknowledge the soul animating the flesh'.[6] Something more is required, something that allows us to experience the shock of violation.

Bachelard speaks of 'desecration', and the implication is clear that we need a vocabulary of the sacred here, a sense almost of 'blasphemy'. It is this that religious doctrine offers to the institutions and dialects of 'human rights', and it is a vital contribution. It is essential that, in an age that is often simultaneously sentimental, utilitarian and impatient, we do not allow the language of rights to wander too far from its roots in an acknowledgement of the sacred. This means, on the one hand, that would-be secular accounts of rights need to hear the arguments against an excessively abstract model of clearly defined claims to be tried before an impartial or universal tribunal. On the other, it means a warning to religious bodies not to try to make anxieties about their freedom to make religiously based ethical judgements an excuse for denying the unconditionality – and the self-critical imperatives – of the language of rights. Too much is at stake for the world's well-being.

PART THREE

Living with Limits: The Environment

Changing the myths we live by

In August 2003, in the middle of all the anxieties about climate change triggered by unprecedented temperatures, George Monbiot wrote in the Guardian that 'We live in a dream world', in which 'the superficial world of our reason' is constantly overtaken and frustrated by the deep, unspoken assumptions that really shape our responses to the world around, those assumptions that make us project 'our future lives as repeated instances of the present'. If we lived rationally, we should be taking instant action about those features of our present life which are making the human future more and more precarious. Since Monbiot wrote, the WHO has estimated that deaths from heat exhaustion (already 20,000 last year in Europe) will double within a decade. No wonder he says that 'The future has been laid out before us, but the deep eye with which we place ourselves on Earth will not see it'.[1]

Yet what his passionate demand for reasonable action both acknowledges and sidelines is that rationality alone doesn't address what this 'deep eye' sees. In an argument no less passionate and angry about our current unreason in respect of the environment, Mary Midgley insists that the problem is with 'the myths we live by' (the title of her outstanding book of 2003 on the stories that have created and sustained the contemporary cultural and technological world). She exposes the way in which reason itself has been co-opted into the great modern project of reducing the world to a store of neutral stuff that can be processed by the mind and will. But she also identifies a further complication, which is the behaviourist picture of mind and will: reason has been made to betray itself by means of a reductive account of material reality, and human reality in particular, in which we have a model of thinking and acting that is essentially no more than a description of loosely interlocking functions. Human thinking is a highly successful way of manipulating the environment, setting an agenda for other mechanical processes or functions. We end up with the very odd idea that mental activity is simply that form of material happening (neurons firing and so on) which has the best record in bringing other sorts of material happening into line with it. We have the worst of all worlds, intellectually speaking: an assumption that human mind and will are independent of the material world so that they can impose their wants and needs upon it; and a further assumption that to describe the problem-solving functions of the human brain is to describe thinking in the only way that matters, the only way that is 'scientifically' defensible. She offers some startling examples of the naked presupposition that what 'really' exists is sets of function-patterns which can be reshuffled at will to produce results yet more malleable to manipulation – including the designing and redesigning of humans as well as of other organisms. Programmes build better programmes, which, presumably, somehow set themselves ever higher 'aspirations' for improvement (that is, functional economy and rapid delivery of goals). And this is thinkable because of the underlying conviction that mental activity is essentially a programme for physical hardware.[2]

Midgley's discussions are invaluable, not least in the way they lay bare the alarming philosophical nonsenses that prevail in these reductive schemes, where metaphor is habitually confused with argument, and the self-destructive import of what is being claimed seems to escape notice. If this is reason, there is a pretty good case for superstition; or rather, as Midgley suggests, there is more than a case, there is an urgent need for different 'myths', a different set of symbols to organize the world of our experience. In Monbiot's language, the 'deep eye' has to learn to see something new. If we are to find any realism or truth in our engagement with the accelerating crisis of our environment, we need more than reason – or at least, more than reason defined in the professedly neutral way that modernity has sought to understand it. In this lecture, I want first to engage with the challenge to change the myth: Midgley is not very positive about what Christianity can offer here, since she tends to assume that what is normatively Christian is a degree of theological distance about 'nature'; and she (rightly) notes that early modern religion is one of the major contributors to the idea that the fate of nature is for it to be bossed around by a detached sovereign will, whether divine or human. But there is at least one radically different perspective that needs to be retrieved in the Christian repertoire of responses, one that, I shall argue, takes us beyond a generalized respect for the natural order. And on the basis of this, I want to suggest some of the Christian reasons we might have for regarding ecology as essentially a matter of justice for the human as well as the non-human world. From this, I shall move on to considering one or two of the most pressing problems facing us, to see how a different myth relates to the actual choices we must make if we are to have a human future compatible with the will and character of God.

First, then, to the 'myth'. The Christian believes that creation exists because God speaks: in both Hebrew and Christian Scripture, the Word of God is the foundation of everything. In Eastern Christian thought especially, this theme was developed in some depth, drawing out the implication that creation is itself an act of communication, a form of language. Creation is an address, an action that expresses an intelligence and asks for intelligent response. Thus the greatest Greek theologian of the seventh century, Maximus the Confessor, says that every existent reality is a *logos* (a word, an intelligible structure) that carries in a specific way the universal and eternal logos in virtue of which everything comes to be, the divine Word spoken of at the beginning of St John's gospel. The further implication is that each existent reality communicates, in and by virtue of the eternal Word, the character of God; and that to respond appropriately to creation is part of responding appropriately to God and indeed of knowing God. Creation itself is an act of divine self-giving, the bestowing of God's activity in and through what is not God; so for the created intelligence, the world is gift, a means of receiving something of the life of God.

In the words of a recent writer on this Eastern Christian perspective, such a vision 'puts material creation no less than intelligible in an intimate and dynamic relation with God'.[3] So to penetrate the workings of the world, to understand its intelligible shape, is to come into contact with a divine action that is reasonable – consistent with itself, accessible in some limited ways to our minds. In the language of Jewish scripture, true thinking, true knowing of the world is becoming aligned with God's wisdom, God's self-consistency in purpose and action, which the Jewish people thought of as a living principle in the universe. But because of this, true thinking is also becoming aligned with the intimate relation of the world in all its variety with God; it is to relate to God by being 'in tune' with the relation of the physical universe to God. If the world manifests the glory and love of God, it is a manifestation that leads to relationship; it is not simply a pattern that we admire, but an ordered life in which we can have a share. And, as the Romanian theologian Dumitru Staniloae has stressed, to understand creation as a gift from God, as something that makes relation with God possible, is also to become able to make creation a gift – to receive it from God in blessing and thanksgiving, to offer it back to God by this blessing and gratitude (that is, to let go of the idea that it is just there for our use), and to use it as a means of sharing the divine generosity with others.

Many Eastern Christian writers have emphasized that this picture gives a distinctive vocation to the human person as the one who is specifically and uniquely given a fully intelligible language in which to speak of God's gift and to celebrate it. Humanity, in the *Genesis* story, names the animals; the calling of the human person is to name the world aright: that is, to acknowledge it as God's gift and to work so as to bring to light its character as reflecting God's character, to manifest its true essence. Thus it is common to describe the vocation of human beings in this context as 'liturgical': human beings orchestrate the reflection of God's glory in the world by clothing material things with sacred meaning and presenting the world before God in prayer. Worship is not only a matter of words, but is a foretaste of the God-related destiny of the world, that longed-for state of creation in which everything can be clearly seen as bearing God's glory and love. And one signal and important aspect of sin is the refusal of human beings to undertake this calling, to refuse to act in a 'priestly' way towards the environment – to refuse to bless and give thanks, to refuse the right use of material things. The great Russian Orthodox theologian, Alexander Schmemann, goes so far as to suggest that the refusal of this calling is the very heart of original sin, which is the replacement of priestly naming and blessing by the attitude of the consumer, who seeks only to dominate and absorb things in such a way that it becomes impossible to treat them as gift.[4] And in case anyone should think that all this is a somewhat fanciful theological interpretation restricted to the Eastern Christian world of the Byzantine era, it is worth noting in passing that most serious scholars of Jewish liturgy would now agree that the layout and ritual of the Jerusalem Temple constituted a highly sophisticated representation of a restored paradise, in which the worship of heaven and that of earth were united, a theme which was deeply formative in the earliest Christian worship also.

To put it at its strongest, what this theology claims is that what most deeply and basically is the self-giving action of God; everything that happens to exist, everything that belongs in the interlocking pattern of the intelligible world, is, and is the way it is, in virtue of this underlying reality which is God's giving. This reality is eternal and self-sufficient in the life of God as trinity, as the everlasting exchange of gift between Father, Son and Spirit; but by God's free decision it is also the ground for what is not God. The secret at the heart of all things is gift, and the purpose of God in so giving a share in his action, an 'analogical' echo of his own life, is that what is not God may be suffused with God's joy. The fundamental myth proposed by Christian theology in this tradition is that

God's self-forgetting and self-sharing love are what animates every object and structure and situation in the world, and that no response to the world that is not aware of this is either truthful or sustainable.

Theology has to add, of course, that the myth is focused on history, on certain events. Our refusal of priestly responsibility is judged and then reversed by the act of Jesus, in whom God's self-giving is fully at work and who gives his entire identity as a sacrificial gift to the Father so that life and joy may return, so that paradise may be inhabited again. The community of Jesus is a priestly community, as the New Testament makes plain, a community whose rationale is blessing and giving, naming the world correctly and offering it thankfully to God in such a way that offering, giving, becomes the determining feature of relations between human beings as well. When the Christian Church celebrates the presence of its Lord at the Eucharist, it takes the material of the world and gives it to God so that it may become a fully and equally shared meal, a means of communion in Christ. The Eucharist manifests the destiny of all material things, which is to be effective signs of an accepting love that uses the material environment to express grace and justice.

For the Christian, intelligent, rational action in the world is precisely not the rationality castigated by Mary Midgley; but neither is it simply the self-evident reasonableness longed for by Monbiot. It is the expression of a radical and, we believe, truthful 'myth', the conviction that what we encounter is gift, so that we shall only tell the truth about the world as and when we treat the world accordingly – which means blessing the world as God's self-communication and asking constantly how we use the matter of the world to reflect the underlying and sustaining act of God. This is why for the Christian the connection between ecology and justice is axiomatic; it is no surprise to read in much contemporary writing on ecology that the irresponsible treatment of the environment both reflects and encourages an oppressive politics. To conscript the resources of the natural world into the struggle for power between humans is nothing new; but what recent decades have made clear is that this process has now reached a point at which the offence against the nature of things is no longer just a matter of moral and theological judgement: it has reached a point at which an offended natural order 'rebels', is no longer able to co-operate with undisciplined human will. The menace of radical climate change with which we began is only one instance; but the effects of irresponsible alteration of the ecology of life-forms in specific habitats (cane-toads in Australia, for example) show the same reality. There is a point beyond which the system cannot continue to operate 'normally'.

Economics can manage for only so long as a science that ignores the limits of material resource. A commentator from the New Economics Foundation observed in 2003 that 'To understand anything real about the world economy ... we have to understand the condition of its owner, the earth, and its biosphere'.[5] While economic analysis still refers to environmental factors in economic activity as 'externalities', the problem remains in the developed world generally of a divided consciousness, scientifically aware of but apparently practically blind to issues such as soil degradation, deforestation and a disrupted food chain. The great advances in corporate social responsibility in the business world, welcome as they are, will not of themselves undo the damage caused by our myths of limitless resource and trust in technology to solve consequent problems. Dominant in the whole picture, however, is the addiction to fossil fuel of the wealthy nations; this is what secures the steady continuance of carbon emissions, but it is also what drives anxieties about political hegemony. Since the oil production of relatively stable and prosperous societies is fast diminishing, these countries will become more and more dependent on the production of poorer and less stable nations. How supplies are to be secured at existing levels becomes a grave political and moral question for the wealthier states, and a real destabilizer of international relations. This is a situation with all the ingredients for the most vicious kinds of global conflict – conflict now ever more likely to be intensified by the tensions around religious and cultural questions. And in a world of severely limited supply, it is also clear that for less economically advantaged countries the chances of equal access to fossil fuel supply is negligible, as current DEFRA statistics plainly imply – which has implications for their economic development and the future of their civil society networks. A country engaged in modest industrialization and the modernization of health facilities can lose its professional class quite quickly if energy scarcities go beyond a certain level. And even within developed nations, there is the risk that, in a phrase of Ivan Illich (writing more than 30 years ago), high energy consumption will mean that 'social relations must be dictated by technocracy'.[6] Inequalities of wealth exist within 'wealthy' nations, and it is worth remembering that issues about access and control arise here too, and that the implications for democracy and justice are not always favourable.

One of the features of addictive behaviour is, classically, denial; we should perhaps not be surprised to find the divided mind I spoke of a moment ago in so much of our economic forecasting. But we learn to face and overcome denial partly by new relationships or new security about relationships enabling us to confront unwelcome truths without the fear of being destroyed by them. This is why myths matter, and why multiplying statistics doesn't of itself change things. That the world is the vehicle of 'intimate and dynamic relation' with the active and intelligent source of all life is some sort of spur to face our sins and absurdities in dealing with it. But we need to bear in mind also that we are talking not just about the respectful conservation of an environment for its own sake. Concrete material processes have, so to speak, caught up with the myth, and we should be able to see that offences against our environment are literally not sustainable. The argument about ecology has advanced from concerns about 'conservation': what we now have to confront is that it is also our own 'conservation', our viability as a species, which is finally at stake. And what is more, in the shorter term, what is at stake is our continuance as a species capable of some vision of universal justice. Not the least horror of our present circumstances is the prospect of a world of spiralling inequality and a culture that has learned again to assume what Christianity has struggled to persuade humanity against since its beginning – that most human beings are essentially dispensable, born to die, in Saul Bellow's harsh phrase. I needn't elaborate on how this makes absolute nonsense of any claim to be committed to a gift-based view of the world and of our individual and social relations.

There is in the long run no choice between this spiralling inequality (and the fortress societies it will create) and some realistic step to deal with our addictions. The Global Commons Institute, based in London, has in recent years been advancing a very sophisticated model for pushing us back towards some serious engagement with this matter of equality, through its proposed programme of 'Contraction and Convergence'. This seeks to achieve fairly rapid and substantial reductions in greenhouse gas emissions – but to do so in a way that foregrounds questions of equity between rich and poor nations. At the moment, rates of emission are fantastically uneven across the globe. In the first 48 hours of 2004, an average American family would have been responsible for as much in the way of emissions as an average Tanzanian family over the entire year. So what is proposed is that each nation is treated as having the same limited 'entitlement to pollute' – an agreed level of carbon emission, compatible with goals for reducing and stabilizing overall atmospheric pollution. Since, obviously, heavily industrialized, high-consumption nations will habitually be using a great deal more than their entitlement and poorer nations less, there should be a pro rata charge on the higher users. They would, as it were, be purchasing the pollution 'credits' of less prosperous countries. And this charge would be put at the service of sustainable development in poorer nations in accord with the Millennium Development Goals. This would be treated not as an aid issue, but as a matter of trading and entitlement.

The hoped-for effect in the medium term would be convergence: that is, a situation in which every citizen of the globe would be steadily approaching the same level of responsibility for environmental pollution. Because such a programme would necessarily challenge over-average users to reduce (otherwise an intolerable tax burden would be imposed), we could look for a reduction in the addictive levels of dependence in wealthier countries and a stimulus to develop renewable energy sources. We should also achieve a dependable source of development income, neither loan nor aid, for the countries suffering most intensely from the existing inequities.

This kind of thinking appears utopian only if we refuse to contemplate the alternatives honestly. Climate change has rightly been described by Sir David King, Chief Scientific Adviser to the Government, as a 'weapon of mass destruction', words echoed by Hans Blix, the former UN weapons inspector. In the current atmosphere of intense anxiety about terrorism, 'rogue states' and long-term political instability, we absolutely cannot afford to neglect what is probably the most deep-rooted source of further and potentially uncontrollable instability in the foreseeable future. We are already aware of the role of fossil fuel supplies in international conflict; we are seeing the beginnings (especially in the Middle East) of serious tensions around water supplies. 'Somehow we must persuade our dreamselves to confront the end of life as we know it' wrote Monbiot in 2003; my main contention here has been simply that fear alone fails to persuade, and that we need to change the dream, the myth, itself. We need a positive vision of the world that compels our love and respect. This is not simply a positive view of human nature. Colin Tudge, at the end of a lengthy and powerfully argued book on the future of food supplies through 'enlightened agriculture', *So Shall We Reap* (2003), appeals to the convergent vision of prophetic religion and evolutionary biology, which, he claims, preserves for us a deep intuition about not taking 'too many liberties with our environment', so that our humanity is fundamentally 'benign'.[7] The point about the convergence of religious and scientific vision is absolutely right, I think, for the reasons already set out – the palpable 'revolt' of the natural order against its distortion by human will. But I still believe that we need that further dimension which insists that the world is simply not understood if it is not seen as related to God.

I have argued elsewhere that the failure of secularism is that it cannot see things clearly in relation to anything other than human needs and perceptions now; the opposite of secularism in this context is not so much a set of systematic religious beliefs as a disposition to be aware of the dimension of unseen relations and connections in and between things and between all things and their source in God, that 'intimate and dynamic' relation evoked by the Greek Fathers. But this means, for the religious believer, that resisting the dominance of secularism is not primarily a political struggle for the rights of religious organizations, but a different sort of political battle – a battle against the reductionism that diminishes both the world and the mind or reason, against the strange versions of human knowledge and labour so scathingly described by Mary Midgely; a battle for the understanding of matter as the raw material of human justice and solidarity. For the Christian, it is, covertly but crucially, a battle for what Gregory Dix in his book on the liturgy famously called *homo eucharisticus*, that species of human being defined by communion rather than consumption.

And the Church's contribution has to consist not primarily or exclusively in public lobbying, though that is important, but in its showing forth of a different myth – the truth of creation's relation with the creator and especially the role of human work and thought within that. This is what is exhibited every time the Eucharist is celebrated. But this puts a considerable challenge before congregations as well: how easy is it to see in our worshipping practice and our habitual life together both a celebration of God's communication in what God has made and a process of conversion from the *homo economicus* towards the new humanity which restores blessing and justice to their proper place? A recent and welcome development has been the growth of 'eco-congregations', local churches or church groups signing up to a set of environmentally responsible policies for their day to day work as individuals and as communities. But there is still a gap in speech and practice at the level of our institutions as a whole. If we commend contraction and convergence, should the Churches undertake an ecological audit of some sort, to contribute to that change in the 'dreamselves' that we are advocating? What is really going on in the Christian's 'deep eye'?

Dumitru Staniloae described the self-communication of God to humanity as 'words turned towards the future of mankind'.[8] To understand the created order in its relation to God is to see what is possible and imperative for the human future, if human beings are not to be living in prolonged and finally suicidal conflict with the natural order. Yes, this is in a sense an anthropocentric perspective; what other could we intelligibly have, after all? But the centrality of the human in this theology is affirmed only in terms of the human calling to liberate and make sense of an environment which is always engaged in a prior relation with God; the humility that is thus enjoined on us is a constant check to the glorifying of the will. And the news for humanity is both joyful and sobering: there is a possible human future – but it will be costly for us. The question is whether we have the energy and imagination to say no to the non-future, the paralysing dream of endless manipulation, that currently has us captive.

Renewing the face of the earth: human responsibility and the environment

1

Some modern philosophers have spoken about the human face as the most potent sign of what it is that we can't master or exhaust in the life of a human other – a sign of the claim upon us of the other, the depths we can't sound but must respect. And while it is of course so ancient a metaphor to talk about the 'face' of the earth that we barely notice any longer that it *is* a metaphor, it does no harm to let some of these associations find their way into our thinking; because such associations resonate so strongly with a fundamental biblical insight into the nature of our relationship with the world we inhabit. 'The earth is the Lord's', says the twenty-fourth psalm. In its context, this is primarily an assertion of God's glory and overall sovereignty. And it affirms a relation between God and the world that is independent of what we as human beings think about the world or do to the world. The world is in the hands of another. The earth we inhabit is more than we can get hold of in any one moment or even in the sum total of all the moments we spend with it. Its destiny is not bound only to human destiny, its story is not exhausted by the history of our particular culture or technology, or even by the history of the entire human race. We can't as humans oblige the environment to follow our agenda in all things, however much we can bend certain natural forces to our will; we can't control the weather system or the succession of the seasons. The world turns, and the tides move at the drawing of the moon. Human force is incapable of changing any of this. What is before me is a network of relations and interconnections in which the relation to *me*, or even to us collectively as human beings, is very far from the whole story. I may ignore this, but only at the cost of disaster. And it would be dangerously illusory to imagine that this material environment will adjust itself at all costs so as to maintain our relationship to it. If it is more than us and our relation with it, it can survive us; we are dispensable. But the earth remains the Lord's.

And this language is used still more pointedly in a passage like *Leviticus* 25.23: we are foreign and temporary tenants on a soil that belongs to the Lord. We can never *possess* the land in which we live, so as to do what we like with it. In a brilliant recent monograph, the American Old Testament scholar, Ellen Davis, points out that *Leviticus* 25 is in fact a sustained argument about enslavement and alienation in a number of interconnected contexts. The people and the land alike belong to God – so that 'ownership' of a person within God's chosen community is anomalous in a similar way to ownership of the land. When the Israelite loses family property, he must live alongside members of his family as if he were a resident alien (25.35); but the reader is reminded that in relation to God, the entire community, settled by God of his own gratuitous gift in the land of Canaan, has the same status of resident aliens. When there is no alternative for the impoverished person but to be sold into slavery, an Israelite buying such a slave must treat them as a hired servant; and if the purchaser is not an Israelite, there is an urgent obligation on the family to see that they are redeemed. Davis points out that the obligation to redeem the enslaved Israelite is connected by way of several verbal echoes with the obligation defined earlier of redeeming, buying back, family land alienated as a result of poverty (vv. 24–28). The language of redemption applies both to the land and to the people; both are in God's hands, and thus the people called to imitate the holiness of God will be seeking to save both persons and property from being alienated for ever from their primary and defining relation to the God of the Exodus.[1]

A primary and defining relation: this is the core of a biblical ethic of responsibility for the environment. To understand that we and our environment are alike in the hands of God, so that neither can be possessed absolutely, is to see that the mysteriousness of the interior life of another person and the uncontrollable difference and resistance of the material world are connected. Both demand that we do not regard relationships centred upon *us*, upon our individual or group agendas, as the determining factor in how we approach persons or things. If, as this whole section of *Leviticus* assumes, God's people are called to reflect what God is like, to make God's holiness visible, then just or good action is action which reflects God's purpose of *liberating* persons and environment from possession and the exploitation that comes from it – liberating them in order that their 'primary and defining relation' may be realized.

Just action, towards people and environment, is letting created reality, both human and non-human, stand before God unhindered by attempts to control and dominate.

2

It is a rather different reading of the biblical tradition to that often (lazily) assumed to be the orthodoxy of Judaeo-Christian belief. We hear regularly that this tradition authorizes the exploitation of the earth through the language in Genesis about 'having dominion' over the non-human creation. As has been argued elsewhere, this is a very clumsy reading of what Genesis actually says; but set alongside the Levitical code and (as Ellen Davis argues) many other aspects of the theology of Jewish Scripture, the malign interpretation that has latterly been taken for granted by critics of Judaism and Christianity appears profoundly mistaken. But what remains to be teased out is more about the nature of the human calling to further the 'redemption' of persons and world. If liberating action is allowing things and persons to stand before God free from claims to possession, is the responsibility of human agents only to stand back and let natural processes unfold?

In Genesis, humanity is given the task of 'cultivating' the garden of Eden: we are not left simply to observe or stand back, but are endowed with the responsibility to preserve and direct the powers of nature. In this process, we become more fully and joyfully who and what we are – as St Augustine memorably says, commenting on this passage: there is a joy in the 'experiencing of the powers of nature'. Our own fulfilment is bound up with the work of conserving and focusing those powers, and the exercise of this work is meant to be one of the things that holds us in Paradise and makes it possible to resist temptation. The implication is that an attitude to work which regards the powers of nature as simply a threat to be overcome is best seen as an effect of the Fall, a sign of alienation. And, as the monastic scholar Aelred Squire, points out, this insight of Augustine, quoted by Thomas Aquinas, is echoed by Aquinas himself in another passage where he describes humanity as having a share in the working of divine Providence because it has the task of using its reasoning powers to *provide* for self and others (*aliis*, which can mean both persons and things).[2] In other words, the human task is to draw out potential treasures in the powers of nature and so to realize the convergent process of humanity and nature discovering in collaboration what they can become. The 'redemption' of people and material life in general is not a matter of resigning from the business of labour and of transformation (as if we could), but the search for a form of action that will preserve and nourish an interconnected development of humanity and its environment. In some contexts, this will be the deliberate *protection* of the environment from harm: in a world where exploitative and aggressive behaviour is commonplace, one of the 'providential' tasks of human beings must be to limit damage and to secure space for the natural order to exist unharmed. In others, the question is rather how to use the natural order for the sake of human nourishment and security without pillaging its resources and so damaging its inner mechanisms for self-healing or self-correction. In both, the fundamental requirement is to discern enough of what the processes of nature truly are to be able to engage intelligently with them.

And all of this suggests some definitions of what unintelligent and ungodly relation with the environment looks like. It is partial: that is, it refuses to see or understand that what can be grasped about natural processes is likely to be only one dimension of interrelations far more complex than we can gauge. It focuses on aspects of the environment that can be comparatively easily manipulated for human advantage and ignores inconvenient questions about what less obvious connections are being violated. It is indifferent, for example, to the way in which biodiversity is part of the self-balancing system of the world we inhabit. It is impatient: it seeks returns on labour that are prompt and low-cost, without consideration of long-term effects. It avoids or denies the basic truth that the environment as a material system is finite and cannot indefinitely regenerate itself in ways that will simply fulfil human needs or wants. And when such unintelligent and ungodly relation prevails, the risks should be obvious. We discover too late that we have turned a blind eye to the extinction of a species that is essential to the balance of life in a particular context. Or we discover too late that the importation of a foreign life-form, animal or vegetable, has upset local ecosystems, damaging soil or neighbouring life-forms. We discover that we have come near the end of supplies (of fossil-fuels, for example) on which we have built immense structures of routine expectation. Increasingly, we have to face the possibility not only of the now familiar problems of climate change, bad enough as these are, but of a whole range of 'doomsday' prospects. Martin Rees's 2003 book, *Our Final Century*, outlined some of these, noting also that the technology which in the hands of benign agents is assumed to be working for the good of humanity is the same technology which, universally available on the internet, can enable 'bio-terror', the threat to release pathogens against a population. This feels like an ultimate reversal of the relation between humanity and environment envisaged in the religious vision – the material world's processes deliberately harnessed to bring about domination by violence; though, when you think about it, it is only a projection of the existing history of military technology.

A. S. Byatt's novel *The Biographer's Tale* tells the story (or rather a set of inter-connected stories) of a writer engaging with the literary remains of a diverse collection of people, including Linnaeus, the great Swedish botanist. Late in the book, Fulla, a Swedish entomologist, holds forth to the narrator and his friends about the varieties of devastation the world faces because of our ignorance of insect life, specifically the life of bees.[3] 'She told fearful tales of possible lurches in the population of pollinators (including those of the crops we depend on for our own lives). Tales of the destruction of the habitats by humans, and of benign and necessary insects, birds, bats and other creatures, by crop-spraying and road-building ... Of the need to find other (often better) pollinators, in a world where they are being extinguished swiftly and silently. Of the fact that there are only 39 qualified bee taxonomists in the world, whose average age is 60 ... Of population problems, and feeding the world, and sesbania, a leguminous crop which could both hold back desertification, because it binds soil, and feed the starving, but for the fact that no one has studied its pollinators or their abundance or deficiency, or their habits, in sufficient detail.' It is a potent catalogue of unintelligence.

Earlier in the book,[4] Fulla has said that 'We are an animal that needs to use its intelligence to mitigate the effects of its intelligence on the other creatures' – a notable definition in the contemporary context of what the Levitical call to redemption might mean. We cannot *but* use our intelligence in our world, and we are bound to use it, as Fulla's examples suggest, to supply need, to avoid famine and suffering. If the Christian vision outlined by Aquinas is truthful, intelligence is an aspect of sharing in God's Providence and so it is committed to providing for others. But God's Providence does not promote the good only of one sector of creation; and so we have to use our intelligence to seek the good of the whole system of which we are a part. The limits of our creative manipulation of what is put before us in our environment are not instantly self-evident, of course; but what is coming into focus is the level of risk involved if we never ask such a question, if we collude with a social and economic order that apparently takes the possibility of unlimited advance in material prosperity for granted, and systematically ignores the big picture of global interconnectedness (in economics or in ecology).

Ecological questions are increasingly being defined as issues of justice; climate change has been characterized as a matter of justice both to those who now have no part in decision-making at the global level yet bear the heaviest burdens as a consequence of the irresponsibility of wealthier nations, and to those who will succeed us on this planet – justice to our children and grand-children (this is spelled out clearly in Paula Clifford's new book, *Angels with Trumpets: the Church in a time of global warming*[5]). So the major issue we need to keep in view is how much injustice is let loose by any given set of economic or manufacturing practices. We can't easily set out a straightforward code that will tell us precisely when and where we step across the line into the unintelligence and ungodliness I have sketched. But we can at least see that the question is asked, and asked on the basis of a clear recognition that there is no way of manipulating our environment that is without cost or consequence – and thus also of a recognition that we are inextricably bound up with the destiny of our world. There is no guarantee that the world we live in will 'tolerate' us indefinitely if we prove ourselves unable to live within its constraints.

Is this, as some would claim, a failure to trust God, who has promised faith-fulness to what he has made? I think that to suggest that God might intervene to protect us from the corporate folly of our practices is as unchristian and unbiblical as to suggest that he protects us from the results of our individual folly or sin. This is not a creation in which there are no real risks; our faith has always held that the inexhaustible love of God cannot compel justice or virtue; we are capable of doing immeasurable damage to ourselves as individuals, and it seems clear that we have the same terrible freedom as a human race. God's faithfulness stands, assuring us that even in the most appalling disaster love will not let us go; but it will not be a safety net that guarantees a happy ending in this world. Any religious language that implies this is making a nonsense of the prophetic tradition of the Old Testament and the urgency of the preaching of Jesus.

But to say this is also to be reminded of the fact that intelligence *is* given to us; we are capable of changing our situation – and, as A. S. Byatt's character puts it, using our intelligence to limit the ruinous effect of our intelligence. If we can change things so appallingly for the worse, it is possible to change them for the better also. But, in Christian terms, this needs a radical change of heart, a conversion; it needs another kind of 'redemption', which frees us from the trap of an egotism that obscures judgement. Intelligence in regard to the big picture of our world is no neutral thing, no simple natural capacity of reasoning; it needs grace to escape from the distortions of pride and acquisitiveness. One of the things we as Christians ought to be saying in the context of the ecological debate is that human reasoning in its proper and fullest sense requires an awareness of our participation in the material processes of the world and thus a sense of its own involvement in what it cannot finally master. Being rational is not a wholly detached capacity, examining the phenomena of the world from a distance, but a set of skills for finding our way around in the physical world.

3

The ecological crisis challenges us to be reasonable. Put like that, it sounds banal; but given the level of irrationality around the question, it is well worth saying, especially if we are clear about the roots of reasoning in these 'skills' of negotiating the world of material objects. I don't intend to discuss in detail the rhetoric of those who deny the reality of climate change, except to say that rhetoric (as King Canute demonstrated) does not turn back rising waters. If you live in Bangladesh or Tuvalu, scepticism about global warming is precisely the opposite of reasonable: 'negotiating' this environment means recognizing the fact of rising sea levels; and understanding what is happening necessarily involves recognizing how rising temperatures affect sea levels. It is possible to argue about the exact degree to which human intervention is responsible for these phenomena (though it would be a quite remarkable coincidence if massively increased levels of carbon emissions merely *happened* to accompany a routine cyclical change in global temperatures, given the obvious explanatory force of the presence of these emissions), but it is not possible rationally to deny what the inhabitants of low-lying territories in the world routinely face as the most imminent threat to their lives and livelihoods.

And what the perspective of faith – in particular of Christian faith – brings to this discussion is the insight that we are not and don't have to be God. For us to be reasonable and free and responsible is for us to live in awareness of our limits and dependence. It is no lessening of our dignity as humans, let alone our rationality and liberty as humans, if we exercise these 'godlike' gifts in the context of bodies that are fragile and mortal and a world that we do not completely control. I recently suggested that the current financial crisis had more to do with pride than with greed – understanding pride as the attempt to forget or obliterate our sense of living within limits and lacking total control. Intelligent life in these circumstances is not the triumphant imposition of human will upon a defeated natural order, but the reasoned discovery of how we live in such a way as not to destroy a balance in the natural order which we sense rather than fully grasp. It is to turn away from denial – from all those denials of our finite condition that were summed up many years since in a famous book by Ernst Becker, *The Denial of Death*, in which he identified the basic pathology of the human mind as the fantasy of being 'self-created'.

Such denial is not properly understood as deliberate refusal of the truth; it is in large part a consequence of the perceived complexity of the global situation, a complexity that produces both paralysis in some areas and a stubborn adherence to failed or out-dated paradigms. Jonathon Porritt, in his magisterial essay on *Capitalism as if the World Matters*, ascribes the 'continuing, utterly perverse denial on the part of politicians' to a failure to grasp that much of the very complexity which makes people stick to policies they think they understand is itself the result of 'the dominant paradigm of progress through exponential economic growth'.[6] Unfortunately, he goes on, too few politicians who *have* grasped the issue have worked out carefully enough what 'transitional strategies' would be possible for the reimagining of a broadly capitalist practice (that is, an economic practice that values risk and innovation and enables increased collective wealth through trade) that was not systematically disastrous for the environment. His book attempts to offer some starting points for such work – noting, soberly, that denial of a different kind afflicts many Green movements, whose campaigning style allows them to be dismissed or at best patronized by actual decision-makers. Among the strategies discussed is the crucial call to alter the way in which we calculate cost and profit so as to include some sort of monetary valuation of the depletion of natural capital and also some way of assessing impacts on individual and social well-being. One consequence of taking this seriously would be one or another form of carbon taxation. In the same way, more positively, we need ways of redefining business excellence in terms of sustainability and deliberate encouragement of low-carbon technologies. An economic world in which environmental responsibility was rewarded, was assumed to be a routine aspect of practice that was both ethically defensible *and* profitable, would have a very different flavour from what we have generally seen for most of the last couple of centuries. And it is also an area in which the pressure of the 'ordinary' consumer can make a perceptible difference. More broadly, Porritt rightly underlines the close connection of all this with what we ought to be saying about 'political virtue'. We must find ways of opening up a proper discussion of how to restore a sustainable democratic politics in a world where unbridled economic liberalism has in many contexts eroded the authority of elected governments and led some to believe that there is no alternative to current global capitalism but economies of the most static and protectionist kind.

All these proposals illustrate what an *intelligent* response to the environmental crisis might look like. Porritt is clear that this needs grounding in carefully defined common values and in the renewal of civil society through the articulating and promoting of such values—including the recognition of the interdependence of all things and of the equal significance of diverse kinds of 'capital' – social and human as much as material or natural.[7] In other words, intelligence comes to life when a kind of empathy and imagination is stirred by a new vision of things: intelligence alone does not generate new vision, and bare argument does not on the whole change things; but vision displayed in new forms of human life and engagement can renew intelligence in the sense I have been giving to the word. And this is where the significance of the perspectives of faith is most obvious.

4

Renewing the face of the earth, then, is an enterprise not of imposing some private human vision on a passive nature, but of living in such a way as to bring more clearly to light the interconnectedness of all things and their dependence on what we cannot finally master or understand. This certainly involves a *creative* engagement with nature, seeking to work with those natural powers whose working gives us joy, as St Augustine says, in order to enhance human liberty and well-being. But that creative work will always be done in consciousness of costs, seen and unseen, and will not be dominated by fantasies about unconditional domination. It is a vision that, in the Christian context, is founded on the idea of humanity as having a 'priestly' relationship with the natural order: the human agent is created with the capacity to make sense of the environment and to move it into a closer relation with its creator by drawing out of it its capacity to become a sign of love and generosity. This entails so using the things of the earth that they promote justice between human beings – making sense so as to make peace, equity and so on, using the skills of negotiating the environment in order to alleviate suffering and spread resources. Used in this way, the raw material of the environment is seen as serving human need – but only by being used in awareness of its own integrity and its own constraints. It remains itself, but in its use for the sake of healing or justice becomes 'sacramental' of the infinite gift from which it originates. The 'face' of the earth becomes an aspect of the face of God. And a good many theologians have started from here in explaining what the actual sacraments of the Church mean – especially the Eucharist – as the first fruits of a world of material things that has been given meaning in the context of communicating divine generosity.

All this echoes what St Paul touches on in *Romans* 8: creation is in some sense frustrated so long as humanity is 'unredeemed'. The world is less than it might be so long as human beings are less than they might be, since the capacity of human beings to shape the material environment into a sign of justice and generosity is blocked by human selfishness. In the doomsday scenarios we are so often invited to contemplate, the ultimate tragedy is that a material world capable of being a manifestation in human hands of divine love is left to itself, as humanity is gradually choked, drowned or starved by its own stupidity. The disappearance of humanity from a globe no longer able to support it would be a terrible negation of God's purpose for a world in which created intelligence draws out the most transformative and rich possibilities in its material home. As is true in various ways throughout the whole created order, humanity and its material context are made so that they may find fulfilment in their relationship. Without each other they are not themselves. And the deliberate human refusal of this shared vocation with and within the material order of things is thus an act of rebellion against the creator.

Which is why Christians are bound to set all this discussion in the context of that divine practice which decisively redeems humankind. God restores relationship with himself through the life, death and resurrection of Jesus: he shows his face to us and, as St Paul says in *2 Corinthians*, our own faces are 'unveiled' as we advance towards God. We are revealed for who or what we are. And in this event we become able to reveal what the entire material world is for, to display it as a sign of love by our loving and just use of it – and by our contemplative respect for it and our capacity to let it be. The grace set free in Christ's work allows us to be liberated from the murderous anxiety that drives us to possessive models of engagement. Liberated ourselves, we become able to act liberatingly towards the world we inhabit and whose materiality we share and depend upon. Our own redemption is the re-creation of our intelligence.

The contemporary Greek theologian, Christos Yannaras, has developed a rich and complex metaphysics of relation, stressing that Christian theology sees the human person as purely abstract if cut off from relation with God and others *and* the material world. He diagnoses the malaise of modern Western society (in politics, philosophy, art and religion) very much in terms of a loss of relation and what goes with it, a loss of the sense of vocation to a sort of 'artistic' transformation of the world. Technology, Yannaras argues, is toxic when it forgets this artistic and transformational dimension – that is (in the terms I've been using here) when it loses its proper human intelligence. But it is a particular image used by Yannaras that perhaps expresses most simply what a Christian account of responsibility in our environment comes down to. In his book of meditations, *Variations on the Song of Songs*, he speaks of how love compels you to see things differently – to love 'the landscapes we have looked at together.' And so if we fall in love with God, even fleetingly, all the sense impressions of this world become part of such a common 'landscape'.[8] We love what we see together with God; and, as I have argued before, if God sees the world he has made as 'very good', I must begin to see it with his eyes and so to sense in it the promise of his beauty. It becomes, in Yannaras's vocabulary, 'a gift of erotic joy' – an encounter with something that generates desire beyond utterance or final fulfilment.

Now it may be a long way from the technicalities of recalculating economic gains in terms of environmental cost to the experience of 'erotic joy' in relation to God. But the distinctive Christian approach to responsibility for our environment has somehow to hold these two languages together. Finally, our care for the world we inhabit is not simply a duty laid upon us, but a dimension of life made whole: a redeeming activity grounded in the character of our own redemption, a revelation of the true 'face' of creation as we ourselves undergo the uncovering of our own human face before God. Going back to the root meaning of the Hebrew word, what we're asked to undertake is in fact a conversion, a turning, *towards* the truth: towards the God who is eternally active and giving in ways beyond our concepts, towards the hidden depths of who we ourselves are – and thus towards the face of the earth, seeing it freshly in its unfathomable interrelatedness. As Psalm 104 (vv. 29–30) has it, when God hides his face, creation is locked in fear and slips towards death; when he breathes on creation (when he 'sends his spirit'), creation happens all over again, and the face of the earth is renewed. That turning of the Spirit towards the earth is the movement that carries our love and intelligence in the same direction, so that we can properly make answer for, be responsible for, our world.

Climate crisis:
fashioning a Christian response

As a matter of fact, I don't want to begin by discussing climate crisis, despite the title of this chapter. I believe that we shall be able to shape a robust and creative Christian response to this or any other of our current crises only if we step back a bit and try to understand why so much of what's wrong has its roots in a shared cultural and spiritual crisis. The nature of that crisis could be summed up rather dramatically by saying that it's a loss of a sense of what life is. I don't mean 'the meaning of life' in the normal way we use that phrase. I mean a sense of life as the web of interactions, mutual givings and receivings, that makes up the world we inhabit. Seeing this more clearly helps us dismantle the strange fictions we create about ourselves as human beings. We are disconnected and we need to be reintroduced to life.

So I'm going to outline some of the ways in which the Jewish and Christian traditions offer a way into this – not least through the remarkable story of Noah. I'm going to try and show how the biblical picture presents us with a humanity that can never be itself without taking on the care and protection of the life of which it's a part. And I want also to make some links to other aspects of our present situation that intensify the feeling of crisis, and to suggest how our responses to the climate crisis and other ecological challenges naturally feeds into our responses to the wider economic and social malaise as well. I'll have something to say about the practical steps we can all take in response to these things; but at the heart is the challenge to live with different images in our minds. The story of Noah is a great archetypal story, one to which we constantly return to learn something of the truth of our own situation and make better sense of it. So let's start with some of the familiar images from that story.

1

If there's one thing most people still remember about Noah and the flood, it's that the ark was full of animals. Thanks to a variety of popular songs – including the children's cantata, *Captain Noah and his Floating Zoo*, which we have probably all heard at primary school concerts, and plenty of picture books and cartoons, you're likely to think of Noah as surrounded by the animals who came in two by two. Forgetting for a moment the complications of the biblical text, with its distinction between the seven pairs of ritually clean animals and the single pair of unclean animals required, the story is clearly about how the saving of the human future is inseparable from securing a future for all living things. It's not just that Noah collects specimens of animal life; he collects breeding pairs, and, when the floodwaters have subsided, they are famously told to go and 'multiply' (*Genesis* 8.17). Noah is made responsible for the continuation of what we would call an ecosystem. In all sorts of ways, the story in Genesis deliberately echoes the story of creation itself, using many of the same words and phrases. The creation stories of *Genesis* 1 and 2 see the creation of humanity as quite specifically the creation of an agent, a person, who can care for and protect the animal world, reflecting the care of God himself who enjoys the goodness of what he has made. With Noah, that care is expressed in terms of saving a future in which humanity and the animal world share the same space.

In the words of the theologian Michael Northcott, 'In contrast to the prideful destruction visited on the earth by his violent neighbours, Noah submits patiently to the humble demands of caring for the many animals he intends to save from destruction.'[1] The image of Noah summoning the creatures to the ark may also be meant to recall God bringing the animals to Adam so that they can be named (*Genesis* 2.19): once on the scene, humanity has to establish its relationship with the animal world, a relationship in which meaning is given to the whole world of living things through the human reflection of God's sustaining care.

I shan't labour the point that reading Genesis as if it licensed the exploitation of the rest of creation is a major mistake. Nothing could be clearer in the biblical text than the belief that humanity is meaningless seen independently of the world of diverse life forms in which it is embedded. The flood story ends with the making of a covenant, a binding treaty, not just between God and humanity, but between God and all living things (*Genesis* 9.8–17): God is committed to life, to the continuance of life on earth, and whatever happens he will not let life disappear. And although the focus in the story of the flood has been on animal life, it is clear that the horizon of the text extends much wider. The one thing we should not imagine is that God's covenant means that we have a blank cheque where the created world is concerned. The text points up that God's promise has immediate and specific implications about how we behave towards all living beings, human and non-human. It is not a recipe for complacency or passivity.

Read in this way, the Bible seems to be saying that creation finds its focus in three things: the possibility of life, the transmission of life and the interrelated diversity of life. So if we focus, as we can hardly help doing, on humanity as the supreme creative possibility – the form of life that reflects the love and intelligence of the creator – this has important implications. The supreme possibility is to show something of the nature of God within the creation, and the 'specialness' of humanity turns out to lie in its role as protecting (through the exercise of that love and intelligence) life overall, not only of human life; it is a crucial part, but still only a part, of the interdependence of all living things. So for humanity to be a point of focus in creation is not for it to be separate from the rest of creation or to have solitary privileges and powers over creation. It is to realize that it is unimaginable without all those other life forms which make it possible and which it in turn serves and conserves. And if that is the case, then respect for humanity, a proper ethical account of humanity, has to be bound up with respect for life itself in all its diversity.

One of the greatest Christian thinkers of the twentieth century, Karl Barth, when he discusses the foundation of ethics,[2] makes very creative use of the idea of respect for life as a basic category. Life, he notes, is something that cannot be owned, only lived.[3] It is something developing through time; something experienced as gift, not possession; something made real by relationship with the creator. He goes on to express his reservations about trying to connect the way this works out ethically in human affairs with any ideas about non-human life in general. But the Noah story suggests that these reservations are misplaced. Genesis tells us that when we are called to relationship with our creator, we are in the same moment summoned to responsibility for the non-human world. That's how we express and activate our relationship with the creator, our reality as made in God's image. In this way, the creator has joined together the sacredness of human life with that of life itself. There is no way in which we can grasp human dignity and value it independently of human life's involvement with all other life, vegetable and animal – the variegated life of the rain forest as well as the multiple species of pollinating bees.

This vision of an ethical perspective based on reverence for the whole of life is not often heard in discussions among Christians about environmental ethics, but perhaps it deserves some further exploration. The Noah story – and the Jewish and Christian ethical insights that can be built upon it – lays out a clear vision, a very specific definition of the human vocation as including the care and preservation of the conditions of all life, care for the future of life. God may promise in the aftermath to the story of the flood that life will not be wholly destroyed, but that does not lift from us the burden of responsibility for what confronts us here and now as a serious crisis and challenge. To act so as to protect the future of the non-human world is both to accept a God-given responsibility and appropriately to honour the special dignity given to humanity itself. In Christian theological terms, it is to accept the renewed human dignity and authority that flows from the self-giving of Christ and his bodily resurrection, which is itself a sign of God's concern with the material world and his commitment to its transfiguration. Thus respect for the living material world and human self-respect belong together. The restoration or salvation of one is bound up with the other.

2

How then do we live as humans in a way that honours rather than endangers the life of our planet? Or, to put it slightly differently, 'How do we live in a way that shows an understanding that we genuinely live in a shared world, not one that simply belongs to us?' This would be a good question even if we were not faced with the threats associated with global warming, with the reduction of biodiversity, with desertification and deforestation, with fuel and food shortages. We should be asking the question whether or not it happens to be urgent, just because it is a question about how we live humanly, how we live in such a way as to show that we understand and respect that we are only one species within creation. The nature of our crisis is such that we can easily fall back on a position that says it isn't worth trying to change our patterns of behaviour, notably our patterns of consumption, because it's already too late to arrest the pace of global warming. But the question of exactly how late it is isn't the only one, and concentrating only on this can blind us to a more basic point. If we are locked into a way of life that does not honour who and what we are because it does not honour life itself and our calling to nourish it, we are not even going to know where to start in addressing the environmental challenge.

Alastair McIntosh in his splendid book, *Hell and High Water*, speaks of what he calls our current 'ecocidal' patterns of consumption as addictive and self-destructive. Living like this is living at a less than properly human level: McIntosh suggests we may need therapy, what he describes (in chapter 9) as a 'cultural psychotherapy' to liberate us. That liberation may or may not be enough to avert disaster. We simply don't know, though it would be a very foolish person who took that to mean that it might be all right after all. What we do know (or should know) is that we are living inhumanly.

Start from here and the significance of small changes is obvious. If I ask what's the point of my undertaking a modest amount of recycling my rubbish or scaling down my air travel, the answer is not that this will unquestionably save the world within six months, but in the first place that it's a step towards liberation from a cycle of behaviour that is keeping me, indeed most of us, in a dangerous state – dangerous, that is, to our human dignity and self-respect. McIntosh writes that 'unless the psycho-spiritual roots of this are grasped, our best efforts will amount to no more than "displacement activity"'.[4] So we must begin by recognizing that our ecological crisis is part of a crisis of what we understand by our humanity; it is part of a general process of losing our 'feel' for what is appropriately human, a loss that has been going on for some centuries and which some cultures and economies have been energetically exporting to the whole world. It is a loss that manifests itself in a variety of ways. It has to do with the erosion of rhythms in work and leisure, so that the old pattern of working days interrupted by a day of rest has been dangerously undermined; a loss of patience with the passing of time so that speed of communication has become a good in itself; a loss of patience which shows itself in the lack of respect and attention for the very old and the very young, and a fear in many quarters of the ageing process – a loss of the ability to accept that living as a material body in a material world is a risky thing. It is a loss whose results have become monumentally apparent in the financial crisis of the last 12 months. We have slowly begun to suspect that we have allowed ourselves to become addicted to fantasies about prosperity and growth, dreams of wealth without risk and profit without cost. A good deal of the talk and activity around the financial collapse has the marks of McIntosh's 'displacement activity' – precisely because it fails to see where the roots of the problem lie; in our amnesia about the human calling.

So some of our habits in the wealthy world have the effect of separating us from our humanity by separating us from the very processes of life itself, from the experience of time and growing and of death itself as something inevitable. We have seen growing evidence in recent years of a lack of correlation between economic prosperity and a sense of well-being, and evidence to suggest that inequality in society is one of the more reliable predictors of a lack of well-being. It looks very much as if what we need is to be reconnected rather urgently with the processes of our world. We shouldn't need an environmental crisis to establish that the developed world has become perilously out of touch with the experience of those living in the least developed parts of the world and with their profound vulnerabilities and insecurities. But it is the case that this crisis has focused as few other things could the real cost of illusion, the cost of the progression traced by Alastair McIntosh, perhaps too dramatically for some tastes, from pride to violence to 'ecocide'.[5] And this means that we have to ask whether our duty of care for life is compatible with assuming without question that the desirable future for every economy, even the most currently successful and expansionist, is unchecked growth. If the effect of unchecked growth is to isolate us more and more from life, from the complex interrelations that make us what we are as part of the whole web of existence on the planet, then we cannot continue to grow indefinitely in economic terms without moving towards the death of what is most distinctively human, the death of the habits that make sense in a shared world where life has to be sustained by co-operation not only between humans, but between humans and their material world.

Just to be clear: we must not romanticize poverty and privation, and we cannot deny that economic growth may be a powerful driver of human liberation. Humanity is undermined just as surely by material wretchedness and privation and the constant struggle for subsistence, and it is right to work for a world in which there is security of work and food and medical care for all, and to try and create local economies that make local societies prosper through trade and innovation. But the question more and more people are asking is whether there are macro-economic models that would allow us to see investment in public infrastructures and the development of sustainable technologies as priorities for a healthy economy, rather than a simple growth in consumer power. The 2009 report, *Prosperity Without Growth*, from the Sustainable Development Commission, outlines what sort of areas would need to be rethought if we took such an approach and tried to balance the need for a stable and productive economy with the need for investment directed towards 'resource productivity, renewable energy, clean technology, green business, climate adaptation and ecosystem maintenance and protection'.[6] It would mean revising a lot of assumptions about the timescale and character of profit and about the balance of private and public good. Without some such rethinking of our current obsession with growth in consumerist terms, we can be sure of two things: inequality will not be addressed (and so the powerlessness of the majority of the world's population will remain as it is at the moment); and the dehumanizing effects of the culture of consumer growth will worsen. Only if we start thinking along these lines can we see our way through the difficulties often referred to about holding together the imperative of environmental care and the imperative of economic development.

Mike Hulme, in a provocative and original book, *Why We Disagree About Climate Change*, argues that the anxieties around global warming and related matters are actually a welcome opportunity for us to look hard at fundamental issues concerning our social and ethical situation. He quotes the somewhat startling remarks of a former Canadian government minister who said that even if the science around climate change was mistaken, the focus on the question had provided the best possible impetus towards more equality and justice in the world.[7] Put like this, the remark is a bit of a hostage to fortune. I'm not sure it would be helpful to make moral capital out of erroneous science, and it is certainly not helpful to give a handle to those eager to encourage scepticism about the science of climate change. But presumably the point is to move us away from seeing the question only in terms of a problem-solving exercise. Hulme suggests that to come at the set of issues around climate change in terms of an agenda to do with fundamental justice has energizing and mobilizing power, more so than an approach based simply on the fear of catastrophe, which can have a paralyzing effect. We need to think about this as a call to do what is in its own right good and life-giving for us, a call to be more human.

Mike Hulme's book is helpful as a warning against too readily buying into extravagant language about 'solving' the problem of climate change as if it were a case of bringing an uncontrolled situation back under rational management, which is a pretty worrying model that leaves us stuck in the worst kind of fantasy about humanity's relation to the rest of the world. Instead, he recommends a deliberately many-faceted approach, recognizing that there is no one ecological problem waiting for a solution and that the various levels of challenge need as wide a variety of creative response as we can muster. I shall be coming back in a moment to look at some of the specifics this involves.

3

To summarize so far: living in a way that honours rather than threatens the planet is living out what it means to be made in the image of God. We do justice to what we are as human beings when we seek to do justice to the diversity of life around us; we become what we are supposed to be when we assume our responsibility for life continuing on earth. And that call to do justice brings with it the call to re-examine what we mean by growth and wealth. Instead of a desperate search to find the one great idea that will save us from ecological disaster, we are being invited to a transformation of individual and social goals that will bring us closer to the reality of interdependent life in a variegated world, whether or not we find we can 'save the planet'.

Hulme is right surely that the scale and complexity of the challenge we face mean that no one solution will suffice. We need to keep up pressure on national governments; there are questions only they can answer about the investment of national resources, the policy priorities underlying trade, transport and industry and the legal framework for controlling dangerous and destructive practices. But we ought to beware of expecting government to succeed in controlling a naturally unpredictable set of variables in the environment or to produce by regulation a new set of human habits. We need equally, perhaps even more, to keep up pressure on ourselves and to learn how to work better as civic agents. Hulme gives the example of the Carbon Reduction Action Groups, first established in 2006, as a means of expressing local civic responsibility by working with the idea of personal carbon allowances and sharing 'skills in lower-carbon living'. To quote: 'CRAGS adopt the position that individuals need not accept the existing political and governance arrangements and can subvert these traditional arrangements through local action'.[8] And in addition to all this, encouraging local government initiatives and legal challenges to bad business practice are just as necessary a part of a comprehensive strategy; pressure in this area needs to be as effective as campaigning directed towards national governments. A campaigning strategy targeted exclusively at the level of national directives or international protocols ignores the potential of a broad platform of tactics in diverse contexts. More importantly, it ignores the potential of the crisis to awaken a new confidence in local and civic democracy, its potential to foster a new sense of what is politically possible for people who thought they were powerless.

The threat posed by climate change and environmental degradation tends to make us think about survival and look for solutions that will guarantee survival.

That's a reasonable response to any threat; but the sheer complexity of this situation and the continuing uncertainty about some of the precise detail (how late is it? have we reached the 'tipping point?) make us especially vulnerable. We are bound to realize sooner or later that easy solutions are not at hand, and that there is no one cause of the whole crisis that will allow us to point to some single scapegoat. This in turn makes us vulnerable to panic on one hand, apathy on the other, and the illusion that someone will both take the blame and assume the responsibility of finding a solution – usually meaning a series of grand technological solutions requiring massive investments of money nobody seems to have.

What if we reframe the question more like this? 'When we find ourselves facing massive insecurity of this sort and when we sense that we have somehow sacrificed our happiness along the way, what is it that we have lost? And how can we work to restore it?' That kind of question can be answered effectively only if we have a robust picture of what human capacity and responsibility should look like. And this surely is the main contribution to the environmental debate that religious commitment can make. With due respect to one recent secular commentator, the role of religion here is not to provide an ultimate authority that can threaten and coerce us into better behaviour; it is to hold up a vision of human life lived constructively, peacefully, joyfully, in optimal relation with creation and creator, so as to point up the tragedy of the shrunken and harried humanity we have shaped for ourselves by our obsession with growth and consumption. In the words of Michael Northcott, 'industrial humans increasingly experience their identity in terms of the things that they have acquired, instead of in their being creatures';[9] and we might recall the words of Karl Barth quoted earlier about life as something to be lived, not owned.

So, without trivializing or minimizing the ravages that have been inflicted on the whole material environment by the consequences of industrialization, we could say that the human soul is one of the foremost casualties of environmental degradation, in the sense that the processes of environmental damage have both reflected and intensified a basic spiritual malaise. Many of the things which have moved us towards ecological disaster have been distortions in our sense of who and what we are, and their overall effect has been to isolate us more and more from the reality we're part of. Our response to the crisis needs to be, in the most basic sense, a reality check, a re-acquaintance with the facts of our interdependence within the material world and a rediscovery of our responsibility for it. And this is why the apparently small-scale action that changes personal habits and local possibilities is so crucial. When we believe in transformation at the local and personal level, we are laying the surest foundations for change at the national and international level. They are not two alternative paths but aspects of one essential impulse, the restoration of a healthy relation with our world.

So whatever we do to combat the nightmare possibilities of wholesale environmental catastrophe has to be grounded not primarily in the scramble for survival, but in the hope of human happiness. The opportunity presented to us is an opportunity of pressing for a deeper and more searching public debate about the character of such happiness, the character of the human good. It is encouraging that an increasing number of social philosophers are moving the discussion in this direction. Michael Sandel's work, *Justice: what's the right thing to do?*, for example, concludes that we have succumbed to thinking about justice essentially in connection with individual rights rather than in the context of asking what actions are in themselves good; and the result, he says, has been an abstract and legalistic notion of rights and a very 'thin' idea of justice itself. If we are to move on from this, he continues, we are bound to accept a greater degree of real argument in our public life about the nature of the good life – which means allowing moral and religious convictions to be far more visible in the public sphere. 'A politics emptied of substantive moral engagement makes for an impoverished civic life'.[10] What is true for our discussion of civil and criminal justice holds equally for our understanding of the moral dimension of the environmental crisis we face – including the issue of environmental justice itself.

We seem to have travelled some way from Mount Ararat. But the crucial thread running through these diverse considerations is the question of what we mean by life and how we honour it appropriately in our practice, individual and social. To be human, in the biblical world view, is to be given a responsibility for the future of life. We become less than human when we stifle possibilities for life, when we ignore the need for balanced diversity – or forget the degree of our ignorance about its detailed workings. Creation, the total environment, is a system oriented towards life – and, ultimately, towards intelligent and loving life, because in the Creator there is no gap between life, intelligence and love. The biblical vision does not present us with a humanity isolated from the processes of life overall in the cosmos, a humanity whose existence is of a different moral and symbolic order from everything else; on the contrary, the unique differentiating thing about humanity is the gift to human beings of conscious, intelligent responsibility for the life they share with the wider processes of the world. Because this life reflects in varying degrees the eternal life of God, we have to say, as believers, that the possibility of life is never exhausted within creation: there is always a future. But in this particular context, this specific planet, that future depends in significant ways on our co-operative, imaginative labour, on the actions of each of us. Just as importantly, our human dignity itself is bound up with these actions. What we face today is nothing less than a choice about how genuinely human we want to be; and the role of religious faith in meeting this is first and foremost in setting out a compelling picture of what humanity reconciled with both creator and creation might look like.

Conclusion

How does this choice become specific? All I want to do by way of conclusion is to remind you of some of the points already touched upon. Successive 'summits' on climate change and environmental issues keep us all aware of the imperative to urge leaders at the most senior level to attend and to create a suitably serious plan for taking forward within a tight time frame protocols about carbon reductions – carbon taxes, investment in new energy-efficient technologies (using the gains from carbon taxes among other things), the international acceptance of accounting regimes that factor in environmental cost. In recent weeks, we have had unexpected signs that the East Asian countries are readier than we might have imagined to put pressure on the economies of the US and Europe. The idea that fast-developing economies are totally wedded to environmental indifference because of the urgency of bringing their populations out of poverty no longer seems quite so obvious a truth; and the realization that unchecked environmental degradation means more poverty for everyone in the (not very) long run is clearly taking root.

Then there are the community options. I mentioned the CRAG initiatives earlier, and that is just one example of the effectiveness of collaborative local action. In the same general territory, each of us can bring pressure to bear on institutions we are connected with to conduct a rigorous carbon audit; for those involved in the Church of England, the website of the Shrinking the Footprint initiative offers help with such projects, detailed suggestions for both study and action.

And last, and anything but least, there is what each of us can do to reconnect with reality, as I put it earlier. There are the various specific choices we can make about our refuse, our travel, our domestic energy use – all fairly familiar by now; and once again there are resources available for more detailed proposals. But I'd want also to underline the need for us to change our habits enough to make us more aware of the diversity of life around us. I once suggested that one necessary contribution to a better awareness of these issues was to make sure we went out of doors in the wet from time to time (a suitable lesson from Noah), and, if we haven't got gardens of our own, make sure we took opportunities of watching the changing of the seasons on the earth's surface. This may seem trivial compared with the high drama of 'saving the world'; but if this analysis is correct, our underlying problem is being 'dissociated', and we ought to be asking constantly how we restore a sense of association with the material place, time and climate that we inhabit and are part of.

The Christian story lays out a model of reconnection with an alienated world: it tells us of a material human life inhabited by God and raised transfigured from death; of a sharing of material food which makes us sharers in eternal life; of a community whose life together seeks to express within creation the care of the creator. In the words used by both Moses and St Paul, this is not a message remote from us in heaven or buried under the earth: it is near, on our lips and hearts (cf. *Romans* 10.6–9, *Deuteronomy* 30.11–14). And, as Moses immediately goes on to say in the Old Testament passage, 'Today I am giving you a choice between good and evil, between life and death ... choose life' (*Deuteronomy* 30.14–15, 19).

PART FOUR

Housekeeping: The Economic Challenge

Ethics, economics and global justice

1

In a conversation late in 2008 at Canary Wharf, a senior manager in financial services observed that recent years had seen an erosion of the notion that certain enterprises necessarily took time to deliver and that therefore it was a mistake to look for maximal profits on the basis of a balance sheet covering only one or two years. There had been, he suggested, a deep and systemic impatience with the whole idea of taking time to arrive at a desired goal – and thus with a great deal of the understanding of both labour and the building of confidence. Either an enterprise delivered or it didn't, and the question could be answered in a brief and measurable time-span. For all the rhetoric about accountability, getting your money's worth, the effect of such assumptions in all kinds of settings has been a spectacular failure to understand the variety of ways in which responsible practice might be gauged – whether in relation to investment in actual production or in relation to new financial products, whose sustainability and reliability can only be proved after the passage of time. Very much the same kind of impatience has also been part of the tidal wave of assault on the historic professions – including the law, teaching and academic research and some aspects of public service. The short-term curse continues to afflict the voluntary sector in the absurd timescales attached to grant-giving; all that is material for a lecture in its own right.

But in connection specifically with the financial crisis, the main point is about what appropriate patience might look like where various financial and commercial enterprises are concerned. The loss of a sense of appropriate time is a major cultural development, which necessarily changes how we think about trust and relationship. Trust is learned gradually, rather than being automatically deliverable according to a set of static conditions laid down. It involves a degree of human judgement, which in turn involves a level of awareness of one's own human character and that of others – a degree of literacy about the signals of trustworthiness; a shared *culture* of understanding what is said and done in a human society. And this learning entails unavoidable insecurity. I do not control others and I do not control the passage of time and the processes of nature; even the processes of human labour are limited by things outside my control (the capacities of human bodies). My lack of a definitive and authoritative or universal perspective means that I may make mistakes because I misread others or because I miscalculate the levels of uncertainty in the processes I deal in. And the further away I get from these areas of learning by trial and error, the further away I get from the inevitable risks of living in a material and limited world, the more easily can I persuade myself that I am after all in control.

Although people have spoken of greed as the source of our current problems, I suspect that it goes deeper. It is a little too easy to blame the present situation on an accumulation of individual greed, exemplified by bankers or brokers, and to lose sight of the fact that governments committed to deregulation and to the encouragement of speculation and high personal borrowing were elected repeatedly in the UK and US for a crucial couple of decades. Add to that the fact that warnings were not lacking of some of the risks of poor (or no) regulation, and we are left with the question of what it was that skewed the judgement of a whole society as well as of financial professionals. John Dunning, a professional analyst of the business world, wrote as long ago as 2004 about what he called the 'crisis in the moral ecology' of unregulated capitalism;[1] and he and other contributors to his book discussed how 'circles of failure' could be created in the global economy by a combination of moral indifference, institutional crisis and market failure, each feeding on the others. Yet warnings went unheeded; people's rational capacities, it seems, were blunted, and unregulated global capitalism was assumed to be the natural way of doing things, based on a set of rational market processes that would deliver results in everyone's interest.

This was not just about greed. At least some apologists for the naturalness of the unregulated market pointed, quite reasonably in the circumstances, to the apparently infallible capacity of the market to free nations from poverty. It may help to turn for illumination to an unexpected source. Acquisitiveness is, in the Christian monastic tradition, associated with pride, the root of all human error and failure: pride, which is most clearly evident in *the refusal to acknowledge my lack of control over my environment*, my illusion that I can shape the world according to my will. And if that is correct, then the origin of economic dysfunction and injustice is pride – a pride that is manifest in the reluctance to let go of systems and projects that promise more and more secure control, and so has a bad effect on our reasoning powers. This in turn suggests that economic justice arrives only when everyone recognizes some kind of shared vulnerability and limitation in a world of limits and processes (psychological as well as material) that cannot be bypassed. We are delivered or converted not simply by resolving in a vacuum to be less greedy, but by understanding what it is to live as an organism which grows and changes and thus is involved in risk. We change because our minds or mindsets are changed and steered away from certain powerful but toxic myths.

Now, you could say that ethics is essentially about how we negotiate our own and other people's vulnerabilities. The sort of behaviour we recognize as unethical is very frequently something to do with the misuse of power and the range of wrong or corrupt responses to power – with the ways in which fear, envy or admiration can skew our perception of what the situation truly demands of us. Instead of estimating what it is that we owe to truth or to reality or to God as the source of truth, we calculate what we need to do so as to acquire, retain or at best placate power (and there is of course a style of supposedly religious morality that works in just such an unethical way). But when we begin to think seriously about ethics, about how our life is to reflect truth, we do not consider what is owed to power; indeed, we consider what is owed to weakness, to powerlessness. Our ethical seriousness is tested by how we behave towards those whose goodwill or influence is of no 'use' to us. Hence the frequently repeated claim that the moral depth of a society can be assessed by how it treats its children – or, one might add, its disabled, its elderly or its terminally ill. Ethical behaviour is behaviour that respects what is at risk in the life of another and works on behalf of the other's need. To be an ethical agent is thus to be aware of human frailty, material and mental; and so, by extension, it is to be aware of your own frailty. And for a specifically Christian ethic, the duty of care for the neighbour as for oneself is bound up with the injunction to forgive as one hopes to be forgiven; basic to this whole perspective is the recognition both that I may fail or be wounded and that I may be guilty of error and damage to another.

2

It's a bit of a paradox, then, to realize that aspects of capitalism are in their origin very profoundly ethical in the sense I've just outlined. The venture capitalism of the early modern period expressed something of the sense of risk by limiting liability and sharing profit; it sought to give limited but real security in a situation of risk, and it assumed that sharing risk was a basis for sharing wealth. It acknowledged the lack of ultimate human control in a world of complex processes and unpredictable agents, and attempted to 'negotiate vulnerabilities', in the terms I used a moment ago, by stressing the importance of maintaining trust and offering some protection against unlimited loss. By sharing risk between investor and venturer, it also shared power.

The problems begin to arise when the system offers such a level of protection from insecurity that risk comes to be seen as exceptional and unacceptable. We take for granted a high level of guaranteed return and so come to prefer those transactions in which the actual business of time-taking and the limits involved in material labour and scarcity of goods are less involved. It has been persuasively argued that things begin to go astray, morally, in the early and intimate association between capitalism and various colonial projects, in which abundant new natural resources and abundant new reserves of labour (notably in the shape of slavery) could be counted on to minimize some kinds of risk.

In the post-colonial climate, it has been the world of financial products that becomes the favoured basis for both personal and social economy. A badly or inadequately regulated market is one in which no-one is properly monitoring the scarcity of credit. And this absence of monitoring is especially attractive when governments depend for their electability on a steady expansion of spending power for their citizens. Increasingly, to pick up the central theme of Philip Bobbitt's magisterial works on modern global and military politics, government rests its legitimacy upon its capacity to satisfy consumer demands and maximize choices – its capacity to defer or obscure that element of the uncontrollable which in earlier phases of capitalist production dictated the habits of mutual trust and shared jeopardy, the habits that made sense of the otherwise morally controversial idea that the use of money was itself in some sense a chargeable commodity, something that needed to be paid for. Maximized choice is a form of maximized control. And it presupposes and encourages a basic model of the ideal human agent as an isolated subject confronting a range of options, each of which they are equally free to adopt for their own self-defined purposes. If an economy resting on financial services rather than material production offers more choice, a government will lean in this direction for electoral advantage, since its claim to be taken seriously is now grounded in its ability to enlarge the market in which individuals operate to purchase the raw materials for constructing their identities and projects.

As I hope will be clear, this is a deeper matter than just 'greed'. It is a fairly comprehensive picture of what sort of things human beings are; and to recognize it as a reasonably accurate model of late modern 'developed' society, especially in the North Atlantic world, is not to suggest any blanket condemnation of market principles, any nostalgia for pre-modern social sanctions and so forth – only to begin to sketch an analysis of where and how certain quite intractable problems arise. As already indicated, the modern market state, in Bobbitt's sense of the term, the state that promises maximized choice and minimal risk, is in serious danger of encouraging people to forget two fundamentals of economic reality – *scarcity* as an inexorable truth about a materially limited world, and concrete *productivity and added value* as the condition for increasing purchasing power or liberty, and thus sustaining any kind of market. The tension between these two things is, of course, at the heart of economic theory, and imbalance in economic reality arises when one or the other dominates for too long, producing an unhealthily controlled economy (scarcity-driven) or an unhealthily hyperactive and ill-regulated economy (based on the simple expansion of purchasing power).

But *forget* that tension and what happens is not stability, but plain confusion and fantasy. We have woken up belatedly to the results of behaving as though scarcity could be indefinitely deferred: the ecological crisis makes this painfully clear. We have woken up less rapidly and definitively to the effects of displacing labour costs to undeveloped economies. The short-term benefits to local employment in these settings and in lower prices elsewhere cannot offset longer-term issues about *security* of employment (jobs will move when labour is cheaper in other places) and thus also the problematic social changes brought by large-scale movement towards new employment patterns that have no long-term guarantees. One effect of this pattern is the creation not of a new consumer class, but of a new group of urban paupers in unstable developing economies – a phenomenon visible in some East Asian contexts.

The move away from a realistic focus on scarcity and productivity/added value and towards the virtualized economy of money transactions has been deeply seductive, and, over a limited time-frame, spectacularly successful in generating purchasing power. Given that credit is not something that is naturally 'scarce' in precisely the same sense that material resources are, inade-quate regulation can, as already noted, foster the illusion that the money market is effectively risk-free; that money can generate money without constraint. In contrast to an economic model in which the exchange of goods is the basic process being analysed or managed, we have increasingly privileged and encouraged a model in which the process of exchange itself has become the raw material, the motor of profit-making. But, to repeat the point made so many times in the last few months, the problem comes when massively inflated credit is 'called in': when the disproportion between actual, measurable material security and what is being claimed and traded on the market is so great that confidence in the institutions involved collapses. The search for impregnable security, independent of the limits of material resource, available labour and the time-consuming securing of trust by working at relationships of transparency and mutual responsibility, has led us to the most radical insecurity imaginable.

3

This is not the only paradox. In a *Prospect* essay of January 2009, Robert Skidelsky discussed why it is that a globalized economy has produced a resurgence of protectionism and nationalism, not to mention the political and economic domination of a single state, the US.[2] We have, he suggests, been seduced into thinking that the mere lack of frontiers in global technology means that we accept a common destiny with other societies and are firmly set on the path to integrated economic operations. 'Globalisation—the integration of markets in goods, services, capital and labour—must be good because it has raised millions out of poverty in poorer countries faster than would otherwise have been possible.'[3] But the Whiggish idea that all this represents an irreversible movement towards an undifferentiated global culture and that a world without economic frontiers is natural, inevitable and by definition benign, rests on several very doubtful assumptions, rooted in an era that is passing – an era in which it was taken for granted that we began from a position of grave scarcity and moved towards unimpeded growth. But we are now in a position of 'partial abundance' (that is, a generally higher standard of living globally) which at the same time is more conscious of the limits of our material and environmental resources. As a result, globalization is less obviously good news for the 'developed' world. 'The economic benefits of offshoring are far from evident for richer states', says Skidelsky: jobs drain away to places where labour costs are cheaper, and we end up paying more to foreign investors than we earn in international markets. And the temptation for such wealthier economies is thus towards protectionism, with all its damaging consequences for a world economy. It is one of the most effective ways to freeze developing economies in a state of perpetual disadvantage; it makes it impossible for poorer economies to trade their way to wealth, as the rhetoric of the global market suggests they should.

Skidelsky argues that we need to take steps to reduce the attractions of relocating and 'offshoring' in the first place, so that countries can focus afresh on their own processes of production so as to keep both internal and external investment alive. As he says, the present situation favours economic agreements that give little or no leverage to workers and that have minimal reference to social, environmental or even local legal concerns. Learning how to use governmental antitrust legislation to break up the virtually monopolistic powers of large multinationals that have become cuckoos in the nest of a national economy would also be an essential part of a strategy designed to stop the slide from opportunistic outsourcing towards protectionism and monitoring or policing the chaotic flow of capital across boundaries.

We have yet to see how much of this is deliverable, but the thrust of the argument is hard to resist, either morally or practically. Morally, protectionism implicitly accepts that wealth maintained at the cost of the neighbour's disadvantage or worse is a tolerable situation – which is a denial of the belief that what is good for humanity is ultimately coherent or convergent. Such a denial is a sinister thing, since it undermines the logic of assuming that what the other finds painful I should find painful too – a basic element of what we generally consider maturely or sanely ethical behaviour. Practically, protectionism is another instance of short-term vision, securing prosperity here by making prosperity impossible somewhere else; in a global context, this is inexorably a factor in ultimately shrinking potential markets.

And the wider agenda sketched by Skidelsky means also that commercial concerns would be prevented from overturning the social and political priorities of elected governments. The arguments around unrepayable international debt a decade ago repeatedly underlined the destructive effects of imposed regimes of financial stabilization that derailed governmental programmes in poor countries and effectively confiscated any means of shaping a local economy to local needs. And we hardly need reminding of the distorting effect on a national economy – and public ethics too – of being seen as a pool of cheap labour and a haven for irresponsible practices.

Several writers have said that a reformed and revitalized WTO ought to be able to move us further towards the monitoring I mentioned a moment ago.

Some would be more specific and argue that for this to work effectively, there needs also to be some regulation of capital flow and exchange mechanisms, and this is where a variety of commentators from very diverse backgrounds see the 'Tobin tax' proposals as having a place taxing currency exchanges in ways that would serve national economies. We should also need some mechanisms by which it could be guaranteed that a recognizable proportion of 'savings', locally generated profits in a national economy, could be ploughed back into investment in local infrastructure, so that we should not constantly have to deal with the consequences of new money in a growing economy roaming around looking for a home and ending up fuelling the pressure on banks to lend above their capacity so as to keep the money moving.

Most such moves would, of course, require a formidable, perhaps unattainable level of global agreement and global enforceability; short of this, they could be counterproductive. But the debate on what kinds of international convergence are possible and necessary is a crucial one. The basic question that Skidelsky and others are posing, however, is how the market as we know it can be restructured so as to make it do what it is supposed to do: that is, to offer producers the chance of a fair and competitive context in which to trade what they produce and become in turn effective investors and developers of the potential of their business *and* their society. The last few months have seen an extraordinary and quite unpredictable shift in the balance, with international financial transactions losing credibility and national governments coming into their own as guarantors of some level of stability. It is a rather ironic mutation of the idea of the market state: when it comes to the (credit) crunch, populations want governments to secure their basic spending power, even if it limits their absolute consumer freedoms. There is also a point, increasingly noticed in ethical discussion in recent years, about securing justice for future generations: any morally and practically credible policy should be looking to guarantee that future generations do not inherit liabilities that will cripple the provision of basic social care, for example. Unregulated 'freedom' in the climate of destructive speculation is not the most attractive prospect, certainly not compared with a guarantee that assets will not be allowed to drop indefinitely in value. The only way of 'maximizing choice' is to make sure that it is still possible to choose and to use *something*, and to secure the possibilities of reasonable choice for our children and grandchildren, even at the price of restricting some options. Without that restriction, nothing is solid: we should face a world in which everything flows, melts, dissolves, in a world of constantly shifting and spectral valuations.

4

If we try to draw some of this together into a few governing principles, what might emerge? The non-economist is bound to be intimidated by the complexity of what we confront, but, as has been said, 'we are all economists now'; the specialists are not more conspicuously successful than others in mapping the territory, and this at least encourages some tentative proposals from the side lines, however broad and aspirational. Certainly, over the last century and a half, Anglican theologians have from time to time taken their courage in their hands and attempted to outline what an ethically responsible economy might look like, and I am conscious of standing in the shadow of some very substantial commentators indeed, from F. D. Maurice to William Temple. In the background too is the formidable legacy of Roman Catholic social teaching, expressed in some powerful statements from the British and American Bishops' Conferences in recent decades and in Pope Benedict's remarkable encyclical, *Caritas in veritate*. So with this heritage in mind, I shall suggest five elements, in descending order of significance, which might provide the bare bones of an economic culture capable of delivering something like an ethically defensible global policy.

(i) Most fundamentally: we need to move away from a model of economics which simply assumes that it is essentially about the mechanics of generating money, and try to restore an acknowledgement of the role of trust as something which needs time to develop; and so also to move away from an idea of wealth or profit which imagines that they can be achieved without risk, and to return to the primitive capitalist idea, as sketched above, of risk-sharing as an essential element in the equitable securing of wealth for all.

(ii) As many writers, from Partha Dasgupta to Jonathon Porritt have argued, environmental cost has to be factored into economic calculations as a genuine cost in opportunity, resource and durability – and thus a cost in terms of doing justice to future generations. There needs to be a robust rebuttal of any idea that environmental concerns are somehow a side issue or even a luxury in a time of economic pressure; the questions are inseparably connected.

(iii) We need to think harder about the role, actual and potential, of democratically accountable governments in the monitoring and regulation of currency exchange and capital flow. This could involve some international conventions about wages and working conditions, and co-operation between states to try and prevent the indefinite growth of what we might call, on the analogy of tax havens, cheap labour havens. Likewise it might mean considering the kind of capital controls that prevent a situation where it is advantageous to allow indefinitely large sums of capital out of a country.

(iv) The existing international instruments (the IMF and World Bank, the WTO and the G8 and G20 countries) need to be reconceived as both monitors of the global flow of capital and agencies to stimulate local enterprise, and provide some safety nets as long as the global playing field is so far from being level. They need to provide some protective sanctions for the disadvantaged – not aimed at undermining market mechanisms, but at letting them work as they should, working to allow countries to trade their way out of destitution.

(v) Necessary short-term policies to kick-start an economy in crisis, such as we have seen in the UK in recent months, should be balanced by long-term consideration of the levels of material and service production that will provide an anchor of stability against the possible storms of speculative financial practice. This is not simply about 'baling out' firms under pressure, but about a comprehensive look at national economies with a view to understanding what sort of production levels would act as ballast in times of crisis, and investing accordingly.

Aspirational these may be; but what I hope is *not* vague here is the moral orientation that lies behind all these points. Ethics, I suggested, is about negotiating conditions in which the most vulnerable are not abandoned. And we shall care about this largely to the extent to which we are conscious of our own vulnerability and limitedness. One of the things most fatal to the sustaining of an ethical perspective on any area of human life, not just economics, is the fantasy that we are not really part of a material order – that we are essentially will or craving, for which the body is a useful organ for fulfilling the purposes of the all-powerful will, rather than being the organ of our connection with the rest of the world. It's been said often enough but it bears repeating, that in some ways – so far from being a materialist culture – we are a culture that is resentful about material reality, hungry for anything and everything that distances us from the constraints of being a physical animal subject to temporal processes, to uncontrollable changes and to sheer accident.

Implied in what has just been said is a recognition of the dangers of 'growth' as an unexamined good. Growth out of poverty, growth towards a degree of intelligent control of one's circumstances, growth towards maturity of perception and sympathy – all these are manifestly good and ethically serious goals, and, as has already been suggested, there are ways of conducting our economic business that could honour and promote these. A goal of growth simply as an indefinite expansion of purchasing power is either vacuous or malign – malign to the extent that it inevitably implies the diminution of the capacity of others in a world of limited resource. Remember the significance of scarcity and vulnerability in shaping a sense of what ethical behaviour looks like.

It is true that modern production creates markets by creating new 'needs' – or, more properly, new expectations. Human creativity moves on, and human ingenuity constantly enlarges the reach of human management of the environment. That isn't in itself an evil; but a mature perspective on this would surely note two things. One is that there is always some choice involved in what is to be developed – and thus some opportunity cost. Not everything can be produced according to the dictates of desire, and so there will still be the need to sort out priorities. Second, we cannot ignore or postpone the question of what we want enlarged management of the environment *for*. The reduction of pain or of frustration, the augmenting of opportunity for human welfare and joy – again, these are obviously good things. They are good because they connect with a sense of what is properly owing to human beings, a sense of human dignity. And thus if the way in which they are secured for some reduces the opportunities of others, the pursuit of them is not compatible with a serious commitment to human dignity.

All this amounts to a belief that pursuing ethical economic growth, while not systematically hostile to new demands and new markets, while indeed acknowledging the way in which new markets can and should help to secure the prosperity of new producers, necessarily means looking critically at our lifestyle. To make it specific, and to use one of the more obvious examples, it has become more and more clear that lifestyles dependent on high levels of fossil fuel consumption reduce the long-term opportunities of basic human flour-ishing for many people because of their environmental cost – not to mention the various political traps associated with the production and marketing of oil in some parts of the world, with the consequent risks to peace and regional stability. Growth as an infinitely projected process of better and cheaper access to fossil fuel-related goods, including transport, would not be an impressive ethical horizon. The question which present circumstances are forcing rather harshly on our attention is how self-critical we can find it in ourselves to be about our lifestyle in the more affluent parts of the world – not in order to adopt a corporate monastic poverty, but in order to arrive at a sense of the acceptable limits to growth in the context of what might be good for the human family overall and the planet itself.

The five broad principles sketched above could only be fleshed out against a background in which people recognized that talking about the need for growth made no sense except in relation to a world of complex social and political relationships and of limited material resources – a background of willingness to ask not what might be abstractly possible in terms of increasing the range of consumer goods, but what might be manageable as part of a balanced global network of forces, basic needs, mutual respect and so on.

5

Basic to everything we might want to say about the financial crisis from the religious point of view is the question, 'what for?' What is growth for? For what and for *whom* is wealth important? If it is essential to invest in certain kinds of productive ventures, how does this relate to the broader and longer-term imperative of securing the funding of social care future by way of sustainable shared resources, accumulated wealth? And so on. But behind such questions as these is the unavoidable issue of what human beings are for; or, to put it less crudely, what the content is of ideas of human dignity and where we look for their foundation or rationale. The principles outlined a moment ago require a context not only of geopolitical and social analysis, not even of pragmatic recognitions of the limits of material resources or the opportunity costs of certain financial decisions, but of a comprehensive sense of *belonging in a world* – and a world that is neither self-explanatory nor self-sufficient, but is transparent to a deeper level of agency or liberty, that level that is called 'God' by the religious traditions of humanity. In Christian belief, the world exists because of a free act of generous love by the creator. God has made a world in which, by working with the limitations of a material order declared by God to be 'very good', humans may reflect the liberty and generosity of God. And our salvation is the restoration of a broken relationship with this whole created order, through the death and resurrection of Jesus Christ and the establishing by the power of his Spirit a community in which mutual service and attention are the basic elements through which the human world becomes transparent to its maker.

The realizing of that transparency is, for religious believers of whatever tradition, the beginning of happiness – not of a transient feeling of well-being or even euphoria, but of a settled sense of being at home, being absolved from urgent and obsessional desire, from the passion to justify your existence, from the anxieties of rivalry. And so what religious belief has to say in the context of our present crisis is, first, a call to *lament* the brokenness of the world and invite that change of heart which is so pivotal throughout the Jewish and Christian Scriptures; and, second, to declare without ambiguity or qualification that human value rests on God's creative love and not on possession or achievement. It is not for believers to join in the search for scapegoats, because there will always be, for the religious self, an awareness of complicity in social evil. Nor is it for believers to make light of the real suffering that goes with economic uncertainty and loss – no less real for the formerly affluent Westerner faced with redundancy than for the powerless farmer or woman worker enduring yet another change for the worse in a battered and injured African or Asian economy.

But the task is to turn people's eyes back to the vision of a human dignity that is indestructible. This is the vision that will both allow us to retain a hold on our sense of worth even when circumstances are painful or humiliating and sustain the sense of obligation to the needs of others, near at hand or strangers, so that dignity may be made manifest.

In conclusion, let me suggest three central aspects of a religious – and more specifically, Christian – contribution to the on-going debate, which may focus some more detailed reflection:

(i) Our faith depends on the action of a God who is to be trusted; God keeps promises. There could hardly be a more central theme in Jewish and Christian Scripture, and the notion is present in slightly different form in Islam as well. Thus, to live in proper harmony with God, human beings need to be promise-keepers in all areas of their lives, not least in financial dealings.

(ii) As we have noted more than once already, the perspective of faith understands human beings as part of creation – not wholly in control, though gifted with capacities that allow real and significant powers over the environment, bound to material identity and unable to escape material need. Living in faith is living in awareness of this created and limited identity without resentment or fantasy.

(iii) Living as part of creation brings with it a sense of the common destiny and common predicament of humanity. But more specifically, the Scriptural understanding of our calling, especially as set out in the letters of St Paul, sees the ideal human community as one in which the welfare and giftedness of each and the welfare of all are inseparable. What is good in God's eyes for human beings, not something that is altered by differences in culture or income; we can't say that what is unwelcome or evil for us is tolerable for others.

So: trustworthiness, realism or humility and the clear sense that we must resist polices or practices which accept the welfare of some at the expense of others – there is a back-of-an-envelope idea of where we might start in pressing for a global economic order that has some claim to be just. It can't be too often stressed that we are not talking about simply limiting damage to vulnerable societies far away: the central issues exposed by the financial crisis are everyone's business, and the risks of what some commentators (Timothy Garton Ash and Jonathon Porritt) have called a 'barbarizing' of Western societies as a result of panic and social insecurity are real enough. Equally it can't be too often stressed that it is only the generosity of an ethical approach to these matters that can begin to relate material wealth to human well-being, the happiness that is spiritual and relational and based on the recognition of non-negotiable human worth. There is much to fear at the moment, but, as always, more to hope for – so long as we can turn our backs on the worlds of unreality so seductively opened up by some of our recent financial history. Patience, trust and the acceptance of a world of real limitation are all hard work; yet the only liberation that is truly worthwhile is the liberation to be where we are and who we are as human beings, to be anchored in the reality that is properly ours. Other less serious and less risky enterprises may appear to promise a power that exceeds our limitations – but it is at the expense of truth, and so, ultimately at the expense of human life itself. Perhaps the very heart of the current challenge is the invitation to discover a little more deeply what is involved in *human* freedom – not the illusory freedom of some fantasy of control.

18

Theology and economics: two different worlds?

1

It is quite striking that in the gospel parables Jesus more than once uses the world of economics as a framework for his stories – the parable of the talents, the dishonest steward, even, we might say, the little vignette of the lost coin. Like farming, like family relationships, like the tensions of public political life, economic relations have something to say to us about how we see our humanity in the context of God's action. Money is a metaphor like other things; our money transactions, like our family connections and our farming and fishing labours, bring out features of our human condition that, rightly understood, tell us something of how we might see our relation to God.

The point doesn't need to be laboured. Monetary exchange is simply one of the things people do. It can be carried out well or badly, honestly or dishonestly, generously or meanly. It is one of those areas of life in which our decisions show who we are, and so it is a proper kind of raw material for stories designed to suggest how encounter with God shows us who we are. All obvious enough, you may think. But we should reflect further on this – because we have become used in our culture to an attitude to economics which more or less turns the parables on their head. In this new framework, economic motivations, relationships, conventions and so on are the fundamental thing and the rest is window-dressing. Instead of economics being one source of metaphor among others for the realities of self-definition and self-discovery, other ways of speaking and understanding are substitutes for economic assessment. The language of customer and provider has wormed its way into practically all areas of our social life, even education and health care. The implication is that the most basic relation between one human being and another, or one group and another, is that of the carefully calibrated exchange of material resources; the most basic kind of assessment we can make about the actions of another, from the trader to the nurse to the politician, is the evaluation of how much they can increase my liberty to negotiate favourable deals and maximize my resources.

In asking whether economics and theology represent two different worlds, we need to be aware of the fact that a lot of contemporary economic language and habit doesn't only claim a privileged status for economics on the grounds that it works by innate laws to which other considerations are irrelevant. It threatens to reduce other sorts of discourse to its own terms – to make a bid for one world in which everything reduces to one set of questions. If we want to challenge the idea that theology and economics do belong in completely separate frames, the first thing we need to do, paradoxically, is to hang on to the idea that there really *are* different ways of talking about human activity and that not everything reduces to one sovereign model or standard of value. Economic exchange is *one of the things people do*. Treat it as the only 'real' thing people do and you face the same problems that face the evolutionary biologist for whom the only question is how organisms compete and survive or the fundamentalist Freudian for whom the only issue is how we resolve the tensions of infantile sexuality.

In each of these reductive contexts, there is something of the same process going on. Each will tell you that your capacity to examine yourself and clarify for yourself who you are in the light of your memory, imagination and varie- gated relationships is a fiction – or at best a small and insignificant aspect of your identity. The face you see in the mirror is not the real thing: you are being activated by hidden motives and calculations, you are unconsciously balancing out the forces that are involved in guaranteeing your chances of survival as a carrier of genetic material or in mediating and controlling the frustrations of Oedipal desire – or in securing the maximal control of disposable resources in a world of scarcity and competition. All of these models leave you with an uncomfortable lack of clarity about whether you can really take intelligent decisions at all on the basis of the kind of person you consciously want to be.

Traditional religious ethics – in fact, traditional ethics of any kind – doesn't require you to ignore the hidden forces that may be at work in any particular setting. It simply claims that being aware of them is part of something more integrated – a habit of picturing yourself as a single self-continuous agent who can make something distinctive out of all this material. Being a human self is learning how to ask critical questions of your own habits and compulsions so as to adjust how you act in the light of a model of human behaviour, both individual and collective, that represents some fundamental truth about what humanity is *for*. Put like this, it is possible to see the various balancing acts we engage in, the calculations of self-interest and security, the resolution of buried tensions, as aspects of finding our way to a life that *manifests* something – instead of just solving this or that problem of survival or profit. It is really to claim that our job as human beings is to *imagine ourselves,* using all the raw material that science, psychoanalysis or economics can generate for us – in the hope that the images we shape or discover will have resonance and harmony with the rhythms of how things most deeply are, with what Christians and others call the will and purpose of almighty God.

If all that is clear to begin with, we can also begin to see economics in its proper place. It is one thing that people do, yes; but perhaps at this stage of the argument we can grant that it has a very special importance. In the last few years, I have found myself repeatedly noting that the term 'economy' itself is in its origins simply the word for housekeeping. And if this is the root or the core of its sense, we ought to be able to learn something about where the whole discourse belongs by thinking through what housekeeping actually is. A household is somewhere where life is lived in common; and housekeeping is guaranteeing that this common life has some stability about it that allows the members of the household to grow and flourish and act in useful ways. A working household is an environment in which vulnerable people are nurtured and allowed to grow up (children) or wind down (the elderly); it is a background against which active people can go out to labour in various ways to reinforce the security of the household; it is a setting where leisure and creativity can find room in the general business of intensifying and strengthening the relationships that are involved. Good housekeeping seeks common well-being so that all these things can happen. And we should note that the one thing required in a background of well-being is stability. 'Housekeeping theory' is about how we use our intelligence to balance the needs of those involved and to secure trust between them. A theory that wanders too far from these basics is a recipe for damage to the vulnerable, to the regularity and usefulness of labour and to the possibilities human beings have for renewing (and challenging) themselves through leisure and creativity.

That is the kind of damage that manifestly results from an economic climate in which everything reduces to the search for maximized profit and unlimited material growth. The effects of trying to structure economic life independently of intelligent choice about long-term goals for human beings have become more than usually visible in the last 18 months, and one reason for holding this conference is the growing force of the question, 'what for?' in our global market. What is the long-term well-being we seek? What is the human face we want to see, in the mirror and in our neighbours? The isolated *homo economicus* of the old textbooks, making rational calculations of self-interest, has been exposed as a straw man: the search for profit at all costs in terms of risk and unrealism has shown that there can be a form of economic 'rationality' that is in fact wildly irrational. And, over the last two or three decades, the impact of a narrow economic rationality on public services in our society has shown how there can be a 'housekeeping' strategy that ends up destroying the nurture and stability that make a household what it is. What we most need, it seems, is to recover that vision of what the Chief Rabbi, Lord Sacks, has called 'the home we build together'.

2

So the question of how we think about shared well-being is the central one before us. If we are not to be reduced to speaking about this only in vague terms of the control of material resources, we need a language that allows us to imagine and criticize our humanity in relation to something more than the immediate environment. Theology does not solve specific economic questions (any more than it solves specific scientific ones); but what it offers is a robust definition of what human well-being looks like and what the rationale is for human life well-lived in common.

Central to what Christian theology sets before us is mutuality. The Christian Scriptures describe the union of those who are identified with Jesus Christ as having an organic quality, a common identity shaped by the fact that each depends on all others for their life. No element in the Body is dispensable or superfluous: what affects one affects all, for good and ill, since both suffering and flourishing belong to the entire organism, not to any individual or purely local grouping. The model of human existence that is taken for granted is one in which each person is both needy and needed, both dependent on others and endowed with gifts for others. And while this is not on the whole presented as a general social programme, it is manifestly what the biblical writers see as the optimal shape of human life, life in which the purposes of God are made plain. Jesus' own teaching and practice make it quite explicit that the renewed people of God cannot exist when certain categories are systematically excluded, so that the wholeness of the community requires them to be invited. St Paul spells out the implications in terms of the metaphor of organic unity in the Body; St John recalls the teaching of Jesus at the Last Supper about the divine purpose of a oneness that will mirror the oneness of Jesus and the eternal source of his being. 'Indwelling' in one another is the ground of Christian ethics. Each believer is called to see himself or herself as equally helpless alone and gifted in relationship.

Helpless alone and gifted in relationship: this is where we start in addressing the world of economics from a Christian standpoint. No process whose goal is the limited or exclusive security of an individual, an interest group or even national community alone can be regarded as unequivocally good in Christian terms because of the underlying aspiration to a state of security in isolation. If my well-being is inseparable in God's community from the well-being of all others, a global economic ethic in which the indefinitely continuing poverty or disadvantage of some is taken for granted has to be decisively left behind. And this, remember, not simply because there is an imperative to be generous to others, but because we must recognize our own need and dependence even on those who appear to have nothing to give. To separate our destiny from that of the poor of the world, or from the rejected or disabled in our own context, is to compromise that destiny and to invite a life that is less than whole for ourselves.

To use a different but perhaps helpful metaphor, our life together reflects the way our very language works. We speak because we are spoken to, and learn to become partakers in human conversation by being invited into a flow of verbal life that has already begun. It is simply and literally impossible for us to learn and use language without acknowledging dependence; aspirations to an isolated life in this context are straightforwardly meaningless. No word or phrase is simply a possession; it is there to pass on, to use in the creation of a shared reality. And the worst abuses and misconceptions of language are those in which words and phrases are 'traded' (an interesting metaphor in this connection!) in ways that do not seek to build that shared reality – whether this is a matter of using language as a weapon, as a way of concealing truth or to manipulate judgement and desire. It is not an accident that in a context where injustice and narrow judgement prevail in economic relations, language itself becomes stale or dead. If we think of how much 'dead' language there is around in our culture (in bad journalistic writing, in advertising, in propaganda, in official jargon), we may get a clear glimpse of just how bad our economic life has become. We talk, in another powerful and significant metaphor, of 'debasing the currency' of our speech. We know that it is possible for us to forget that we need *living* language – honest language, fresh metaphors, new puzzles and challenges – for our life to be as it should. We depend on others generating this living speech and we need to be able ourselves to contribute to it: the silence of cliché and cynicism is the diabolical mirror image of the silence that comes on the far side of the most creative speech. The silence of cliché is what happens when there seems no point in listening for the new, and no energy for active response to what is said. You might as well say x as say y: everything is exchangeable. Which is itself a characteristic of the market mentality: everything can be measured and thus replaced by something of equivalent significance as far as material profit and security are concerned. Paying the right kind of attention to the corruptions of language in our age is inseparable from attending to the corruptions of our economic exchanges; and it is no less of a religious obligation.

In sum, faith educates us in dependence and in the authority of the giver at the same time. In our current climate, this particular balance is one of the hardest to achieve. But if our economic life is indeed 'one of the things we do', it will be marked in its actual operations by just the same constraints and buried rhythms or tensions that appear in other aspects of what we do. If theology has something to say about those rhythms and tensions, it has something to say to economics.

3

If what we have said so far makes sense, theology contributes two things to the discussion of an ethical economic future. It challenges, as we have seen, the idea that there is a mysterious uniqueness about economic life that takes it out of the normal scope of our discussions of intelligent choice and the humane evaluation of options. It proposes a model of human life together that insists on the fact that we are all involved in the fate of any individual or group and that no-one is exempt from damage or incapable of gift within the human community as God intends it. But the second aspect worth noting is that, by underlining the fact that we do have the capacity for truthful self-understanding and thus for intelligent scrutiny of alternative courses of action, the Christian theological vision also offers a critical account of what human personality can be. It provides a basis for talking about character and thus about virtue (as I have suggested elsewhere). It takes for granted that we have a proper interest in the continuity, the intelligibility, of our lives; that we have a proper interest, to use a slightly different idiom, in integrity – in being recognizable to ourselves from moment to moment, and being answerable for ourselves from moment to moment. It is clear enough, alas, that regulation alone is ill-equipped to solve our problems: the issues need to be internalized in terms of the sort of life that humans might find actively desirable and admirable, the sort of biographies that carry conviction by their self-consistency. And this means recovering the language of the virtues and the courage to speak of what a good life looks like – as well as the clarity to identify what has gone wrong in our society when we fail to set out a clear picture of the good life as it appears in trade and finance as much as in the classical professions.

This means, in turn, rescuing the concept of civic virtue, and thus the idea of public life as a possible vocation for the morally serious person. The discussion we have embarked on in this conference is not simply about the theological grounds for a more just social order, though it is at least that; it is also a matter of grasping that 'well-being' involves the capacity, in the words that some contemporary philosophers like to use, of bearing one's own scrutiny – being able to look at yourself without despair or contempt. This is not at all the same as looking at yourself with complacency or self-congratulation. It is to do with developing a discerning self-awareness that is awake to possible corruptions, able to ask questions of all sorts of emotional and self-directed impulses, and capable of developing habits of honest self-examination. It depends not on the confidence of getting or having got things right, but on the confidence that it is possible steadily to expose yourself to the truth, whatever your repeated failures to live in and through it. Well-being entails a dimension of hopeful honesty that keeps alive the conviction that learning and change are real in human life and that there can be a story to be told that will hold a life together with some sort of coherence.

So the contribution of theology to economic decision-making is not only about raising questions concerning the common good, questions to do with how this or that policy grants or withholds liberty for the most disadvantaged. These are obviously necessary matters, and a sound theological stress on mutuality, on the balance of dependence and gift sketched earlier, is crucial to our public discussion of economics. But we need also to look with the greatest of care at what is being assumed and what is being actively promoted by our economic practices about human motivation, about character and integrity. This impacts of course on the integrity of business practice; but it also has to do with assumptions about competition, about the priority of work over family, about what advertising appeals to and what behaviour is rewarded. If we find, as a good many commentators and researchers have observed in recent years, that working practices regularly reward behaviour that is undermining of family life, driven or obsessional, relentlessly competitive and adversarial, we have some questions to ask. As well as working for a global economic order that is just and mutual, we need habits in the actual workings of the financial 'industry' that do not destroy what I called earlier 'discerning self-awareness' and the capacity for humane relationships.

4

Economic activity is something people do, one kind of activity among others; and as such it is subject to the same moral considerations as all other activities. It has to be thought about in connection with what we actively want for our humanity. And questions about what we want will take us beyond 'pure' economic categories just as surely as talking seriously about politics or technology will take us outside a narrowly specialized discourse once we want to know what they're for. Human life is indeed a tapestry of diverse activities, not reducible to each other. It is not the case that all motivation is 'really' economic, that all relations are actually to do with exchange and the search for profit. Yet it can be said with some reason that economics in the sense of house-keeping is a background for other things; and because of that, it is particularly important to keep an eye on its moral contours. Get this wrong and many other things go wrong, in respect of individual character as well as social relations.

Thus we are bound to look for the sort of language that will keep our imagination and our critical faculties alive in this enterprise, that will keep us alert to the dangers of all sorts of reductionism. Theology in one way does represent a 'separate' frame of reference, one that doesn't at all depend on how things turn out in this world for its system of values. That's why it isn't in competition with other sorts of discourse. But that is also why it is so important – so indispensable, a believer would say – a register for talking about such a range of activities. It recalls us to the idea that what makes humanity human is completely independent of anyone's judgements of failure or success, profit or loss. It is sheer gift – sheer love, in Christian terms. And if the universe itself is founded on this, there will be no sustainable human society for long if this goes unrecognized.

PART FIVE

Justice in Community

19

Sustainable communities

What comes to mind when we hear a term like 'sustainable community'? As with 'sustainable development', it's surely about living in an environment that has a future we can imagine. And to talk of a future we can imagine is to talk of certain plans and hopes that are shared. 'Sustainability' is not a matter of how we create something that never has to change; it's to do with how we cope with change in a way that has integrity and continuity, that secures for us a background of trustworthiness that encourages a bit of creativity. Sustainable development is development that does not wreck and deplete the environment so seriously that there is no secure background for human labour and society. So perhaps we should be thinking of sustainable community as the sort of social environment that does not wreck and deplete human capital so much that there is no energy left for initiative and discovery.

If we are going to plan sustainable communities, then, we have to have a good nose for what depletes human capital. And I want to suggest that one major threat to human capital is the sense of living without landmarks in time or space. A friend of mine once said that he thought airport lounges were a device to make us ready to be shipped into outer space because they were designed to be 'nowhere in particular'. But how much building and development in recent decades has proceeded as if the aim was indeed to create an impression of nowhere in particular? Human beings from their earliest days work out their identity by learning to cope with a specific set of triggers and stimuli, the geography of a room, the rhythms of feeding and sleeping, a face that becomes familiar. As their awareness expands, they still work out and define who they are in relation to patterns of activity in time and to a differentiated space; their mental world is in part a set of routes between familiar points. We inhabit a map. It is most dramatically expressed in the Australian aboriginal idea of the 'song lines' that give structure to the world: the aborigine knows the landscape as a series of songs to be sung as you move from this point to that. Geography is a set of instructions for responding with this or that song to the visual triggers you encounter.

Now of course any landscape, any physical environment, has such triggers. But it seems fairly clear that a physical environment that is repetitive, undifferentiated, can fail to give adequate material for a person to develop. A varied environment with marked features, that perhaps have narratives and memories attached to them, offers multiple stimuli to respond to. There is a local geography that is more than just an abstract plan of the ground: it invests places with shared significance. But for this to happen, places must be distinguishable, differentiated. A landscape which proclaims its sameness with countless others, in its layout, building materials, retail outlets and so on, is a seedbed for problems. If it's true that I can't answer the question 'Who am I?' without at some level being able to answer the question 'Where am I?', the character of a built space becomes hugely important. There will always be small scale domestic answers to 'Where am I?' because we all imprint distinctiveness on our homes and are 'imprinted' by them; but when this is restricted to the domestic, we should not be surprised if there is little sense of investment in the local environment outside the home.

So the first challenge for the building of sustainable community is whether a development has thought through its geography in such a way as to be somewhere in particular. We have been through a good many false starts in the last hundred years or so. So much of the philosophy of the interwar suburban developments and the post-war municipal growth assumed that absolute homogeneity was what was required. Communities were created that looked essentially like warehouses for people, areas which, while not technically anonymous, could have been called anything. And because all the pressure was towards increasing 'zoning', old urban centres became increasingly stripped of any residential element, and retail outlets in new developments were often in unattractive and vulnerable clusters. More recently, we have seen the challenge of massive new developments (like the Thames Gateway) offering new opportunities to disadvantaged communities, but with the risk of swamping them and making them more and more anonymous.

Functioning communities need to develop a sense of place, and that means developing variety, a real landscape, not just a territory covered with 'machines for living'. In the last decade, we have seen major shifts in some areas of response to the challenge. Simple things like variety in building styles and materials in new developments have made some difference; there has been something of a return to the older town centres; there have been several developments, notably in a number of dockland or waterfront locations, that have clearly set out to maximize the particularity of a setting. So it is a good time to take stock and to try and outline how the communities of the next generation can be saved from the curse of living nowhere in particular. I have no blueprint, but here are a few thoughts on the possibilities.

First, something is contributed to a sense of place by using, where possible, local building materials or at least making use of local styles. This is not to condemn builders to an endless round of pastiche: fresh things can be done and have been done in this connection; and the advantage of such a strategy is both to offer some sort of continuity with a visible local history and to offer a visible set of marks for recognition of a specific location in the present. It affirms that the community now is here because of a past, because of other lives, other stories. It is not locked into itself in a sterile eternal present. This is one of the things, after all, that may prompt people in the present to act so as to leave a legacy – to 'imagine a future', as I put it earlier.

Second: we need some thinking about how retail outlets are to be planned. In spite of recent reversals in policy which favour town-centre retail sites, it is unlikely that we shall see a significant reversal in the drift to large-scale out-of-town malls and supermarkets – and town-centre sites are in any case likely to be dominated by retail chains and fast-service smaller-scale supermarkets. For the foreseeable future, most shopping that is not done via the internet will still be done in such a setting. But there need to be challenges to at least some of the assumptions behind this, and some strategies that limit the cost of this. I am thinking not only of the devastation of small businesses it can represent, but also of the straightforward environmental cost of shopping habits entirely dependent on private motor transport. This might be addressed in two ways. One is by careful planning of public transport facilities in relation to large-scale retail parks, following through the existing provision of courtesy buses by some large retail outlets: we need a standard policy of tenants in such environments making provision for travel or accepting a levy that would subsidize public transport. Another is to ask about further incentives for certain sorts of outlet to remain in smaller clusters within residential areas. But such clusters would need to be something more than the single depressed-looking parade of shop fronts we see in most mid-twentieth-century suburbs and estates. Clusters would need some landscaping, and some leisure space comparable to what many malls offer; and they would need to be fairly well distributed, with an eye to what a neighbourhood might look like, with a focal space inside a certain walking distance. Being bold and fanciful, I wonder whether the arcade format ought to be looked at again, as something that could provide sheltered space and might be combinable with fairly dense residential development around.

Third: increasingly, schools in newly built areas see themselves as a major community resource in terms of space and other facilities, and are designed as such. The school is still in many significant ways a necessarily public space, practically the only one in some environments. Designing schools with this dimension in mind is imperative – and once again there are some good examples. A school is ideally somewhere where the affirmation of a community can be fostered, and it needs to be committed to holding on to memories older than simply the creation of this particular housing development. If it is well designed and has a thoroughly positive attitude to community access, it contributes enormously to 'a future we can imagine'. If I had a specific dream around this area, it would be of planning that integrated school buildings with some of the common space for small-scale retail development that I've just been speculating about. This could conceivably mean the making of a really common space: leisure facilities, educational and arts facilities, the simple availability of places for both personal and group meeting, all in physical proximity, would help to shape a civic landscape which gave the message that people were naturally expected to want to meet, to relax in common and to learn together, from childhood onwards. It is always worth looking at a plan for any building and any complex of buildings and asking, 'What does this take for granted about what people most want?' The answers in respect of an awful lot of development over three quarters of a century suggest a pretty diminished view of human aims and desires – dwellings that are both undifferentiated and mutually isolated (just as true in the executive estate as in the tower block), an assumption that living space is almost exclusively domestic space and that common public space is a thing of the past. A creative use of educational buildings (which are bound to be on a certain scale) is one of the simplest ways of restoring something of a public square.

Fourth, you won't be surprised to hear something on the significance of religious provision in the planning of communities. This is partly because, despite the never very large statistics for religious practice, two facts have to be clearly kept in view. First, the majority of the population, whatever their practice, continue to affirm some sort of religious belief, and to be sympathetic to the visible presence of religious institutions among them – not least in church schools, but also in the availability of church buildings of some kind. Second, in an increasingly culturally varied society, the visibility of communities of faith becomes significant in a new way. If this cultural variety is more than a faint background to what is essentially a unified body of secular consumers, it must leave space for faith to be a tangible aspect of variety; after all, for non-Western believers (Christian and non-Christian), faith is not a picturesque extra to the essentials of life, whose proper place is domestic or at least behind locked doors. The ultimate denial of real cultural plurality is this insistence on religious invisibility. It may be argued (indeed, it is argued) that only a rigorously neutral public space can prevent us from falling into violent tribal rivalries between faith groups. But this is anything but uncontroversial as an assumption, and it seems to take it for granted that constructive statements of honest difference cannot be contained in a single society. The evidence is not exactly clear on that. And it is often in the very process of working at common belonging, civic and civil space, which we have been thinking about that constructive and co-operative variety can appear. People who have a sense that the deepest roots of their motivation can be stated and respected in public are more likely to want to engage in civic and civil labour. Tell them that their contributions are welcome, but only if they rigorously censor the expression of their most serious commitments, and some will not be eager to close on the bargain.

And last, planning should, then, look seriously at how the reality of faith becomes part of the landscape – how religious buildings figure among the landmarks of a community. But this is not only a question of attending to the pragmatic needs of religious groups. Like it or not, there are unsought experiences that communities share, trauma and celebration which call out for the kind of space that carries no political or sectional agenda, that is not for anything but the expression of certain serious and complex emotions. I recall an incident during my time in South Wales, when a teenager had been murdered on the way home from school on the edge of a large modern estate. The local curate had talked to some of the girl's classmates and as a result had opened the church on a Friday evening for a few hours, for anyone who wanted to drop in. The small building was packed; something could be said, felt, expressed there that did not have a home anywhere else. And whether we are thinking about personal trauma or collective (marking the anniversary of a fire or disaster, responding to a national crisis or an international challenge such as the tsunami), it is emphatically true that a very large number of people, far larger than the statistics of regular worshippers, urgently need a place for certain things to be voiced. What is offered by a space dedicated to worship is essential – somewhere where events may occur that belong to a whole locality, where solidarities of a mysterious but very important kind can be reinforced.

This is only a sketch of the sort of considerations that might arise for planners and funders if they believed that people needed more than a determined block of living space within a flattened landscape. And as my last point implies, and as I hinted earlier, the problem is one of undifferentiated time as well as undifferentiated space. Communities are rendered unsustainable not only by flattened space, but by 'flattened time'. Our age is one in which a mixture of aggressive commercialism and unbroken global communication technology have between them ironed out for many people what once seemed obvious rhythms in our lives – day and night, work and rest. Communities that work well, I suggest, need differentiated time as well as differentiated space – that is, they need some sort of calendar. The round of religious festivals has shrunk to a very residual awareness of Christmas and Easter, and neither could be said to be observances for a whole community. Religious practitioners of all backgrounds will of course maintain their own calendars, but they will not represent a rhythm that is natural and taken for granted in the wider society. It is not strictly a question for planners; but it is worth asking, if we are interested in a community's health and survival capacity, how we break up time into significant units, how we punctuate the simple duration of our days with events that locate us in more than the space immediately under our eyes. We have some guidelines nationally when major events are constructed for anniversaries – commemorating the end of the last war, the Holocaust or 9/11. How do smaller local communities do something similar? The remarkable persistence in some places of Remembrance Sunday, and the creation or revival of quite large scale corporate acts of remembrance speak of a need for public 'liturgy', acknowledging (however vaguely) something overwhelmingly costly behind the apparent securities of the present. Local observation of such global traumas or of the date of some purely local event that has deeply marked the history of an area are obvious ways of affirming some common roots for the present social settlement that go beyond current solidarities of ideas or interests.

Ultimately, questions about belonging lead us either to a view of solidarity and identity based on tightly negotiated interests in common, and often therefore to a highly anxious and adversarial stance towards other communities – or to a view in which solidarity comes from a sense of living in a landscape that has its own solidity, its own dimensions in time and space, independent of the current interests of the particular group that happens to live there at the moment. Solidarity of the second kind is perhaps less likely to be easily manipulated into artificial rivalry with other communities. The most mindless and most passionate conflicts are often – not by any means always, but often enough to be worth remarking – between groups that are very similar in their practice and culture, because it is then easy to argue that a very similar group must be a threat to your own uniqueness and to the security of your territory. Communities and societies that have a sense of who and where they are that is positive and internal to themselves will not need to reinforce themselves in the way that virtually indistinguishable groups have to, by stressing who they are not. So a community that is committed to replenishing and not depleting human capital is one that is aware of being in a real place that has its own integrity, character and memory. Memory cannot be manufactured; but any new development needs to build, metaphorically as well as literally, on genuinely local ground, on an area and its history and human geography.

There are no infallible recipes for sustainable communities. But there are ways of identifying what depletes our resources and of combating those factors with some urgency and energy. It has taken time to spot some of the worst offenders; but I hope that after a longish period of what was in many ways a deeply anti-human set of assumptions about living environments, we have acquired a few skills. Little I have said here will be new, and I am well aware of the way in which many of the points I have been making are being taken on board by developers, planners and builders. Round the corner from Lambeth Palace, you can see some of the work of Coin Street Community Builders – a development trust originally set up in the early 1980s to offer alternatives to the building of more office blocks along the South Bank. It has sponsored business development and social housing, leisure space, improved facilities for public transport, intensive management of parks and walkways, an important community arts festival, multi-purpose neighbourhood centres, incorporating space for educational, play and meeting opportunities; and it has fostered co-operative management of its housing projects, with training in the requisite skills. There are plenty more examples of this kind of social enterprise. If there are no infallible recipes, at least there is abundant good practice.

But the more we continue to set this against a backdrop of serious thinking about what human beings need space for (and thus about what human beings are for), the more committed we shall be to resisting that shrinkage of human space that has so often blighted urban and suburban development in the past century (and more). There are things we can do to give new development 'a local habitation and a name', to build as though we understood how human beings become themselves in loyalty to a set of local landmarks and stories and idioms, how they need space for deep conviction to become visible and deep emotion to be allowed expression. If we can act in this way, we shall be planning for communities that can in turn act and plan for a shared future. We shall have shaped a human environment that nourishes imagination – and in the widest sense, nourishes faith.

20

The gifts reserved for age: perceptions of the elderly

A lot of human cultures have a very structured idea of the process of human ageing. It's most vividly illustrated perhaps in the traditional Indian idea that, having raised a family and discharged your duty to society in this way, you should abandon your home and devote yourself to meditation or pilgrimage, become a wandering *sannyasin*.

We probably find this very strange. Although admirable organizations like Saga Tours have made the wandering life a real possibility for some beyond the first flush of middle-age, I suspect this isn't quite what classical Hinduism has in mind. But what underlies the Indian idea? I think it is the belief that there comes a stage in people's lives when they no longer have to justify their existence; when it is right and proper for them to spend time reflecting on what they have been and what they have done and trying to make better sense of it. We used to talk, even in European culture, of having time to 'make your soul' as you move closer to death. It's a very telling phrase, suggesting that most of us in our working lives will have had little time to give substance and depth to who we really are.

In a spiritually sensitive culture, then, it might well be that age is something to be admired or envied. A person is released from the pressure to justify himself or herself, free to discover who they are – and perhaps to pass on to the rest of us something of what they discover. Looking around, my own sense is that there is a certain amount of double vision in our environment. There is a degree of jocular envy directed towards the retired; people will both express their wish that they had the leisure they imagine the retired have, and affect a cheerful scepticism about how 'retired' people actually are, a cheerful scepticism encouraged by the retired themselves ('I bet you find it hard to sit around all day'; 'I'm busier now than I've ever been').

But on the other hand, age in itself is not so positively seen. In sharp contrast to the idea that this stage of life is enviable, we hear high levels of anxiety about getting old, anxieties about health, mobility, access to facilities, simple routine care and attention. What's more, in a climate where media and marketing concentrate on the young to a staggering degree, the images of what age might be are seldom encouraging. What is there to aspire to in age? What does the good life look like for those who don't have the opportunities, for financial or social or health reasons, to live as the marketing industry seems to assume you ought to live? The point's been made often enough that a global advertising culture breeds both unreal aspiration and bitter resentment among the economically disadvantaged. But it's a point worth pondering in the context of our images of youth and age as well; what does this global culture say about – and say to – the elderly? It isn't surprising if the prospect of age is unattractive to many people. When Shakespeare's King Lear mocks the attitude of his business-like daughters by offering to admit that 'age is unnecessary', he foreshadows with uncanny accuracy the fear that surrounds this area: being old is being dispensable. And it's worth noting that he also reminds us that prejudice or contempt for the elderly is not a purely modern matter, even if it has become culturally more prevalent. When T. S. Eliot used the evocative phrase I have borrowed for my title today, he was being ironic: he goes on to enumerate those experiences of remorse and helpless self-doubt or self-dislike that memory in old age can bring – a salutary reminder that 'making your soul' is never as straightforward as we might like it to be. What if age is largely about mourning, loss and bitterness?

Of course, ageing brings much that is bound to be threatening; of course it entails the likelihood of sickness and disability and that most frightening of all prospects, the loss of mental coherence. But if this is combined with an unspoken assumption that the elderly are socially insignificant because they are not prime consumers or producers, the public image of ageing is bound to be extra bleak; and that is the message that can so easily be given these days. In contrast to a setting where age means freedom from having to justify your existence, age in our context is often implicitly presented as a stage of life when you exist 'on sufferance'. You're not actually pulling your weight; you're not an important enough bit of the market to be targeted in most advertising, except of a rather specialized and often rather patronizing kind. In an obsessively sexualized world of advertising and other images, age is often made to look pathetic and marginal. And in the minds of most people there will be the picture of the geriatric ward or certain kinds of residential institution.

To borrow the powerful expression used of our prisons by Baroness Kennedy, this is 'warehousing' – stacking people in containers because we can think of nothing else to do with them. From time to time, we face those deeply uncomfortable reports about abuse or even violence towards the vulnerable. Terrible as this is, we need to see it as an understandable consequence of a warehousing mentality.

As the Friends of the Elderly make plain in their literature, even if not precisely in these terms, the question of how we perceive age is essentially a spiritual one. If you have a picture of human life as a story that needs pondering, retelling, organizing, a story that is open to the judgement and mercy of God, it will be natural to hope for time to do this work, the making of the soul. It will be natural to ask how the life of older people can be relieved of anxiety, and how the essentially creative work of reflection can be helped. It is not an exaggeration to say that, in such a perspective, growing old will make the greatest creative demands of your life. Furthermore, if we are all going to have the opportunity of undertaking reflection like this, it will be important that older people have the chance to share the task with the rest of us. The idea that age necessarily means isolation will be challenged. There is a sense that what matters for our own future thinking through of our life stories doesn't depend on the sort of things that go in and out of fashion. That is why, in most traditional societies, the term 'elder' is a title of honour – as it is, of course, in the Christian Church, where the English word 'priest' is an adaptation of the Greek for 'elder'. A person who has been released from the obligation to justify their existence is one who can give a perspective on life for those of us who are still in the middle of the struggle; their presence ought to be seen as a gift.

Incidentally, one of the most worrying problems in the impact of Western modernity on traditional culture is that it quite rapidly communicates its own indifference, anxiety or even hostility about age and ageing. Generation gaps open and it is no longer clear what there is to be learned. On our own doorsteps, we now have to confront a situation in, for example, the British Muslim community, where the status of older family members has been eroded by the prevailing culture around, creating a vacuum: of course, it is natural and in many ways healthy for the young to examine and explore the received wisdom of their elders as they move towards maturity, but when younger members of a community are left without signposts, they are more easily shifted towards extreme behaviour of one sort or another. It is as if, in the crises of these communities and the challenge they pose to the rest of our society, we see an intensified image of the tensions and unfinished business in our whole attitude to age and ageing.

We must not be sentimental. Age doesn't automatically confer wisdom, and the authority of 'elders' of one sort or another can be oppressive, unrealistic and selfish. But when we completely lose sight of any idea that older people have a crucial role in pointing us to the way we might work to make better sense of our lives, we lose something vital. We lose the assumption that there is a perspective on our human experience that is bigger than the world of production and consumption. Work, sex, the struggle to secure our position or status, the world in which we constantly negotiate our demands and prove ourselves fit to take part in public life – what is there outside all this that might restore some sense of a value that is just given, a place that doesn't have to be earned? A healthy attitude to the elderly, I believe, is one of the things that can liberate us from the slavery of what we take for granted as the 'real' world. Giving dignity to the elderly – and dignity is a crucial word for the mission of groups such as Friends of the Elderly – is inseparable from recognizing the dignity of human beings as such. Contempt for older citizens, the unthinking pushing of them to the edges of our common life, is a sure sign of a shrivelled view of what it is to be human.

That is why I've said that how we perceive age is a spiritual issue. And if it is the kind of spiritual issue I've tried to outline, we need, in response, to think hard about how we resource policies for the elderly that will not only secure the dignity we have been speaking of, reducing as far as possible the anxiety that ought to be lifted from the elderly, but will also help us see how the relationship between older people and the rest of society can be best nourished, on the assumption that the rest of society actually needs its older citizens. Quite a few science fiction stories have played with the idea of a society where people's lives are terminated after a certain (not very advanced) age; but they all suggest that such societies are in one way or another mad. And their madness is the effect not simply the cause of their rejection of the process of ageing.

So the challenge we face in supporting the dignity and security of the elderly is far more than a practical one of raising enough resources; it is about identifying the underlying assumptions that keep elderly people marginal, challenging the shortage of positive pictures of ageing. And to do this effectively, we have to develop a view of human flourishing and human justice that is not content with the criteria of producing and consuming alone. Properly understood, a positive attitude to ageing is an act of faith in human freedom from the mechanical processes of work and the anxieties that go with this.

Developing viable and intelligent attitudes to ageing is not, of course, an academic issue, given the demographic facts. We are an ageing population.

The percentage of young people in the total population is falling fast, and we have hardly begun to think through what this might mean as far as resource allocation is concerned. Can we envisage a situation in which this could be seen as a good thing? Can we envisage resisting the temptation to regard the demographic pattern of the future as primarily a threat to economic efficiency? Well, only if our current attitudes undergo a fair amount of reshaping. And every successful effort in giving the elderly choice, dignity and a respected place in the conversation of society is an essential element in that reshaping.

It is not easy to specify everything that needs doing as we work through all this. But, in the light of our society's history, we could venture a few obvious areas. Housing has become a focal concern; we are more and more conscious of the danger of assuming that there are only two real alternatives for the elderly – living alone (and therefore at risk) or living institutionally. One of the notable shifts in the pattern of life for older people in the last three decades has been the development of different levels of sheltered and partly communal housing. It would make quite a difference if the planning of new housing developments routinely incorporated questions about this element of the social mix. This is the case in some contexts, but not all; and the bringing of this issue more clearly and explicitly into the purview of planners and private developers would be a welcome sign of vision. What we do about planning and housing will speak volumes about whether we actually believe older people should be visible in society; so often we act and plan as if they shouldn't.

Training for professionals and volunteers is also going to be of importance. Volunteer home support is a crucial part of what Friends of the Elderly offers, but it needs constant encouragement and resourcing. If we are to see a society in which real friendship with older people matters, where they are actively encouraged to be part of the wider social network, we shall need more of the already developing co-operation and partnerships with social services, education and the NHS to equip younger people to carry this forward effectively. It is work that has begun very impressively in some areas, but it should be clear that it will make heavier demands as time goes on. If we genuinely want to give older people choices about where and how they live, and if it is best for some to continue with a degree of independence, we have to work to create the best conditions for this.

This instance brings into focus what ought to be obvious – in this as in other areas of social concern. Making sure that older people are part of networks and neighbourhoods is not a job that can be done exclusively or even primarily by statutory bodies. The demands are unpredictable, the goals often hard to quantify. But a thriving culture of voluntary help needs public affirmation. Should we be looking to government to sponsor something like a nationwide set of benchmarks for the care of the elderly; a full and comprehensive 'charter', if you like, for older citizens? Despite all the difficulties I have already mentioned, there is still widespread public sympathy for the challenges facing the elderly – most people, after all, have to deal with these in their own families. The sense that our government institutions were declaring some responsibility for standards here, and were actively encouraging and supporting training projects would be another welcome development in the eyes of most citizens.

To digress just for a moment, I want to mention one specific kind of enterprise that crosses several frontiers in addressing the needs of older people. I have seen at close quarters some of the positive effects of oral history projects. Such a project can involve very young people, schoolchildren especially; it affirms the value of older people's memories; it allows them a chance to do some of that work we have already been thinking about, of ordering and reflecting on a life history. It is one of those aspects of an integrated approach to the elderly that charities concerned in this area should welcome and foster as best they can. I'd go so far as to say that any list of positive standards and expectations for the elderly should include the possibility of recording and talking through memories with younger people.

But mention of memory at once raises the dark shadow that is for most of us one of the most deeply threatening aspects of ageing. As the 2005 annual review of Friends of the Elderly points out, a generally ageing population means an increase in the number of people likely to be afflicted with dementia. A large percentage of the population (and I should say that I am among them) has experience of the dilemmas of care that arise here. So far, a lot of what I have said might presuppose a more sunny prospect for older people than is in fact the case for a significant proportion of them.

Our understanding of dementia conditions is growing all the time, and we have seen a number of promising theories developed about contributory causes or about aspects of lifestyle that might defer or prevent the onset of these distressing states. But much is still mysterious, and we are not remotely likely to have resolved the problems in the next few decades. Here perhaps we are most challenged; it is not a matter of respecting age because older people are free to reflect and share their reflection. The question is whether we can respect and love those who may seem to have no clear picture of themselves or others at all.

These are the people who most of all have no obvious stake in society, no justi-fying role. Yet how we treat them is as clear an index of our social vision as is the issue of how we treat children – almost more so, since these are not people who will grow and change in obviously positive ways. Are we truly committed to giving place and respect to those who can return nothing (as it seems)?

Instinctively, we recognize that even the often deeply harrowed and disturbed consciousness of those who suffer from dementia is a human consciousness whose confusion and anguish do not make it any the less a proper subject for our compassion and service. Once again, increasingly sophisticated training is called for; and Friends of the Elderly can congratulate themselves on the pioneering work done in this field, with the imaginative developments in mapping behaviour, planning sympathetic physical environments and flexible timetables, and resourcing respite care. It is, I think, dangerous to imagine that in this area especially voluntary provision alone will meet the needs we are likely to confront in a couple of decades. It is all the more important to think ahead, to set standards for expectations, and to develop training programmes for both volunteers and professionals.

As I have said, this poses the toughest challenge to our willingness to take the elderly seriously. But if we begin from the spiritual priorities I have tried to outline, we should have to say that, even in a disturbed consciousness there is something going on that calls for our patience. One of my own most vivid and indeed painful recollections of my mother's condition in the last months of her life is of the feeling that she was still struggling to communicate, to make some sort of sense; I couldn't understand or help, but I knew that at the very least I owed her my presence and my efforts to listen.

Yet in the harsh world of limited funding and personnel, how do we go on defending the expenditure of money and skill on such situations? As we've seen, there is always the temptation to 'warehousing' in substandard geriatric care. But I have to say too in this context that the current drift towards a more accepting attitude to assisted suicide and euthanasia in some quarters gives me a great deal of concern. What begins as a compassionate desire to enable those who long for death because of protracted pain, distress or humiliation to have their wish can, with the best will in the world, help to foster an attitude that assumes resources spent on the elderly are a luxury. Investment in palliative medicine, ensuring that access to the best palliative care is universally available, continuing research not only into the causes, but into the behavioural varieties of dementia and so on – how secure would these be as priorities if there were any more general acceptance of the principle that it was legitimate to initiate a process designed to end someone's life? I am certainly not ascribing to the defenders of euthanasia or assisted dying any motive but the desire to spare people unnecessary suffering. But I think we have to ask the awkward question about how this might develop in a climate of anxiety about scarce resources.

I do not have a quick solution to the undeniable problem of resources. Nor, frankly, does anyone, independently of a deepened motivation to guarantee just treatment and high quality care for all, a motivation that honestly faces the demands on public and private finance that this will make. The fundamental question is whether we see this as expenditure that honours a human dignity we care about, or whether it is thought of as at best an unwelcome and rather irrational obligation. What I have tried to do in these brief observations is to argue that age deserves honour in any society which is serious about two things – about the fact that we all have the task of making sense of our lives by telling our stories without pressure, and about the fact that the value of our lives is not ultimately linked with the level of how much we produce or how much we consume.

If we do not accept that we ought to be serious about these things, we shall not only fail the elderly and treat them more and more as marginal to the real business of human communities: we shall run the risk of building into our society a far wider disregard for the disadvantaged, those who are not in the forefront of producing and consuming. The Friends of the Elderly first came into existence because of the recognition that people living lives of poverty needed literal friends and advocates; the current profile of the charity reflects the awareness that older citizens are still constantly among the most high risk groups where economic and social privation are concerned. Taking the poor seriously means taking the elderly seriously, even those older people who do not suffer the most obviously acute forms of material deprivation.

Friends of the Elderly has for the last century had the task of speaking and acting for the sake of what we now fashionably call 'social inclusion' – speaking for the poor, but more and more speaking for those whose lives are now lived outside the realm of 'getting and spending'. And this has meant speaking against certain things, against the over-functional narrowness that fails to see inherent dignity in everyone, against any idea that people don't deserve space and respect to become themselves more deeply and lastingly as they grow older. The task remains; it has not got easier and it is not likely to. But we should remember the millions of people who still have the instinctive feeling I described earlier, the feeling that something is owed to our older citizens and that something crucial can be learned from them. Our job is to affirm that instinct without reservation or apology and to keep it linked to a whole sense of what we properly are as men and women – people who live in time, who learn who they are as they pursue both inner and outer dialogues, who need to be released from the tyrannies of producing and performing which so dominate our lives. The respect we learn and practice with our seniors is not something slavish or immature; it is a mark of our own maturity, indeed, our respect for our own humanity. Showing that and sharing that will give us work for a good many more centuries.

Reforming punishment

1

'Responsibility' is always in danger of being a rather grey word; it can be used repressively and even menacingly. Because it has come to be the counterweight to talk about rights, it is liable to sound like the bad news after the good news – rights and responsibilities, we say, to remind ourselves that there are no free lunches. I suspect that this rather sombre colouring to the word is the result of understanding responsibility primarily as being accountable to others, to society, authority and so on. 'You must act responsibly' is what the world around says to us, to me; it is about restrictions, about the proper negotiating of our purposes in full awareness of the claims of others.

This is true as far as it goes, but the cost of thinking only in these terms is high. It leaves out of account that other aspect of responsibility to which I want to draw attention here, which is responsibility for: it isn't just that we are responsible to others, and that others have a right to demand certain kinds of behaviour from us; we are also responsible for each other. Each of us has to answer for someone else's welfare as well as our own – and that means that there must also be someone else who is there to answer for us, whose concern is our welfare. This is a theme deeply rooted in our Judaeo-Christian ethic. From the question of God to Cain – 'Where is your brother?' – to St Paul telling us to 'bear one another's burdens', this ethical tradition affirms that the most fruitful and peaceful common life depends on willingness to speak and act for each other in this way. It isn't simply that we are all responsible to a common and impersonal set of claims; the relation is horizontal as well as vertical, and we are in the business of speaking up for, defending and enriching the lives of other people. A good legal culture, on this definition, will be one that allows and encourages this kind of mutuality, not simply one that reinforces the general claims of the other and the community. It is a culture in which it is taken for granted that everyone should have a voice, and that where voices go unheard for whatever reason, there will be others who accept that they must make sure this silence is broken. It is not perhaps a self-evident feature of liberal or democratic society if those terms are thought of only as securing various kinds of freedom from outside interference or unchallengeable top-down authority. But if liberal and democratic societies are to be more than assemblies of atoms, we need something like this biblical dimension of responsibility for each other to come into play.

So yes, the doublet of rights and responsibilities is unavoidable. But it is not a matter of balancing what's due to me with what's due to society or other people in general. My responsibility to speak for you is inseparable from someone's responsibility to speak for me: no one is left isolated, and no-one's welfare is finally to be separated from that of all others. Responsibility is good news as well as bad, if you must think in that sort of framework. And what a healthy legal culture promotes is – if you allow this general moral background, what you could call a 'liberal-plus' approach – individuals growing into better mutual awareness, so that their speaking for each other and taking on the task of another's welfare may be just, well-informed and solidly motivated.

In what follows, I want to apply these principles to the Criminal Justice System as we know it in the UK at present and to ask where the most urgent need lies for action to equip it better for this kind of purpose. If a healthy legal culture is defined as I have suggested, how healthy is our current climate? Reform in this area naturally asks the question of whose interests are suffering at any given moment, whose voice is unheard. And perhaps the strongest new groundswell of popular opinion in the last couple of decades has been to do with the rights of victims. The way in which our legal processes have often had the effect of 'revictimizing' those who have suffered from crime has been a constant refrain, especially where crimes against women and children or otherwise vulnerable people are concerned. Stress is also laid on the need of victims for some sense of closure, and for some sense of involvement in a legal process that, after all, is only happening because they have suffered. This arises in part from a very natural reaction against sentimental attitudes to offenders on the part of well-meaning liberal reformers, reflecting a lack of any concern with that aspect of crime, which is about more than the guilt of an individual but involves others because it is a breaking of relationship. It is all too easy to work from a notion of crime that is wholly bound up with the individual responsibility and punishment of the offender as a means of asserting those impersonal social and communal claims that have been denied. But crime has effects that spiral outwards from the single act or group of actions at its centre, into the lives of many specific people; how do we attend to the mending of all that has been broken in this process?

2

Hence the new emphasis on the welfare of victims and the creation of groups like Victim Support; hence the questions asked about how those aspects of legal process that intimidate victims might be modified; the calls for the introduction of an ombudsman for victims of crime, and for various benefits to be available for victims whether or not an offence has been through the criminal justice system. In terms of redressing a balance and attending to a seriously neglected dimension of criminal justice policy, all this was and remains welcome. International standards for the care of crime victims – the EU Framework Decision of 2001 is a good example – have been transformed. 'Most trial processes—whether civil or common law based—leave victims feeling cheated and too many offenders fail to take responsibility for their actions' wrote Helena Kennedy in her 2004 book, *Just Law*.[1] Change was scandalously overdue.

But it is the same Baroness Kennedy who points out the problems associated with this new emphasis. It can be, she says, 'a Trojan horse'[2] for those who believe that offenders' rights, and indeed the rights of any accused person in the system even before sentencing, need to be reduced. It can stereotype the needs of victims and confuse the function of legal processes (which are not designed to be about compensation first and foremost). And in spite of concerns about the experience of victims in the legal process, some of the political advocates of victim rights have often sidestepped the immediate practical issues about how victims can be better prepared for the experience of the courts and what special provisions are desirable for the most vulnerable in particularly sensitive cases such as rape and abuse.

Most disturbing, though, is the insidious way in which the legal system, like so many other areas of our public life, comes to be consumerized in this climate. Brian Williams, Professor of Community Justice at De Montfort University, in an excellent recent study of victims and the justice system, says, of the developments in the 1990s and the early years of this decade, 'Victims were increasingly being characterised in policy debates as users, or even as clients or consumers, of the criminal justice system, although a number of observers have argued that this is a false analogy: victims have little choice about using criminal justice services and most would prefer not to be in the position of having to do so.[3] The most extreme versions of this focus on the supposed needs of victims and on the 'client' model have been in evidence in the US, with the involvement of victims in the parole process, and in some contexts the invitation to relatives of a murder victim to witness the murderer's execution. American jurists are beginning to worry about the disproportionate leverage exercised on the legal process by this degree of participation.

In the light of the general principles sketched out here, what does this say about responsibility? First of all, like every attempt to do justice to the perspective of the victim, it runs the risk of imagining the victim as perennially passive, someone things are done to, whether good or evil things. The shift towards the concerns of victims began with the recognition that the existing system left victims feeling powerless; the danger is of creating a culture in which they remain powerless – powerless to change or move forwards or exercise their freedom in a civic or communal way, and endowed only with a rather strange variety of consumer power, faced with choices that others have determined for them. A system that was at the mercy of organized lobbying on behalf of the victim would not serve the real interest of the victim because it could never break out of the stress on the victim role at just the point where someone might need help to shed that. And, as Brian Williams notes,[4] there is a temptation to politicize the whole situation, with tough sentencing policies being presented as the best way to address victims' needs. Such research as there is on 'victim satisfaction' is very far from giving anything like clear support to this. Should we not be thinking about policies that looked towards the restoring to the victim of some renewed capacity to engage responsibly? To make fuller use of the empathy that can be nurtured through reflecting on experienced injustice and trauma?

3

If some of the language around the needs of victims has these rather ambiguous implications, how do we begin to think about the needs of offenders in a way that avoids what I earlier called the sentimentality and individualism of some penal reformers in the not too distant past? If the underlying problem in crime is a breakage in relationship, this means that the offender has lost the active sense of being answerable for others. That sense is, as I've suggested, inseparable from the assurance of having others who are answerable for you. The most unhelpful and indeed damaging way of treating this is thus surely a system that leaves the offender without any grounds for believing that he or she is the object of anyone's responsibility.

This is emphatically the message that much of our present system still gives to the offender. The statistical likelihood is that an offender will be accommodated in overcrowded conditions, deprived of privacy; that contact with family will be vulnerable to unpredictable moves and varying policies in different institutions; and that informal personal support (such as the excellent work of the Samaritans, for example) will be at best patchy. Families of prisoners, including, very disturbingly, remand prisoners, who die in custody thankfully now have the assurance of transparent investigation into their deaths, though the anchorage of this in legislation is less than perfect (there was no mention of prisons in the Corporate Manslaughter Bill of 2006, an omission that the Joint Home Affairs and Work and Pensions select committees agreed to be indefensible). And of course prisoners are still deprived of the vote.

Since 2004, the National Offender Management Service has been developing, in the light of the 2002 report from the Social Exclusion Unit, a far more integrated approach to continuity within the custodial period and in the context of resettlement, and is addressing resettlement needs in far sharper focus than was once the case, commissioning more comprehensive service packages around housing, work, family support, substance abuse risks and so on. Likewise the Prison Service at the moment understandably prides itself on the quality of some rehabilitation and detoxification programmes in prisons, and on the fact that primary health care is supposed to work to the same level as the NHS in general. All this is welcome evidence of the recognition of the urgent need to provide stable and reliable services for offenders at every stage of their progress through the system and back into the community. But plenty of issues remain about delivering these new aspirations and standards, and much of this work is still embryonic. The risk of some fragmentation when services are contracted to private providers is still a contested aspect of the developing pattern of offender management. And the quality of services within prisons poses the uncomfortable question of why so many people with drug problems and (especially) mental health problems are in custody in the first place, and why prison is expected to supply what ought to be available in the community at large for vulnerable individuals. If certain kinds of care and treatment are in practice available to some people only in custodial conditions, the message is still that there is a deficit in responsibility somewhere.

The populist complaint that facilities are available in prison that are not accessible to people outside has, ironically, a point to it, though not exactly the point that the populist wants to make. It is not that prisoners are 'privileged', but that prison is being asked to plug gaps in an overstretched welfare regime. And given that the Prison Service itself is overstretched and that sustained attention to prisoners' health and education needs is in any case almost impossible to effect with shorter sentences (further reduced by remand delays), the standards that some institutions can properly boast do not mean, alas, that we can take it for granted that prison, corporately and generally, always involves attention to the most pressing needs of the offender. It is said so often that it is virtually a cliché, but it has to be said again: custodial sentencing means that you are punished by being deprived of your freedom, not that your subsequent welfare is a matter of indifference.

If we seriously want to address the problem of reoffending, it is clear that a penal culture in which there is no real attention to how offenders change is worse than useless – literally worse than useless, in that it reinforces alienation, low self-worth and the lack of any sense of having a stake in the life of a community. Once again, this has been recognized in recent policy developments, and programmes directed to changing offending behaviour are now a mainstream part of the overall 'paths to resettlement' defined by the NOMS and are beginning to show some effects in reoffending rates. The then Home Secretary said in his 2005 lecture to the PRT – a lecture in which he gave strong support both to community sentencing and to a greater involvement of prisons in the civic life of an area – that 'clear goals right from the start' and a commitment to a distinctive 'package of support and interventions for each offender' had to be the keystones of a really effective penal policy. It was a lecture that quite rightly signalled the need for a substantial culture change.

4

To create another kind of culture in the Criminal Justice System, one that is committed to building responsibility, the first thing we must do is to get rid of the tacit assumption that managing the needs of victims and the needs of offenders is a zero-sum game. As I have outlined it, the history of recent policy debates shows how easy it is to become trapped in such a model. Isolate offenders' needs from those of victims, and there is a predictable reaction in the direction of treating victims as the primary beneficiaries of a process in which they are to be given something like a veto in some circumstances and are imagined as customers who must be satisfied. Isolate victims' needs from those of offenders and you have another reaction which will leave victims without information or interaction in regard to offenders, and which will risk making the rehabilitation of offenders a narrowly focused therapeutic exercise. As many people, probably the overwhelming majority of those who work with either offenders or victims, recognize, we are very unlikely to move away from this stand-off within the framework of our current practice. Adversarial forensic processes and the custodial fundamentalism of a lot of new law will inexorably combine to keep appropriate responsibility from both parties. I say nothing – though a great deal could be said, and indeed has been said in the last week or so – of the way in which the custodial obsession, the creation of more and more offences with a custodial tariff, simply chokes the prison system and compounds all the failures in responsibility for prisoners that I listed a few minutes ago. Nor will I elaborate on the cost to taxpayers of an ineffectual and overloaded system, and the wider cost in patterns of reoffending because of the inadequacy and unevenness of responsibility-building services in such a context.

But naturally, new models do not spring to life ready-made. The main tools of a policy that will avoid the zero-sum deadlock are, of course, community justice and restorative justice. But, to paint with a very broad brush, community justice (non-forensic hearings and negotiations outside a court system, involving 'stakeholders', direct and indirect) can still be seen as a vehicle for addressing victim concerns at the expense of offenders; and restorative justice (mediation, conferencing, confrontation between offenders and victims, attempts to achieve some kind of emotional closure by apology or reparation) can be seen as giving offenders the chance to avoid appropriate punishment by going through certain motions, not too difficult to learn, which may or may not be of any use to victims and in fact risk some damage to them.

Yet it would be disastrous if such negative or suspicious perceptions stopped us thinking through both these models more carefully – models which, in fact, have a good deal in common. Both take seriously the notion that those most directly involved in a criminal event have the largest stake in containing and dealing with its consequences. Both assume that penal custody as the default solution to the effects of crime is inadequate – though both accept that it is in a good many serious cases a necessary part of the whole strategy. Both attempt to find ways of treating crime that move things on, that create new situations and relations, instead of simply removing people from the social scene. So let me try to outline some of the considerations that may help us keep both in focus together and that could answer some of the concerns about reintroducing the victim-offender stand-off under a new guise.

The first is obvious, but needs articulating nonetheless. We must think about these models on their own moral merits, not as economic or political shortcuts. Community justice needs to be separated from any suggestion of franchising or privatizing the operation of the law. The idea that offender management should be put out to tender is one that could sit very comfortably with some sorts of talk about community justice if we are not careful; and this buys into a very questionable understanding of genuine collective responsibility fully owned by the state – a properly common moral discourse about crime and punishment. And it is essential that both community and restorative programmes are seen as genuine responses to a problem, not dismissed as simply attempts to evade the punitive dimension, the necessary vindication of a society's values. It is an easy vote-catcher to describe alternatives to custody in this way. It would be welcome – though it feels at times like crying for the moon – if politicians and commentators could refrain from speaking as if punishment were essentially about the expression of disapproval and the infliction of legally controlled suffering and not much more. In itself, such an approach changes nothing; but any crime surely indicates that something needs to change in a person's awareness and conscience.

Secondly, we need clarity and honesty about what offences can and cannot be appropriately dealt with under the non-custodial and reparative model. Where serious crimes of violence and abuse are concerned, and where a continuing threat to public safety is involved, we have to think less about alternatives to custody and more about what can be achieved in the custodial setting, admitting that custody is an unavoidable element in society's response to the crime. But this means thinking very carefully about the tariff for many kinds of theft, for economic crimes more generally, for a good deal in the area of petty vandalism and drug offences – to offer a few examples. Custody certainly carries a distinctive stigma, and it is regularly argued that this on its own is a uniquely powerful deterrent. But there are problems with this. It is not at all obvious that the 'stigma' sanction works for those among whom petty criminality related to theft and drug usage is relatively common – those with educational deficit or mental health challenges. There is something of a vicious circle involved in repeated use of custody for those who manifestly do not see it as a sanction of great significance. And, paradoxically, brief custodial sentences are likely to be the least effective in changing or challenging behaviour, given those characteristics of the contemporary prison experience already listed – overcrowding, frequent movement, uneven provision of rehabilitative services and so on. There is good evidence that reoffending rates are proportionately higher among short-sentence prisoners.

It should be clear too in this general context that the impact of custody on women, especially women with heavy family responsibilities, is disproportionately severe and destructive. It is worth remembering that two thirds of women in custody have children under 16. Helena Kennedy gives a heartrending case to do with a teenage Bengali girl, pregnant as a result of rape within her family, who tried in panic to dispose of her new-born baby and was charged with attempted murder.[5] She rightly asks why a child who is the victim of crime should be prosecuted in this way. In a case like this a custodial sentence for the crime of which the girl was accused might 'send a message' of a kind, but would both traumatize and criminalize a vulnerable individual, as well as leaving guilty persons untouched (fortunately the judge in the case agreed).

So we need to continue to work to define with greater and greater clarity where custody is going to be destructive, and where the primary need is to address some of the deficits in education, capacity and empathy that stand behind crime. We should also note in passing that the case Baroness Kennedy cites shows some of the potential pitfalls of an uncritically 'communitarian' approach: the terror of the young woman in this story was intensified by the attitudes of her family and immediate community to pregnancy outside marriage. Any community justice programme worth the name needs the closest monitoring and the most stringent training to prevent its becoming a vehicle for group or local prejudice. Community justice needs to work in such a way that it represents a local group of 'stakeholders' taking responsibility not simply for their immediate environment, but for the application of standards, liberties and dignities agreed by the whole of their society – which is why the popular delegating and franchising (privatizing) options need to be unmercifully scrutinized.

Third, community and restorative models need to gain consent from both offenders and victims. That is, they have to define and deliver outcomes that will be attractive enough to hold the confidence of those involved – some sorts of reparation and closure for victims, some sorts of new empowerment and opportunity for offenders. This takes time. What victim and offender believe they need may not in fact be what will most help them. There will be some victims for whom reparation can mean something like revenge; there will be offenders who confuse empowerment with an escape from guilt. Victims (or their advocates) may, as we have seen, want to control the fate of offenders, offenders may want to accumulate merit marks to secure better treatment (early parole, if they are within the custodial system). Faced with these difficulties, the temptation is to cut corners; Brian Williams in his study of both models of procedure refers to numerous studies in the last five years that will have a very sobering effect on anyone who is inclined to be messianic in their attitude to alternatives to custody. There can be community programmes that are just as careless of victims' needs as any classical forensic process; there can be restorative schemes that fail to implement or monitor agreements reached and become both hurtful for the victim and useless formality for the offender. To use that painfully well-worn phrase, there has to be a 'desire for change'. Victims may want to move on with the sense that they have been properly heard and attended to. Offenders may want to find the right kind of help in altering destructive patterns of behaviour. Those different sorts of desire then have to be taken seriously and worked with by those who administer such schemes, whether the police, the custodial institution or whatever local consortium is involved.

5

How this desire is fostered is the crucial question; dealing with this is the key to the other two considerations I have raised. The whole complex of penal issues is less likely to be abused and exploited by politicians and commentators if there is wider ownership of an approach that asks how the criminal justice system helps to bring about change. The law encodes our respect for human dignity in general; but this should not be taken to mean that the function of the justice system is only to flatten out a bumpy surface or to restore a disturbed situation to the status quo. It must also be the guarantor of possibilities, clearing the way for individual citizens to exercise their dignity by taking part in the processes of shaping the conditions of their lives.

This does not mean that the law in itself is the agent of moral change – a tempting but dangerous idea as you can see when it gets into the wrong hands. The law cannot prescribe reconciliation and it cannot effect forgiveness; what happens if a penalty is completed or remitted in some way is not forgiveness but only discharge. Mended relationships need more than this, and what they need the legal system does not and should not try to provide. But a system that actively works against reconciliation, against the development of those involved in a criminal event towards something more adequately and resourcefully human, is in its way just as dangerous. It can serve human dignity only in a formal and rather abstract way: punishment is calculated on the basis of its effectiveness in expressing social disapproval, and in some measure on its deterrent capacity. These are components in any nuanced theory of punishment; but they do not create conditions in which a society can move forward in lessening the chances of disruptive and abusive behaviour. Somehow, the law has to play its part in energizing such movement. To put it slightly differently, the legal system of a society cannot enforce morality; but a society that has no corporate energy for improvement is going to waste human and material resources in a way that undermines its credibility and legitimacy. And, on present showing, it will do nothing to halt rising levels of serious crime. The state through its legal processes will not make us good, but it will, if it's doing its job, give room to and support a range of other processes and factors that prompt and sustain moral decisions. If democracy is more than a dreary plebiscite for apathetic consumers, it should be nourishing empathy, awareness and critical change.

And this amounts to suggesting that the problems of the criminal justice system are inevitably problems generated by a wider context than this alone. In a setting where volunteering is not encouraged, where the ideals of public service are not reinforced and where the 'customer' paradigm prevails in most areas of public transaction, it is not surprising if we have a penal system that too often appears chaotic and ineffectual. It will not be possible to build responsibility in the criminal justice system unless the sense of being answerable for each other is strengthened in the whole of our social fabric. Which does not mean, of course, that prison reform can be postponed until we have solved the bigger problem; the special significance of this area of our difficulties is that it brings into such sharp focus the cost of a climate of non-responsibility. It pinpoints how desperately hard it becomes to spring people out of destructive cycles when that aspiration is not in the bloodstream of a culture. And (sadly) it reminds us also that it is almost impossible to move some things forward when they lack obvious electoral rewards; this is how a downward spiral of expectation is created.

That downward spiral of expectation is, of course, one of the things that sustains those assumptions about the needs of victims which can trap victims of crime in a reactive posture, and allows concern about victims' needs to be exploited by those who want to reinforce alarmist messages about 'soft' treatment of offenders. In a different climate, well-managed processes of restorative justice have the potential to restore dignity to the victim as well as the offender. And in a community justice framework of the right kind, the chosen involvement of victims in dealing with the broader fallout of a criminal event means that they are able once again to exercise their dignity actively in what I earlier called the shaping of the conditions of their lives.

That raising of the level of expectation in relation to victims of crime necessarily entails a similar raising of the sights of what is expected from offenders. If crime can be not only punished but challenged, this puts the offender in a position where he or she has to make sense of their actions in some way; and this is a vital part of the fostering of responsibility. Making sense of your actions involves understanding where they come from and where they go to – motives and consequences; it means seeing what you do in a wider context than how you feel or what you want. Responsibility grows when actions can be planned that will play a part in this wider context, where goals are imagined that are more than just release of feeling. To be helped to be answerable for what you do is to be helped to understand deeper levels of your own worth or significance; there is some aspect of another person's good that depends on you. To allow people to see that realization as the root of empowerment is one of the great challenges of a renewed criminal justice culture, and it is not clear that it can be achieved simply by the cognitive-behavioural therapies that tend to be the favoured option at the moment. In the most practical terms, it can be fostered also and importantly by further exploring volunteering programmes for prisoners along with the more protracted work that goes on in restorative conferencing, anger management and so on in a properly sustained rehabilitative scheme. And the potential for the 'civic presence' of prisons needs more flesh on it, not least in regard to the possible role of local groups, including faith communities, in sustaining community chaplaincy provision to facilitate the transitions between custody and freedom and to help balance the difficult tension between guaranteeing a community's safety and pushing the boundaries of what is possible for the ex-offender. If the care of offenders after release is focused too tightly on managing risk, there will be less opportunity for trust and therefore responsibility to be built up. It is a point worth pondering for the probation service.

In recent years, the restorative model has become more and more deployed in the Youth Justice System; and, in spite of some false starts and awkwardnesses, it is beginning to prove its worth. Now is the time for 'mainstreaming' it. The commitment of the Home Office to developing community prisons is in many ways welcome. But it has to go side by side with alternatives to custody – and therefore with some long hard thinking about the multiplication of custodial tariffs when new legal offences are created. This is a long shot I realize, but I wonder if the time has not come for a comprehensive commission on penal policy and non-custodial options. We cannot for much longer manage with an expanding prison population whose levels of reoffending are so high.

In conclusion, though, let me repeat – the crisis in the penal system is bound up with the wider question of whether our social imagination in general is being fed by the vision of mutual responsibility. It is unhappily easy for the sceptic to suppose that the religious perspective on these matters is essentially and even exclusively about underscoring guilt and penalty. I have been trying to suggest that the most distinctive contribution such a perspective may bring is a stress on finding our adult liberty in carrying the responsibility for someone else's welfare. If at least that dimension of the religious ethic that has grown out of our tradition can be revitalized for our society, it is not only our attitudes to penal policy that will be regenerated and transformed.

Big society – small world?

I intend in this chapter to reflect a little on the implications of our current discussions around the 'Big Society'. My hope is to suggest ways in which it can be a vehicle for serious rethinking of our national and international priorities at a time when some of our conventional pictures of left and right in politics are under question. This certainly doesn't mean that we should see it as a sort of halfway house between different sets of principles. I believe the possibilities are more radical than that, involving the development of a new set of principles – or perhaps, as I shall also be suggesting, not so new after all. A politics, national and international, of local co-operation and 'mutualism', rooted in a sense of political virtue and appealing to human empathy – this is, as far as I can see, a large part of what Christian faith has always looked towards. I hope that what I say will have some resonance with those who don't begin where I begin, in this commitment of faith, and may even suggest that there is some significant intellectual and moral capital to be discovered in the world of theology as we seek for ways forward for a society currently facing the likelihood of pretty high levels of anxiety and disorientation.

1

The theme of the Big Society has found its way into a wide range of contexts in the last couple of years. Reactions have been varied; but we should not be distracted from recognizing that – whatever the detail of rationale and imple-mentation – it represents an extraordinary opportunity. Introduced during the run-up to the last election as a major political idea for the coming generation, it has suffered from a lack of definition about the means by which ideals can be realized. And this in turn has bred a degree of cynicism, intensified by the attempt to argue for devolved political and social responsibility at exactly the same time as imposing rapid and extensive reductions in public expenditure. The result has been that 'Big Society' rhetoric is all too readily heard by many as aspirational waffle designed to conceal a deeply damaging withdrawal of the state from its responsibilities to the most vulnerable.

But cynicism is too easy a response and the opportunity is too important to let pass. As the financial crisis of the last few years became more serious, a good many voices were being raised to say that the traditional map of British, and indeed global, politics had become obsolete. The apparently irresistible advance of largely unregulated financial transaction had been tolerated by left and right because of its apparent ability to secure high levels of individual prosperity and a satisfactory, if not exactly spectacular, tax income to support national defence and welfare. It had, of course, done little to liberate struggling younger economies or deeply indebted countries, but a modest degree of government-to-government aid, allied with exhortations and some conditionalities around more transparent governance, was part of the routine expenditure of adminis-trations in the developed world. But this had in effect loaded the responsibility for both individual and social welfare on to a set of feverishly active but very fragile instruments, and had to a greater or lesser extent shaped the fiscal possi-bilities for elected governments. Thus it had also vastly increased the actual insecurity of both individuals and societies: variations in the financial market had the potential to change the value of the savings and pensions of millions. And when those variations became substantially more feverish than usual as a result of an accumulation of reckless debt-trading, the result was dramatic, and its longer effects are now dictating policy on health, education and much more.

Strictly economic remedies and alternatives of various sorts have already been much discussed. But along with this, there has been a more clearly *political* response – political in the sense that it asks questions about the proper location of power, about where the levers of change and control lie in society. And this in turn generates a crucial set of questions about political ethics or political virtue: if we need to explore where power lies, we need also to explore what we want power to *do* and why. It is in this context that discussion has been developing about, for example, the proper definitions of wealth and well-being, about individual and communal goals, about the sort of human character that is fostered by unregulated competition and a focus on individual achievement, and about where we derive robust ideas of the common good and the social compact. It is in this context that the 'Big Society' theme has to be understood.

2

'Character': another term that is easy to treat cynically, because we readily associate it with caricatures of clergy and schoolteachers talking about 'character-building' activities: that is, usually unpleasant or strenuous things that no normal person would actually want to do left to themselves. But there is a growing recognition that we do after all need the language of character and of virtue; and no amount of exhortation to pull our weight in society (big or otherwise) is any use without some thinking about what kind of people we are, want to be and want others to be; what are the habits we want people to take for granted, what are the casual assumptions we'd like people to be working with? We have as a society allowed those habits and assumptions to drift steadily towards a preoccupation with the individual's power to maximize choice, so that 'freedom' comes to be defined as essentially a state in which you have the largest possible number of choices and no serious obstacles to realizing any of them. And politics has accordingly been driven more and more by the competition to offer a better range of choices – a marketizing of public discourse thoroughly analysed by many observers in the last decade or so. But as our current debates seem to indicate, we have woken up to the fact that this produces a motivational deficit where the idea of the common good is concerned. It's interesting that part of the repertoire of a certain kind of reactionary journalism is the abuse of 'bleeding-heart' liberals or reformists or whatever; as though the idea that *empathy* might be a proper driver of action and change is automatically laughable.

Now, the point about empathy is that it implies a particular kind of emotional awareness. It lets us know that what we feel is not just a private affair: communication with others is possible because emotions can be shared in language and imagination. And the conclusion is that I am able to learn more about myself from others – to have my horizon extended by listening to the words of others, to develop a sense of different possible worlds and different ways of understanding or seeing myself. What I feel, and my capacity to externalize what I feel, are not the end of the story – arguably not even the beginning of the story. They must lead into a real mutuality of concern. And 'character' is one of the words we use to describe what happens when we begin to construct a serious, long-term account of who we are as persons, in conversation with others, instead of staying within the territory of what we think we are sure of (our own felt life) and assuming the absolute priority of this in our policies or decisions.

Some of the philosophical basis of this is spelled out with great eloquence in the second chapter of Oliver Davies's fine study of the theological centrality of compassion.[1] 'Character' is something to do with learning to scrutinize ourselves, to become, in a constructive sense, strangers to ourselves, wondering about how and why we react to our environment, searching for resources to make that response more adequate and more alive.

There is now a substantial literature on the development of emotional intelligence, some of which has thrown into sharp relief the ways in which social and relational signals in early life can create long-term distortion of the capacity for empathy, sometimes, it is argued, in ways that are even neurologically traceable. And, if we pursue the connections within this research, empathy is linked with the capacity to inhibit those unquestioned emotional responses that can, unchecked, result in wreckage; connected with the capacity to see an integrated picture of the environment in which immediate emotional response is not everything. Iain McGilchrist's bold and wide-ranging writings on the functions of the hemispheres of the brain make the point very forcefully that a culture in which one kind of cerebral function is disproportionately privileged over the other (where analytic functions predominate over more holistic perspectives) is in some trouble. If we live in a milieu where a great many signals discourage empathy and self-scrutiny, and thus emotional awareness, we shall develop habits of self-absorption, the urge for dominance, and short-term perspective. Our motivation to change anything other than what we feel to be our immediate circumstances will be weak, because our sense of ourselves as continuous, reflective agents will be weak. And the clear implication of all this is that, without an education of the emotions (which means among other things the nurture of empathy), public or political life becomes simply a matter of managing the competition of egos with limited capacity to question themselves. It will amount to little more than the kind of damage limitation that arises when we have nothing robust to appeal to except universal entitlements.

Now we need the language of human rights, and it is not useful to try and unravel it; but we need also to make sure that this language is grounded in a clear sense of the dignity of the other, not simply of the claims of the self. In other words, language about 'rights' becomes a fully *moral* affair when and only when it is connected with empathy, with the sense of the dignity of the other and thus of some sort of mutual nourishing or cherishing. The recognition of rights as a moral affair, grounded in mutual personal recognition, is thus one crucial dimension of character as we have been defining it.

Sue Gerhardt, in her book in *The Selfish Society*, quotes a quite well-known story of how the people of a small French Protestant village in the Second World War systematically set out to rescue French Jews from the occupying German forces;[2] and in particular, she refers to the words of one of the villagers (in fact, the pastor's wife) about the imperative of helping those who needed rescue. 'You see', she said, 'it is a way of handling myself'; in other words, as Gerhardt adds, 'an attitude that she did not question, a response that she trusted.' It is this response, the kind of response that you don't have to think about, but which represents an abiding sense of who you really are, that allows us to recognize each other as potential partners in human converse and co-operation, and thus as comparably vulnerable in the face of crisis or threat. The difficulty that can haunt a narrow discourse of rights is that the other is potentially a rival; the humanizing and moralizing of rights is the acceptance that the other is potentially someone with whom I can *compare* what I experience.

3

Back to the public question with which we began. These thoughts about empathy are meant to underline the fact that the relocation of political decision making from state to locality may be worthy or desirable in itself, but is doomed to failure unless it is accompanied by some sustained thinking about how character, and in particular civic character, is formed, and how a system of social relations can be shaped by the mutual recognition we have just been thinking about. One modern writer said of the moral exhortations of Christian faith that they could not be understood just as simple and universal commands to which we said yes or no, because they presupposed a specific kind of human awareness that took time to grow; they were, he said, 'addressed to people who do not yet exist'. The same might be said of exhortations to civic responsibility. It is at this point that we can see most clearly the connection between 'Big Society' language and those institutions that still prize and try to nourish character, above all the communities of faith, and very specifically (I make no apology for foregrounding this) the sometimes fragmented or marginal but still visible communities of the established Church, with its commitment to continue its presence in every locality in the nation.

Now, the Church is frequently seen as a divided, fractious and inward-looking body, and there is far too much that makes this a perfectly fair

assessment in many circumstances. But its central images and commitments
rest on something very close to the empathic recognition that we have seen as
essential to social vitality. The familiar language of the 'body' as a focal image for
Christian community carries with it the acknowledgement that no one element
in the social order can know itself accurately without knowing its dependence
on others and also its responsibility towards others. Mutuality is written in.
And whatever the routine perceptions of the Church in some vocal quarters of
modern British society – dismissive, hostile, patronizing – it remains true that
it is still *expected* to behave in accord with this, and so value in a particular way
whoever comes to its doors. I have a vivid recollection of sharing years ago in
an event organized by the National Union of Mineworkers at a time of intense
pressure and uncertainty, and being told by a very secular speaker on the same
platform on a *very* wet day in Merthyr Tydfil, that I was there to remind others
of all those who did not have the institutional solidarity of unions to support
them and so depended on the solidarity offered by the Church – the elderly, the
children, the disabled, those who had never worked, all who were beyond the
arithmetic of social 'usefulness'. It was a salutary insight into how much implicit
theology there is in parts of our society to call the Church to account.

But for the Church to step up to these expectations, the Church needs to be
a place in which the formation of character, the enabling of human recognition,
is of first importance. And I would venture to say that this is its primary responsibility in our present context. It is right that the Church should be challenged,
along with other civil society networks, to build the capacity of local communities to solve their problems. It is definitely not right for this to be a matter of
hiving off moral questions to the private sphere. If the Church is in the business
of building character and empathic maturity, it will be building the character of
citizens: that is, of people who have the power to vote and thus in some measure
to shape public policy. There may be an attempt to delegate public responsibility
for 'welfare' (I use that unhelpful word advisedly, as representing what seems to
be the attitude of some to the question) to those who may be expected to feel
the responsibility more acutely than some others. But if the Church is actually
nourishing empathy, mutual recognition, then it is nourishing people who will
continue to ask difficult questions in the wider public sphere; questions, for
example, about how the priorities are identified when cuts in public expenditure
are discussed; about the supposed absolute imperative of continuous economic
growth; or about levels of reward unconnected with competence in areas of the
financial world.

And, to digress very briefly on a theme that will be of some interest in the university, these difficult questions should also include challenges about how higher education is *publicly* valued, and about what balance should be struck between rewarding material profitability in research and supporting those disciplines that might be thought to have some connection with the nourishing of empathy. A university is not a Church; but it has historically had something in common with some aspects of the Church's life and priorities. It has assumed that the life of the mind is rooted in a fundamental passion for truth and the maturing of intelligence, in such a way that what is immediately profitable is not necessarily the only proper goal for intellectual labour. It has assumed that the sheer understanding of human behaviour in more than mechanistic ways is a necessary dimension of any intellectual institution worth the name. And through these assumptions, the university has consistently helped to nurture a particular kind of civic awareness, one in which this *personal* intelligence and humane imagination has kept empathy alive. God help us (literally) when the humanities and the pure sciences come to be seen as luxuries in higher education, or indeed education at any level.

4

Both Church and academy, when they are operating freely and confidently, and are understood for what they are in society, are committed to enabling what I have been calling 'recognition', the awareness of a common human location and task that limits our suspicions and our tendency to self-protection and allows us to compare with one another what it is like to be human – and so to clarify what we can and cannot do together. A 'Big Society' programme that does not acknowledge the absolute importance of nourishing this recognition (which also includes nourishing trust in public life and its institutions) is a waste of time. If, on the other hand, it works with an awareness that good 'localism' can, with the right kind of statutory support and resourcing, play back into the debates and decisions of the national polity, it might yet achieve something remarkable.

The least happy outcome would be if the split between a moral private sphere and a pragmatic public sphere, virtuous 'community' and neutral 'government', were reinforced. The best outcome would be if the virtue of the local and voluntary genuinely inspired a different kind of national politics. Thus, instead of hiving off the building of sustainable community to voluntary bodies (leaving central government to balance the books however they can), a localist agenda could revitalize pressure from below on government and statutory bodies to re-engage with a morally robust programme for the common good, nationally and internationally. By a 'morally robust programme', I mean a realistic debate about taxation, about investment in a real not a virtual economy (that is, an economy that actually produces *things* and specific services rather than paper profits alone), about the appropriate rewarding of work in health and education, about the support offered in public policy to children and families, about the extent of commitments to the development of poorer economies and much else. And somewhere near the centre of these concerns might well be, in the immediate future, the urgent question of how we develop the proposals around a 'Big Society Bank' that have been set out in the Government's strategy for *Growing the Social Investment Market* (2011), with the promise of capitalization from 'dead' assets in bank accounts and a further injection of £200 million from the main British banks. Such capitalization will provide resources for projects developed with the help of specialist intermediaries. And one obvious challenge and possibility for voluntary bodies (including, for this purpose, the Churches) is to assist in connecting visionary projects with the sort of advice and support they need to become 'investment-ready'. This and other proposals for encour-aging social investment have some real potential for allaying at least to some extent the feared social cost of the current cuts. This is one area where turning elevated aspiration into monetary reality may now be a serious possibility.

And my mention a moment ago of international development issues raises some further searching questions in relation to the Big Society vision. We are told that centralism is to be deplored and that the heart of true and transform-ative politics is the building of local capacity. As we have seen, this broad-brush position may need some qualification; but insofar as it recognizes the dangers of directive centralism in creating a dependent rather than a creative political culture at every level of society, insofar as it gives a proper place to the devel-opment of political virtue in actual persons, it is a serious and attractive vision, which a Christian theologian has many reasons for applauding. However, it is just those reasons that will make the Christian theologian pursue the issue of global power relations as well as local. If it is the case that the workings of the global market take power decisively away from local economies (and locally elected governments) there is a question to be asked. As things stand, the defenders of the globalized economy claim that it is only the operation of the market that will finally liberate local economies to lift themselves out of endemic poverty; and in theory they have much on their side. In practice of course, things are very different. Both hidden and overt forms of protectionism are at work; indebted countries have regularly been pressed to deal with their debts by accepting a particular style of liberal deregulation from international financial institutions, with the frequent effect of distorting a country's productive capacity and driving up the prices of essentials (though these drastic techniques are not quite so popular with the World Bank and IMF as once theywere). Whatever the current system, it cannot reasonably be presented as one that delivers substantial decision-making power to local agents.

5

So once again, what is needed is to ask the strictly political questions: where is power wielded and to what ends? And if the answer to this is what it seems to be in the contemporary global economy, the next question is who has the capacity to change things in a direction that will restore some genuine decision-making ability to localities. There are, I believe, at least three significant elements to a creative response to this, and they relate to our discussion so far.

First, there is the matter of the destination of international aid. A creditable, and in its initial context defensible, policy of channelling aid through governments in developing countries has predominated, with the goal of strengthening governments and building up national coherence. However, the number of failed and failing states in the less prosperous world has increasingly made this policy problematic. In a way that closely mirrors the Big Society analysis of our national needs, many have come to realize that government-channelled aid alone cannot easily produce the changed relationships and enhanced perception of one's capacities that will secure lasting change – quite apart from the problems of corruption and bureaucratic waste or a focus on prestige or short-term projects unconnected with sustainable local benefit. If aid is directed to creating lasting capacity at the grass roots, a great deal of what we have been doing for the last few decades has been a monumental failure. But the alternative is not to leave everything to private charity, with its risks of reinventing wheels and duplicating efforts, or to the vagaries of financial enterprise; it is to involve in the development process whatever dependable and durable institutions of civil society there are around, with good track records of delivery in local contexts. And once again, Churches and other communities of faith are among the most demonstrably effective and wide-reaching agents of change (not least for women, as the work of the Mothers' Union worldwide across the Anglican Communion shows). A 'Big Society' model for international development will aim to strengthen not government in isolation, but the self-confident nurturing of local political capacity through civil society that will in due course support a lasting participatory politics at national level. In other words, what is required is an engagement with the government of developing countries that will work seriously at building a healthy political culture through the encouragement of local initiative. And the role of Churches and educational institutions as educators of critical citizens is even more clear here than in the domestic context.

Second, one of the most powerful tools in this process is the building of microcredit institutions in alliance with civil society bodies. The small-scale investment needed to give impetus to small businesses is best handled in this mode; and the running of microcredit schemes is itself a profoundly important learning vehicle for those involved. Once again, a fresh model for the delivery of aid and development will be focused on what sustains this kind of capacity. It is not just a matter of rewarding success, important as this may be; it is necessarily also to do with assessing what needs to happen to create a mindset of achievement in a context where powerlessness is what is normally experienced; and investing systematically in small-scale credit schemes should be a major priority. The 'Five Talents' scheme, a significant Christian-based microfinance initiative, speaks about the imperative need to provide social and spiritual capital along with loans, so as to strengthen confidence and to combat the sense of paralyzing social invisibility. Equally, the creation of credible supervisory and regulatory regimes for microcredit is needed to avoid intensifying debt.

And third, this connects with some of the proposals much discussed in the last couple of years about an innovative tax on financial transactions – what has been called a 'Robin Hood tax', imposing a levy of something like 0.05% on transactions in currency, stocks and derivatives between major financial institutions (that is, not High Street banks). It is estimated that this level of taxation at present levels of business would generate £20 billion per annum for the UK alone. And the proposal is further to hypothecate the profits, dividing the revenue between domestic public services and international development projects. On its own, this idea might too easily be taken for another variety of 'stateist' problem-solving; but united to a coherent programme of capacity-building in local communities, here and worldwide, understood in the context of the two priorities already outlined, it still has the potential to deal effectively with the acute current dangers of paralysing the voluntary sector through heavy cuts in their public budgetary support. It may also be that a thought-through model for the operation of a 'Big Society Bank' could accommodate the handling of revenue from a transaction tax, and so offer an integrated resource for local and co-operative ventures of the sort we have been discussing.

Now, these elements of a response to global poverty and exclusion illustrate the kind of synergy between government and civil society that we need to be encouraging. It is not an either/or in this context any more than it is domestically. Examples abound: certainly the most effective development work that has been done in Sudan has come from a mixture of partnerships, with Churches collaborating at grass-roots level in delivery of food to children provided through the World Food Programme. And in Zimbabwe, the 'Farming God's Way' project, funded by the 2009 Zimbabwe Appeal of the Archbishops of Canterbury and York, works with local communities, promoting organic methods to boost food production. It uses the 'Umoja' model, widely adopted by African Churches and supported by Tearfund and a number of Anglican aid agencies, which encourages not only learning about existing skills and resources and developing local capacities, but also raising awareness of what people are entitled to claim from government.

6

The priority is to keep a clear focus on the need to guarantee that power in the global economy does not simply continue to flow towards those who are already secure and wealthy. What I am here arguing for is a thoroughly coherent account of what 'Big Society' ideals might mean, in such a way that the theme of a transfer of power is pursued at every level, national and global. One important thing to bear in mind is that we can easily be misled into thinking that the suspicion of centralism must involve a systematic hostility to state provision of services. But if we approach the question by way of thinking about where power lies, we have to consider carefully those areas in which local effectiveness can be sustained *only* by the broader public provision of infrastructure. National transport networks are the obvious example; but the same principle applies to all those aspects of common life where justice requires us to avoid 'postcode lotteries' – in other words, those aspects of common life where national *parity of standards* guarantees that no-one's local liberties or possibilities are unduly limited by contingent local factors to do with prosperity, mobility, local natural resources and so on. In this light, there is no alibi for the state in securing equality of excellence, so far as is humanly possible, through the national resourcing and monitoring of health care and education, not to mention pensions and disability provision, housing security for the destitute and the care of children in every context where they are present.

There probably wouldn't be much disagreement about this, expressed in these terms; but we need to spell it out with the greatest possible clarity in the present climate. Localism does not mean the dissolution of a complex national society, let alone a complex international network of societies, into isolated villages. It means, for one thing, the familiar principle of 'subsidiarity', so important in Catholic social thought – the principle that decisions need to be taken at the appropriate level. But an implication of this that is not often enough brought out is that there *are* issues appropriately dealt with at state level – not least because local freedom to take effective action depends on such issues being addressed at more than the local level. Similarly, pursuing the analogy with the international situation, local economies will not blossom and function as they might without attention to the terms of international trade and finance. It is vacuous to suggest that a national economy, once introduced to the saving truths of global capitalism, will at once begin to produce, spend and save its way out of poverty by its own efforts only. If it is entering an already slanted, protectionist environment, and still more if it has inherited unpayable debt contracted in the past, it will need something from the international instruments of finance to secure and strengthen what it can do. And, as already noted, even microfinance initiatives will need some measure of international regulation and quality assurance if they are to be long-term agents of empowerment.

In short, we should be thinking about *both* elements in the title of this address. We look for and, I hope are willing to work for, a society in which the bonds created by civil society groups, including very particularly the Church and other religious bodies, guarantee – so to speak – a thick-textured social life, in which people have many communal identities enriching their experience, from the more functional (like belonging to a credit union or a political party, a neighbourhood watch or a food co-operative) to the more imaginative and creative (a choir, a sports club, a Bible-study group). Out of those identities will come the energy and empathy to be ready to organize communities for mutual security and support. At the same time, the world *is* getting 'smaller', not only in the sense that communications bring other people's reality closer to us all the time, but in the sheer practical impact of changes elsewhere in the globe on local conditions, most particularly in economic matters. Unless we can think intelligently about what really does need doing and can only be done at national and international level, localism risks becoming a rather sinister programme in which every local community sinks or swims according to its immediate local capacity. And that's not only a morally and theologically insupportable picture; it is also a wholly unreal one, given the more and more sophisticated kinds of interdependence that bind us together.

The localism that is gaining traction at the moment reflects a deep impatience with what some would see as the legacy of Fabian corporatism - the belief that the state is invariably best placed to be the immediate provider of all services, with the result that what I called a moment ago the 'thick texture' of social life is impoverished, a proper civic pride is flattened out by a uniform bureaucracy, and 'public service' is reduced to the servicing of this bureaucracy. The reaction against this has been powerful in British politics since the 1980 - though it has been accompanied by a paradoxical increase in bureaucratic surveillance and control, through the vehicle of the regulation of various activities and the pressure for compliance with regulatory standards in areas where they were previously informal. But this reaction itself has generated some damaging mythologies about state and community. The combination of a starry-eyed conviction of the market's ability to maximize everyone's welfare and a suspicion of professional vested interests produced not a localism of community and plural texture of belonging, but an attempt to squeeze all social activities into the terms of market exchange. Being a citizen was what guaranteed you the vote; being a consumer was what guaranteed you local and personal freedom.

The Big Society vision, so far as its content can be teased out, seems to represent another and potentially more promising reaction, recognizing the dangerously 'thin' account of humanity produced by this 'market' mythology. And the remarkable opportunity of this moment in political history is that it is possible to think and talk about a social model that is neither Fabian nor Friedmanite, neither statist nor consumerist. My concern is that we use this opportunity to the full - and particularly that we do not treat the enthusiasm around some sorts of localism simply as a vehicle for disparaging the state level of action to secure the vulnerable, nationally and internationally. It is welcome that there is a concern to think about relocating power; but, as we have seen, for this to work well depends on being reasonably clear as to what you want power to do – which includes the 'backwash effect' of serious localism in re-energizing national and international policy, to the extent that it is building real civic virtue.

This potentially productive tension between the local and the global is not unfamiliar to the theologian. Committed to a deep scepticism about the claims of the isolated and autonomous self, s/he is also bound to take seriously the vertiginous nature of personal freedom; the trinitarian and sacramental schemes within which theology works have much to say about the presence of the whole within the life of the particular and the fulfilment of the particular in communion with the whole. Nick Boyle, in his remarkable collection of essays, *Who Are We Now?*, says that, as a Christian commentator on our cultural situation, he expects 'a strengthening of our awareness of global responsibility— of the extent to which we are made up by structures relating us to millions of people we have never met—and so of the need to make individual choices in the context of a global ethic'; but in tandem with this, he also hopes for and expects 'a revival of the doctrine of the soul, ... the doctrine that our identity lies in the good things that we do, perhaps in the virtues that we acquire, something more akin to the notion of karma than of the ego'.[3] These visions belong together, and theology's claim to an honoured place among the threatened humanities rests on its capacity to illuminate that belonging. If we can keep this dual vision clear, we may yet make something of the Big Society in this shrinking world.

PART SIX

Religious Diversity and Civil Agreement

23

Analysing atheism:
unbelief and the world of faiths

In the year 156 of the Christian era, Polycarp, Bishop of Smyrna, was arrested and brought before the magistrate, charged with being a Christian. He was in his eighties, and his age and frailty prompted the magistrate to offer him a quick discharge if he would acknowledge the divine spirit of the emperor and say 'Away with the atheists.' The latter, at least, you might think would not be difficult for a bishop; but of course at this period an atheist was someone who refused to take part in the civic cult of the empire, to perform public religious duties and take part in the festivals of the Roman city. Christians were atheists, by this definition; Polycarp had a problem after all. His response, though, was an elegant turning of the tables. He looked around slowly at the screaming mob in the amphitheatre who had gathered for the gladiatorial fights and public executions, and, says our eyewitness chronicler, he groaned and said, 'Away with the atheists.'

The magistrate did not fail to grasp the theological point, and Polycarp was duly condemned to be burned alive. But this poignant story is one well worth pondering for reasons beyond the study of early Christianity. It is a reminder that 'atheism' may be a less simple idea than either its defenders or its attackers assume. People often talk as though 'atheism' were a self-contained system, a view of the world which gained its coherence from a central conviction – that there is no transcendent creative power independent of the universe we experience. But the story of Polycarp reminds us that to understand what atheism means, we need to know which gods are being rejected and why.

Thus an early Christian was an atheist because he or she refused to be part of a complex system in which political and religious loyalties were inseparably bound up. 'Atheism' was a decision to place certain loyalties above those owed to the sacralized power of the state. But, moving across the world of faiths, Buddhists are sometimes described as atheists by puzzled observers, aware of the fact that

Buddhist philosophy has no place for a divine agent and that Buddhist practice concentrates exclusively upon the mind purifying itself from self-absorption and craving; here, 'atheism' is a strategy to discipline the mind's temptation to distraction by speculative thought. Whether or not there is a transcendent creator is irrelevant to the mind's work; preoccupation with this is a self-indulgent diversion at best, and at worst a search for some agency that can do the work only we can do.

Neither of these has much in common with the atheism characteristic of Western modernity, which draws much of its energy from moral protest. The God of Jewish and Christian faith is seen as an agent who has the power to prevent the world's evil yet refuses to do so, so that there is the appearance of a moral incoherence at the heart of this tradition. Or he is seen as an arbitrary tyrant whose will is inimical to the liberty of human creatures; or else as an impotent and remote reality, a concept given a sort of ghostly existence by human imagination. In all these instances, it is clear that the refusal of belief in God is something essential to human liberation. We cannot live with a God who is responsible for evil; we cannot grow up as human beings if what is demanded of us is blind obedience; we cannot mortgage our lives and our loving commitment to an animated abstraction. Atheism here is necessary to maturity, individually and culturally.

Even those who argue at length about the simply conceptual inadequacies, as they see it, of Western religion, classically, writers in the Bertrand Russell style, will frequently deploy the language of moral revolt as well. 'Protest atheism', as it is often called, has become a familiar element in the armoury of modern intellectual life, perhaps more often repeated than expounded, but culturally very powerful. The more austere objection to belief found in the positivism of the early to mid-twentieth century (that it is equally without meaning to affirm or to deny the existence of an agency whose existence could never be empirically demonstrated) has an ironic resonance with Buddhism, but is another component in the mind of Western modernity, even when the philosophical system from which it arises no longer has much credibility. This is atheism as the mark of supreme intellectual detachment, with the intellect defined as a mechanism for processing checkable information only, with everything else reduced to emotive noise. But the other great modern version of atheism is that which exposes religious talk as ideological – as an instrument of social control whose surface conceptual structure is designed to obscure its real function and to divert thought, emotion and energy from real to unreal objects. This is the essence of Marxist atheism, but it also has some relation to Nietzsche's unforgettably eloquent polemic against Christian faith.

The point is that atheism is to be defined as *a* system only by some dramatic intellectual contortions. A number of intellectual and spiritual policies involve or at least accompany the denial of certain versions of the divine, especially the divine as an active and intelligent subject; but in each case the denial is not intelligible apart from a specific context of thought and image, representation and misrepresentation of specific religious doctrines, and the overall system of which the denial is a part is not necessarily shaped by it. This is why the recent proposal in the UK that religious education in schools should give attention to 'atheism and humanism' as 'non-faith belief systems' alongside the traditional religions was based on some serious conceptual confusions and category mistakes. In the background is the pervasive assumption of modernity that the intellectual default position is non-religious; but what this fails to see is that non-religiousness is historically and culturally a complex of refusals directed at specific religious doctrines, rather than a pure and primitive vision invaded by religious fictions. And if this is so, either religious education has to locate non-religious positions in relation to what it is that they deny, or it will end up treating atheism as the only position not subject to critical scrutiny and the construction of a proper intellectual genealogy: not a welcome position for a rationalist to be in.

In fact, the incorporation of critical positions into religious education is to be applauded. To see where the points of strain are to be found in a religious discourse, and to seek to understand how a thoughtful and self-critical tradition can respond to them, is essential to a proper grasp of religious identities. One of the weaknesses of the kind of religious education now common in schools (in the UK at least) is that it tends to describe the positions of faith communities as finished systems for which questions have been answered rather than (to borrow Alastair MacIntyre's phrase) 'continuities of conflict', in which the moral, spiritual and intellectual tensions constantly press believers towards a fuller, more comprehensive statement of their commitments.

'If you meet the Buddha, kill him' is a well-known Zen dictum, from a tradition deeply aware that personal agenda and history are easily capable of distorting any supposedly clear vision of where enlightenment is to be found. Any conceptual form that can be given in the abstract to the Buddha (that is, to the enlightened awareness) will take its shape from the *unenlightened* awareness, and so has to be dissolved. But this is not that different from the conviction of much Hindu thought, that the divine is 'not this, not that', never identifiable with a determinate object, or from the principle, deeply rooted in the

Abrahamic faiths, that God cannot be given an 'essential' definition, classified as a kind of object. This may be expressed in the form of the apophatic theology of an Ibn Sina, Maimonides or Nicholas of Cusa: Ibn Sina (like Aquinas and all that flows from him) insists that there can be no answer to the question, 'What makes God divine?' as if some 'quiddity' could be identified that grounded a divine definition. God is God by being God – by being the necessary, uncaused active reality he is; nothing else. But the same point is made in wholly different idioms by twentieth-century writers such as Karl Barth and Simone Weil. For Barth, all systems for which God is an object are unsustainable: he always speaks before we have words to answer, acts before we can locate him on some intellectual map. He is never 'available', though always present. And Simone Weil, in an argument of some complexity, concludes that when the human ego says 'God', it cannot be referring to any reality to which the name might be truthfully applied. Because the 'I' that says 'God' is always self-directed and so wedded to untruth, God cannot properly be spoken of. Any God my selfish mind can conceive is bound to be a false, non-existent God. The true God is known only in ways that cannot be reduced to theory or third-person language. If you meet God (in the language of systematic theology or metaphysics), kill him.

It seems that, in differing degrees, most major religious discourses require and cultivate unbelief: that is, unbelief in a divine agent who can be thought about as an agent among others, an instance of a type, a kind of life that can be defined in terms of something other or prior. Thus when we try to consider and understand atheism of any kind, our first question has to be what it is about some particular piece of speech about God that is causing trouble, and whether it is in fact essential to a religious tradition's understanding of what it means by God or the divine. It may be, of course, that what is objected to really is what a religious tradition believes; but even if it is, it is crucial to explore where the points of strain are felt, so that convictions may be tested and if possible reinforced. So the challenge of atheism in its various guises is one that has the potential to deepen what is said about our commitments; not for nothing did Olivier Clement, the French Orthodox theologian, write in the 1960s about 'purification by atheism'. To come to the point where you disbelieve passionately in a certain kind of God may be the most important step you can take in the direction of the true God.

But what I want to suggest specifically in connection with the dialogue between the world faiths is that we spend more time looking at what is *disbelieved* in other religious discourses. A few years ago, an American theologian wrote a book about Christian doctrine as a series of 'unbeliefs':[1] what does Christianity commit you to denying about God and Christ? I wonder if the same method might not be illuminating as we look across the faiths. Just as in the case of atheism generally we learn what we are and are not really committed to, so in dialogue or trialogue or whatever between faiths, we might be able to learn from each other's disbeliefs, to be 'purified' by encountering and examining the protests and denials, the 'atheisms', of each other's views.

Let me try to illustrate; I shall concentrate chiefly upon the Abrahamic faiths, but it should be clear at the very start of this reflection that Buddhism is of special significance in its denial of any personal agency outside the bounds of the world. If we ask why such a denial is made, we must conclude, as suggested earlier, that there is an anxiety that projection on to an external deity fatally weakens the incentive to dealing with our own distraction and selfishness; and there is an anxiety that the very act of affirming the existence of such a deity constitutes an escape from the severely practical analysis of the mind's liberation. In response to this, all three of the Abrahamic faiths have to examine themselves carefully. If we believe in a source of energy, forgiveness and love independent of ourselves, how exactly do we prevent it from becoming a belief that weakens our responsibility and imprisons us in fantasy? We shall need (to say no more in detail) to establish that we are not looking for a supernatural agent to fill the gaps in our imperfect self-awareness and willingness to change, a consoling personality who is there to serve the needs of our idle and needy selves. We shall need to examine carefully those aspects of our language which themselves warn against just such a misunderstanding – and those which might most easily suggest it or nourish it. Our faith becomes self-aware in a fresh way; even if we end by saying, as we probably shall, that the Buddhist refusal of a personal God assumes that ascribing personality and objectivity to God must always be a simple projection of our need, and if we argue, as we probably shall, that nothing is served by denying the fact of our dependence on what lies beyond the world, we shall have been warned, sharply and constructively, of just how we may use our faith to reinforce what is least converted in us.

But how might this apply to the conversation *between* the Abrahamic traditions? Here are some suggestions.

The Jew disbelieves propositions like the following: God is free to disregard or rewrite the solemn promise made to a specific people at a point in history; God makes no specific demands on those God chooses to hold in the closeness consequent upon such a promise; God cannot deal adequately with the world by revealing the divine will, but has to intervene in allegedly more 'intimate' or direct ways.

The Christian disbelieves propositions like these: God needs to be persuaded by our virtue to love us or to act on our behalf; God is a solitary individual with a personality comparable to that of a human individual; God is metaphysically incapable of acting in and as a created and dependent being; God's action can have no impact upon physical processes.

And the Muslim disbelieves propositions like these: God is the compound of several distinct divine agents (whether an indeterminate number or just three); God wills that the divine purpose be realized only in the lives of a limited segment of society or humanity; God's will can be divorced from the supposed cultural limitations of its earliest definitive and complete expression (the Qur'an); God is known by a complex of human approximations to truth.

As will be evident, there is overlap in these configurations; and all three traditions agree in disbelieving in a God who is one of the items that exists within the universe, who is subject to time and change as finite beings are, who shares the same conceptual territory as do the limited agents we are familiar with. Although Christianity and Judaism have increasingly been willing to entertain images suggesting vulnerability and suffering in the divine life, this is largely a modern development whose conceptual relation to the definitive doctrines of the religions is a rather uneasy business. Powerful devotional metaphors require careful handling in this context, and they should not obscure one of the most significant convergences that exists between the Abrahamic faiths – and indeed between these faiths and others – on the conviction that God is not a member of any class of existent beings. You'll recall the earlier reference to Ibn Sina, echoed to the letter by Aquinas.

That being said, however, the respective systems of disbelief I have sketched so briefly pose equally significant mutual challenges. Faced with the disbeliefs of another discourse, each of the three participants in the Abrahamic conversation should be prompted to ask whether the God of the other's disbelief is or is not the God they themselves believe in. If the answer were a simple yes, dialogue might be a great deal more difficult than it is; the reality of dialogue suggests that we do not in fact have to do with a simple 'atheism' in respect of the other's models of God. And part of the fascination and the spiritual significance of dialogue is the discovery of how one's own commitments actually work, and specifically how they work under pressure. Is Christianity that which

Judaism as such denies? Is the affirmation of Christianity identical to the denial of what Jews believe *as Jews*? And so with Islam also; one of the darkest and most tragic parts of our history in relation to other faiths ('our' history being, for these purposes, the history of all the Abrahamic faiths) is the construction of the other as the opposite. To pick up an idea which I have tried to develop elsewhere, we have to put behind us a picture of the world of faiths in which each is seen as answering the same questions, so that the respective 'perfor-mance' of different traditions can be categorized in terms of right and wrong answers to these questions. Binary oppositions do not serve us at all here.

So to some of the particulars, though we can only take a few examples. I begin with two Muslim disbeliefs and their impact on Christian-Muslim encounter. The Muslim disbelieves in a plurality of divine agents: so the Christian has to ask whether his or her belief is properly so characterized – and if it is not, to examine why and how it could come to be read that way. Thus the Christian may say, in the tradition of Augustine and Aquinas, that belief in the Trinity is not belief in three self-subsisting individuals sharing a divine nature; it is to claim that the life that is divine life exists as three utterly interdependent 'streams' of agency, which cannot be reduced to each other – an originating agency, a responsive agency, an excess of creative and eternal agency always free to replicate the pattern of origin and response. The Greek tradition avoids calling them 'persons' and prefers 'subsistents' (*hupostaseis*). This is a very abstract rendering indeed of the doctrine of the trinity, but one which avoids the distorting impression that Christians believe in some kind of divine society of individuals; and there are aspects of both theology and popular devotion that can give such an impression of a belief which Muslims (and Jews) find incom-prehensible and inconsistent with belief in the oneness of God. The important clarification for the Christian is that divine oneness is not the oneness of an individual (where there may logically be more than one of its kind) – and this is actually something that can be agreed by the Jew and the Muslim, who (at least in the shape of their mainstream philosophical systems) would equally deny that God is an individual in that sense. The Muslim challenge pushes the Christian, now as in the Middle Ages, to clarify a fundamental point of belief.

Imagine, next, the Christian picking up a Muslim unbelief and challenging it. The Muslim does not believe in a 'church' that is socially a separate body from the political community at large as organized by divine law. The Christian, however, has a long tradition of expecting the body of believers to be in significant respects different from political society (think of Polycarp again).

Is the Muslim attitude not tantamount to saying that nothing but a theocracy can express Islam? To which the Muslim might respond by saying that if God is a God who has the capacity to make known the divine will, and if there is ultimately one good for human society which is to be found in following that will, there can be no stability or justice in a society that is not founded upon revealed law. But this does not at all mean that 'religious' authorities must dominate the state, or that the free exercise of different faiths is unthinkable.

First, there are no simply religious authorities in the Western and Christian sense: there is a community (a political community, naturally, since that is how communities organize themselves) of those who have willingly submitted to revealed law. Second, only free submission to God's law is a proper foundation for the 'House of Islam': it may be necessary to combat the unbeliever as a political assailant, but this is not to deny the liberty in principle of any human being to be subject to God or not. Even the issue of voluntary abandonment of Islam is a subject that needs to be looked at with nuance; this is by definition a *political* offence, yet it is not wholly clear in Muslim jurisprudence that it merits an extreme political penalty. But the Muslim might emerge from the discussion conscious of a question about why and how the Christian might see this as a denial of human liberty; and the upshot could be a deeper recognition of the logic of free submission, and the unavoidably paradoxical nature of a political community governed by law which also assumes that loyalty and obedience to this community cannot be secured by external sanctions that seek to constrain the will by threat. And so the Muslim, challenged about a disbelief by the Christian, is taken back to the most fundamental defining question of Islam, the character of obedience.

Is what the Muslim denies what the Christian affirms? It seems less obvious than at the beginning of the argument. The Muslim is not a theocrat as the Christian West might understand the term: the denial of a 'secular' space is not a claim to impose religious authority over some other kind, but the acknowledgment that only one basis exists for coherent political life of any kind. The Christian may in fact agree; but will argue that in the realities of a historical existence where levels of submission to God are varied (to say the least), there is bound to be a tension between the community which lives professedly by God's law and the turbulent and unstable succession of social orders which arise in turn around it. Dealing with the Muslim's refusal of belief in any 'church-like' body, existing as a distinct entity within civil society may clarify both the Muslim's view of freedom and obedience and the Christian's eschatological reserve about any historical political order. And as in my first instance, a language for the conversation appears as this clarification advances, a language about God's will to be known and the necessity of such knowledge for a social life free from incoherent rivalry, struggle and injustice.

So, to the disbelief of the Jew. Both Christian and Muslim apparently hold that God *is* at liberty to revise the divine promises; and in such a God the Jew cannot believe. A God who changed his mind would be precisely a God whose freedom would be subject to limit and negotiation, a God whose word once spoken could be rescinded. Hebrew scripture explicitly rules out such a thought, and Jewish philosophy understandably regards the mutability of divine election as diminishing God. Is this a fair perception of the God of Muslims and Christians? The Christian, of course, has the entire argument of Christian Scripture to appeal to, especially the complex arguments of Paul in Romans. The promise is made to Abraham's children, but God has extended the definition to include those who become Abraham's children by imitating his faith, not simply by lineage; thus those who enter the Christian Church are honorary or adoptive Jews. God *is* faithful – a point insisted upon by Paul against those who would indeed argue that God's mind has changed and the Jewish people are rejected. The Muslim will go back to the story of Abraham in the Qur'an, accepting that there is a history of some sort of covenant (though with Ishmael as well as Isaac); but what constitutes covenantal obligation on the human side is that obedience which is now given final form in Muslim revelation, of which all earlier prophecy and theophany is a foreshadowing.

Neither Christian nor Muslim believes in a mutable God; but both will be properly challenged by the Jew to look at the coherence of their own stories, especially in the light of the persistence of Jewish religion and nationality. The question about God becomes intimately associated with a question about power. If the Christian and the Muslim are incorporating Jewish history into their narrative, does the Jew have the right to speak for himself or herself, and to be heard? Jewish disbelief in a changeable God is linked (in a way that does not apply to Christians and Muslims) with Jewish self-belief, the confidence of the Jewish people that they are immutably a people. If Christian and Muslim theologies, even when they confess an immutable God, presuppose the mutability of Jewish identity or legitimacy, they claim a very specific kind of power, a power to declare someone else's history over. Jewish disbelief challenges at the deepest level the way such claims may and do emerge in the histories of the younger faiths. Can Christianity and Islam sustain themselves against the accusation of promoting a theological imperialism that has, from a Jewish point of view, nakedly and often murderously political implications?

And once again, there are answers that may emerge. Christians (Christians other than the extreme dispensationalist Christian Zionists anyway) will often find difficulty in offering a theologically positive valuation of the continuing identity of the Jewish people, but may still believe that it is necessary to work at this, if only in terms of the people of Israel as the radical sign of the Church's incompleteness and the priority of the covenant people into whom non-Jews are now believed to be incorporated. The Muslim (paradoxically, more than the Christian in some respects) has a powerful sense of a shared prophetic history, but is unlikely to compromise over the supersession of Torah by Qur'an. Yet the Muslim will also understand the inseparability of law and people in ways that a Christian might find harder, since it bears a certain similarity to the Muslim denial of neutral secularity and of a separated religious society; hence the often exemplary record of Muslim toleration of Jews as a nation within the nation.

Many other comparable exercises could be carried out in respect of the impact of 'disbeliefs' upon dialogue between the Abrahamic faiths, but I hope that the point of the discussion may be emerging. I am proposing that there is some analogy between the significance of particular unbeliefs upon the self-understanding of religious discourse in general and the significance of the 'unbeliefs' of particular religious discourses for each other. There is no such thing as a global system of 'atheism': there are denials of specific doctrines on varying grounds, and the examination of where the points of stress are in the exposition of these doctrines very importantly allows us to test the resources of what we say as believers – and, ideally, to emerge with a more robust sense of those resources. But equally, conversation between faith traditions can sometimes give the impression that part of the essence of one religious idiom is its disbelief in the God supposedly revealed in another so that binary oppositions dominate our attitudes. Treat these disbeliefs, I am suggesting, as we might imaginatively and sensitively treat atheism; that is, try to see why what is denied *is* denied, and whether that denial is directed against what another tradition in fact claims. And in the light of that, try to discover what your own tradition commits you to and how it answers legitimate criticism from outside – criticism which often (as in the case of the mutability of God) could be raised intelligibly *within* the native tradition. What emerges is frequently a conceptual and imaginative world in which at least some of the positive concerns of diverse traditions are seen to be held in common.

But this is not at all to condemn interfaith dialogue to the sterile and abstract task so often envisaged for it, of identifying a common core of beliefs. The exercise I have been describing is not about finding a common core at all; it is about finding the appropriate language in which difference can be talked about rather than used as an excuse for violent separation. Just as in an encounter with atheists, it is sometimes possible to grasp the positive sense or expectation that leads an atheist to reject what he or she imagines is God, so that the conversation does not simply end in the positing of affirmation and denial, so here. We should certainly not be looking for a common core of belief between believer and atheist, but for a language in which to acknowledge and understand the difference. And in interfaith conversation, we continue to make the claims we make out of conviction of the truth, but seek to break through the assumption that everything can be reduced to whether people say yes or no to a set of simple propositions. Only in the wake of such a move can true dialogue proceed; it does not in fact happen when the 'common core' model is at work, because the hidden assumption is that what is common is bound to be what matters – in which case, difference is not really interesting, intellectually or spiritually. Nor does it happen when the relation between the faiths is seen as one between a set of correct answers and several sets of incorrect ones.

This chapter began as a reflection on the slippery character of the word 'atheism', and the need to resist the elevation of atheism to the level of a system – a danger which has been very publicly around in educational debates in the UK in the last few years. But the more we recognize the variegated sense of atheism, the more important it may appear to approach the denials made by atheists as a way into understanding more thoroughly what doctrines and commitments do and don't entail. And on the basis of this, we have moved on to look at the denials, the unbeliefs of certain religious traditions, denials often assumed (both within and beyond a tradition) to be necessarily connected with the refusal of the truth of another faith, seen as a system constructed on the basis of what one tradition or another denies. To allow atheistic schemes to be examined as more than just the elaboration of a single denial, and to allow religious faiths to be examined as more than a map of mutual exclusions and incompatibilities are closely connected. Hence the suggestion, not after all so paradoxical, that we can learn better how to understand other religious believers if we learn better how to understand unbelievers. If both enterprises lead us back to an enhanced appreciation of the resource and complexity that our own faith both offers us and demands of us, so that we are more and not less confident in dialogue, we shall not have wasted our time.

24

Religious diversity and social unity

If you believe what some commentators have to say, one of the major factors provoking conflict in our world is the sheer fact of different religious convictions: in our own country, it seems to be assumed by many that if we could only get the relation between 'faith communities' right, social harmony would inevitably follow. And conversely, any expression of a belief that one's own religious loyalty is absolute, any statement of the belief that I, as a Christian, Muslim, Buddhist or whatever, am speaking the truth, is regarded as threatening and unacceptable. Surely the problem lies with this contest over the truth; surely, if religious people would stop speaking about truth and acknowledge that they were only expressing opinions and conditional loyalties, we should be spared the risk of continuing social conflict and even violence.

But what this hopeful fantasy conceals is an assumption that talking about truth is always less important than talking about social harmony; and, since social harmony doesn't seem to have any universal self-evident definition, it is bound to be defined by those who happen to hold power at any given time – which, uncomfortably, implies that power itself is more important than truth. To be concerned about truth is at least to recognize that there are things about humanity and the world that cannot be destroyed by oppression and injustice, which no power can dismantle. The cost of giving up talking of truth is high: it means admitting that power has the last word. And ever since Plato's Republic political thinkers have sought to avoid this conclusion, because it means that there is no significance at all in the witness of someone who stands against the powers that prevail at any given time; somehow, political philosophy needs to give an account of suffering for the sake of conscience, and without a notion of truth that is more than simply a list of the various things people prefer to believe, no such account can be given.

So the fact of disagreement between religious communities is in fact crucially important for the health of our common human life. Because these communities will not readily give up their claims to truth in response to the appeal from the powers of the world around to be at one for the sake of social harmony, they testify that power, even when it is apparently working for the good of a majority, cannot guarantee that certain values and visions will remain, whatever may happen. But does this concern for truth mean that there is always going to be damaging conflict wherever there is religious diversity? What about the cost of religious diversity to 'social cohesion' – to use the word that is currently popular in British political rhetoric? Does disagreement about truth necessarily mean the violent disruption of social co-operation? I shall be arguing that it does not, and that, on the contrary, a robust view of disagreement and debate between religious communities may (unexpectedly?) play a major role in securing certain kinds of social unity or cohesion.

The first point I want to make is about the very nature of religious language. To believe in an absolute religious truth is to believe that the object of my belief is not vulnerable to the contingencies of human history: God's mind and character cannot be changed by what happens here in the world. And the logic of this is that an apparent defeat in the world for my belief cannot be the end of the story; God does not fail because *I* fail to persuade others or because my community fails to win some kind of power. Now if I believe for a moment that my failure or our failure is a failure or defeat for God, then my temptation will be to seek for any means possible to avoid such an outcome; and that way lies terrorism and religious war and persecution. The idea that any action, however extreme or disruptive or even murderous, is justified if it averts failure or defeat for my belief is not really consistent with the conviction that my failure is not God's. Indeed, it reveals a fundamental lack of conviction in the eternity and sufficiency of the object of faith. In plain English, religious violence suggests religious insecurity. When different communities have the same sort of conviction of the absolute truth of their perspective, there is certainly an intellectual and spiritual challenge to be met; but the logic of belief ought to make it plain that there is no defence for the sort of violent contest in which any means, however inhuman, can be justified by appeal to divine sanction. The divine cannot need protection by human violence. It is a point uniquely captured in the words of Jesus before the Roman governor: 'My kingdom is not of this world. If it were, my servants would fight' (*John* 19.36).

So the rather paradoxical conclusion appears that the more religious people are utterly serious about the truth of their convictions, the less they will sanction all-out violence; they will have a trust that what truly is will remain, whatever the vicissitudes of society and history. And they will be aware that compelling religious allegiance by violence is tantamount to replacing divine power with human; hence the Quranic insistence that there can be no compulsion in matters of religious faith. It is crucial to faith in a really existing and absolute transcendent agency that it should be understood to be what it is independently of any lesser power: the most disturbing form of secularization is when this is forgotten or misunderstood. And the difficult fact is that it has been so forgotten or misunderstood in so many contexts over the millennia. It has regularly been confused with cultural or national integrity, with structures of social control, with class and regional identities, with empire; and it has been imposed in the interest of all these and other forms of power. Despite Jesus' words in John's gospel, Christianity has been promoted and defended at the point of the sword and legally supported by extreme sanctions; despite the Quranic axiom, Islam has been supported in the same way, with extreme penalties for abandoning it and civil disabilities for those outside the faith. There is no religious tradition whose history is exempt from such temptation and such failure.

Like others, I have sometimes been very critical of the heritage of the European Enlightenment where it has been used to appeal to timeless and obvious rational truths that are superior to the truths claimed for revelation and imparted in the historical processes of communal life. But it should be granted that the Enlightenment had a major role in highlighting some of the inner contradictions of religious language and behaviour in the wake of an age when so much violence had been justified by the rhetoric of faith. After the wars of religion in Europe, it was plausible and important to challenge those habits of thought which had made it seem natural to plunge whole societies, indeed, the greater part of a whole continent, into murderous chaos on the pretext of religious dispute. For the major thinkers of the Enlightenment, the contrast was between absolutes that could be defended only on the basis of arbitrary religious authority and absolutes that were established by universal reason; and it was obvious that the latter promised peace because they did not need any reference to authorities that, in the nature of the case, could be accepted only by certain groups. By forcing religious authorities to acknowledge that they could not have the legal and civic right to demand submission, Enlightenment thinkers in a sense obliged believers to accept what was in fact an implication of their own religious faith – that power in this-worldly terms was an inappropriate vehicle for faith.

But the Enlightenment dream of a universal rationality proved in the event as vulnerable and questionable as any religious project. It became entangled in theories and discourses of racial superiority (supported by a particular reading of evolutionary biology) and the economic determinism of capitalist theory and practice; it developed a complex and unhealthy relationship with nationalism, which was, increasingly, seen as the practical vehicle for emancipation and rationalization; and its own account of universal reason was undermined first by Marxian and Freudian theories, then by the structuralist and postmodernist revolutions. European rationality – and its American manifestations in the Declaration of Independence and the political philosophy flowing from that – came to seem as local and arbitrary as any other creed; in the world of global politics, it depended on force as much as argument. And if you come to believe that the values of a certain culture, whether Western democracy or any other, are absolute and impossible for rational people to argue about, then, when some groups resist or disagree, you have a theory that licenses to suppress them; what is more, because you have no transcendent foundation for holding to these values, you may come to believe that any and all methods are justified in promoting or defending them, since they will not necessarily survive your failure or defeat.

Thus the hope of universal harmony on the grounds of reason can become a sophisticated version of the priority of force over everything else, a journey back towards the position that Plato exerted all his energy to refute in the Republic. If the power of argument proves not to be universal after all, sooner or later we are back with coercion; and when that happens, it becomes harder and harder to hold firm to the classical liberal principles that are at the heart of the Enlightenment vision, harder and harder, for example, to maintain that torture or the deliberate killing of the innocent in order to protect the values of society can never in any circumstances be right. It is one of the great moral conundrums posed by the experience of recent years: what if the preserving of civil liberties and the preserving of the security of a liberal society turn out not always to be compatible?

The reality of religious plurality in a society declares, as we have already seen, that some human groups hold to their convictions with an absolute loyalty, believing they are true and thus non-negotiable. If they thought otherwise about these convictions, they might be involved in negotiations about merging or uniting in some way; there would be no ground for holding on to a distinct identity. Yet they do hold to their claims to truthfulness, and so declare to the society around that certain things are not liable to be changed simply because of changes in fashion, political theory or political convenience. The lasting plurality of religious convictions is itself a mark of the seriousness of the convictions involved. Some things are too important to compromise. But if a religious community is as serious as it ought to be about its beliefs, this refusal to compromise is accompanied by the confidence that, whether or not these particular beliefs prevail in any society, they will still be true, and that therefore we do not have to be consumed with anxiety about their survival. The religious witness is able to confront possible political failure, even social collapse, in the trust that all is not and cannot be lost, even when the future becomes unimaginably dark; what it will not do is to sanction any policy of survival at all costs (including the cost of basic humane conventions and moral boundaries).

Thus my first point about the role of plural religious communities in society is that they both underpin the notion that there are values which are not negotiable, and that at the same time they prohibit any conclusion that such values can ultimately be defended by violence. They challenge the drift from Enlightenment optimism to the postmodern enthronement of power and interest as the sole elements in political life; that is, they allow societies as well as person to fail with grace and to find space beyond anxiety. That is not at all the same as saying that they require passivity, resignation to the unprincipled power of others. But they allow human beings the dignity of accepting defeat in certain circumstances where the alternative is to abandon the moral essence of a society in order to win: they suggest the subversive but all-important insight that failure might be preferable to victory at the cost of tolerating, say, torture or random military reprisal as normal elements in political life. By being absolute and thus in a sense irreconcilable, they remind society that a unity imposed by force will always undermine the moral substance of social and political life. There is no way of finding a position outside or beyond diverse faith traditions from which to broker a union between them in which their convictions can be reconciled; and this is not bad news but good – good because it does two things at once. It affirms transcendent values; and by insisting that no other values are absolute, it denies to any other system of values any justification for uncontrolled violence. Transcendent values can be defended through violence only by those who do not fully understand their transcendent character; and if no other value is absolute, no other value can claim the right to unconditional defence by any means and at all costs. Thus the rationally irreconcilable systems of religious belief rule out any assumption that coercive power is the last resort or the ultimate authority in our world.

And if that is the case, we can see how religious plurality may serve the cause of social unity, paradoxically but genuinely. If we are prohibited from claiming that social harmony can be established by uncontrolled coercive power – that is if we are obliged to make a case for the legitimacy of any social order – but are also prohibited from solving the problem by a simple appeal to universal reason, we are left with a model of politics which is always to do with negotiation and the struggle for mutual understanding. Politics is clearly identified as something pragmatic and 'secular', in the sense that it is not about absolutes. As the world now is, diverse religious traditions very frequently inhabit one territory, one nation, one social unit (and that may be a relatively small unit like a school, a housing co-operative or even a business). And in such a setting, we cannot avoid the pragmatic and secular question of 'common security': what is needed for our convictions to flourish is bound up with what is needed for the convictions of other groups to flourish. We learn that we can best defend ourselves by defending others. In a plural society, Christians secure their religious liberty by advocacy for the liberty of Muslims or Jews to have the same right to be heard in the continuing conversation about the direction and ethos of a society that is characteristic of liberal polity in the broadest sense of the word.

Diverse religious communities thus approach each other in these social units with a powerful interest in finding what sort of values and priorities can claim the widest 'ownership'. This is not an effort to discover the principles of a generalized global ethic to which different traditions can sign up, tempting as this vision is; the work is more piecemeal and less concerned with programmatic agreed statements – though it is certainly a significant moment when diverse communities can take responsibility for common declarations of some kind. The Alexandria Declaration was one such, laying down the limits of what could be defended in the name of religion within the conflicts of the Holy Land; in the same context, more recently, the declaration made by the Chief Rabbis of Israel and the representatives of the Church of England in October 2007 outlined the protocols which both sides believed to be essential in defending each other, and other religious bodies, against physical attack or malicious misrepresentation. It is highly desirable that communities of faith continue to work at joint statements of witness about the environmental crisis (still an area that needs far more interfaith collaboration). And the levels of joint witness over matters around bioethics, for example, are significant wherever a narrowly and aggressively non-religious rationality presses for certain kinds of change. At the same time, where each community recognizes that no one religious tradition can claim to control the processes of public life, this may bring a realism about what the state can and cannot be expected to take for granted and thus a willingness to find, once again, strategies that can win maximal rather than ideal levels of ownership.

A certain pragmatism about what can be agreed as common moral 'property' combined with a strong advocacy of each community's freedom both to practise its faith and to express and argue it in public – this is what religious plurality in a contemporary society may look like. It suggests and helps to secure a state of affairs in which the definition of public policy is never carried through in abstraction from the variety of actual convictions that is evidenced in society – not because any one of these asserts its right to dictate, but because all claim the freedom to join in public argument in ways that insist on the need for what I have been calling maximal ownership. So, if a society seeks to legislate for euthanasia, for the absolute equivalence of marriage and any other kind of partnership, for discrimination against minorities in the name of social cohesion, religious bodies may be expected to argue, not for their right to settle the matter, but for a settlement that manifestly respects their conviction to the extent that they can defend it as legitimate even if not ideal. The notion that social unity can be secured by a policy of marginalizing or ignoring communities of faith because of their irreducible diversity rests on several errors and fallacies, and its most serious and damaging effect is to give credibility to the idea of a neutral and/or self-evident set of secular principles which have authority to override the particular convictions of religious groups. And, as I have argued at length in other places, this amounts to the requirement that religious believers leave their most strongly held and distinctive principles at the door when they engage in public argument: not a good recipe for lasting social unity.

Religious diversity in the modern state can thus be seen as a standing obstacle to any enshrining of a state absolutism (even a purportedly liberal variety) in ways that could pretend to legitimize coercion in the name of (non-religious) values; and it can be seen as a guarantor of the fullest argument and consultation in a democratic society, insisting that communities of faith have a stake in the decisions of the state and its moral direction. This last is important not only in the largely negative instances I have quoted, but also in the pressure that communities of faith can bring to bear in order to persuade the state to act beyond some of its normal definitions of self-interest – for example in addressing international debt and poverty, securing the best possible deal for refugees and migrants, and setting itself some clearly moral aims in foreign policy. This sort of thing will only happen, of course, if religious groups can persuade an electorate to 'own' such a vision. Governments in democratic societies have to be responsive to what electorates want; and if no religious group in a religiously plural context can insist on its preferences as of right, it is still true that the organs of debate in democratic society allow people of faith to be heard in public argument and thus to attempt persuasion.

But there is one more aspect of the plurality of religious presences that is important for social integrity and harmony (a harmony which includes, as mature political harmony must, the processes of honest disagreement and negotiation). Plural religious traditions are a reminder that for most of the human race the values of society are still shaped by one or another history of religious belief. The narrowly 'modern' approach, which takes it for granted that social values and priorities are timeless, turns its back on the history that forms our convictions. All religious practice declares that we inherit certain kinds of insight and perspective, and that to understand why we think as we do, we need to be aware of history. So much is true of any society in which there is a strong and visible cultural presence of religion. But when this is a diversified presence, with distinct convictions and practices in evidence, it turns the argument in fresh directions. A society in which religious diversity exists is invited to recognize that human history is not one story only; even where a majority culture and religion exists, it is part of a wider picture. And very frequently the engagement of different religions in dialogue and co-operation will open up and highlight the many ways in which diverse traditions share a heritage at various points in history. The histories of religion intersect, in their texts and their social development and their political encounters.

Religious diversity when studied with care and sympathy shows us a historical world in which, whatever we say about the claims of diverse religions to truth, there is no possibility of claiming that every human question is answered once and for all by one system. Religions have defined themselves in dialogue and often intellectual conflict with each other; but that very fact implies that there will always be other ways of posing the fundamental questions that human beings confront. Diversity of faith points us towards a past in which there is a kaleidoscope of human perceptions, sometimes interacting fruitfully, sometimes in profound tension. Yet the encounter in history of these diversities shows that diversity cannot help being interactive; and that it in itself can prompt us to think of social unity as the process of a constantly readjusting set of differences, not an imposed scheme claiming totality and finality. Religious diversity becomes a stimulus to find what it is that can be brought together in constructing a new and more inclusive history – to find some fuller sense of the ways in which apparently divergent strands of human thought, imagination and faith can weave together in the formation of each other and of various societies.

Thus in what has been historically a majority Christian culture in the UK, the present diversity of religions within a mostly fairly secular social environment means that the UK has had to think through its history again in the consciousness of how it has engaged with those others who are now on its own doorstep or within its walls – which means recognizing how even a majority Christian culture has been affected by the strand of mathematical and scientific culture stemming from the Islamic world of the early Middle Ages and how aspects of medieval Christian discourse took shape partly in reaction to Islamic thought. The apparently alien presence of another faith has meant that we have had to ask whether it is after all as completely alien as we assumed; and as we find that it is not something from another universe, we discover elements of language and aspiration in common. The fuller awareness of a shared past opens up a better chance of shared future, a home that can be built together, to borrow the compelling image used by the Chief Rabbi in one of his most compelling books. Indeed Lord Sacks offers a very helpful framework for understanding the kind of social unity I have been imagining in this lecture. As he points out, the truth of many contemporary societies is that there is no straightforwardly prevailing religious position dominating society, and, with migration and growing ethnic diversity, no ready-made shared history to which everyone can look in the same way. In such a world, a stable and robust social unity comes from the sense of a common project which all can learn to inhabit equally. Diverse communities resolve to enter a kind of 'covenant' in which they agree on their mutual attitudes, and thus on a 'civil' environment, in every sense of the word; and they build on this foundation a social order in which all have an investment. They build a society governed by law – law as a system in which strangers can become partners by accepting the same context of duty and entitlement in the common project of constructing their social world.

And this happens most fruitfully, so Jonathan Sacks argues, when we begin from acknowledging what he has elsewhere called 'the dignity of difference', from taking seriously the experienced diversity of conviction – not from a utopian and potentially even oppressive set of assumptions that boil down to the belief that everyone who is 'reasonable' is bound to have the same view. Throughout this lecture I have been arguing that different religious convictions, all held in depth and with passion, give a necessary human fullness to the moral practices of a society. They give the resources needed to preserve the idea that some principles are non-negotiable and they also declare as plainly as possible to the society around them that there are therefore elements of the human condition which cannot be ignored or sidelined in the search for lasting human welfare and justice. To extend and alter the scope of my title a little, religious diversity tells us that the unity of actual human beings, the integration of their experience into a meaningful whole that takes in all aspects of their reality, is impossible without reference to the relation of human beings to the sacred – without reference to the 'image of God' in Jewish and Christian terms. Any society that marginalizes religious communities or denies them the liberty to share honestly in public debate is fragmenting not only the human subject, but human society by demanding that we ignore one overwhelming dimension of what it is to be human.

In conclusion, then, I would maintain that the presence of diverse religious groups in a society, allowed to have a voice in the decision-making processes of society without embarrassment, is potentially an immense contribution to a genuinely active and interactive social harmony and a sense of moral accountability within the social order. It is not something to be afraid of. This argument, of course, does not directly address the details of interfaith dialogue or its methods; but it does suggest that when honest and careful dialogue is going on, this will be for the ultimate good of any society. As I have said, none of this implies for a moment that dialogue entails the compromise of fundamental beliefs or that the issue of truth is a matter of indifference; quite the opposite. But there is a proper kind of humility which, even as we proclaim our conviction of truth, even as we Christians proclaim that all human beings are called to union with God the Father in Jesus Christ by the gift and power of the Spirit, obliges us to acknowledge with respect the depth and richness of another's devotion to and obedience to what they have received as truth. As we learn that kind of respect for each other, we remember that we have none of us received the whole truth as God knows it; we all have things to learn. And it is that expectant and positive attitude to our mutual encounter that makes the relation between passionately convinced Christians, Muslims, Jews, Hindus, Buddhists, Sikhs, whatever else, finally a gift and not a threat to a thoroughly contemporary and plural society and its hopes for coherence, justice and peace.

25

Faith communities in a civil society

On September 11th 1906, Mohandas Gandhi addressed a meeting of some 3,000 people in the Empire Theatre in Johannesburg to protest against the introduction of registration and fingerprinting for all Indians in South Africa – part of the first wave in the terrible history of legal racism in South Africa which ended at last in the final decade of the last century. It was a Muslim in the audience, Haji Habib, who first proposed that the decision for non-violent resistance to the legislation should be taken 'in the name of God'. Gandhi stressed the great solemnity of such a form of words, but the meeting rose to affirm this as their will. The *Satyagraha* movement was born, the movement of 'soul force' whose central principle was that our behaviour must witness to truth whatever the cost – and that this witness to truth can never, of its very nature, involve violence or a response to oppression that simply mirrors what has been done by the oppressor. In Gandhi's vision, Christ's prohibition against retaliation came together with his own Hindu heritage to inspire a lifetime of absolutely consistent labour on behalf of this 'soul power'; and on that day in Johannesburg, as at many other points in his life, Gandhi was wholeheartedly supported by his Muslim allies.

The ironies don't need to be spelled out. September 11th is now the anniversary of an act of nightmare violence, which has set in motion a further chain of retaliation, fear and misery. In 1906, the convergence of traditions and disciplines of faith signalled the possibility of escaping from the calculations of ordinary political struggle, the world in which we simply go on imitating the behaviour that has damaged us in the insane hope that we might somehow arrive at a point where someone has a sufficient monopoly of the power to generate fear to guarantee stability. More than a century later, that system of political calculation seems stronger than ever in much of our world; and worse still, religious communities are regularly blamed for its persistence and power. If we ask whether the coming together of religious groups works today as a sign of hope, the response from a good part of the educated public is not very encouraging. Part of our agenda, then, both in the working of the Christian-Muslim Forum and in the discussions of this meeting, has to be to recover that sense of a convergent belief in the possibility of liberation from the systems of violent struggle, in a way that genuinely opens doors in our world.

Gandhi's own conversion to a consistent philosophy of non-violence was, he tells us in *My Experiments with Truth*,[1] greatly assisted by an insight that brought together legal training with his study of the *Gita*: 'I understood the Gita teaching of non-possession to mean that those who desired salvation should act like the trustee, who, though having control over great possessions, regards not an iota of them as his own.' This offers a very useful way into the question of what it is that makes or ought to make the perspective of religious faith liberatingly distinctive in human society – both in the sense Gandhi intended and in a much wider and more radical sense. Gandhi is reflecting on the emphasis in the *Bhagavad-Gita* on detachment: our natural or instinctive way of operating in the world is to imagine ourselves as controlling both our own destiny and the conditions in which we live, so that we struggle for the conditions that promise us such control. But the divine imperative is that our actions should be determined not by this, but by the fixed resolve to act in accordance with the truth: that is, with the truth of who and what he actually is both in society and in the universe itself. When we have learned to act in this way, we are free from fear; we give up the anxious effort to master our circumstances by force. Who we are and what we have come to us from God, and what they communicate to us of God's goodness can never be lost; so it is possible for us to see both who we are and what we have as given for the sake of others. Hence we are trustees: we own nothing absolutely, but are commissioned to communicate to others in spiritual and in directly practical ways the assurance that God has given us.

Gandhian *Satyagraha* is thus rooted in an attitude that, in his eyes, should be fundamental to all religious practice and belief worth the name, an attitude that relativizes the claim of the self to absolute possession or absolute control. But it does not entail – as the superficial observer might think – absolute passivity or the acceptance of injustice; as Gandhi's witness so consistently shows, it is rather that it dictates the way in which we resist. We do not resist in such a way that we appear to be seeking the same kind of power as is now injuring or frustrating us. We do not imitate anything except the truth: our model is the divine communication of what is good. But beyond this obvious principle is the further point which Gandhi implies but does not fully state: belief itself is not a possession, something acquired by the ego that will henceforth satisfy the ego's needs for security and control. To believe in God is to be a 'trustee' of God's truth. My belief is not a thing I own; I might say, truthfully enough, that it 'owns' me, that I am at its service, not that it is at mine. When I claim truth for my religious convictions, it is not a claim that *my* opinion or belief is superior, but a confession that I have resolved to be unreservedly at the service of the reality that has changed my world and set me free from the enslavement of struggle and rivalry. To witness to this in the hope that others will share it is not an exercise in conquest, in signing up more adherents to my party, but simply the offer of a liberation and absolution that has been gratuitously offered to me. When Gandhi reminded his Johannesburg audience that a promise made in the name of God was a serious matter, he was underlining for them the fact that commitment to God in their work for justice involved them in an act of renunciation in the name of truth, the renunciation of any style of living and acting that simply reproduced the ordinary anxieties and exchanges of force that constitute the routine of human society.

Now not all of us are going to agree about how far the claims of Gandhi's legacy extend, how far he was able to see their full implications within his own Indian context or how they are to be implemented in our contemporary setting. But if we are asking about the place of religious commitment in modern civil society, it seems to me that these aspects of his vision of *Satyagraha* are a very suggestive starting-point. What he is asserting is that the religious witness is at its most clearly distinctive in society when it most plainly declares itself answerable to an order quite beyond the balances and negotiations of social conflict and its containments; and when it thus renounces the claim to have a place among others in the social complex.

This is, I grant, a startling way of putting it; surely what any religious believer wants is to have the voice of faith heard within the pluralist debate, to have a guaranteed place at the table? Surely that's why we are discussing the whole question of faith and civil society and why we want to answer once and for all the reproach that religion is a dangerous and destabilizing presence in our culture? Well, yes; but the point which Gandhi invites us to consider is that we shall persuade our culture about this only when religion ceases to appear as yet another human group hungry for security, privilege and the liberty to enforce its convictions. To have faith, Gandhi might say, is to hold something in trust for humanity – a vision of who and what humanity is in relation to a truth that does not depend on worldly victory. And to witness to a truth that does not depend on worldly victory – a truth that, in Plato's terms, is not just the interest of the strong or successful – implies that we do not battle for its survival or triumph in the way that interests and parties do in the world around us. In a paradox that never ceases to challenge and puzzle both believers and unbelievers, it is when we are free from the *passion* to be taken seriously, to be protected or indeed to be obeyed that we are most likely to be heard. The convincing witness to faith is one for whom safety and success are immaterial, and one for whom therefore the exercise of violent force against another of different conviction is ruled out. And the nature of an authentically religious community is made visible in its admission of dependence on God – which means both that it does not fight for position and power*and*that it will not see itself as existing just by the license of human society. It proclaims both its right to exist on the basis of the call of God and its refusal to enforce that right by the routine methods of human conflict.

All this is, for the Christian believer, rooted in the gospel narrative and in the reflections of the first Christians. Jesus himself in his trial before Pilate says that his royal authority does not derive from anything except the eternal truth which he himself embodies as the incarnate Word of God; only if his authority depended on some other source would his servants fight (*John* 18.36–7). Earthly authority needs to reinforce itself in conflict and dominance. If the community of Jesus' followers reinforced itself in such a way, it would be admitting that its claims were derived from this human order. The realm, the *basileia*, of God, to which Jesus' acts and words point is not a region within human society any more than it is a region within human geography; it is that condition of human relationships, public and private, where the purpose of God is determinative for men and women and so becomes visible in our history – a condition that can be partially realized in the life of the community around Jesus, but waits for its full embodiment in a future only God knows. And for the first and second generations of believers, the community in which relation with the Risen Jesus transforms all relationships into the exchange of the gifts given by Jesus' Spirit has come to be seen as the historical foretaste of this future, as it is here and now the embodiment of Jesus' own identity – the Body of Christ – to the extent it shows this new quality of relation.

The Church is, in this perspective, the trustee of a vision that is radical and universal, the vision of a social order that is without fear, oppression, the violence of exclusion and the search for scapegoats because it is one where each recognizes their dependence on all and each is seen as having an irreplaceable gift for all. The Church cannot begin to claim that it consistently lives by this;

its failure is all too visible, century-by-century. But its credibility does not hang on its unbroken success; only on its continued willingness to be judged by what it announces and points to, the non-competitive, non-violent order of God's realm, centred upon Jesus and accessible through commitment to him. Within the volatile and plural context of a society that has no single frame of moral or religious reference, it makes two fundamental contributions to the common imagination and moral climate. The first is that it declares that, in virtue of everyone's primordial relation to God (made in God's image), the dignity of every person is non-negotiable: each has a unique gift to give, each is owed respect and patience and the freedom to contribute what is given them. This remains true whether we are speaking of a gravely disabled person – when we might be tempted to think they would be better off removed from human society; or of a suspected terrorist – when we might be tempted to think that torture could be justified in extracting information; or of numberless poor throughout the world – when we should be more comfortable if we were allowed to regard them as no more than collateral damage in the steady advance of prosperity for our 'developed' economies.

But the point of this first contribution, as it affects civil society, is this: the presence of the Church, not as a clamorous interest group but as a community confident of its rootedness in something beyond the merely political, expresses a vision of human dignity and mutual human obligation which, because of its indifference to popular success or official legitimation, poses to every other community a special sort of challenge. 'Civil society' is the recognized shorthand description for all those varieties of human association that rest on willing co-operation for the sake of social goods that belong to the whole group, not just to any individual or faction, and which are not created or wholly controlled by state authority. As such, their very existence presupposes persons who are able to take responsibility for themselves and to trust one another in this enterprise. The presence of the Christian community puts to civil society the question of where we look for the foundation of such confidence about responsibility and trustworthiness: does this set of assumptions about humanity rest on a fragile human agreement, on the decision of human beings to behave as if they were responsible, or on something deeper and less contingent, something to which any and every human society is finally answerable? Is the social creativity which civil society takes for granted part of a human 'birthright'?

The second major contribution made by the presence of the Church is what we might in shorthand call 'universalism' – not in the technical theological sense, but simply meaning the conviction that every human agent is involved in either creating or frustrating a common good that relates to the whole human race. In plainer terms, we cannot as Christians settle down with the conclusion that what is lastingly and truly good for any one individual or group is completely different from what is lastingly and truly good for any other. Justice is not local in an exclusive sense or limited by circumstances; there are no classes or subgroups of humanity who are entitled to less of God's love; and so there are no classes entitled to lower levels of human respect or compassion or service. And since an important aspect of civil society is the assumption that human welfare is not achieved by utilitarian generalities imposed from above, but requires active and particularized labour, the fact of the Christian community' presence once again puts the question of how human society holds together the need for action appropriate to specific and local conditions with the lively awareness of what is due to all people everywhere. This is not only about a vision of universal human justice as we normally think of it, but also applies to how we act justly towards those who are not yet born – how we create a just understanding of our relation to the environment.

In short, the significance of the Church for civil society is in keeping alive a concern both to honour and to justify the absolute and non-negotiable character of the human vision of responsibility and justice that is at work in all human association for the common good. It is about connecting the life of civil society with its deepest roots, acknowledged or not. The conviction of being answerable to God for how we serve and respect God's human and non-human creation at the very least serves to ensure that the human search for shared welfare and responsible liberty will not be reduced to a matter of human consensus alone. And if the Church – or any other community of faith – asks of society the respect that will allow it to be itself, it does so not because it is anxious about its survival (which is in God's hands), but because it asks the freedom to remind the society or societies in which it lives of their own vulnerability and their need to stay close to some fundamental questions about the nature of the humanity they seek to nourish. Such a request from Church to society will be heard and responded to, of course, only if the Church genuinely looks as though it were speaking for more than a self-protecting set of 'religious' concerns; if it appears as concerned for something more than self-defence. To return to what was said earlier, it needs to establish its credentials as 'non-violent': that is, as not contending against other kinds of human group for a share in ordinary political power. To put it in severely condensed form, the Church is most credible when least preoccupied with its security and most engaged with the human health of its environment; and to say 'credible' here is not to say 'popular', since engagement with this human health may run sharply against a prevailing consensus. Recent debates on euthanasia offer a case in point; and even here, it is surprisingly often claimed that the Churches are concerned here only to sustain their control of human lives – which sadly illustrates what all too many in our society have come to expect of the Church.

I have spoken so far, as I was invited to do, about the Christian understanding of the role of faith in civil society, and have attempted to connect it with some of the most fundamental elements of the Christian revelation – the absolute*difference*of the power and action of God as against human power (embodied in the fact of Jesus' crucifixion as the climax of God's incarnate work), and the universal promise offered in the Resurrection (embodied in the mission of the Church as mediating Christ's living presence). In doing this, of course, it is impossible not to be aware of the distinct ways in which other religious traditions understand their role in relation to the ambient society. As many have observed, Islam takes as central the conviction that the law and public practice of a society ought ideally to conform to revealed law; Muslims are often puzzled by what they see as the Christian insistence on separation between the religious and the political, and it might well be thought that the vision outlined here is so antithetical to the Islamic frame of reference that there is no possible convergence. Yet there are three considerations that should make us hesitate before settling for this conclusion. The first is that, in understanding divine law as universal and equally applicable to all, Islam, like Christianity, refuses to make faith either subservient to the social order or simply an aspect among others of social life: it is something that offers transformation to the entire range of human activity. The second is that Islam itself recognizes the reality of potential conflict between political power and faithful obedience to revealed law; nothing in Islamic tradition suggests that there could be a guarantee of fidelity to God simply through formal allegiance to Islam by the ruling authority, and the legitimacy of passive resistance to unjust authority is acknowledged. And third, the Quranic dictum that there is no compulsion in religion is the foundation for any Muslim account of the imperative of non-violence. This stands, of course, alongside the no less significant tradition of the imperative to *jihad* as the duty to defend the Muslim community wherever its integrity and survival are at risk; but the question which is bound to arise in our day is whether, given the complex realities of today's world, there would ever now be the kind of situation which would justify the samesortof defensive *jihad* that was envisaged in the earliest days of Islam – or whether those commentators are right who insist that the only *jihad* now justifiable is the struggle against evil in the heart and the resistance to a culture of cruelty and indifference to suffering, a struggle which of its nature must be non-violent.

I look forward to hearing reflection on this and related issues; but my chief point is that the convergence that occurred on this day in Johannesburg in 1906 was not an illusory or opportunistic affair. Both our faiths bring to civil society a conviction that what they embody and affirm is not a marginal affair; both claim that their legitimacy rests not on the license of society but on God's gift. Yet for those very reasons, they carry in them the seeds of a non-violent and non-possessive witness. They cannot be committed to violent struggle to prevail at all costs, because that would suggest a lack of faith in the God who has called them; they cannot be committed to a policy of coercion and oppression because that would again seek to put the power of the human believer or the religious institution in the sovereign place that only God's reality can occupy. Because both our traditions have a history scarred by terrible betrayals of this, we have to approach our civil society and its institutions with humility and repentance. But I hope that this does not mean we shall surrender what is most important – that we have a gift to offer immeasurably greater than our own words or records, the gift of a divine calling and a renewal of all that is possible from human beings.

PART SEVEN

Rediscovering Religion

26

Religious lives

A religious life is a material life. Forget for a moment the arguments we might have about the definition of the 'spiritual'; living religiously is a way of conducting a bodily life. It has to do with gesture, place, sound, habit – not first and foremost with what is supposed to be going on inside. The whole idea of an 'inner life' is, properly, what we put together from a certain reading of visible lives; it is not a self-evident category, a cluster of intangible experiences or mental dispositions, but what comes to light as the sense, the intelligibility, of a certain pattern of acts. It's a point made more economically by the Apostle James in refusing to accept a smooth demarcation between belief and action. The devils in hell, he notes, have all the right ideas, their problem is not that they are mistaken about the nature of the universe and its maker; but it would be eccentric to call them 'believers' – or, in the terms I'll be using here, it would be eccentric to say that their beliefs entitle them to be called livers of religious lives.

I'm labouring the point because of the persistent cultural error of treating questions about 'religion' as questions about beliefs that may be more or less justifiable at the bar of public reason. The indignation of the media columnist is easily aroused over religious education in schools because it has to do, they maintain, with inculcating beliefs that have no evidence; as one such writer elegantly put it a few weeks ago, it is on a par with believing in the tooth fairy. But – leaving aside the failure so far of belief in the tooth fairy to generate martyrdom or the *Divina Commedia* – the fundamental mistake is to consider belief itself, in its corporate religious context, as more or less exclusively a mental event: an eccentric, 'vagrant' mental event, a virus, to use another analogy that has found some popularity. In this chapter, I want to look at what is involved in approaching religious life in terms of gesture and habit; how religious conversion is recognized, brought into speech; and what, in such a light, a religious life claims for itself. Part of my agenda, I confess, is to put some questions against what is fast becoming a cliché – the cultural currency of 'spiritual' identity as something favoured in opposition to 'religious' belonging. I don't deny that the statistics bear out the judgement of cultural popularity; but I suspect that there are lurking confusions in the use of the salient words, and that certain issues are effectively silenced by so easy a polarity.

At the most prosaic level, religious lives are indeed recognized as habits of behaviour – ritual words and acts, the mapping of an undifferentiated duration within narratives of sacred time. For the religious practitioner, these habits are not chosen as such, not created in order to express an attitude; they are acquired as habitual responses to what is presented. They connect with the habits and gestures that demonstrate in other areas – indeed, you could say, in the whole field of knowledge acquisition – an acquaintance with what is there to be 'negotiated'. Knowledge, it has been said, is first knowledge of how to move in a territory in which you are not the only agent or presence. Children learn to avoid walking into chairs and touching hot surfaces; chess players learn not to move on to the pawn's immediate diagonal; experimental scientists learn what impedes the collection of useable data – what 'laboratory conditions' are. Most religious persons would say that their ritual actions are more like these things than they are like the devising of conscious symbols.

We are here, of course, close to the uncomfortable frontier with magical thinking, and so to a source of potential embarrassment for the modern believer. But courage: the frontier is real, however fine. The believer may say that these gestures, these words, are the appropriate, even the natural, way of negotiating a territory; most would add that a mistake, a solecism or a simple refusal here does not of itself bring disaster. It simply empties out from your behaviour a particular dimension of meaning (more of this later) and leaves you without a compass in the territory of the heart. Acquiring the bodily habits of religious practice both is and isn't a matter of technique: this is how to respond; but this is not how to manipulate or control.

This is abstract. What I am talking about can be far better put:

> And there is God. The girl who could not kneel but learned to do so on the rough coconut matting in an untidy bathroom. Such things are often more intimate even than sex. The story of the girl who gradually learned to kneel is something I would love to write in the fullest possible way.[1]

Etty Hillesum, who died in Auschwitz in 1943, left behind her a journal for the two years before her deportation and death, an extraordinarily full and absorbing document which chronicles a complex sexual and emotional life, a deepening immersion in Rilke and Dostoevsky and a religious conversion of a very unconventional order. Her Jewishness is both a matter of immense significance – this is Holland in the 1940s, after all – and curiously muted as a religious theme. Like others, it is as if she travelled to her roots by a long detour through the religion and imagination of modern Europe. But amongst much that is arresting in what she writes, the repeated references to 'learning to kneel' give a clue to something of what she understood by learning to say 'God' without embarrassment. Of her mentor and (briefly) lover, the psychoanalyst Julius Spier, she notes[2] his observation that 'it took quite a long time before he dared to say "God" without feeling that there was something ridiculous about it. Even though he was a believer'; and she notes too her mother's '"Yes, actually, I am religious"', commenting, 'That actually is the giveaway'.[3] Finding the courage to say the word – without an 'actually' – is a sort of counterpoint to responding to the compulsion to kneel.[4]

Spier, she says, taught her this courage. Yet she is at first inhibited in asking him what he does when he prays. 'I know the intimate gestures he uses with women, but I still want to know the gestures he uses with God ... Does he kneel down in the middle of his small room? ... Does he kneel before he take his dentures out or afterward?'[5]

Praying is a physically intimate matter. In 1942, she records the sheer difficulty of writing about the urge to kneel which 'sometimes pulses through my body, or rather it is as if my body had been meant and made for the act of kneeling ... It has become a gesture embedded in my body, needing to be expressed from time to time'.[6] And to say this is more embarrassing 'than if I had to write about my love life'. The gesture is demanded by some inner 'welling-up', a sense of 'plenitude' which transforms the grey landscape of dawn into spaciousness.[7] And it is accompanied by a 'listening in' to the self;[8] she observes much later that she needs the German *hineinhorchen* to express what is going on.[9] It is an attentiveness to nothing external; and the dogmatically keen-eyed will notice the passages where she seems to settle for a highly subjectivized model ('what is deepest inside me, which for the sake of convenience I call God', or 'The externals are simply props'[10]). Yet this listening, *hineinhorchen*, is and is not a simple scrutiny of the self: 'it is really God who hearkens inside me. The most essential and the deepest in me hearkening unto the most essential and deepest in the other. God to God': loving attention to others is a clearing of 'the path toward You in them'.[11]

It is not easy to disentangle exactly what is being said in all this. Etty Hillesum can speak of thanking God for indwelling her[12] and writes in relation to St Augustine, 'Truly those are the only love letters one ought to write: love letters to God'.[13] God is regularly invoked as source and giver. It would be wrong to read her as simply identifying God with a dimension of the self, something contained in the self; yet it is clear that her sense of God is inseparable from the sense of something growing 'inside'. She quotes approvingly Rilke's *Stundenbuch: Auch wenn wir nicht wollen:/ Gott reift* – 'Even if we don't want it: God ripens'[14] – the conclusion of a long section dealing with the growth of a sort of divine image in us. What the journals present is a process of impassioned discovery. She can write in July 1942, during a crucial period of development when she is coming to terms with separation from Spier, 'I haven't finished with You by a long chalk, oh God, or with this world'.[15] Her prayers, in the entries for these days, are exceptionally vivid and immediate; again we find the emphasis on kneeling, 'almost naked, in the middle of the floor, completely "undone"',[16] the struggle to be 'faithful' to God (and a complex awareness that something in the relation with Spier means something less than entire faithfulness,[17] and above all the sense of accumulating something, growing in a way that carries a sort of responsibility. This is a life in which a task is accepted: a task that can be defined only as that of allowing God to 'ripen' in increasingly visible ways.

What this involves comes more plainly to light in the harrowing letters from the transit camp at Westerbork. She had written earlier of accepting suffering as 'passive activity',[18] of the need to accept suffering that is in no sense chosen, including the trials that come from genetic and temperamental givens.[19] She quotes Andre Suares on Dostoevsky: 'Pain is not the site of our longing, but the site of our certainty',[20] meaning that suffering is neither to be mastered nor to be fled, but to be utilized and transformed. The 'site' is given: unavoidable suffering is what it is, not a stimulus to a longing for a better place or a pedagogy for moral improvement, but a datum which our humanity must humanize. And some months before her going to Westerbork, she says of Spier that his stature lies in having 'given shelter' in his person to 'a portion of life and suffering and God':[21] suffering is to be made at home in the human self, neither romanticized nor denied.

It is a comment that perhaps helps us understand what is going on in her thinking about God: the self develops as a place where certain realities can find a home, realities that are in one sense very much the inner business of the self and yet are unsought, not generated by the will or the imagination, but implanted – could we say? – by a life history.

Life can educate one to a belief in God. And experiences too are what bring this about; but I don't mean visions and other forms of sense experience which show us the "existence of this being", but, e.g., sufferings of various sorts. These neither show us God in the way a sense impression shows us an object, nor do they give rise to conjectures about him. Experiences, thoughts–life–can force this concept on us. So perhaps it is similar to the concept of "object".

That is Wittgenstein, in 1950;[22] and the significance of this in the present context is his surprisingly strong language about a concept being 'forced'. Etty Hillesum's writing about kneeling exhibits precisely what such force might look and feel like. But as we follow her to Westerbork, the nature of the imperative shifts subtly. She is conscious of just this need to 'give shelter', to accommodate, the reality of suffering so that what, if anything, is saved in or from the camps is not a matter of bodily survival but a mode of preservation that can become an offering, a word of intelligibility, in the post-war world; hence her apprehension about denying or ignoring the worst around.[23] She sets herself to chronicle the unbearable (disease, the lack of sanitation; what is done to children – there are letters of August 1943 of particular horror[24]), while saying that her life is now 'an uninterrupted dialogue' with God.[25] Uninterrupted? The first edition of her writings appeared under the title *An Interrupted Life*; but she read it as the 'ripening' of something, the expansion of herself to 'shelter' what must not be lost. The interruption of the nightmare situation at Westerbork forces her to a level of consistency or fidelity in her perception of herself, her 'speaking' of herself in action or attitude. It is not simply that, in Wittgenstein's words, a concept has been forced upon her; more that an identity has been imposed and accepted. The brutal imposition of the identity of a subhuman, the process which she chronicles with painfully dry irony in many journal entries, is woven into the identity already accepted, the identity of someone who kneels to God only. The kneeling embodies something imposed from within, yet not devised or preferred by the ego; and this makes possible the peculiar freedom she notes when face to face with her Gestapo custodians.

It is a freedom that has slightly chilled some readers, as it alarmed some of her friends. Relatively early, in February 1942, she describes her experience of such an encounter,[26] recording her sense of pity for the 'sullen ... driven and harassed' young soldier who is supervising a large crowd of Amsterdam Jews being registered for deportation, her sense of his weakness and the contingency of his humanity ('Did you have an unhappy childhood, has your girlfriend let you down?'). He, as much as any person in the hall, is being shaped by the situation they all share, prisoner or guard: the space is the same, what matters is how you comport yourself within it, how much room you can make for the others in the shared space and their particularity. Again, a month or so later, she writes about giving space for grief in a way that rules out cluttering the inner space with hatred or vengefulness:[27] space for grief absorbs sorrow, hatred generates more sorrow. She notes more than once the arguments she has with those who want her to echo their hatred or to dehumanize Germans in their turn, but she is clear that this is a futile response.

A perceptive commentator has candidly reported her occasional frustration at the lack of what might be thought a proper anger here; I am less sure. The letters from Westerbork leave no ambiguity about her sensations of horror and disgust and, I think, anger, at the atrocities she witnesses. But we have to take very seriously the imagery of giving space. She is wholly persuaded that she has a task of internal housekeeping for her imagination and emotion that is to do with guaranteeing that certain things do not disappear from the human landscape. If anger drives out grief, something has disappeared that has the capacity to remake broken human bonds, because grief can be recognized and shared across a conflict and anger can't (and yes, the echo here is very strong of Simone Weil on the Iliad, and Priam's appeal to Achilles). Most decisively, what she believes she is doing is what can best be described as taking responsibility for God in the situation.

> You cannot help us, ... we must help You to help ourselves. And that is all we can
> manage these days and also all that really matters: that we safeguard that little piece of
> You, God, in ourselves.[28]
>   There must be someone to live through it all and bear witness to the fact that God
> lived, even in these times. And why should I not be that witness?[29]

Perhaps the language jars; though no more than Bonhoeffer's well-known poem on going to God in God's need rather than running to God out of one's own helplessness; or even Teresa of Avila's account in her autobiography of a conversion prompted by encountering the image of Christ at the scourging pillar, and recognizing a call simply to be in some sense visibly where he is. This is not, in any of the cases mentioned, a speculative statement about some imagined metaphysical limit on God's liberty; all of those listed are clear that God is where God chooses to be. But God's nature and action entail that

God is not an item in the world, battling for advantage. The religious life, on this account, would be taking on the task of ensuring a habitation for God, a God who does not guarantee for himself a place in the created world, a place alongside other agents, and so is visible only when a human life gives place, offers hospitality to God, so that this place, this identity, becomes a testimony. And another of Wittgenstein's aphorisms, from 1937 this time, echoes this, when he says that belief in Christ is something other than the acceptance of a historical record: it is the 'result' of your own biography, and so you must 'make a quite different place in your life for it'.[30]

Paul Ricoeur, in an essay on 'The Hermeneutics of Testimony',[31] argued that testimony, the event that manifests a presence otherwise unthought or unknown, always 'gives something to be interpreted',[32] because it proposes a story that must be heard and weighed against other stories (testimony and trial belong together) and is not susceptible to generalizing methods or a reduction to the terms of a system. There is a hint here of Kierkegaard's arguments also, that the 'religious' 'cannot speak',[33] cannot, that is, argue and defend and even demonstrate in the ways that are appropriate to the realms of the aesthetic and the ethical. It is not, for either Ricoeur or Kierkegaard, that faith is therefore an irrational decision as opposed to a rational one – as if the human subject were faced with a set of parallel possibilities for belief, some well-supported and some not, with religious belief being just one of those things that the unpredictable will might settle upon. The religious life, the life of testimony, is generated by events of a certain kind, and it becomes itself an event of a certain kind. Its belief content is neither a reasoned conclusion nor an arbitrary mythology, but the necessarily gradual and complex outworking of the nature of the wider landscape implied in these events.

Back to where I began. A religious life is a material life in a particular place, marked by particular material patterns and rhythms. Its goal is for the place it inhabits to be place in which certain realities become visible. It takes responsibility for the appearing of God; in doing so it equally embodies responsibility to God. It makes a bid to be fairly 'tried' as a narrative among others; and what it has to show is that it is indeed a distinctive place, not a version of some other discourse. So the religious person describing herself has to do so in a manner that somehow makes concrete the sense of replying to uninvited initiatives. And with due respect to Kierkegaard's distinction between aesthetic and religious, this is comparable to what the creative artist will say of their 'self-positioning' by way of the realized artistic work: this is where I stand, not by my choice but because this is what had to be done or achieved. This is the appropriate response to how the environment and my embodied imagination have met each other.

Etty Hillesum learned to kneel. The physical position is part of a whole protracted story of how she 'places' herself in the world in such a way as to become a symbol and an event, the witness to the fact that God lived during a certain epoch of terror, dehumanization and the apparent absence of God. The role of physical discipline in religious life has probably never been less significant than in the modern Western world (how many people actually kneel in churches now?), but it is at the very least a statement that what is encountered in religious life is, as we noted earlier, no less a matter of negotiating our way around the bare thereness of something than the techniques of mapping our path through a world of material objects. The pattern of a physical life traces the outline, so to speak, of a discovered object, which is made visible only by the continuing process of 'tracing'. Beginning with the conscious practice of such a pattern, a whole biography can take on the same character, to become a symbolic outline. Etty Hillesum learns to kneel, and learns in due course to plot her location within the tumultuous spiritual geography of the Gestapo office and the camp at Westerbork. And those religious traditions that lay special emphasis on material disciplines would say that the planned engagement with the processes of your own body that constitute Sufi or Zen or hesychast contemplation is a training for a free engagement with an entire material and historical environment – for a liberated life. We begin to learn how to be a sign inhabited by God's meanings as we accept a shape for our physical practice that arises in response to the sort of pressure Etty Hillesum charts, the pressure of a passion for transparency to oneself and truthful feeling, the pressure Wittgenstein seem to speak of.

Where does this leave us with the fashionable disjunction between the religious and the spiritual? I accept entirely that the language here is rather arbitrary; it so happens that the public (well, the questionnaire-answering public) associates the religious with limits, with doctrine and regulated corporate life, the spiritual with self-development, wisdom and loose communal structures. There are other idioms, especially among theologians, which would point in a different direction – those, for example, that oppose the religious to the biblical, that is, the sphere of securely controlled practice to the sphere of transforming obedience to revelation. The shadow of Karl Barth hangs over this discussion, and I have myself used such an opposition to the detriment of 'religious' identities in this particular sense.

But what I have been suggesting in the present context is that 'religion' under-stood precisely as the realm of limit and physical determination, including community and language, carries with it a different order of freedom from a spirituality that is focused on the nurture of the inner life as such. The 'spiritual' as a category which can be applied to a range of phenomena or traditions of speech and action seems in current usage to work with a model of the self -selecting from this range a vocabulary and a set of practices which might serve an existing sense of need, and which may add to the self's repertoire a degree of access to further experience. Whether we are speaking of versions of traditional practices (the reshaped Kabbala popular with some or, rather more seriously, the revisionist Sufism of 'traditionalists' like Frithiof Schuon) or of more obviously constructed practices (the world of New Age communities of divers kinds) the point is the same. What is to the fore is not so much the possibility of locating yourself in a territory so as to become a sign of an alien or exiled presence as the deployment of skills to settle and assure the self.

That this is no ignoble or wicked enterprise, I don't dispute; but I am concerned to look for ways of distinguishing it clearly from something poten-tially more radical. Teresa of Avila wrote of her need to distinguish experiences beginning in God and terminating in the self, and those beginning in the self and terminating in God; the latter left the self altered in unpredictable and sometimes alarming ways, but had the effect of enlarging it rather than simply consoling it.[34] This strikes me as similar to what I have been trying to discern. And, put in this way, it helps also to clarify a point that might be made against the formulation I have used. D. Z. Phillips, in his book on *The Problem of Evil and the Problem of God*,[35] has some observations on the difference between what he calls 'temporal' and 'eternal' covenant: a temporal covenant is one in which human beings implicitly make a conditional contract with God – a commitment to believe provided that certain things do not happen; and eternal covenant is one in which the only point of loving God is loving God, and no conditions are specified, no outcomes regarded as invalidating the agreement. 'The point of loving God is not that hope should not perish or that the world should be a meaningful place. The point of loving God is not even to be found in the persistence of belief in him on earth'.[36] The eternal covenant is a habit of life in which all that happens is in advance located within the practice of the love of God.

Now I have spoken of Etty Hillesum's notion of the religious life giving place to God on earth, taking responsibility for God's appearing; is this to settle for a temporal covenant, committed to 'the persistence of belief'? I think not. Etty Hillesum does not decide that the world would be a better place if belief in God persisted and so decide to make her life a locus for God. Something unarguable is happening to her apprehension of who she is, something exhibited in her material life; and whatever happens becomes part of that uninterrupted conversation with God, that listening to a foreign voice in the heart of the self, which becomes habitual. She does not follow the practice of loving God so that a particular outcome may be guaranteed; if she dies, the responsibility for God's appearing on earth in one sense dies with her. That place is occupied, built over by the violence that kills her. But the pressure towards testimony is part of the pressure to exhibit – by kneeling, by speaking to God, by refusing to occupy inner space with hatred or revenge – what the world cannot deliver, cannot produce, cannot master and thus (in another sense) cannot destroy or kill. The point of it all, or, in Teresa's language, the terminus, remains God, not the success of the self. Testimony may or may not persuade; but it remains. And the 'eternal covenant' is expressed in its attempt to include an entire biography, irrespective of its success in compelling assent.

It asks to be read and interpreted. Stanley Cavell pursues the question of why we seem to need just this metaphor, of reading, as we try to make clear what it is we understand of a body (a body as opposed to a mass of material), and observes that it has something to do with seeing, with 'being advised', with a tone that relates to narrative or history.[37] A life that claims, like Etty Hillesum's, to 'give shelter' to God and love and suffering invites a particular kind of interpretative labour. Why should we think that God, love and suffering were concepts that had become homeless in the first place? Her language presupposes that they are at risk. So we cannot read without knowing a larger history that might explain such a risk. What is it to 'give shelter'? We should need to attend to what she has to say about the economics of the emotional and imaginative life, about what habits of mind and speech make it impossible to go on entertaining certain categories. We should need to look at the record of the material habits that embody a grammar of response to the non-negotiable, what it might mean to say that a life was receiving its shape rather than creating it in a vacuum. We might – though probably not in this case – conclude that the claims were misplaced. The situation is not so serious, and the concepts are not homeless after all; or the record of habits suggests an element of willed symbolization or even dramatization. But we should have the tools, I believe, to begin to recognize what sort of claim it might be that a life was a religious one – rather than a spiritual one or a moral one. And it would have a lot to do with how we saw a life offering itself, so to speak, into the context of a possible language about God, becoming a 'word', a sacred text.

Etty Hillesum is engaged with several concrete texts – the Bible (notably the Psalms and Matthew's gospel), Augustine, Dostoevsky, Rilke. Some of these are orthodox Christian texts, some not. Her practice engages with an aspect of traditional discipline, kneeling, thanksgiving, and so on, but it is not part of a corporate Jewish or Christian discipline and its relation with classical Christian ethics is a nice question (I think not only of her idiosyncratic – though never exactly casual – approach to sexual encounter, but of the difficult pages in which she describes her efforts to induce a miscarriage: an episode which later entries imply she had second thoughts about.[38] Is she in this respect, at the end of the day, another selective modern, with an isolated contemporary soul, so that we have finally to let her go as an apostle of communal religious identity? It is a question that needs care. I believe that her idioms are often those of the modern soul, but that the outcome of the story is something for which the modern individualistic or voluntarist account of religious experience will not provide an adequate vehicle. What is distinctive and angular is that she has elected to be identified, not to identify God simply in her terms, to be a word, a sign. If the religious, as distinct from the simply spiritual, is about responsibility to and for a foreign and transcendent presence, there can be little doubt where to place her.

To make oneself a sign: the phrase echoes, deliberately, what a noted French theologian early in the twentieth century said of Jesus in his last days – that he 'placed himself in the order of signs'. The Christian narrative – not exclusively among religious traditions, but with a marked force and priority – deals with a biography regarded as wholly and without interruption an offering 'into' language, a place wholly occupied by God, yet without qualification a human locus in history. As such, it determines how the Christian tradition understands holiness, the perceptible alignment of a life with God. I do not want to embark on a theological essay here, nor to argue what might be in common between different accounts of holiness in diverse religious discourses. But the idea that the paradigm religious life is one that 'gives shelter' to a vulnerable divine presence, a narrative that seeks to embody God, to take responsibility for the appearing of God (and of suffering and love), has a particular resonance with Christian and Jewish tradition, and illuminates why a life like Etty Hillesum's is hard to read without that tradition in mind.

And it also focuses a difficult question about secularized or secularizing cultures. Could there be a cultural environment in which the religious in this sense was no longer accessible? Assuming a continued decline in allegiance to traditional religious bodies in the post-Christian West, and bracketing for a moment the issue of how Islamic religiousness constructs its stories in such an environment, could we come to a point where Etty Hillesum's self-descriptions would no longer be understandable? Answering the question without recourse to theology, we might have to say that yes, this was a possibility; but we should need then to consider the implication that human lives might lose the possibility of 'sheltering' certain things; that the possibility of suffering meaningfully, for example, might vanish. Remember that for Etty, the self's 'safeguarding' of God is inseparable from that careful attention to what is given room in the self's encounter with itself: making space for sorrow, without its being crowded out by anger or hate, is bound in with the self's hospitality to God. Indeed, a self conscious of the idea of God and taking no responsibility for the rest of its inner ecology would be only very questionably religious. If responsibility for the persistence of God and for the possibility of radical sorrow (and its issue in compassion) belong together, a culture in which awareness of God at this level was not understood would atrophy in its freedom to feel and show grief and pity; and a culture in which grief and pity were pushed aside by cultivated and socially nurtured resentment would have little capacity to understand what 'God' might mean. The answer (if answer there is) is not, though, a campaigning for religious dominance or security; it is simply to conserve narratives like these, in the hope that their cross-references will open some doors of comprehension.

Olivier Clément wrote that any renewed religiousness in the modern and postmodern West had the primary task of *promouvoir le gratuit, l'inassimilable, ce qui ne sert a rien mais eclaire tout*: 'to bring to prominence the gratuitous, what resists assimilation and serves nothing yet clarifies everything.'[39] To give over a life, in any circumstances, not only the dramatic and terrible context of Westerbork and Auschwitz, to making a habitation for grief and for God is the most effective resistance possible both to a secular reduction of human meaning to the level of arbitrary choice and commodified feeling or imagination, and to a pseudo-religiousness, a spirituality, in which religious symbolism itself becomes a fashion accessory for the postmodern self. There is a significant difference between a symbolism borrowed to illustrate the choices of the ego for a short season and the bestowal of a life to become a symbol. The latter is ineluctably a matter of cost, a foregoing of certain freedoms that results, so it is believed, in a different sort of freedom, the sort that allows the enemy to be seen with pity and human curiosity, and that seeks to lay a foundation for peace in shared grief. It serves no externally or publicly determined purpose, but neither does it serve the agenda of an ego; it is in what is beyond or between these that religious people try to locate the concept of the will and purpose of God. What Etty Hillesum determines to embody and welcome is the intuition that a life given over in this manner makes speech possible at a new level, because it seeks to live from that inner space in which all human seriousness is grounded. But to talk of this as a place where God is lodged – and remember her insistence on letting go of the embarrassment at the word 'God' – this is to perform the most radical relativizing possible of the individual ego, to say that I am answerable for all I do and say to what I do not control or grasp. A religiousness that 'clarifies everything' perhaps costs everything also; which is why it is reducible neither to mere orthodoxy nor to spirituality, neither of which clarify in Clément's sense.

'God is in safe hands with us despite everything', she wrote, in September 1943. She died in November. To see that what matters is not that you are – in any easy sense – safe in the hands of God, but that God is safe in your hands is to turn upside down any consolatory version of faith, to stake yourself indeed on an 'eternal covenant'. On this kind of inversion, we do not decide. Doors open, because of how life is in our times; through them something enters that we do not understand. A life is shaped, to the extent that we call it a home, a shelter, for something. And we argue for it or commend it not by dialectical nimbleness, but by fidelity in some very prosaic things; perhaps we might even start by practising how to kneel.

Acknowledgements

The chapters of this book were first given as lectures on the following occasions:

Part One – Secularism and its Discontents

Chapter 1

Given as 'Has Secularism Failed? Notes on the Survival of the Spirit', Raymond Williams Lecture, given on 1 June 2002 at the Hay-on-Wye Festival; first published in *Scintilla 7* (2003), pp. 9–20

Chapter 2

Given on 23 November 2006 at the Pontifical Academy of Social Sciences, Vatican City

Chapter 3

The Chatham Lecture: given on 29 October 2004 at Trinity College, Oxford

Chapter 4

Given as 'Law, Power and Peace: Christian Perspectives on Sovereignty', the David Nicholls Memorial Lecture, on 25 September 2005 at University Church of St Mary the Virgin, Oxford

Chapter 5

Given on 26 January 2008 at Liverpool Cathedral, during Liverpool's year as European Capital of Culture

Chapter 6

Given as 'Religion, culture, diversity and tolerance: shaping the new Europe', on 7 November 2005, at the European Policy Centre, Brussels

Chapter 7
Given on 17 April 2008, Westminster Cathedral; first published in *Faith and Life in Britain: the Cardinal's Lectures 2008* (Chelmsford, 2008), pp.35–48

Part Two – Living within Limits: Liberalism, Pluralism and Law

Chapter 8
Given on Wednesday 16 May 2007 at the Toynbee Hall, London

Chapter 9
The Isaiah Berlin Lecture: given on 16 November 2010 at the Hampstead Synagogue

Chapter 10
The Chevening Lecture: given on 15 October 2010 at the British Council, New Delhi

Chapter 11
The James Callaghan Memorial Lecture: given on 29 January 2008 at the House of Lords.

Chapter 12
Given on 1 May 2008 at the London School of Economics, Westminster

Chapter 13
Given as 'Human Rights and Religious Faith' on 28 February 2012 at the World Council of Churches, Ecumenical Centre, Geneva

Part Three – Living with Limits: The Environment

Chapter 14
Given on 5 July 2004 at Lambeth Palace, London

Chapter 15
The Ebor Lecture: given on 25 March 2009 in York Minster

Chapter 16
Operation Noah Lecture: given on 13 October 2009 in Southwark Cathedral

Part Four – Housekeeping: The Economic Challenge

Chapter 17
Given on 7 March 2009 in the Temple of Peace, Cardiff

Chapter 18
Given as part of the Trinity Institute Conference on 25 January 2010 at Trinity Wall Street, New York

Part Five – Justice in Community

Chapter 19
Given at the New Neighbourhoods Conference on 16 March 2005 in Chatham, Kent

Chapter 20
Given to Friends of the Elderly on 6 September 2005 at Church House Westminster

Chapter 21
Given on 1 February 2007 to the Prison Reform Trust, at the Institute of Directors

Chapter 22
The Commemoration Oration: given on 21 March 2011 at King's College London

Part Six – Religious Diversity and Civil Agreement

Chapter 23
Given as part of the Pacem in Terris Lecture series, on 29 March 2004 at Georgetown University, Washington DC

Chapter 24
Given during the sixth Building Bridges Conference on 6 December 2007 in St Andrew's Cathedral, Singapore

Chapter 25
Given at a Christian–Muslim Forum Conference on 10 September 2007 in King's College Chapel, Cambridge

Part Seven – Rediscovering Religion

Chapter 26
The Romanes Lecture: given on 18 November 2004 in the University Schools, Oxford

Notes

Chapter 1

1   W. Stein: *Criticism as Dialogue* (Cambridge, 1969), pp.183–246
2   ibid., pp.199–200
3   R. Gaita: *A Common Humanity: thinking about love and truth and justice* (Melbourne, 1999), p.24
4   ibid., p.26
5   Wendy Wheeler, 'One-Dimensional Politics', *Soundings*, xiv, (Spring 2000), p.110
6   J. Barrell, ed., *Samuel Taylor Coleridge: On the Constitution of Church and State* (London, 1972), pp.98–9
7   (Cambridge, 2002)
8   A. Shanks, *'What is Truth?' Towards a theological poetics* (London, 1972), p.139
9   Gaita, op. cit., pp.283–4
10   D. Kennedy: *New Relations: the refashioning of British poetry 1980-94* (Bridgend, Seren, 1996), pp.236–52
11   ibid., p.247
12   ibid., p.249

Chapter 2

1   M. Ignatieff: *Isaiah Berlin: a life* (New York and London, 1998), p.226
2   R. Bhaskar: *Philosophy and the Idea of Freedom* (Oxford, 1991), p.72
3   N. Boyle: *Goethe: the poet and the age – Volume 2: Revolution and Renunciation, 1790-1803* (Oxford, 2003), p.33
4   D. Mathew: *Acton: the formative years* (London, 1946), p.170
5   See R. Hill: *Lord Acton* (New Haven and London 2000), pp.414–6
6   C. Taylor: *Philosophical Arguments* (Cambridge, MA and London, 1995), p.221

Chapter 3

1 W. Cavanaugh: *Theopolitical Imagination: Christian practices of space and time* (London, 2003), p.43
2 ibid., p.46
3 M. Malik: 'Muslims and Participatory Democracy', in M. Siddique Seddon, D. Hussain and N. Malik, eds: *British Muslims: loyalty and belonging* (London, 2003), pp.69–85
4 ibid., p.9
5 See T. Winter: 'Muslim Loyalty and Belonging' in *British Muslims*, p.20, for a very helpful brief discussion of this.
6 S. Hauerwas: *With the Grain of the Universe: the Church's witness and natural theology* (Grand Rapids MI, 2001), p.131
7 Cavanaugh: *Theopolitical Imagination*, p.71
8 ibid., p.122
9 Malik: 'Muslims and Participatory Democracy', p.80

Chapter 4

1 D. Nicholls: *The Pluralist State: the political ideas of J. N. Figgis and his contemporaries* (London, 1975; 2/1994), p.113
2 ibid., p.77
3 O. O'Donovan: *The Desire of the Nations: rediscovering the roots of political theology* (Cambridge, 2/1999), p.233
4 See C. Insole: *The Politics of Human Frailty: a theological defence of political liberalism* (London and Notre Dame IN, 2004), pp.1–14
5 *Citizenship, Community, and the Church of England: Liberal Anglican Theories of the State Between the Wars*, Oxford Historical Monographs (Oxford, 2004)

Chapter 5

1 C. Dawson: *Religion and Culture* [Gifford Lectures] (New York, 1948), p.233

Chapter 6

1 'Is Europe at its end?' (an intervention at the Sant' Egidio International Meeting, Lyons 2005): www.archbishopofcanterbury.org/articles.php/1180/
2 T. Ramadan: *Western Muslims and the Future of Islam* (Oxford, 2005), p.53
3 ibid., p.55
4 ibid., pp.43–8
5 ibid., pp.65–77
6 ibid., p.145
7 Quoted in E. Skidelsky: 'Habermas vs the Pope', *Prospect*, 20 November 2005, p.15

Chapter 7

1 Quoted from N. McCormick: *I Was Bono's Doppleganger* (Penguin, 2004), p.114
2 D. Zohar and I. Marshall, *Spiritual Capital: wealth we can live by* (London, 2004), p.3
3 See for example Martin's essay, 'Central Europe and the Loosening of Monopoly and the Religious Tie', in *On Secularization: towards a revised general theory* (London, 2005), pp.112–19
4 ibid., pp.115–16
5 Zohar and Marshall, *Spiritual Capital*, pp.61–3, 73
6 ibid., p.142
7 D. Martin, *Does Christianity Cause War?* (Oxford, 1997), pp.153–4
8 ibid., p.159

Chapter 8

1 (Aldershot, 2004)
2 J. Clark: *Our Shadowed Present: modernism, postmodernism, and history* (London, 2003), p.85
3 'Muslims and Participatory Democracy', in Seddon *et al*: *British Muslims*, pp.69–85
4 Gorringe: *Furthering Humanity*, pp.233–7
5 N. Boyle: *Who Are We Now? Christian humanism and the global market from Hegel to Heaney* (Edinburgh and Notre Dame IN, 1998), p.314

Chapter 9

1 I. Berlin, 'Two Concepts of Liberty' [1958], in *Four Essays on Liberty* (Oxford, 1969), incorporated into H. Hardy, ed.: *Isaiah Berlin: Liberty* (Oxford and New York, 2002)
2 I. Berlin and R Hausheer, eds: *The Proper Study of Mankind: a anthology of essays* (London, 1997), p.224
3 ibid., p.361
4 ibid., pp.241–2
5 ibid., p.264
6 See for example R. Jahanbegloo: *Conversations with Isaiah Berlin* (English translation of original French 1991, London, 1992, 2/2007), pp.47–8
7 ibid., p.242
8 C. Taylor: *A Secular Age* (Cambridge MA, 2007), p.701
9 ibid., p.702
10 Reprinted in *Proud to Be a Mammal: essays on war, faith and memory* (London, 2010)
11 ibid., pp.186–7
12 Berlin: *Proper Study*, p.497

Chapter 10

1   See fn.50
2   Francis X. Clooney: *Comparative Theology: deep learning across religious borders* *(Chichester,* 2010), p.8
3   ibid., p.16
4   ibid., especially chapter 9
5   This point is well made by Amartya Sen in his essay on 'The Indian Identity' in *The Argumentative Indian: writings on Indian history, culture and identity* (London, 2005), pp.334–56
6   ibid., p.356
7   ibid., p.32

Chapter 11

1   D. Nash: *Blasphemy in the Christian World: a history* (Oxford and New York, 2007), esp. pp.25–34
2   ibid., p.34
3   See G. D. Nokes: *A History of the Crime of Blasphemy* (London, 1928), p.48; R. Webster: *A Brief History of Blasphemy: Liberalism, Censorship and the Satanic Verses* (Southwold, Suffolk, 1990), p.23; and Nash, op. cit., pp.160ff
4   'The Question of Freedom of Religion or Belief and Defamation', *Religion and Human Rights,* 2 (2007), 113–118
5   Webster: *Brief History,* p.129
6   ibid.
7   ibid., p.134
8   Nash: *Blasphemy,* pp.34–6
9   'Faith and the State of Jurisprudence', in P. Oliver, S. Douglas Scott and V. Tadros, eds: *Faith in Law: essays in legal theory* (London, 2000), pp.129–49, esp. p.137

Chapter 12

1   *After Virtue: A Study in Moral Theory* (London, 1981; 3/2007), pp.66–7
2   R. Ruston: *Human Rights and the Image of God* (2004)
3   *Summa theologiae:* IIa IIae 104.5
4   *The Hedgehog Review* 9.3 (Fall 2007), pp.32–48 [a special issue on human dignity and justice]
5   ibid., p.47
6   D. Jones: *Epoch and Artist* (London, 1959), p.90
7   *Hedgehog Review,* pp.68–9
8   ibid., p.65
9   S. Lovibond: *Realism and Imagination in Ethics* (Minneapolis MN, 1983), p.215

Chapter 13

1   S. Bachelard: 'Rights as Industry', *Res Publica*, xi/1 (2002), pp.1–5
2   ibid., p.4
3   (London, 2004)
4   See, for example, Ruston: *Human Rights*, pp.100–3
5   ibid., p.279
6   Bachelard, p.279

Chapter 14

1   *Guardian*, 12 August 2003
2   See, for example, M. Midgley: *The Myths We Live By* (London and New York, 2003), pp.110–3
3   E. Theokritof, 'Embodied Word and New Creation', in J. Behr, A. Louth, D. Conomos, eds: *Abba: the Tradition of Orthodoxy in the West* (New York, 2003), p.223
4   A. Schmemann: *Of Water and the Spirit: A Liturgical Study of Baptism* (New York, 1974), p.96
5   A. Simms: 'Real world environmental outlook', in Ann Pettifor, ed.: *Real World Economic Outlook: the legacy of globalization, debt and deflation* (Basingstoke and New York, 2003), p.60–74
6   Quoted by Andrew Simms in the *New Statesman* for 28 June 2004
7   pp.390 and 391
8   In A. M. Allchin, ed.: *The Tradition of Life: Romanian Essays in Spirituality and Theology* (Oxford, 1971), p.67

Chapter 15

1   E. F. Davis, *Scripture, Culture and Agriculture*, an agrarian reading of the Bible (Cambridge, 2009), ch.5, esp. pp.90–94
2   *Asking the Fathers* (London 1971, R/2010), p.92
3   A. S. Byatt: *The Biographer's Tale* (London, 2000), pp.243–4
4   p.205
5   P. Clifford: *Angels with Trumpets: the Church in a time of global warming* (London, 2009)
6   J. Porritt: *Capitalism as if the World Matters* (London, 2005), p.215
7   See ibid., p.293, for a summary of the argument of Part 2 of Porritt's book.
8   C. Yannaras: *Variations on the Song of Songs* (Boston MA, 2005), p.67

Chapter 16

1   M. Northcott: *A Moral Climate: the ethics of global warming* (London and New York, 2007), p.73

2   *Church Dogmatics*, III.4 [Doctrine of Creation, part 4], #55.1 (Edinburgh, 1961), pp.324–97
3   ibid., p.329
4   A. McIntosh: *Hell and High Water: climate change, hope and the human condition* (Edinburgh, 2008), p.219
5   See esp. ibid., chapter 5
6   Sustainable Development Commission: *Prosperity without Growth? – The transition to a sustainable economy*, p.82. An updated and expanded version of the report has been published in book form: T. Jackson: *Prosperity Without Growth: Economics for a Finite Planet* (London, 2009)
7   M. Hulme: *Why We Disagree About Climate Change: understanding controversy, inaction and opportunity* (Cambridge and New York, 2009), p.354
8   ibid., p.307
9   Northcott: *Moral Climate*, p.186
10   M. Sandel: *Justice: what's the right thing to do?* (London, 2009), p.243

Chapter 17

1   J. Dunning: *Making Globalization Good: the moral challenges of global capitalism* (Oxford, 2004), p.357
2   R. Skidelsky: 'Where do we go from here?', *Prospect*, 17 January 2009
3   ibid., p.39

Chapter 21

1   *Just Law: the changing face of justice – and why it matters to us all* (London, 2005), p.224
2   ibid., p.223
3   B. Williams: *Victims of Crime and Community Justice* (London, 2005), p.25
4   ibid., p.26
5   Kennedy: *Just Law*, pp.305–6

Chapter 22

1   O. Davies: *Theology of Compassion: the metaphysics of difference and the renewal of tradition* (Norwich and Grand Rapids MI, 2001)
2   S. Gerhardt: *The Selfish Society: how we all forgot to love one another and made money instead* (London, 2010), p.184. The story is told in Philip Hallie's classic, *Lest Innocent Blood Be Shed: the story of the village of Le Chambon and how goodness happened there* (London, 1979)
3   Boyle: *Who Are We Now?*, pp.92–3 (see fn. 48)

Chapter 23

1   C. Morse: *Not Every Sprit: dogmatics of Christian disbelief* (London, 2008)

Chapter 25

1   M. Gandhi: *An Autobiography: the story of my experiments with truth* (Eng. trans., Boston MA, 1957), p.195.

Chapter 26

1   K. A. D. Smelik, ed.: *Etty. The Letters and Diaries of Etty Hillesum, 1941–1943* [Eng. trans by A. J. Pomerans of *Etty: de nagelaten geschriften van Etty Hillesum 1941–1943* (Amsterdam, 1986)] (Cambridge and Grand Rapids MI, 2002), p.148
2   ibid., p.181
3   ibid., p.209
4   Cf, ibid., pp.223, 225, 516
5   ibid., p.198
6   ibid., p.320
7   ibid., p.216
8   ibid., p.212
9   ibid., p.519
10   ibid., pp.494 and 463 respectively
11   ibid., p.519
12   For example, ibid., p.237
13   ibid., p.546
14   ibid., p.192
15   ibid., p.496
16   ibid., p.497
17   ibid., p.493
18   ibid., p.27; the phraseology is Spier's
19   ibid., pp.160–1
20   ibid., p.183
21   ibid., p.564
22   L. Wittgenstein: *Vermischte Bemerkungen* (Frankfurt 1977): Eng. trans. by P. Winch, *Culture and Value* (Oxford, 2/1980), p.86
23   *Etty,* p. 586–7
24   ibid., pp.642–3 and 644–5
25   ibid., p.640
26   ibid., p.258–9
27   ibid., pp.308–9
28   ibid., p.488

29 ibid., p.506
30 *Culture and Value*, p.32
31 *Essays on Biblical Interpretation* (Minneapolis MN, 1980), pp.119–54
32 ibid., p.144
33 *Fear and Trembling* (published pseudonymously, 1843), p.124
34 Teresa of Avila: *Interior Castle*, IV.1.4–5
35 *The Problem of Evil and the Problem of God* (Minneapolis MN, 2005)
36 ibid., pp.161–2
37 S. Cavell: *The Claim of Reason: Wittgenstein, skepticism, morality and tragedy* (Oxford and New York, 1979), pp.363–4
38 See *Etty*, pp.168–9 and 293
39 O. Clément: *Anachroniques* (Paris, 1990), p.62

Index